BOLLINGEN SERIES LXXXV

Selected Works of Miguel de Unamuno

Volume 4

Edited and Annotated by
Anthony Kerrigan and Martin Nozick

Miguel de Unamuno

The Tragic Sense of Life

in Men and Nations

Translated by Anthony Kerrigan

With an Introduction by
Salvador de Madariaga
and an Afterword by
William Barrett

Bollingen Series LXXXV · 4
Princeton University Press

THIS IS VOLUME FOUR OF THE
SELECTED WORKS OF MIGUEL DE UNAMUNO
CONSTITUTING NUMBER LXXXV IN BOLLINGEN SERIES
SPONSORED BY BOLLINGEN FOUNDATION.
IT IS THE SECOND VOLUME OF THE
SELECTED WORKS TO APPEAR

Printed in the United States of America
by Princeton University Press

Table of Contents

Translator's Foreword

The Tragic Sense of Life in Men and Nations is the Great Pine, the Attis-Adonis pine tree, of Miguel de Unamuno's work. It is also an *Amanita* (whose host tree south of the forty-fifth parallel is ultimately the pine, as Pliny held), an *Amanita muscaria*, the deadly mushroom which killed Claudius (administered with the help of the Spanish philosopher Seneca, as Robert Graves has submitted), a dangerous cultivation but also a spontaneous growth identified with lightning and the divine poison of sacred madness. Unamuno meant to plant the poison of doubt; but from the mature plant he expected the fruit of belief to grow. He sowed the same seeds elsewhere, everywhere, but this potent tree took the strongest root.

Closely related seeds for this particular specimen of thought, of a book, the cousin-german seeds, are to be found scattered in the *Diario íntimo*, the keeping of which saved him from the temptation of suicide (as Unamuno wrote Dr. Gregorio Marañón). The diary was locked away and is just now first published in Spain (three distinct editions, 1970-1971) after being unpublished and out of sight (*inédito* even in Spanish), for some 70 years: a secret and mostly spiritual diary. (All this time it has been kept under lock and key in a standing roll-front wooden cabinet in his workroom in Salamanca.) The *Diario* was an adumbration and served as a preliminary sketch, twice removed, for *The Tragic Sense of Life*: the conflict between asserting heart and denying reason, with Unamuno physiologically requiring belief in continuity of self. The coincidental point of departure in time for the *Diario* was the evolution, or disintegration, of one of his children, a mere babe in a crib who slept by his side, blasted by disease and growing up retarded, thus bringing into question, close to home, the whole of Creation. The first word in the *Diario* is the Greek for hydrocephaly, and it serves by way of epigraph. A real-life event *would* be the natural fodder—yes, fodder, in this case: psychic straw, hay—for Unamuno's mind. He lived in the flesh as all other men must, but he also lived in the flesh *spiritually*, as a whole man, *nada menos que todo un hombre*, altogether a man; a seminal father and no Spanish Don Juan, his natural adversary, whether in life or literature; a thinking life-sized entity, and no *thinking reed*, like Pascal's man, "the weakest in nature"; an all-around polemical thinker, and no objective pedant, no mere professor, not a savant at all, as he repeatedly proclaimed. The opening chapter of our book is titled "The Man of Flesh and Blood," and it was as such a man that he considered and meditated man's fate. (It must be admitted, though, that Unamuno considered Don Quixote—and Don Juan—to be as real as Cervantes—and Tirso—and the characters in his own fiction as alive as himself.)

Perhaps no other thinker ever conceived his greatest book on the basis of such a phenomenon: an imperfect child, a human, all-too-human, mis-conception.

If he, as father, had created a permanently imperfect thing, it was only to be expected that the Father of Creation was directly involved. (The last full entry, dated January 15, 1902, in the *Diario íntimo*, is a "*Padre nuestro*" of Unamuno's own composition, which reads, cryptically: "Father always engendering for us the Ideal. I, projected to an infinity, and you, projecting yourself to infinity, meet; our parallel lives meet in infinity and my infinite I is your I. . . ."). He also thought he himself might be to blame. His faith was by now dubious; and Reason—Reason in religion was a plague. It was the principal cause of his downfall. (For the *Diario* includes no questioning of tradition; quite the contrary: it is an almost compulsive devotional, an evocation of given Belief. Unamuno fell back on the reactions of his infancy, of a primitive infancy, of the infancy of his Basque people and of Christian Europe.) In a letter to the novelist Leopoldo Alas, a bare half-year before the birth of the doomed boy, he wrote: "My faith in an intimate, organic Catholicism, wellspring of reflex actions, is precisely what turns me against it when it is concretized in formulas and concepts." And to the same correspondent he had spoken of a proposed "fictional" character (much like himself, he noted) who, "since he carries God in the marrow of his soul has no need to believe in Him: it is a reflex action."

Few thinkers in history-as-written-down must have taken as point of departure for their thinking their condition as fathers; a few have thought as Fathers, as Fathers of the Church, or simply as Fathers in the Church, but their thinking has been necessarily disembodied. In any case, "Spinoza and Kant and Pascal were bachelors; they were never, apparently, fathers; and neither were they monks in the Christian sense of the word." Yes, and (Unamuno characteristically does not mind repeating himself): "Spinoza was, like Kant, a bachelor, and may have died a virgin."

Miguel de Unamuno y Jugo de Larraza (or "U. Jugo de la Raza," as he called himself, as author, in *Cómo se hace una novela*, a name which translates as "U. Marrow of the Race"), Unamuno—even if he must have conducted himself in the sexually abstracted manner of his total opposite, Valéry's Monsieur Teste—Unamuno y Jugo de Larraza y Unamuno (to give him his full set of surnames in Spanish: twice an Unamuno) was no virginal nonbegetter.

This thinker of the living (and dying) thought was Rector-for-Life of the University of Salamanca, and he was, naturally enough in Spain, removed: three times in all. The first time he was removed (on orders from Madrid), he never learned the reason why. After his reinstatement, he was again removed, by the Republican government in Madrid on August 22, 1936; then also—thus making him a total outcast banished by both camps in the Civil War— on October 22, by the other side, the Nationalist government (and this time by his "own colleagues"—his fellow professors—"a fact often forgotten," as Emilio Salcedo points out in his lovingly detailed journalistic biography of Unamuno): Azaña signed the decree, as President, for the Republic, expelling Unamuno from the University and forbidding him to act in any capacity; exactly two months to the day later, Franco signed—this time at the behest of the University council of professors—a similar decree. Victim-by-association of all these decrees, these official curses, Unamuno's Rector's House (*Casa Rectoral*) has never again been officially occupied, has remained unoccupied by any other rector since Unamuno's death on the last day of the first year of the Spanish Civil War: kept open (and now declared National

Patrimony, not to be touched except by some higher authority) as if for *him*, with his brass bed and his books (and his antique washbowl, too) intact and in place, as if awaiting his return—in the flesh.

And he preferred the "resurrection of the flesh in the Judaic manner, rather than the immortality of the soul in the Platonic manner." And he didn't care in which age of his "seven ages" he would reappear, for he liked the tale in Matthew (22:23-32) in which a woman had married, in accord with Hebraic Law, each of seven brothers, in turn; each time she was widowed by the previous brother, and they had "all had her." The Sadducees—aristocrats who conceived of no descent beyond their own families, no descent at all beyond the tomb—ironically asked whose wife she would be "at the end," when they all came face to face, a question which presented no problems for Unamuno, any more than it had for Jesus Christ (Matt. 22:30; Mark 12:18-27).

In any case, Unamuno did not care if he was mad, mad enough to ignore all such "reasonable" cavils, wished in fact that he were mad: "If I were mad, it would be with the holy madness of Christ. Would to God I suffered such an ill!" he writes in the *Diario íntimo.*

The novelist Camilo José Cela has pointed out that, in the internationally famous incident in the *Paraninfo* (the general *Aula Magna*) at the University of Salamanca, in the third month of the Spanish Civil War, on the occasion of the *Día de la Hispanidad*, or *Día de la Raza* (Day of Hispanity, or of the Race), with Unamuno presiding, as Rector and in representation of the (Rebel) Head of State, when the founder-general of the Spanish Foreign Legion, Millán Astray, cried out (or is said to have cried out: there are no sure witnesses, none but a few contradictory ones—only the foreign press was sure) "Long Live Death!", the *"Viva la muerte!"* which was the Legion's battle-cry, this cry (or supposed cry: in any case, he might well have uttered such a cry) was not, precisely, un-Unamunian: it was rhetorically paradoxical, and it was, in a deeper sense, a cry of faith, of faith beyond, even if against, life. (And back before Unamuno, Saint Teresa, the Jewess of Avila, that incandescent and realistic woman of Spain, had cried *"Muero porque no muero"*: "I die because I do not die"—and Unamuno had seized upon that cry and used it as an epigraph for his *Agony of Christianity*.) Unamuno was, nevertheless, affronted: for the cry, Unamunian or non-Unamunian, or whether it was not precisely that cry but another, was launched against Unamuno, and he was led from the platform, away from the submachine-gun-armed legionnaire bodyguard standing behind the rampant General, led away on the arm of Carmen Polo de Franco. The outraged Unamuno was hearing an echo of quintessential non-European Hispanity from his all-too-Hispanized audience, his altogether Hispanic classroom.

Unamuno proclaimed: "To have a great Orthodoxy we must have a great Heterodoxy." And he vindicated all the heresies by consideration, and doubted, and sowed doubt in his own paradoxes, his own Paradox. He questioned the heresies as he did the orthodoxies. One of the pertinent orthodoxies he rejected was the latest, for him and for us: iconoclastic, liberal orthodoxy, which has "brought us a new Inquisition: that of science and culture, which turns its weapons of ridicule and contempt against whoever does not submit to its orthodoxy." And he blamed anterior heresies for the new orthodoxy: for it was "The Renaissance and the Reformation . . . along with their daughter the Revolution," which had brought us this new Inquisition. (In his obdurate Castilian resistance to Italian—Florentine—estheticism, his non-recognition of the humanist Renaissance, of comprehensive Catholic incorporation of Antiquity and the eternal myths, Unamuno ironically matched the German obduracy of the Reformation's Renaissance-hating Luther.) At the end (at the end of one period of his life) he favored taking the field, like a modern Don Quixote, against "modern, scientific, inquisitorial orthodoxy, in the interests of a new and impossible Middle Ages, dualistic, contradictory, impassioned." The presentation in English of Miguel de Unamuno's disquieting meditation—or attitude—and record of near-mystic combat is a polemical (Greek *polemichos*: warlike) enterprise, and we have embarked upon it with the present series of volumes.

"Men seek peace, they say, but do they—really? They are also said to seek liberty. Not at all. They look for peace in time of war—and for war in time of peace. They seek liberty under tyranny—and tyranny when they are free."

Replete with paradox though it may be, Unamuno's message is highly pertinent (not to use the momentarily tainted adjective "relevant") in the Age of Liberal Acquiescence, of relativist absolutes, the new dogmatic epoch which sees the publication of this edition.

In Unamuno's eyes the evil man was not the "true atheist" (who in any case was "madly enamored of God"), not the man who did not believe in the existence of God, but the man who did not want God to exist. The sin against the Holy Ghost, that ever mysterious sin in Christian literature, consists, for Unamuno, in "not desiring God, in not longing to be made eternal."

So that it was natural that Unamuno, in self-exculpation of this mysterious sin, thought of this book, when it was a work in progress—perhaps already a third approach to or draft of the overall idea—as *Tratado del amor de Dios*, and first used this working title in 1905, although most notably in a letter to Ortega y Gasset almost exactly a year later, on May 17, 1906. In this same letter he plaintively asks—asks himself, he says—why, when he is a man of passion, a man of his own anarchism, the only true anarchism, "not the anarchism of those anarchist millionaires who ruin everything," (as he added in a later letter), why, when he was a man of consoling (and combative) despair, a *desesperado*, they have tried to make him out to be "a scholar, a pedagogue, an educator, and a parcel of other such nonsense? *Basta*." We can translate his provisional title as *Treatise on the Love of God*: the use of the word *Love* in a work by a modern thinker situates him in the mystic tradition, and, even more to the point, serves to underline the passional—even physical—basis of his thought. (And the Great Pine—which we called this book at the beginning—is the fecundating Tree of Love, and of immortality. Jung makes it personify the Mother, a figure primary to all Unamuno's sentient thought.) It serves to show that this man of our age, an "existentialist" *avant la parole*, an existentialist *sui generis* (I die, therefore I am, and must survive), was exactly what he said he was, a passionate meditator, a mystic lover suffering the vicissitudes of passion, and no professional philosopher or systematic scholar at all. It serves to show how Unamuno, the non-systematizer, the "non-philosopher" (in the opinion of most of his commentators as well as his own), covered the bones of his thought with the passions of his heart and soul.

Here, *in situ*, in Unamuno's rooms—books, washbasin, vine-covered terrace, and all—the Notes to this, the first edition of any amplitude in any language, including Spanish, were compiled.

We went through the books and the letters and the mementos. The letters received by Don Miguel are catalogued and readily available and mostly in holograph: those from Ezra Pound and Jorge Luis Borges and Nicholas Kazantzakis (who came to Salamanca when the Civil War raged, to see Unamuno) and Ortega y Gasset and dozens of other figures of the day. (Perhaps most surprisingly missing from any part of the house, among the books or the letters, is the name or presence of Simone Weil, the other, contemporary obsessive, driven by a similar hunger, even though, like Unamuno's, unique: she her own heresiarch. In a remarkable essay on Unamuno—in *La voluntad de estilo*, Barcelona, 1957—the Spaniard-in-America, Juan Marichal, points out that Simone Weil, "who doubtless knew [Unamuno's] *The Agony of Christianity*" paraphrased Unamuno's quintessentially Spanish phrase, "The finality of life is to make oneself a soul," with the quintessentially French phrase "The aim of life is to structure an architecture within the soul." An existential world of difference, and each world true to itself: vital Spanish improvisation as against formal French organization.) His books were handled, opened particularly to their marked pages, and the tracery of his reading followed, rather than his reading traced, for our work was one of foraging where Unamuno had foraged, rather than one of thesis-making. Unamuno had distilled his own fighting brew and we stoutly imbibed it. It was significant that our predecessor as translator had been a publican and not a pedagogue. The first man to have put Unamuno into English had, indeed, kept a public house, but long before this had happened, Unamuno, in the last single line of the *Diario íntimo*, refers us to Matthew 21:28-32, where Jesus eulogizes "publicans and harlots" over the authorities. We did not set out to prove that Unamuno was "once a Marxist always a Marxist," or a crypto-Protestant, or a host of things he—tirelessly—said he was *not*. This very book, indeed, is his politics: "My political program is in my book *The Tragic Sense of Life* and in my commentaries on *Don Quixote*," he said when he was drafted to stand for the Spanish Parliament— and was not elected. In a "Portrait of Unamuno" by Jean Cassou, written in French, which Unamuno himself was happy to translate into Spanish and preface to his own *Cómo se hace una novela*, Cassou characterized Unamuno by noting that "a professor himself . . . he professed above all else a detestation of professors." Of course Unamuno was equipped for his whims: he was a Doctor of Philosophy himself, from the Central University of Madrid, for a thesis on the origin of his own Basque race.

The Tragic Sense of Life is, among many other things, a cry from the Depths. Unamuno himself thought it a combination of metaphysics and poetry, his own amalgam of his thought in both, his own chief work. It is a gloss on Unamuno's chance— though not accidental—and contradictory reading. Ezra Pound understood the approach. (It was Pound —another non-professor, or anti-professor, but true educator in his early years—who, not surprisingly, was the first to offer Unamuno an international platform, in English, in the old *Dial*: the first American, perhaps, to want to see Unamuno put before a regular English-reading public. Among the letters Unamuno saved are a couple from Pound—one of them partially in a Poundian brand of Italianate medieval Spanish— who, characteristically, was aware of Unamuno's value, somewhat before the rest of the world. Pound invited him—from Paris: Hôtel de l'Elysée, 3 rue de Beaune: 1920—to contribute to the *Dial* and make it "your representative organ in the United States": the contributions would be translated by "mi amigo il poeta W. C. Williams, hijo d'una española": Pound also asked if Unamuno knew of any young Spanish writers of talent who were in "grave" need of money, for there are always those one can help, to the benefit of literature, by paying them, as he added in his own Spanish. Unamuno answered, agreeing, and Pound hoped, on 5 July 1920, for a "pleasant relationship between yourself and The Dial.")

Unamuno was one of the few great readers Spain has had since the expulsion of the Jews—and almost uniquely a reader in all the languages. This "pure" Basque left over from some Atlantis-civilization— who at the same time embodied his own semitic "Christ out of Tangiers" and the Castilian Celt-Iberian warrior disguised in the so-called *Dama de Elche* stone-figure—annotated and translated fragments of everything which came his way, from pieces of Langston Hughes's Negro religious verse to Blake's "Milton" and Yeats's "The Wheel" which ends

> Nor know that what disturbs our blood
> Is but its longing for the tomb

(the "Irish death-wish" exposed to the Iberian gaze!),
and he needed to look up in his dictionaries only three
words in "Easter, 1916" where he noted more of the
exalted Irish idea of the dead, of their metamorphoses

> MacDonagh and MacBride
> And Connolly and Pearse
> Now and in time to be,
> Wherever green is worn,
> Are changed, changed utterly:
> A terrible beauty is born.

All this in English only. The range of his reading
in other languages is suggested in our Notes. All
Unamuno's friends among bookmen were, like himself, "*Liberales*" on the basis of their reading alone,
of their solidarity as universal readers (though from
a non-Spanish point of view many of the Spanish
"Liberals" are seen to be something quite different
when viewed in the frame of the larger world: an
Ortega y Gasset, for example). In any case, their
breed was not numerous in their generation and the
survivors of the Civil War few, Madariaga and Amé-
rico Castro, most notably. Other Spanish literary men,
whenever they wanted a book, wrote one (such natural creative talents as Baroja and Valle-Inclán, for
example; and these writers were not liberals from
any point of view). None of them, in any case, was
of the warrior-caste, who lived in "warlike idleness,"
or *espadones*, the sword-wearers of a type who had
held Spain since the Jews were expelled. Yet all of
them were combative, more ready for combat than the
contemporary *señoritos* who wore the swords. (It is
worth noting that not one of these Spanish Liberals
was ever associated with the Spanish Communist
Party, which was led by semi-literates and produced

only grotesque caricatures out of García Lorca at best
—quite unlike the *Parti Communiste* next door.)

Unfortunately, like Pound—as the same W. C.
Williams asserted of his "amigo"—Unamuno was
tone-deaf; and if he thought Bach a poor argument
for Protestantism, it was because he was insensitive
to music. Unamuno's closest counterpart in France,
perhaps, Gabriel Marcel, could say of Bach that he
was the first to nourish him religiously, and that "he
has meant more in my life than Pascal or St. Augustine or any author whatsoever," and add "God is the
symphony of spirits," a final thought Unamuno might
have penned, but without any musical sense to animate the literary rhetoric.

Still, our book is a poetic—sometimes lyric—gloss
on Unamuno's reading during the most crucial years
of his life, a gloss of his own library in the medieval
city of Salamanca. And this was a fact to be discovered in the very rooms which were his own Library of Libraries, his Library of Babel, his "universe, which others call the Library . . . ," as Jorge
Luis Borges puts it.

Borges (who also wrote Unamuno and sent him all
his early books, signed and dedicated, for the Master's approval), one of Unamuno's descendants and
in some ways one of Unamuno's own glosses, Borges
has glossed many of Unamuno's original glosses.
Borges wrote Unamuno—from Paris likewise: Hôtel
Bayard, 11 rue Richer: undated—to say that he
wished to convey his "signal gratitude" to Unamuno
for writing such poems as "The Atheist's Prayer"
(*La Oración del Ateo*) and such lines as "And I
shall live in hopes of you, Hope." (*Y viviré esperán-
dote, Esperanza*). Borges adds: "I almost deplore

the renown which causes your name to travel from mouth to mouth, so many mouths, lavished about and glorious; for if the contrary were the case, I should be able to tell you of my constant concern with your verses, tell it to you more freely and from soul to soul." He finishes by telling Unamuno he would "celebrate your not denying to me by present silence the many things your verses have already said to me in the past." (He had just asked whether Unamuno did not feel moved by his, Borges', verse, sent to him from Buenos Aires.) Borges went on to gloss much of Unamuno, as he retrieved from Unamuno's *intrahistoria* and the collective sources common to both of them the pivotal notions which the original or primitive author had not developed.

In Chapter X of the present book, "Religion, Mythology of the Beyond, and Apocatastasis," Unamuno sowed seeds, in the course of planting a series of Unamunian questions, which flowered in Borges: "May we not, rather, perhaps imagine that this earthly life of ours is to the other life what sleep is to waking? May not our entire life be a dream and death an awakening? But an awakening to what? And what if everything were but a dream of God and God were to wake some day? Would He recall His own dream?" Borges was perhaps thirteen when these lines were first written.

Borges had recognized Unamuno as soon as he caught sight of him in print. In his early twenties, Borges wrote (in *Nosotros*, Buenos Aires, 1923): "The man Miguel de Unamuno, under compulsion to his time and place, has thought all the essential thoughts. . . . For a good spell now, my spirit has lived on terms of passionate intimacy with his verse."

Again, in his book *El lenguaje de Buenos Aires* (B.A., 1968), reiterating what he had first declared in a talk in 1927: "Don Miguel de Unamuno is the only Spaniard who feels and senses metaphysics; and thus, and because of other sensibilities, is a great writer." In 1937 on the news of Unamuno's death, he penned a quick obituary: "The leading writer in our language is dead. . . . He was, before all else, an inventor of splendid argument. He debated the I, immortality, language, the cult of Cervantes, faith, ethics, the regeneration of vocabulary and of syntax. . . . I know of no better homage than to continue the rich discussion he began and to go on to plumb the secret laws of his soul."

Borges was true to his idea of homage and tribute. There is no clearer precursor to the quintessential piece by Borges titled "Borges and I" than Unamuno's characteristic cry: "Am I not on the point, perhaps, of sacrificing my most personal I, my divine individuality, whatever I am in God, the person I should be, to the 'Other,' the other I, the historic I, the I which moves and acts in its own history and with its own history?" (1926). The entire idea—and of much else in Borges—is contained in Unamuno's drama *El Otro* (written in exile in 1926). Either of them might have written "To dream that one exists. . . . Well and good! But to be dreamt by someone else . . . !" By chance, it was Unamuno, as long ago as 1914. Borges speaks of "prophetic memory" and Unamuno had spoken of "the memory of the future," which is of the same potential as "the hope in the past." No man comes from Nowhere, and Borges came from Unamuno, among other places and worlds.

In their present form, the Notes to this edition

would not have existed but for Professor Martin Nozick, co-editor but master-reader and chief redactor, author of critical writings on Unamuno, in which he insistently traced the Master's equivocality, political and otherwise. Professor Nozick also particularly traced the vein of Unamuno's gloss of nineteenth-century German theology: a rewarding source not hitherto much tracked or much noted in Unamuno studies in English, though documented in Spanish, mainly in the chronology of Unamuno's own letters, where Unamuno makes it clear that he came to be repelled by these German readings of his, as he noted, for example, in another letter to Ortega y Gasset—to such an unlikely recipient of its contents as Ortega—in 1912, on the eve of our book: "I cannot, no, cannot stand the *purity* of it all: pure concept, pure cognition, pure will, pure reason, all that purity leaves me breathless. . . . And I want to descend to the lowest depths, where the air is heavy and I can clutch at the earth covered with the flowers of passion, illusion, lucky deceits, consoling superstitions (yes, even superstitions), old lullabies from infancy. After some of this reading I cross myself, say an Our Father and a Hail Mary and dream of an impure glory and a *material* immortality *in saecula saeculorum* where I find my mother, my children, my wife and the surety that the human soul, this poor soul of mine, of my people, is the finality of the universe. And reasoning doesn't help. No, no, no! I will not resign myself to reason."

The group working at Salamanca also included Elaine Kerrigan, née Gurevitch, who picked out passages for us all to read and place in the context of the Notes. Some were in German, where even Yiddish—yes, precisely: Yiddish—helped, and some in

Portuguese, which Professor Nozick commands, and some in Danish, where we fell back upon Princeton University Press, whose editions of Kierkegaard were indispensable. For, though Unamuno learned Danish by first learning Norwegian in order to read Ibsen— even as James Joyce, whom Unamuno dubiously qualified as "a bad paterfamilias"—we were in no position to learn Danish merely as an exercise in reading the endless dozens of passages marked in the fourteen-volume edition of the original, which Unamuno devoured far in advance of the vogue, probably the first man in Spain to do so. (The biographer Salcedo maintains that Unamuno first heard of Kierkegaard from a Danish seaman in Bilbao!) Moreover, several of the volumes we found to be absent without leave one summer's working week, for they had been taken away by a professor of philosophy in Salamanca (long ago assistant to Don Miguel) without any specific authorization from the non-specified authorities who guard Unamuno's House as Monument—or the Monument of his own Rector's House to Unamuno— merely for the amazement of his students. Such we found life and work to be in no-longer medieval Salamanca, the exhilarating and pure ex-medieval city of Salamanca, quintessence and heart of Castile, tangentially bounded by Burgos, the walls of Avila, and Philip II's Escorial, center of another century, and by Unamuno's Portugal, *"mi Portugal,"* our Salamanca (where we spent a month three summers in a row in the last years of the 1960s, lodged among waves of errant Portuguese, and the permanent and hermetic bull-breeders of the *Gran Hotel* whom Unamuno religiously shunned). Felisa de Unamuno, Don Miguel's daughter, keeper of her father's papers, books and letters, left the door to the Rector's House on the latch for us, and handed us the keys to the flush doors which formed part of the paneling. She and her sister, Professor María de Unamuno, passed on to us family legend as lived and experienced. At Princeton University Press itself we had the invaluable help of George Robinson, serving the project as copy editor but who in reality knew the fine points and proved more knowledgeable in several quarters than the present two-man Board of Editors, survivors of an original Board of three (including Unamuno's disciple in direct line, Federico de Onís [1885-1966], sometime head of the Spanish department of Columbia University, anthologist, and editor who determined the chronology of our many-volumed edition in English), a Board which had later grown to four in membership. A dire blow was the death of Sir Herbert Read, whose interest in the Unamuno project as proposed by the undersigned was aroused by Edward Dahlberg, *franc-tireur* among men of letters, and the initial catalytic agent of this edition of Unamuno in English. The intervention of Sir Herbert, an original member of the first Board of Editors, founded in Madrid in 1962, assured the existence of the project when it was endangered. *Herbert Read: A Memorial Symposium* (London, 1970) expresses our homage and that of a number of his great contemporaries. (As for Dahlberg, he had corresponded as far back as the Spanish Civil War with Emma Goldman [1869-1940], perhaps *the* Anarchist in American history, who wrote him that Unamuno was the most important Spaniard—and a fascist. But Dahlberg suspected better. His lack of Spanish was compensated for by a more informed intuition than her misinformation, also rather intuitive.)

In the background of this, the second English version, the presence of J. E. Crawford Flitch was felt at every turn. Crawford Flitch was a remarkable amateur, the first translator of Unamuno into English, and his 1921 version, the third language version chronologically, was collated with every sentence of our own—and wherever his word was superior, it was used. His letters to Unamuno, moreover, were there before us, his consultation recorded, his memory still fresh with Salvador de Madariaga—who helped with that first English version—from the time J.F.C. Flitch, "Landlord," kept a public house and inn (the "Trout Inn," Godstow, Oxford): for our translator-traveler-essayist was a man of many facets. Like the French translator of the same book, he thought of Unamuno more than once "in the trenches" where he learned of death and its sensation of "infinite peace." At his home, Stonegrave, York, Herbert Read (trench soldier: The Green Howards, 1915-18, D.S.O. and M.C.) bade us promise not to forget Flitch and his pioneering effort, and when we met on the last two occasions, first in Dublin, and last of all in Azeitão, Portugal, Sir Herbert repeated that we should help rescue Crawford Flitch from the forgetfulness of time, at least in so far as a Translator's Foreword can help, and at least to the extent of a mention of some of his books in the Unamuno library.

There are three books by or involving Crawford Flitch in the library of Unamuno (himself a translator, of, for example, Carlyle's lengthy and Baroque *French Revolution*; and of much Herbert Spencer, whom he later disowned as a thinker, when he liberated himself from the influence of the "unemployed engineer," in Papini's epithet). Most remarkable is Flitch's translation of, and Introduction to, *Angelus Silesius: Selections from the Cherubinic Wanderer*

(London, 1932), consisting of 355 verse selections from the German seventeenth-century mystic, Johann Scheffler of Breslau, together with a long (97 pp.) incisive biographical essay on Scheffler.

The "Tragic Sense of Life" (a phrase almost colloquially used now by such writers as, say, the colloquial Henry Miller) is definable in a variety of ways. For Unamuno, who invented the concept, it was illustrated by the truth, obvious to him, that "everything vital is not only irrational but anti-rational, and everything rational is anti-vital." Theoretically the tragedy lay in the excruciating balance between the equal, contradictory, demands of reason and of vital feeling: an exquisite antinomy. But in practice, in his case, his heart tended to outbalance his head. Not to feel this tragic pull, this anguish of contradiction, not to live like an intellectual *desesperado*, a desperado of the mind and soul, not to feel the tragic sense of life, was not to feel at all, not to live life. For unless one sensed immortality, one was already a victim of mortality— and in fact already as good as dead.

Not only individuals, but an entire people feel and are affected by the tragic sense of life. Unamuno related this sense to his concept of the "Agony of Christianity," where "Agony" means struggle, in accord with the original Greek, and the re-enactment by the prot-*agonists* (necessarily ant-*agonists*) of the Divine Tragedy (as exemplified by Christianity), which is also perhaps the tragicomedy of life. For the Tragedy may also be a Comedy in the end, which Unamuno, given his life style, or merely his temper (in the *Diario íntimo* he noted with obviously horrified awe that his idiotized child did nothing but laugh), could scarcely bring himself to hope was the case (though he also missed in his bones the medieval world in which the believer Dante's *Divine Comedy* was not a Tragedy because "it contained hope"; or at worse was a comic tragedy, and not a divine one, since Dante's damned still live on, still *live*), but which many of those who read this book must hope may be, even now, a final possible uncertainty. As for Don Miguel de Unamuno, his heart had its reasons—*hope against hope*—of which Reason knew ought.

Salamanca   ANTHONY KERRIGAN
1970-71

The legal position of the *Casa Rectoral de Miguel de Unamuno* in Salamanca is worth clarifying. Unamuno left his own books to the University, which stamped them with their own blazon—and then returned them to the Rector's House. So that at first glance it appears that Unamuno had appropriated the University Library's books. The Unamuno family sold the archives and furniture and some medianly important paintings (a Darío de Regoyos, etc.) to the University for a pittance, but they all remain in place. In the late 1960s the Spanish State declared the Rector's House, with all its Unamuniana, to be National Patrimony, with ownership vested in the University.

Of related interest is the public monument to Unamuno in Salamanca: a giant over-lifesize bronze, composed of a series of angular thrusting planes, by Pablo Serrano, one of Spain's great contemporary sculptors. Serrano's Unamuno is somewhat reminiscent of Rodin's tortuous Balzac in Montparnasse, near the site of the now demolished Café La Rotonde, "la de Trotzki," as Unamuno writes that it was called in his time, because Trotsky used to go there during his own Paris exile, and where Unamuno went in turn to the daily "tertulia" with other expatriate Spaniards. Much persistence was needed to obtain authorization for the Salamanca statue's emplacement in the small (nameless) plaza between the Ursuline Convent and the house in which Unamuno died one New Year's Eve of a heart attack (in the course of expostulating with a young law professor, Bartolomé Aragón, who had returned from a trip to Mussolini's Rome a convinced neo-socialist corporative syndicalist—an Italian-type fascist, in short), a plaza which could and should be called Plaza de Unamuno.

Introduction

Unamuno Re-read

As I RETURN to Unamuno, forty years after I first wrote an introductory essay to his *Tragic Sense of Life*, I am struck by a certain incongruity between the way his work is nearly always approached and the spirit of the work itself. We read about his "thought," his reading, and of course, the "influences" he is supposed to have undergone. In all the discussion lurks the fallacy he constantly fought against: the belief that thought presides over the council of ministers of the soul and decides what a man writes. Whereas, of course, for Unamuno (as for most of us, at any rate for most Spaniards) thought is not at the origin but at the end of the creative line of our lives. At the origin there is I.

I, *yo*. The most important word in the Spanish language. Pretty important, despite appearances, also in English—possibly second only to Spanish in granting this importance, for the English, though masters in striking a balance between the social and the individual poles of the self, are possibly the most individualistic of Europeans after the Spanish. Think how insignificant is the French *je*, so insignificant that it often has to be propped up with *moi: et bien, moi, je vous dis.* . . . But the way best to test the strength of our Spanish *yo* is to compare it with its (it would appear) identical Italian *io*. The Italians stress the *i*, as we would expect them to do, since *i* is the key vowel of their language and character, while we stress the *o*. They make it two syllables and thus render it both more flexible and weaker. They say *io*; and we *yo*, imbuing that *o* with the full force of the voice of the self. *Yo* in Spanish is so strong that it is seldom used, like a loaded revolver.

*   *   *

The *yo* of Unamuno was formidable. You could see that at first sight. Ortega was impressive enough to meet: wide magnetic eyes above a vast jaw surprisingly strong in an intellectual, a smile of more light than warmth, in which, by the way, that voluntary jaw fully shared, an inner masculine strength wrapped in a smooth suavity almost feminine in its grace; and one would look and look, charmed and admiring. But his counterpart, Unamuno, was not content to remain there standing in front of you, passively to be looked at and spoken to. He stood aggressively, as if ready to launch an attack, features taut, eye glaring, mouth set into an earnest, unyielding, locked straight line which no smile ever would bend. Unamuno was a challenge on legs. You felt on meeting him that he had begun to contradict you before you had spoken.

And this may well be the master key to his life and work. Unamuno "was against." He was against by nature, even before that which he was to be against had turned up. He was born *anti*. He was the anti-everything. Why? There is no why. Above all, seek not for motives: "resentment," "inferiority complex," all those seemingly deep, at bottom naïve labels of so-called modern, so-called scientific, so-called psychology. Why should men have to be explained when stars, roses, and worms can shine, bloom, and crawl without explanations? His portraits as a youth show him already tense, earnest, unsmiling, defiant, anti-world.

Yes: Anti-world. For the world is that thing out there which is not me. And for Unamuno what mattered was his I, his *yo*. In a nation of *yo*-ists, he was the most *yoist* of all. If we accept as one, and possibly the most significant, of the many Spanish realities for which Don Quixote is a symbol, the deep tendency of the Spaniard to deny reality the right to be itself and to dare force it to adjust itself to our inner dream, Unamuno is one of the most forcible incarnations of Don Quixote which Spain has given forth.

What that dour face is saying is: "I do see you but I do not accept you. You need not speak, still less argue; your words will be drowned by mine, and all arguments are vanities. I am I. Take it or leave it." This attitude was, so to speak, the shape of his being; not his thought, not his philosophy; but the root-cause of his philosophy and of his thought, as it was also of his faith and of his religion, and indeed of his lack of faith and of his doubts.

It is a sheer waste of time to endeavor to discover where Unamuno picked up this or that idea, or what philosopher influenced his thought. It all came from within; and not merely, indeed not mainly, from his brain, but from that *attitude*, that *inner shape of his soul* which was born with him. That is why he is, on the one hand, a fierce, contemptuous adversary of that rationalism which was so widespread in the Europe of his day and, on the other, a mind so irreducible to any definite form of the several "philosophies" which arose in the nineteenth and twentieth centuries as reactions to it.

This refusal to be labeled or classified has been criticized, depicted even as a shortcoming of the men of his epoch. There may be some substance in the reproach as far as other men are concerned; but as for Unamuno, could he help it? He meant to be no philosopher; he was simply Miguel de Unamuno, and the ready-to-leap attitude of his mind did not allow him honestly to wear any label. The chances are that if you challenged him, confronted him on behalf of Kierkegaard or Bergson, with an attack against rationalism, he would fight for rationalism with the utmost vigor and sincerity, for, among other things, he was also a rationalist.

Yet, of course, no cynic, no dilettante. The idea of either would have horrified this earnest soul. He was a rationalist in so far as he felt his reason as a live organ of his spirit and self, with as much right to be heard as the other organs of perception and understanding living in him. And he would not defend rationalism as a philosophy in itself, or as a means to attain truth, but as a living part of a living Unamuno whom you were attacking by the mere fact of attacking rationalism. He would willingly have paraphrased Terence: "Nothing Unamunian do I consider alien."

Who but Unamuno could have invented that title *Nada menos que todo un hombre* (*Nothing Less than a Whole Man*)? That man standing there, staring at you in full earnest, was nothing less than a whole man and wished you to be in no doubt about it. He was aware of his contradictions, indeed he

gloried in them for they were tokens of his existence
as a human being, since a creature without contradictions could be no more than a contrivance of mere intellect. And precisely because he felt all these contradictions in himself and even nurtured them, he had
a way of standing firmly on his feet as if ready for
your attack, knowing it would be an attack since, no
matter what you would say, he would feel it as an
aggression on this or that part of his many-sided self.

*   *   *

This it was that made him so argumentative. It was
one of the many paradoxes of his life (more substantial if less numerous than those in his writings) that
this advocate of the irrational and the vital, this con-
temner of logic, should be a veritable addict of verbal
discussion. Here, as we say in Spain, appetite and
hunger came together, for he loved both discussion
and talk—on condition, that is, that he did the talking. It was typically Spanish of him that he should
grant so much importance to the Word; for in this,
Spaniards preach, so to speak, what they do and do
what they preach. He thought, we all think, that
thought is at its best at the moment it is uttered, because it is then that it comes alive out of the spirit
that has begotten it. And this opinion is but natural
in a people that thinks while talking.

In his addiction to verbal argument, therefore,
Unamuno gave vent at the same time to his intellectual combativeness and to that tendency to think
while talking which grants so much spontaneity and
unexpectedness to the talk of a worthwhile Spanish
mind. The truth in this observation may serve to
excuse Spaniards for the reverse of the coin: their

tendency to turn their talk into a monologue. I have known but very few prominent Spaniards who were wholly free from this foible. Unamuno was not one of them.

There was a lot of him to be lived, and life is short. So there he went for all he was worth. He was endowed with a fair share of those formidable qualities we all readily acknowledge in the Basque: stubbornness and strength. Unamuno will at times strike the reader as persistent and insistent even beyond the needs of the case, just for the love of pounding on; and his style does at times also suggest the hammer of the stonecutter rather than the chisel of the goldsmith. It is all part of the urge of that passionate *yo* imprinting itself on nature.

When he happened not to be ready with a home-made version of the world to oppose to God's own, rather than conform to God's he would turn it upside down. This was the cause of his taste for paradox, a necessity in him of which, however, he came to make a habit and later a practice. He would pick up a well-known formula, say, "Faith is believing what we do not see," and he would at once start to prove that in fact it was the other way about: "Faith is seeing what we do not believe." It was all part of his initial position: Unamuno versus the world.

It was part also of his anarchical, undisciplined, spontaneous nature which led him to trust in intuition rather than in concentrated thought—something that was all to the good, for this tendency made him ever fresh, inventive and stimulating—but led him also at times to mistake for intuition what was no more than caprice, and to indulge in caprice for its own sake. Thus he often had recourse to mere sonority and to what were no more than puns. For instance, not only would he turn the definition of faith upside down, "Faith is believing what we do not see," but at another moment he would turn it into a parallel formula: "Faith is creating what we do not see," based on the pun *creer* (believe) and *crear* (create). Nor was this frivolous game always sterile, for rich is the world of the mind, and his own skill to move among ideas considerable. The trouble here is that he played without a smile, as if he were in dead earnest, which in fact he was.

*   *   *

There was strength in it, but also a weakness due partly to anarchy, partly perhaps also to an aversion for any intellectual pursuits requiring discipline. Thinking aloud, improvising *more hispano*, was for him a more attractive occupation than building up a well-poised edifice requiring a scrupulous calculation of its logical stresses. He would no doubt retort that many such edifices have been built through the ages so that they now form an imposing Philosophy Avenue, but that no one can live in them who is really alive; and, sad to say, he would be right.

Nevertheless, the admiration he deserves as, with Ortega, the most eminent Spanish man of letters of our century, must be tempered by a recognition of his lack of discipline and of his arbitrariness. Discipline is no prominent feature of great artists. There was not much of it in Shakespeare, or in Lope de Vega; on the other hand, too much of it spoils, one fancies, the all too perfect work of Racine. Be that as it may, there are too many moments in which Unamuno is undisciplined not because life surges in him with so much strength that he cannot canalize it (Shakespeare's case), but because he just lets himself go, thinking no doubt that all that shines in him is gold.

Within every author, a critic must be on the watch. Unamuno's self-critic was not up to the mark. There were at least three reasons for this. The first was his "nothing-less-than-the-whole-man" attitude: everything that was thrown up had to be accepted. The second was his irrational vent: if what turned up was absurd, so much the better. The third was Unamuno's pronounced masculinity, a typical Basque feature. He was more of a genius than a talent, in contrast with Ortega who was more of a talent than a genius. In the work of creation, genius is the fecundating, masculine force; talent, the feminine, shaping capacity. Unamuno was lacking in that subtle critical talent which exerts itself prenatally on the work of art and sees that its body is shapely.

*   *   *

The chief paradox of Unamuno's life, however, may well be that this apostle of life, this eloquent advocate of irrationality and experience versus reason and intellectualism, lived mostly in the mind, gathered but little outward experience, and often mistook his thoughts on life for life itself. He was a professor of Greek; he lived a regular, middle-class simple man's life, in the bosom of an exemplary family: regular meals, regular walks, regular classes; he now and then vibrated with the "high frequency" of hectic political events, knew exile but found no interest in Paris and secluded himself in Hendaye, returned to Spain, passed through the Republic like something between a meteor and a ghost, and on finding that the events of 1936 did not let him carry on his quiet way of living in his beloved retreat of Salamanca, he died.

His life was all within. His experience was inner experience. Not for him those excursions to foreign lands, those adventures in the realms of danger, passion, the strange, the unfamiliar, the irregular, the shocking, the crags, peaks, and abysses which surround, fascinate, attract, and repel other men, and out of which they form their thoughts, thoughts fed with the sap of reality. Unamuno spoke and wrote about life far more than most, but he lived far less than most.

Could it be that this formidable man, the uncompromising stand, the proud uplifted head, the glaring eye, and the stubborn mouth, could it be that this challenger was deep down a shy man? Yes. It could be. In fact he was. The forbidding mask hid untold shyness and even tenderness within. His search for retreat, solitude, the quiet of the countryside, the reflective and inward looking contemplation, possibly even that negation of outer life and that wish to *unamunize* it rather than accept it within— what were they but consequences of the over-sensitiveness of the man within? Look more closely at those portraits of him, all immediately so impressive as images of a dour, aggressive man. That man is on the defensive.

His concentration on his own self, on his inner world, is for him one of the ways of escape from an outer world which he fears. He will roam in the vast spaces of his inner self, whose dangers he knows well and he can face, rather than risk adventures in that outer reality he does not actually know and he prefers to deny. Hence that feature, often observed in his novels and in his plays: the indrawn quality of characters and places. In Unamuno's works, details of time and place are seldom given. Everything happens in people's minds rather than in their fields, backyards, rooms, or kitchens.

Furthermore, in Unamuno's works every character speaks and feels like Unamuno. He is so many people himself that the several Unamunos of his plays and novels do not necessarily strike a note of monotony. They are saved by his intensity, and so is the reality he paints, a projection of outer reality onto his inner cavern.

*   *   *

This is yet another paradox. The aggressive man, who seemed eager to conquer the outer world and to *unamunize* it, lets himself be invaded by the outer world, and everything he describes really happens within. But does he actually let in reality—such as it is? For reality to enter a man, he must be ready to give himself to it. The bridge must lend itself to a two-way traffic. On reading him, one is struck by the depth, the liveliness, the ever-renewed vigor of ideas, rather than by any familiarity with things as they actually are.

Nor was it only a lack of familiarity. There was bias as well. The chief virtue of the true artist is passivity. He must allow the river of life to flow through him without meddling, without altering or regulating its course. Later, when the hour of talent arrives, he will have to take an active part in the work, to shape the emotions received; but he should not intervene too soon and try to influence the impressions before they form. Unamuno often falls into this error, impelled by his eagerness to express the thought which dominated all his life. His life was polarized by this one thought which, in one way or another, conditions, determines, and orientates all his works—survival. He must survive. There must be another life.

For him, it need hardly be said, this is not an idea. It is a want, a need, a hunger, an urge, an obsession. It does not generate in his mind but in the recesses of his being. What would you expect? Philosophy? An abstract, objective, "horizontal," concatenated study of the problem of life after death and of the existence of God? Not from Unamuno. The issue is not one between perceptions and logic, but one between Unamuno and non-Unamuno, including God.

Unamuno must live on after death. That is his will. And the will of God must adjust itself to that fact. Nor will he be content with some vapid form of spiritual life:

> The other world . . .
> The other world is that of pure spirit.
> Of pure spirit . . .
> Oh dreadful purity,
> inanity, void.

He must have his flesh and bone, and in this he reveals himself a true Catholic. He wants the other world to be as much of the senses as this, and sighs for the resurrection of the body. Nothing less than the whole man.

*   *   *

So here is the picture of Unamuno as an artist. Weak in his sense of form through an excessive masculinity and an overbalance of genius as against talent; weak also in that his passivity and his impartiality are disturbed by his obsession with his own personal survival; he is strong in his sensuous enjoyment of the whole of his life as a man of flesh and bone; strong also in the spontaneous flow of his thoughts and feelings, in the "vertical," so to speak, spring-like vigor of his utterance.

Unamuno must therefore be considered above all as a lyrical poet. True, his argumentative, didactical tendency was so strong that it often led him to the essay and to the novel, which, for him, is at times an argument between a number of Unamunos of both sexes. But at times his novels are also poems, and he himself once defined a novel as a poem. His way of presenting reality, not directly and in itself, but reflected or, better still, re-lived in his own inner world, and so transfigured and *unamunized*, could lead to no other result than that of turning his novels into poems.

And it is above all as a lyrical poet that he will remain—a case not dissimilar from that of Kierkegaard and Nietzsche: men who felt more than they thought; whose thoughts were, in fact, mere flowers of the sap of feeling; and, therefore, only universal insofar as they are profoundly individual, only meaningful insofar as they convey the aroma and the shape of the individual spirit that lives in them.

It follows that Unamuno, despite his shortcomings, will have his place in Spanish literature as one of the greatest poets in the language of Castille. This he owes to the dimensions of his spirit—depth, width, height; the freshness and spontaneity of his language and style, which in his truly poetical pages, whether in prose or in verse, are of the noblest, most diaphanous and luminous in Spanish letters; to the universal, human quality and greatness of his themes; and to the transparent sincerity which shines in his life and works.

*　　*　　*

The earnestness, the intensity, and the oneness of his predominant passion are the main cause of the strength of Unamuno's philosophic work. They remain his main asset, yet become also the principal cause of his weakness as a creative artist. Great art can only flourish in the temperate zone of the passions, on the return journey from the torrid. Unamuno, as a creator, has none of the failings of those artists who have never felt deeply. But he does show the limitations of those artists who cannot cool down. And the most striking of them is that at bottom he is seldom able to put himself in a purely aesthetical mood. In this, as in many other features, Unamuno curiously resembles Wordsworth—and was, by the way, one of the few Spaniards to read and appreciate him. Like him, Unamuno is an essentially purposeful and utilitarian mind. Of the two qualities which the work of art requires for its inception—earnestness and detachment—both Unamuno and Wordsworth possess the first; both are deficient in the second. Their interest in their respective leading thought—survival in the first, virtue in the second—is too direct, too pressing, to allow them the "distance" necessary for artistic work. Both are urged to work by a lofty utilitarianism—the search for God through the individual soul in Unamuno; the search for God through the social soul in Wordsworth—so that their thoughts and sensations are polarized, and their spirit loses that impartial transparence to nature's lights without which no great art is possible. Once suggested, this parallel is too rich in sidelights to be lightly dropped. This single-mindedness which distinguishes them explains that both should have consciously or unconsciously chosen a life of semi-seclusion, for Unamuno lived in Salamanca very much as Wordsworth lived in the Lake District—

> in a still retreat
> Sheltered, but not to social duties lost,

hence in both a certain proclivity toward plowing a solitary furrow and becoming self-centered. There are no doubt important differences. The Englishman's sense of nature is both keener and more concrete; while the Spaniard's knowledge of human nature is not barred by the subtle inhibitions and innate limitations which tend to blind its more unpleasant aspects to the eye of the Englishman. There is more courage and passion in the Spaniard; more harmony and good will in the Englishman; the one is more like fire, the other like light. For Wordsworth, a poem is above all an essay, a means for conveying a lesson in forcible and easily remembered terms to those who are in need of improvement. For Unamuno, a poem or a novel (and he holds that a novel is but a poem) is the outpouring of a man's passion, the overflow of the heart which cannot help itself and lets go. And it may be that the essential difference between the two is to be found in this difference between their respective purposes: Unamuno's purpose is more intimately personal and individual; Wordsworth's is more social and objective. Thus both miss the temperate zone, where emotion takes shape into the molds of art; but while Wordsworth is driven by his ideal of social service this side of it, into the cold light of both moral and intellectual self-control, Unamuno remains beyond, where the molten metal is too near the fire of passion, and cannot cool down into shape.

Unamuno is therefore not unlike Wordsworth in the insufficiency of his sense of form. We have just seen the essential cause of this insufficiency to lie in the non-aesthetical attitude of his mind, and we have tried to show one of the roots of such an attitude in the very loftiness and earnestness of his purpose. Yet, there are others, for living nature is many-rooted as it is many-branched. It cannot be doubted that a certain refractoriness to *form* is a typical feature of the Basque character. The sense of form is closely in sympathy with the feminine element in human nature, and the Basque race is strongly masculine. The predominance of the masculine element—strength without grace—is as typical of Unamuno as it is of Wordsworth. The literary gifts which might for the sake of synthesis be symbolized in a smile are absent in both. There is as little humor in the one as in the other. Humor, however, sometimes occurs in Unamuno, but only in his ill-humored moments, and then with a curious bite of its own which adds an unconscious element to its comic effect. Grace only visits them in moments of inspiration, and then it is of a noble character, enhanced as it is by the ever-present gift of strength. And as for the sense for rhythm and music, both Unamuno and Wordsworth seem to be limited to the most vigorous and masculine gaits. This feature is particularly pronounced in Unamuno, for while Wordsworth is painstaking, all-observant, and too good a "teacher" to underestimate the importance of pleasure in man's progress, Unamuno knows no compromise. His aim is not to please but to strike, and he deliberately seeks the naked, the forceful, even the brutal word for truth. There is in him, however, a cause of formlessness from which Wordsworth is free—namely, an eagerness for sincerity and veracity which brushes aside all preparation, ordering or planning of ideas as suspect of "dishing up" intellectual trickery, and juggling with spontaneous truths.

Setting Unamuno next to Wordsworth has shown them both as typical spirits of their respective nations. A similar effect would be obtained by comparing Unamuno with Valéry, for both might well stand as, again, typical spirits of their respective nations. Valéry was above all an intellect, a shape-giving, feminine spirit. Unamuno was a nothing-less-than-a-whole-man, a seed-providing, masculine spirit, with all that non-intellectual, vital sap which goes into a work, even into a work of "mere" thought, all the life-element without which, for Unamuno, a work would be worthless, all that which would be brushed aside by Valéry as mere dross, a muddying of the pure waters of the intellect; while the perfection of form, consciously sought and painfully attained by the Frenchman—a perfection, by the way, utterly beyond the powers of Unamuno unless he struck it by chance—would have been for the Spaniard mere vanity and waste. Finish for the Frenchman, finicking for the Spaniard.

Passionate versus dispassionate; a man living from his roots up, giving forth his "works" as a chestnut tree its "candles," versus a goldsmith patiently chiseling his jewels; Unamuno versus Valéry symbolizes the secular tension between the spirit of Spain and the spirit of France, between fullness and perfection, substance and shape, power and care, hunger and fear, a beginning and an end.

* * *

Historically, Unamuno must be counted as one of the chief pioneers of the worldwide rebirth of spiritual forces which set in during the nineteenth century, precisely as a reaction against the rationalistic atheism of that epoch. His originality in this attitude cannot be disputed. He discovered Kierkegaard when his own way of thinking had come to full maturity and was already well known. Nor, had it been otherwise, would it matter at all; for there was no man less apt to borrow from another (a process in any case which is definitely "horizontal") than our "vertical" Unamuno. To put it in the language of Ortega, he was an "Adamic" Spaniard, i.e., a man who, though immensely well read, starts all over again from Adam as if no one had ever written a word since. His reading is incredibly wide; but he only spots in books that which he is already thinking; and his attitude to the problem which obsessed him remains original in its purity and nobility because he is above all determined to keep it true. True even if it must lead him to contradictions. Hence his satisfaction when he found himself backed in this by Walt Whitman: "Do I contradict myself? Very well then, I contradict myself."

Historically again, Unamuno occupies in Spanish culture a place somewhat singular and isolated. "Our brother enemy," Ortega said of him once. He was definitely on the side of Spanish liberals, a liberal himself in the best and most profound sense. But perhaps because he had meditated so deeply on the roots of liberalism, he could hardly accept the line all too frequently taken for granted around him as the frontier between "right" and "left," i.e., with or against the Catholic Church. "I'd rather talk to a canon than to a lieutenant colonel," he once said on a somewhat resonant occasion.

What he meant was perhaps twofold. First, that of the two institutions, both based as they were on discipline, the Church was more capable than the Army to open out toward freedom, because the very basis of the Gospels is the freedom of the human soul; and then, that liberalism can only rest on the divine origin of man, for if man's soul is not divine there is no reason why it should be respected.

In thus seeking a synthesis of liberalism and religious faith, Unamuno was a precursor as much as he had been in his attitude toward nineteenth-century rationalism. Looking back on the struggles Spain has lived from 1808 on to this date, it is possible to wonder whether their true cause, a too black-or-white attitude on both sides, would not have been avoided had more Spanish leaders openly advocated, by no means a middle course, but a loftier perspective such as Unamuno managed to command throughout his exemplary life.

SALVADOR DE MADARIAGA

London, 1970

*The Tragic Sense of Life
in Men and Nations*

I. The Man of Flesh and Blood

HOMO SUM; *nihil humani a me alienum puto*, said the Latin playwright. For my part I would rather say: *Nullum hominem a me alienum puto*: I am a man; no other man do I deem a stranger. For in my eyes the adjective *humanus* is no less suspect than its abstract substantive *humanitas*, humanity. I would choose neither "the human" nor "humanity," neither the simple adjective nor the substantivized adjective, but the concrete substantive: man, the man of flesh and blood, the man who is born, suffers, and dies— above all, who dies; the man who eats and drinks and plays and sleeps and thinks and loves; the man who is seen and heard; one's brother, the real brother.

For there is something else called man, the subject of many lucubrations, more or less scientific, and he is the legendary featherless biped, the ζῷον πολιτικόν of Aristotle, the social contractor of Rousseau, the *homo economicus* of the Manchester school, the *homo sapiens* of Linnaeus, or, if you like, the vertical mammal. Such a man is a man from nowhere, from neither here nor there, neither of this age nor of another, who has neither sex nor country, who is, in short, a mere idea. That is to say, a no-man.

Our man is the other one, the man of flesh and

[*The asterisk alongside any page's number indicates that there is material on that page which is annotated in the *Notes* at the end of this volume.]

blood: you and I, that man yonder, all of us who walk firmly on the earth.

And this specific man, this flesh-and-blood man is both the subject and supreme object of all philosophy, whether certain self-styled philosophers like it or not.

In most of the histories of philosophy that I know, philosophic systems are presented to us as if growing out of one another spontaneously, and their authors, the philosophers, appear as mere pretexts. The inner biography of the philosophers, of the men who philosophized, is assigned a secondary place. And yet it is precisely that inner biography which can mean most to us.

It behooves us to say, before all else, that philosophy lies closer to poetry than to science. All philosophic systems constructed as a supreme concatenation of the end results of the individual sciences have, in every age, possessed much less consistency and life than those which expressed the integral spiritual yearning of their authors.

For the fact is that the sciences—though they concern us so greatly and are, indeed, indispensable for our life and thought—are in a certain sense more foreign to us than philosophy. Their end is more objective, that is, farther removed from us. Fundamentally they are a matter of economics. A new scientific discovery, of the kind called theoretical, is like a mechanical discovery—that of the steam engine, the telephone, the phonograph, the airplane—in that it serves some purpose. Thus, the telephone may serve us to communicate with our beloved some distance away. But as for her, what purpose does she serve? A man takes an electric tram to go to hear an opera,

and might well ask: "Which is the more useful, the
tram or the opera?"

Philosophy responds to our need to form a complete and unitary concept of life and the world and,
following on our conceptualization, the impulse which
engenders an inner attitude or even action. But the
fact is that the impulse in question, instead of being
a consequence of this conception, is the cause of it.
Our philosophy, that is, our mode of understanding
or not understanding the world and life, springs from
our impulse toward life itself. And life, like everything affective, has roots in our subconscious, perhaps in our unconscious.

It is not usually our ideas that make us optimists
or pessimists, but our optimism or pessimism—of
perhaps physiological or pathological origin, the one
as well as the other—that makes our ideas.

Man, they say, is a reasoning animal. I do not
know why he has not been defined as an affective or
feeling animal. And yet what differentiates him from
other animals is perhaps feeling rather than reason.
I have seen a cat reason more often than laugh or
weep. Perhaps it laughs or weeps within itself—but
then perhaps within itself a crab solves equations of
the second degree.

And thus, in a philosopher, what need most concern us is the man.

Take Kant, the man Immanuel Kant, who was
born and lived at Königsberg, at the end of the eighteenth century and the beginning of the nineteenth.
In the philosophy of this man Kant, a man of heart
and head, that is to say, a man, there is a significant
"leap," as Kierkegaard, another man—and such a
man!—would have said: the leap from the *Critique*

of Pure Reason to the *Critique of Practical Reason.*
In the latter he reconstructs what he destroyed in the
former, whatever those who do not see the man himself may say. After having examined and pulverized
with his analysis the traditional proofs of the existence
of God, of the Aristotelian God, who is the God corresponding to the ζῷον πολιτικόν, of the abstract God,
the immovable prime mover, he reconstructs God
anew. But now it is the God of conscience, the Author
of the moral order: in short, the Lutheran God. This
leap by Kant exists already in embryo in the Lutheran
notion of faith.

The one God, the rational God, is the projection
to external infinity of man as he is by definition: that
is, of abstract man, of the man who is no-man; the
other God, the God of feeling and volition, is the projection to internal infinity of man in life, of the specific man, the man of flesh and blood.

Kant reconstructed with his heart what he had
overthrown with his head. And in truth we know,
from the testimony of those who knew him, as well
as from his own, from his letters and private declara-
tions, that the man Kant, the more or less selfish old
bachelor who taught philosophy at Königsberg at the
end of the century of the Encyclopedia and of the
goddess of Reason, was a man much preoccupied
with the Problem: I mean the only real and vital
problem, the problem which strikes closest at the root
of our being, the problem of our personal and individual destiny, of the immortality of our soul. The
man Kant was not resigned to die utterly. And because he was not resigned to die utterly he made that
leap, that immortal leap, from the one Critique to
the other.

Whoever reads the *Critique of Practical Reason*

attentively and without blinkers will see that, strictly speaking, the existence of God is there inferred from the immortality of the soul, and not the immortality of the soul from the existence of God. The categorical imperative leads us to a moral postulate which necessitates, in turn, in the teleological or, rather, eschatological order, the immortality of the soul, and, for the purpose of sustaining this immortality, God is introduced. All the rest is the jugglery of the philosophy professional.

The man Kant felt that morality was the basis of eschatology, but the professor of philosophy inverted the terms.

Another professor, the professor and man William James, has already said somewhere that for the generality of men God is the provider of immortality. Yes: for the generality of men, including the man Kant, the man James, and the man who writes these lines, which you, reader, are reading.

Talking to a peasant one day, I suggested to him the hypothesis that there might indeed be a God who governs heaven and earth, a Consciousness or Conscience of the Universe, but that even so it would not be sufficient reason to assume that the soul of every man was immortal in the traditional and concrete sense. And he replied: "Then, what good is God?" And that was the response, in the secret tribunal of their consciousness, of the man Kant and the man James. But in their role as professors they had to justify rationally an attitude in itself so little rational—which does not mean, of course, that such an attitude is absurd.

Hegel made famous his aphorism that all the rational is real and all the real rational; but there are many of us who, unconvinced by Hegel, continue to believe that the real, the really real, is irrational, that reason builds upon irrationalities. Hegel, a great framer of definitions, attempted to reconstruct the Universe with definitions, like that artillery sergeant who said that a cannon was made by taking a hole and enclosing it in steel.

Another man, the man Joseph Butler, the Anglican bishop who lived at the beginning of the eighteenth century and whom Cardinal Newman declared to be the greatest name in the Anglican Church, wrote—at the end of the first chapter of his great work, *The Analogy of Religion*, a chapter which deals with a future life—these pregnant words:

> This credibility of a future life, which has been here insisted upon, how little soever it may satisfy our curiosity, seems to answer all the purposes of religion, in like manner as a demonstrative proof would. Indeed a proof, even a demonstrative one, of a future life, would not be a proof of religion. For, that we are to live hereafter, is just as reconcilable with the scheme of atheism, and as well to be accounted for by it, as that we are now alive is: and therefore nothing can be more absurd than to argue from that scheme that there can be no future state.

The man Butler, whose works were perhaps known to the man Kant, wished to save the belief in the immortality of the soul, and with this object in mind he made it independent of belief in God. The first chapter of his *Analogy* deals, as I say, with the future life; and the second, with God's government by means of rewards and punishments. And the fact is that, in all truth, the good Anglican bishop infers the existence of God from the immortality of the soul. And, inasmuch as the good Anglican bishop made this inference his point of departure, he did not need to make the leap which the good Lutheran philosopher had to make at the end of the same century. Bishop Butler was one man, and Professor Kant was another.

And to be a man is to be something concrete, unitary and substantive: it is to be a thing, *res*. Now, we know what another man, the man Benedict Spinoza, the Portuguese Jew who was born and lived in Holland in the middle of the seventeenth century, wrote about the nature of things. The sixth proposition of Part III of his *Ethics* states: *unaquaeque res, quatenus in se est, in suo esse perseverare conatur*: that is, everything, in so far as it is in itself, strives to persevere in its own being. Everything in so far as it is in itself: that is, in so far as it is substance, for according to him substance is *id quod in se est et per se concipitur*, that which is in itself and is conceived by itself. And in the next proposition, the seventh, in the same part, he adds: *conatus, quo unaquaeque res in suo esse perseverare conatur, nihil est praeter ipsius rei actualem essentiam*, that is, the effort with which everything strives to persevere in its own being is nothing but the actual essence of the thing itself. This means that your essence, reader, and mine, and that of the man Spinoza, and that of the man Butler, and of the man Kant, and of every man who is a man, is nothing but the endeavor, the effort, which he makes to continue to be a man, not to die. And the proposition that follows these two, the eighth, states: *conatus, quo unaquaeque res in suo esse perseverare conatur, nullum tempus finitum, sed indefinitum involvit*, that is: the effort with which everything strives to persevere in its own being does not involve finite time, but indefinite time. That is to say:

9

you, I, and Spinoza wish never to die, and this longing of ours never to die is our present essence. Nevertheless, this poor Portuguese Jew, exiled in the mists
of Holland, could never succeed in believing in his
own personal immortality, and all his philosophy was
but a consolation invented to make up for lack of
faith. Just as other men have a pain in their hand
or foot, a heartache or a headache, so had Spinoza
a God-ache. Unhappy man! Unhappy men, the rest
of us!

And as for man, this thing—is he a thing? However absurd the question may seem, it is one that
some men have asked. Not long ago a certain doctrine
called Positivism was in vogue, a doctrine which
wrought much good and much ill. And among the
ills it wrought was the introduction of a method of
analysis by which facts were pulverized, reduced to
a dust of facts. Most of what Positivism labeled facts
were really only fragments of facts. In the field of
psychology its effect was deleterious. There were even
scholastics who played at literature—I will not say
philosophers who played at poetry, for a poet and
a philosopher are twins, or perhaps even one and the
same thing—and who carried the Positivist psychological analysis into the novel and the drama, where
the principal task is to put concrete men, men of flesh
and blood, into motion. And the Positivists, by dint
of focusing on states of consciousness, made consciousness disappear. The same thing happened to
them that is said often to happen in the examination
and testing of certain complicated, organic, living
chemical compounds when the reagents destroy the
very body under examination and the only results obtained are the products of the object's decomposition.

Taking as their point of departure the obvious fact

that mutually contradictory states pass through our consciousness, they ended by no longer seeing consciousness itself, the I. To ask a man about his I is like asking him about his body. And note that in speaking of the I, I speak of the concrete and personal I, not of the I of Fichte, but of Fichte himself, the man Fichte.

And that which determines a man, that which makes him a certain man, one man and not another, the man he is and not the man he is not, is a principle of unity and a principle of continuity. A principle of unity, first, in space, by virtue of his body, and next in action and intention. When we walk, one foot does not go forward and the other backward, nor when we look about us does one eye gaze to the North and the other to the South—as long as we are normal, that is. We are animated by some purpose at every moment in our life, and it is to this purpose that the synergy of our actions is directed, even though in the next instant we may alter our purpose. And in a certain sense a man is that much more a man the more unitary his action. There are people who follow a single course of action throughout their life, whatever their purpose may be.

Then there is a principle of continuity in time. Without entering upon a discussion—an idle discussion—of whether or not I am the same person I was twenty years ago, I nevertheless think it is beyond question that the person I am today derives, by a continuous series of states of consciousness, from the person who was contained in my body twenty years ago. Memory is the basis of individual personality, just as tradition is the basis of the collective personality of a people. We live in memory and by memory, and our spiritual life is simply the effort of our memory to persist, to transform itself into hope, the effort of our past to transform itself into our future.

I know very well that all this is sheer platitude; but in going about the world one meets men who seem to have no sense of themselves. One of my best friends, with whom I have strolled every day for years, used to say to me, every time I spoke to him of the sense of one's own personality: "Well now, I don't have any sense of myself. I don't know what you mean."

On one occasion this friend remarked to me: "I'd like to be So-and-So," and here he mentioned a certain man. I said: "Now that's something I've never understood: that one should want to be someone else, anyone at all. To want to be someone else means that one wants to cease being who one is. I can understand one's wanting to have what someone else has, his wealth or his knowledge. But to be someone else: that's something I don't understand." It has often been said that every man who has suffered still prefers to be himself, with all his misfortunes, than someone else, even without those misfortunes. For the fact is that unfortunate men, as long as they keep their sanity in the midst of their misfortune, that is, as long as they still strive to persist in themselves, prefer misfortune to non-being. Of myself I can say that when I was a young man, even when I was a boy, I was not to be moved by the pathetic pictures of Hell that were drawn for me, for even at the time nothing seemed as terrible as Nothingness. I was already possessed of a furious hunger to be, "an appetite for divinity," as one of our ascetics put it.

To propose to a man that he be someone else, that he become someone else, is to propose that he cease to be himself. Every man defends his own personality, and will agree to a change in his way of thinking or of feeling only in so far as the change can fit into the unity of his spirit and mesh with its continuity, in so far as this change can harmonize with and be integrated into the rest of his mode of being, thinking, and feeling, while at the same time it can be linked with his memories. Neither a man nor a people (in a certain sense a people is also a man) can be asked to make a change that will break the unity and continuity of the person. A man can be greatly changed, almost completely in fact, but only within the stream of his continuity.

It is true that so-called changes of personality take place in certain individuals; but these are pathological cases, and the proper concern of mental pathologists. In these changes of personality, memory—the basis of consciousness—is completely destroyed, so that the victim is left only with his physical organism as substratum for his individual continuity, which now ceases to be personal. For the victim, this ill is the equivalent of death; it is not the same as death only for those who are to inherit his fortune, should he have one. Such an infirmity is a revolution, a veritable revolution.

In a certain sense, any infirmity is an organic dissociation; it is a rebellion by some element or organ of the living body which breaks the vital synergy and which conspires toward an end different from that sought by other elements coordinated to it. Its end, considered in itself—that is, in the abstract—may be more elevated, more noble, more anything you like; but it is different. To fly and breathe in the air may be better than to swim and breathe in the water; but if the fins of a fish took it upon themselves to change into wings, then the fish, as fish, would perish. And it is no good saying that the fish would, in the end, become a bird, unless there were some process of continuity in the becoming. I am not sure, but perhaps it could happen that a fish might engender a bird, or another fish that would be closer to a bird than the first fish was; but a fish, the fish in question, cannot itself, during its own lifetime, turn into a bird.

Everything that conspires in me to break the unity and continuity of my life conspires to destroy me and, therefore, to destroy itself. Every individual who conspires among a people to break the spiritual unity and continuity of that people tends to destroy it and to destroy himself as a part of that people. Another nation, you say, is better than our own? Very possibly; though in all truth we don't rightly understand what is meant by better or worse. Richer? Granted. More cultured? Granted likewise. They are happier? Happiness, now . . . Well, all right, granted. They are a conquering people (what is called conquering) while we are a conquered people? Congratulations to them. That's all very well, but they are *another* people. And that's enough! Because for me to become another, to break the unity and continuity of my life, would be to cease being who I am: that is, simply, to cease to be. And that—never. Anything rather than that!

Another, you say, might fill my role as well or better? Another might fulfill my social function? Yes. But he would not be I.

"I, I, I, always I," some reader will exclaim. "And who are you?" I might reply in the words of Obermann, that great man: "In the eyes of the Universe, nothing. In my own eyes, everything." But I would rather recall a doctrine stated by the man Kant: to wit, that we ought to think of our fellowmen, of the rest of humanity, not as means but as ends. For it is not a question of me alone; it is a question of you, protesting reader; it is a question of the other man, of each and every other man. Singular judgments have the value of universal judgments, the logicians say. The singular is not particular; it is universal.

Man is an end, not a means. All civilization is directed toward man, toward each man, toward each I. For what is that idol called humanity—or whatever else they may call it—to which all men and each individual man should be sacrificed? I can sacrifice myself for my fellow man, for my countrymen, for my children, and all of these, in their turn, may sacrifice themselves for theirs, and their sons sacrifice themselves for theirs, and so on in an unending succession of generations. And who is it, now, who receives the fruit of this sacrifice?

Those who talk to us of this fantastic sacrifice, of this dedication without object, are wont to talk also about the right to live. What is this right to live? They tell me I am here to realize I know not what social end; but I feel that I, like each one of my fellow men, am here to realize myself, to live.

Yes, yes, I see it all! One vast social activity, a mighty civilization, a great deal of science, a deal of art, of industry, of morality and then, once we have filled the world with industrial marvels, with great factories, with highways, museums, and libraries, we shall fall exhausted at the foot of it all, and it will all remain—for whom? Was man made for science or was science made for man?

"Wait now!" the same reader will exclaim again; "we're back to what it says in the Catechism: '*Q.* For whom did God create the world? *A.* For man.' " Very well, then: yes. And that's the way any man who is really a man ought to reply. An ant, if it took any notice of these things and were a person conscious of itself, would answer: "For the ant," and that would be the right reply. The world is made for consciousness, for each consciousness.

"One human soul is worth the entire Universe," someone said, and said magnificently. A human soul, mind you! Not a human life. Not this life. And the less a man believes in the soul—that is, in his conscious immortality, personal and concrete—the more the worth of this poor transitory life is exaggerated. And this exaggeration is the source of all that effeminate mawkishness against war. Of course, one ought not to want to die, not die the spiritual death. "Whosoever will save his life shall lose it," says the Gospel; but it does not say "whosoever will save his soul," his immortal soul—or the soul we believe and want to be immortal.

And all the definition-mongers of objectivism do not notice, or rather do not wish to notice, that when a man affirms his "I," his personal consciousness, he affirms man, concrete and real man, affirms the true humanism—the humanism of man, not of the things of man—and in affirming man he affirms consciousness. For the only consciousness of which we are conscious is that of man.

The world is made for consciousness. Or rather, this "for" of ours, this notion of finality—or even better than "notion," this feeling of finality—this teleological feeling does not occur except where consciousness exists. In the end, consciousness and purpose are the same thing.

If the sun were possessed of consciousness, it would doubtless think that it existed in order to illuminate the various worlds; but it would also and above all think that the worlds existed so that it might illuminate them and take pleasure in so doing and thus live. And it would be right to think in this wise.

And this whole tragic struggle of man to save himself, that immortal longing for immortality which caused the man Kant to make the immortal leap mentioned above, all of it is no more than a fight for consciousness. If consciousness is no more—as some inhuman thinker said—than a flash of lightning between two eternities of darkness, then there is nothing more execrable than existence.

Some reader may see a basic contradiction in everything I am saying, as I long on the one hand for unending life, and on the other hand claim that this life is devoid of the value assigned it. A contradiction? I should say so! The contradiction between my heart which says *Yes*, and my head which says *No*! Naturally there is a contradiction. Who does not remember those words of the Gospel which say: "Lord, I believe; help thou mine unbelief"? Contradiction? Indeed there is! Since we live solely from and by contradictions, since life is tragedy and the tragedy is in the perpetual struggle without hope or victory, then it is all a contradiction.

The values we are here discussing are, as you see, values of the heart, and—against values of the heart, reason does not avail. For reasons are only reasons, that is, not even truths. There exists a class of pedantic definition-mongers, pedants by nature and by grace, who remind me of that gentleman who, proposing to console a father whose son had just died in the flower of his youth, told him: "Patience, my

friend, we all have to die!" Would you be surprised
if this father were annoyed at such a piece of impertinence? For it surely was an impertinence. And there
are times when even an axiom constitutes an impertinence. Often enough we might well say:

> Para pensar cual tú, sólo es preciso
> no tener nada más que inteligencia.

There are people, in fact, who appear to think only
with their brain, or with whatever else the specific
thinking organ may be. And there are others who
think with their whole body and soul, with their
blood, with the marrow of their bones, with their
heart and lungs and viscera, with their whole life.
And the people who think only with their brain turn
into definition-mongers; they become professionals of
thought. And you know what a professional is? You
know what a product of the division of labor is?

Take a professional boxer, for example: he has
learned to hit with such economy of effort that he puts
all his force into one blow, bringing into play only
those muscles necessary to achieve his immediate end
and concentrated purpose: to down his opponent. A
blow given by a non-professional may not have as
much immediate, objective efficacy, but it will have
much more vital effect on the man delivering it, causing him to bring into play almost his entire body. One
blow is that of a boxer, the other that of a man. And
it is notorious that the Hercules of the circus, the ath-
letes of the ring, are not generally sound of health.
They floor their opponents, they lift enormous
weights, but they die of tuberculosis or dyspepsia.

If a philosopher is not a man, he is anything but a
philosopher; he is above all a pedant, and a pedant is
a caricature of a man. The cultivation of any branch

of science whatever—of chemistry, physics, geometry, philology—may be a labor of differentiated specialization (and even then, it may be that only in a very restricted sense and within very narrow limits); but philosophy, like poetry, is a labor of integration and synthesis, or else it is merely pseudo-philosophical erudition.

All knowledge has an ultimate object. Knowledge for the sake of knowledge is, say what you will, nothing but a dim begging of the question. We learn something either for an immediate practical end, or in order to complete the rest of our knowledge. Even the learning which appears most theoretical to us, that is, that knowledge having the least immediate application to the non-intellectual necessities of life, answers to a need no less real because it is intellectual, to reasons of economy in our thinking, to a principle of unity and continuity in our consciousness. But just as a bit of scientific knowledge has its finality in the rest of knowledge, so the philosophy that we would make our own has also its extrinsic object—it has reference to our whole destiny, to our attitude toward life and the universe. And the most tragic problem of philosophy is to reconcile intellectual needs with the needs of the heart and will. For it is on this point that all philosophy which attempts to undo the eternal and tragic contradiction underlying our existence falls to pieces. But is this contradiction always faced?

Little can be expected from a ruler, for example, who has not at some time or other concerned himself, even though only dimly, with the first beginning and final end of all things, most especially of man, with his first why and his final wherefore.

And this supreme preoccupation cannot be purely

rational, it must involve the heart. It is not enough to think, we must also feel, our destiny. And the would-be leader of his fellowmen who affirms and proclaims that things above the rooftops leave him cold, does not deserve to lead them. Though, of course, this does not mean that any ready-made solution need be demanded of him. A solution? Is there indeed any solution?

For my part, I would never willingly follow or bestow my confidence on any popular leader who is not impregnated with the idea that whoever leads a people leads men, men of flesh and blood, men who are born, suffer, and, even though they would not die, do die; men who are ends in themselves, not merely means; men who must be whoever they are, and not anyone else; men, in short, who seek what we call happiness. It is inhuman, for example, to sacrifice a generation of men to the generation that follows them, without any regard for the destiny of those sacrificed: not just regard for their memory or their names, but regard for the men themselves.

All the talk about a man living on in his children, or in his works, or as part of the Universe, is but vague lucubration satisfactory only to people who suffer from emotional stupidity—though these same people may also possess a certain intellectual distinction. For one may boast a great talent, what we know as a great talent, and be a dunce as regards feeling, and even a moral imbecile. There have been instances.

The affective dunces with talent are wont to say that it is useless to try and delve into the unknowable or to wrestle against thorns. It is as if one were to tell a man whose leg has been amputated that it is no good thinking about it. And all of us have suffered some amputation; some of us feel it, and others simply do not. Or, some pretend they do not feel anything, and these are the hypocrites.

A pedant who beheld Solon weeping for the death of a son said to him: "Why do you weep thus, if weeping is of no use?" And the wise man answered: "Precisely for that reason, because it's no use." Of course, weeping does have some use, even if only to give relief, but the profound sense of Solon's reply to his impertinent questioner comes through. And I am convinced we would solve many questions if we only went out into the streets and bruited our sorrows—which would probably turn out to be one single common sorrow—and joined in weeping and crying out to Heaven and calling upon God, even if He did not hear us—though He would certainly. The holiest attribute of a temple is that it is a place where men weep in common. A *Miserere* sung in common by a multitude flailed by destiny is worth a whole philosophy. To cure the plague is not enough, it must also be lamented with bitter tears. Yes, we must learn to weep! Perhaps that is the supreme wisdom. Wherefore? Ask Solon.

There is something which, for want of a better name, we shall call the tragic sense of life, and it carries along with it an entire conception of the Universe and of life itself, an entire philosophy more or less formulated, more or less conscious. And this sense may animate, and does animate, not only individual men, but entire peoples. And this sense does not so much flow from ideas as determine them, even though later these ideas react upon it and corroborate it. Sometimes it may originate in a chance illness, dyspepsia, for example; but at other times it is constitutional. And it is no good talking, as we shall see, of men sound and unsound. Apart from the fact that there is no normal standard of health, no one has ever proved that man must necessarily be joyful by nature. But there is more to it than that: man, because he is man, because he possesses consciousness, is already, in comparison to the jackass or the crab, a sick animal. Consciousness is a disease.

There are many examples of flesh and blood men who have been instinct with the tragic sense of life. I think at once of Marcus Aurelius, St. Augustine, Pascal, Rousseau, René, Obermann, James Thomson, Leopardi, Vigny, Lenau, Kleist, Amiel, Quental, Kierkegaard—men weighed down with wisdom rather than with knowledge.

There may be those who believe that any one of these men adopted his attitude—as if such attitudes could be adopted, as one adopts a posture—in order to call attention to himself or perhaps to ingratiate himself with those in power, with his superiors, perhaps. No one is more petty than the man who sets out to reconstruct the intentions of others. But *honni soit qui mal y pense.* And I make use of a French proverb so as not to set down a much more energetic one in Spanish, which, however, borders on coarseness.

And there are also, I believe, whole peoples who possess this tragic sense of life as well.

It is to this question that we must now turn our attention, beginning with the matter of health and disease.

II. The Point of Departure

MY REFLECTIONS up to this point may strike some people perhaps as rather morbid in character. Morbid? But what after all is disease? What, for that matter, is health?

Perhaps disease itself is the essential condition of what we call progress, and progress itself a disease.

Who does not know the mythical tragedy of Paradise? Our first parents lived there in a state of perfect health and perfect innocence, and Yahweh let them eat from the Tree of Life and created all things for them. But He ordered them not to taste the fruit of the Tree of Knowledge of Good and Evil. But tempted by the serpent—a model of prudence for Christ—they tasted the fruit of the Tree of Knowledge of Good and Evil, and became subject to all diseases, and to the crown and consummation of them all, death, and to labor and progress. For progress, according to this legend, springs from original sin. And thus it was that the curiosity of woman, of Eve, of the being most subject to organic necessity and the conservation of life, brought about the Fall, and with the Fall, man's redemption, which put us on the road to God, to attain to Him and to be in Him.

Would you prefer some other version of our origin? Very well. There is one which holds that man is no more, strictly speaking, than a variety of gorilla, or orangutan, or chimpanzee, or the like, a hydrocephalic or something similar. Once upon a time an

anthropoid ape gave birth to a diseased offspring—
as seen from the strictly animal or zoological point of
view—really diseased, and if the disease represented
a weakness, it also proved an advantage in the struggle for survival. At last, the only upright mammal—
man—stood erect. His new posture freed him from
having to use his hands to walk, so that he could
counterpose his thumb to the other four fingers and
thus grasp objects and manufacture utensils; and
hands are great forgers of intelligence, as is well
known. And the upright position allowed his lungs,
trachea, larynx, and mouth to develop the power of
articulate speech, and speech is intelligence. And the
same position, allowing the head—site of the mind—
to weigh vertically upon the trunk, facilitated its development and increase of weight. Inasmuch as
stronger and more resistant pelvic bones were now
needed than those of species whose head and trunk
rest upon all four extremities, it then devolved upon
woman, author of the Fall, according to Genesis, to
give birth to larger-headed offspring through a harder
frame of bones. For having sinned, woman was condemned by Yahweh to bring forth her children in
pain.

The gorilla, the chimpanzee, the orangutan, and
their kind must look upon man as a poor sick animal
who goes so far as to store up his dead: store them
to what end?

And this primary sickness and all those that follow from it—are they not, perhaps, the main element
of progress? Arthritis, for example, infects the blood,
introducing scoriae, a kind of residue from an imperfect organic combustion. But may not this very im-
purity serve to stimulate the blood? Chemically pure

water is undrinkable. And may not physiologically pure blood be unfit for the brain of the upright mammal who must live by thought?

The history of medicine, moreover, teaches us that progress consists not so much in expelling the germs of disease, or more precisely the diseases themselves, as in accommodating them to our organism and thus perhaps enriching it, in dissolving them in our blood. What else do all the serums and vaccines demonstrate, what else is immunization over a period of time?

If the idea of health were not an abstract category, something which strictly speaking does not exist, we might say that a perfectly healthy man would no longer be a man but an irrational animal: irrational for want of any disease to ignite his reason. A real disease, and a tragic one, is the one that arouses in us the appetite to know for the sole pleasure of knowing, the delight of tasting the fruit of the Tree of Knowledge of Good and Evil.

Πάντες ἄνθρωποι τὸν εἰδέναι ὀρέγονται φύσει: "All men strive by nature to know." Thus does Aristotle begin his *Metaphysics*. And a thousand times since it has been repeated that curiosity or the desire to know—which, according to Genesis, led our original mother to sin—is the beginning of knowledge.

But we must differentiate between the desire or appetite to know—apparently and at first sight for the love of knowledge itself, the zeal for tasting the fruit of the Tree of Knowledge—and the need to know in order to live. The latter, which gives us direct and immediate knowledge, and which in a certain sense might be called, if it does not seem too paradoxical, unconscious knowledge, is common to both men and animals, while what distinguishes us from them is reflective knowing, the knowledge of knowing itself.

Men have long debated and long will continue to debate—the world having been given over to their debates—concerning the origin of knowledge. But, leaving aside for the moment the question of what may constitute quintessential knowledge, it is certainly clear that in the apparential order of things, in the life of beings endowed with a certain more or less cloudy faculty of knowing and perceiving, or who at any rate appear to act as if they were so endowed, knowledge is exhibited to us as bound up with the necessity of living and of procuring the wherewithal to maintain life. It is consequent to that very essence of being, which according to Spinoza consists in striving to persevere indefinitely in its own being. Speaking in terms in which concreteness borders on vulgarity, we might say that the brain, in so far as its function is concerned, is in dependence on the stomach. Among beings who rank lowest in the scale of living things, the actions which demonstrate willfulness, those which seem to be connected with a more or less clear consciousness, are actions directed toward procuring nourishment for the being performing them.

Such then is what we may call the historical origin of knowledge, whatever may be its origin in other regards. Beings apparently endowed with perception perceive in order to live, and only to the degree that they need to perceive in order to live. But perhaps once this knowledge has been stored up, knowledge which at first was useful and is no longer so, it constitutes a fund far exceeding that required by life.

Thus we have, first of all, a need to know in order

to live, and then, arising from the first need, what we may call a superfluous or *de luxe* knowledge, which in its turn may come to constitute a new need. Curiosity, the so-called innate desire to know, is only awakened and becomes operative after the need-to-know-in-order-to-live is satisfied. Even though sometimes it may not occur in this order, given the present level of our human lineage, and instead curiosity take precedence over need, and knowledge over hunger, nevertheless the primordial fact is that curiosity sprang from the need to know in order to live, and this is the dead weight and gross matter which all knowledge and science carries in its womb. Aspiring as they do to knowledge for the sake of knowledge and truth for the sake of truth, science and knowledge are forced by the needs of life to place themselves at the service of these needs. And men, believing they seek the truth for its own sake, in fact seek life in the truth. The variety of knowledge and science depends upon the variety of human needs, and men of science usually work, willingly or unwillingly, knowingly or unknowingly, in the service of those in power, or in the service of a nation requiring from them confirmation of its drives.

But does all this really constitute a dead weight and gross matter as far as science is concerned, or is it not rather more likely the source of its redemption? In truth, it is just that, and it is folly to presume to rebel against the human condition.

Knowledge remains at the service of the need to go on living, primarily at the service of personal survival. And this need and this instinct have created in man the organs of knowledge and given them the range they have. Man sees, hears, touches, tastes, and smells whatever he must see, hear, touch, taste, and smell in order to go on living. The weakening or loss of any one of these senses increases the risks which hedge in his life, and if in the present state of society the risks are not augmented, it is because some people nowadays see, hear, touch, and smell for other people. A blind man alone, without a guide, could not live very long. Society constitutes an added sense, the true "common sense."

Man, then, in his condition of isolated individual, only sees, hears, touches, tastes, and smells what he needs in order to live and survive. If he does not perceive colors below red or beyond violet, it is perhaps because those between red and violet suffice for his purposes of self-preservation. And the senses themselves constitute an apparatus for simplification which eliminates from objective reality everything we do not need to know in order to utilize objects for the preservation of life. The animal that does not perish in complete darkness ends by becoming blind. Parasites living in the intestines of other animals on juices they find already processed for them do not need to see or hear, and so they do not see or hear, but instead, having turned into a species of sack, adhere to the being from whom they live. For these parasites neither the visual nor the audible world need exist. It is enough for them that the animals in whose intestines they live can see and hear.

Knowledge, then, is primarily at the service of the instinct of self-preservation, which is indeed, as we agreed with Spinoza, its very essence. And thus it may be said that the instinct of self-preservation itself makes the world's reality and truth perceptible to us. For it is this instinct which chooses—from the unfathomable and limitless world of the possible—everything that exists for us. What exists for us, in fact, is precisely what we need to know, in one or another way, in order to go on existing. Objective existence is, in our minds, dependent on our own personal existence. And nobody can deny that facets of reality unknown to us today and perhaps unknowable at any time—simply because they are not necessary to us for conserving our own present existence—could very well exist and perhaps do exist.

But man neither lives alone nor is he an isolated individual, but is rather a member of society; there is a good deal of truth in the proverb which says that an individual, like an atom, is an abstraction. Of course: divorced from the Universe the atom is as much an abstraction as the Universe divorced from atoms. And if the individual survives through his instinct for self-preservation, society owes its being and its continuance to the instinct for perpetuation in the individual. And, from this instinct, or rather from society, springs reason.

Reason, what we call reason, reflex and reflective knowledge, the distinguishing mark of man, is a social product.

It owes its origin, perhaps, to language. We think articulately, that is, reflectively, thanks to articulate language, and this language arose from the need to communicate our thought to our neighbors. To think is to talk with oneself, and each of us talks to himself because we have had to talk with one another. In everyday life it frequently happens that we hit upon an idea that we were seeking, we succeed in giving it form, that is, securing it, extracting it from the mist of dim perceptions for which it stands in representation, because of the efforts we have made to present the idea to others. Thought is interior language, and interior language originates in outward language. So that reason is properly both social and common, and this fact is fraught with consequences, as we shall see.

And if there exists a reality which, in so far as we know it, is the product of the instinct for self-preservation and of the senses at the service of this instinct, must there not also exist another reality, no less real than the first, the product, in so far as we know it, of the instinct for perpetuation, the instinct of the species, and of the senses at the service of this instinct? The instinct for self-preservation—hunger—is fundamental to the individual human being; the instinct for perpetuation—love—in its most rudimentary, physiological form—is fundamental to human society. And just as man knows what he needs to know in order to continue living, so society, or man to the degree that he is a social being, knows what is needful to know in order to perpetuate man in society.

There is a world, the perceptible world, which is the offspring of hunger, and another, the ideal world, which is the offspring of love. And just as there are senses employed in the service of knowing the perceptible world, so there are also senses—dormant for the most part today, since social consciousness has scarcely yet stirred—employed in the service of knowing the ideal world. For why should we deny objective reality to the creations of love, of the instinct for perpetuation, inasmuch as we' grant it to those of hunger or the instinct of self-preservation? For if it is said that the creations of love are no more than figments of our imagination, devoid of objective value, might it not equally be said of the creations of hunger that they are no more than the figments of our senses? Who can assert that there does not exist an invisible and intangible world, perceived only by the inner sense which lives at the service of the instinct of perpetuation?

Human society, *qua* such a society, boasts senses which the individual, but for the existence of that society, would lack, just as the individual man—who is in his turn a kind of society—boasts senses which are lacking in the cells of which he is composed. The blind cells of hearing, in their obscure consciousness, must of necessity be unaware of the existence of the visible world, and if you were to speak to them of it, they would doubtless consider it an arbitrary creation of the deaf cells of sight, while the latter in their turn would consider the audible world created by the hearing cells a complete illusion.

We have previously remarked on how those parasites which live in the intestines of the higher animals, feeding on the nutritive juices supplied by these animals, do not need to see or hear, so that for them neither the visible nor audible world exists. And if they were possessed of a certain degree of consciousness and paid any heed to the fact that the host at whose expense they live believed in another world, one different from theirs, they would perhaps regard it as a derangement of the imagination. In the same way there are social parasites, as Mr. A. J. Balfour admirably observes. These parasites receive from the society in which they live the basis for a moral conduct and they go on to deny that a belief in God and a future life are a necessary foundation on which to base a permissible life and good conduct—but society has already prepared for them the spiritual nutriment upon which they feed. A single individual can endure life and live it well and even heroically without any belief at all in either God or the immortality of the soul; nevertheless, he will be living the life of a spiritual parasite. What we call the sense of honor is, even in non-Christians, the fruit of Christianity. And I say more: if it happens that faith in God is joined in a man to a life of purity and high morality, it is not so much the belief in God that makes him good, but that his being good, thanks be to God, makes him believe in Him. Goodness is the best source of spiritual clairvoyance.

I am not unaware, of course, that all this talk about man creating the world of his senses and love creating the ideal world and about the blind cells of hearing and the deaf cells of sight and about spiritual parasites and so on may well be said to be pure metaphor. For so it is, and I am attempting no more than to reason by means of metaphor. The fact is that the social sense, offspring of love, creator of language and reason and of the ideal world which springs from this sense, is basically no more than what we call fantasy or imagination. And out of fantasy comes reason. And if we understand fantasy to be a faculty fashioning images capriciously, I will ask: what is caprice? In any case, reason and the senses are also fallible.

And we shall have to look into this quintessential social faculty: the imagination which makes everything personal and which, placed at the service of the instinct for self-perpetuation, reveals God and the immortality of the soul to us, so that God is a social product.

But we will leave this until later.

And now then, why does man philosophize? That is to say, why does he investigate the first causes and the ultimate ends of things? Why do we seek disinterested truth? To say that all men have a natural tendency to know is true. But why?

Philosophers search for a theoretical or ideal point of departure for their human task, the task of philosophizing. But they tend to neglect the search for the practical and real point of departure, the purpose. What is the purpose of making philosophy, of thinking it out and then expounding it to one's fellows? What does the philosopher seek in it and through it? The truth for truth's sake? The truth in order to subject our conduct to it and to determine in relation to it our spiritual attitude to life and the Universe?

Philosophy is the product of each philosopher's humanity, and each philosopher is a man of flesh and blood who addresses himself to other flesh-and-blood men like himself. And let him do what he may, he philosophizes not with his reason alone but with his will, with his feeling, with his flesh and blood, with his entire body and soul. It is a man that makes philosophy.

I do not want to use the word "I" here and say that in philosophizing it is "I" and not the man who philosophizes. For I would not want this concrete, circumscribed I, the I of flesh and blood who suffers from toothache and does not find life bearable if death is really the annihilation of the personal consciousness, I would not want this I confused with that other "I," the contraband I, the theoretical I which Fichte smuggled into philosophy, nor confused even with the Unique, also theoretical, of Max Stirner. It is better to say we; meaning we who are circumscribed in our space.

Knowledge for the sake of knowledge! Truth for truth's sake! That is inhuman. And if we say that theoretical philosophy is directed toward practice, truth toward goodness, science toward ethics, I will ask: And wherefore goodness? Is it perhaps an end in itself? Only whatever contributes to the conservation, perpetuation, and enrichment of consciousness is good. Goodness is directed toward man, toward the maintenance and perfection of human society, which is composed of men. And wherefore is this so? "Act in such wise that your action may be a pattern for all men," Kant tells us. Very well: but wherefore? It is necessary to seek a wherefore.

There is a wherefore at the point of departure of all philosophy, at the true point of departure, the practical and not the theoretical. The philosopher does not philosophize merely for the sake of philosophizing. *Primum vivere, deinde philosophari*, says the old Latin adage; and inasmuch as the philosopher is a man before he is a philosopher, he must live before he can philosophize, and in fact he philosophizes in order to live. Usually he philosophizes so as to be able to resign himself to life, or to seek some end-purpose, or to distract himself and forget his woes, or by way of sport and games. A good example of this last is that terrible Athenian ironist who was Socrates, of whom Xenophon in his *Memorabilia* relates that he was so skillful in describing to Theodata, the courtesan, the artifice she should employ in luring lovers to her house that she invited the philosopher to be her companion in the chase, συνθηρατής: in a word, her pimp. The truth is that philosophy oftentimes tends to become a pimping art, albeit spiritual. And sometimes it is used as an opiate to alleviate pain.

I pick at random a book of metaphysics, the closest to hand, *Time and Space, a Metaphysical Essay*, by Shadworth H. Hodgson. I open it, and in the fifth

34*

paragraph of the First Chapter in the First Part, I read: "Metaphysics is, properly speaking, not a science but a philosophy; that is, it is a science whose end is in itself, in the gratification and education of the minds which carry it on, not in any external purpose, such as the founding of any art conducive to the welfare of life." Let us examine this. And we will see, first, that metaphysics is not, "properly speaking," a science, "that is," it is a science whose end, etc. And this science, which is properly speaking not a science, has its end in itself, in the gratification and education of the minds that carry it on. Which is it then? Is the end of metaphysics in itself? Or is its end the gratification and education of the minds which carry it on? It is either one or the other! Hodgson next adds that metaphysics does not have any kind of external purpose as end, as for instance the founding of an art conducive to well-being in life. Still, is not gratification of mind for the philosopher part of the well-being of his life? Let the reader consider this passage from the English metaphysician, and then tell me if it is not a tissue of contradictions.

All this contradiction is inevitable when an attempt is made *humanly* to define the theory of a science, a knowledge, whose end-purpose is in itself, of knowing for the sake of knowing, of truth for truth's sake. Science does not exist except in personal consciousness and thanks to it: astronomy, mathematics have no more reality than what they possess as knowledge in the minds of those who learn and cultivate them. And if one day all personal consciousness on earth must come to an end, if one day the human spirit must return to nothingness, that is, to the absolute unconsciousness from which it sprang, and if there is not to be any longer a human spirit to avail itself of all our accumulated science—then wherefore this science? For we should not lose sight of the fact that the problem of the personal immortality of the soul involves the future of the entire human race.

The series of contradictions into which the Englishman falls, as he sets about explaining the theory of a science whose end lies in itself, becomes easily understandable as something natural to an Englishman who is before all else a man. Doubtless a German specialist, a philosopher who made philosophy his specialty, first murdering his humanity and burying it in the specialty, would explain much better all this about a science whose end lies in itself and the theory of knowing for the sake of knowing.

Let us take the man Spinoza, the Portuguese Jew exiled in Holland. Read his *Ethics* for what it is, a desperate elegiac poem, and tell me if you do not hear, beneath the unadorned, but seemingly serene, propositions set forth *more geometrico*, a mournful echo of the prophetic psalms. This is not the philosophy of resignation but of despair. And when he wrote that a free man thinks of everything but death and that his wisdom consists in meditating on life itself and not on death—*homo liber de nulla re minus quam de morte cogitat et eius sapientia non mortis, sed vitae meditatio est* (Ethics, Part IV, Prop. LXVII)—when he wrote that, he felt, as we all feel, that we are slaves; and in fact he was thinking of death, and he wrote as he did to free himself—though his attempt was in vain—of this thought. Not even when he wrote Proposition XLII of Part V, to the effect that "blessedness is not the reward of virtue, but virtue itself," did he believe, surely, what he wrote. For men make philosophy precisely to convince themselves of what they say, though they do not succeed. And this desire to convince oneself, that is, to do violence to one's own human nature, is often the true point of departure for not a few philosophies.

"Whence do I come, and whence does the world in which and from which I live? Whither am I going and whither everything around me? What is the meaning of it all?" These are the questions man asks himself as soon as he frees himself from the brutalizing necessity of having to labor for his material sustenance. And if we look closely, we shall see that beneath these questions lies the desire to know not so much the Why as the Wherefore, the wish to know not so much the cause but the finality. Cicero's definition of philosophy is well known, where he called it "the science of things divine and human and of the causes contained in them": *rerum divinarum et humanarum, causarumque quibus hae res continentur.* But in reality these causes are, for us, ends. What is the Supreme Cause, God, but the Supreme End? We are interested in the Why thinking only of the Wherefore. We want to know whence we come only the better to ascertain whither we are going.

This Ciceronian definition, which is the Stoic definition, is also found in that formidable intellectualist who was Clement of Alexandria, canonized by the Catholic Church, and he expounds it in the Fifth Chapter of the first of his *Stromata*. But this same Christian philosopher—was he Christian?—in Chapter 22 of his fourth *stroma*, tells us that for the gnostic (that is, the intellectual), knowledge, *gnosis*, should suffice; and he adds:

> For I will dare aver that it is not because he wishes to be saved that he, who devotes himself to knowledge for the sake of the divine science itself, chooses knowledge. For the exertion of the intellect

by exercise is prolonged to a perpetual exertion. And the perpetual exertion of the intellect is the essence of an intelligent being, which results from an uninterrupted process of admixture, and remains eternal contemplation, a living substance. Could we, then, suppose any one proposing to the Gnostic whether he would choose the knowledge of God or everlasting salvation; and if these, which are entirely identical, were separable, he would without the least hesitation choose the knowledge of God, deeming that property of faith, which from love ascends to knowledge, desirable, for its own sake.

May He, may God himself, whom we long to possess and enjoy eternally, deliver us from this gnosticism or Clementine intellectualism!

Why do I want to know whence I came and whither I am going, whence and whither everything around me, and the meaning of it all? Because I do not want to die utterly, and I want to know if I am to die definitively or not. And if I am not to die altogether, what then is to become of me? If I am to die altogether, then nothing makes any sense. There are three solutions: a) I know I am to die utterly, and then my despair is incurable, or b) I know I will not die utterly, and then I resign myself, or c) I can not know either one thing or the other, and then I am resigned to despair or despairing in resignation, a despairing resignation or a resigned despair, and therein the struggle.

"The best thing to do with what can not be known," some reader will suggest, "is to let it be." But is that possible? In his beautiful poem "The Ancient Sage" Tennyson wrote:

> Thou canst not prove the Nameless, O my son,
> Nor canst thou prove the world thou movest in,
> Thou canst not prove that thou art body alone,

Thou canst not prove that thou art spirit alone,
Nor canst thou prove that thou art both in one:
Nor canst thou prove thou art immortal, no,
Nor yet that thou art mortal—nay, my son,
Thou canst not prove that I, who speak with thee,
Am not thyself in converse with thyself,
For nothing worthy proving can be proven,
Nor yet disproven: wherefore thou be wise,
Cleave ever to the sunnier side of doubt,
Cling to Faith beyond the forms of Faith!

Yes, perhaps, as the Sage says:

> nothing worthy proving can be proven,
> nor yet disproven

And yet, can we repress the instinct which drives man to want to know, to want to know, above all, whatever will lead him to live, to live forever? We say to live forever, not to know forever like the Alexandrian gnostic. For to live is one thing and to know is another, and, as we shall see, there may be such an opposition between the two that we may say that everything vital is, not only irrational, but anti-rational, and everything rational is anti-vital. And herein lies the basis for the tragic sense of life.

The defect in Descartes's *Discourse on Method* does not lie in the methodical prior doubt, in the fact that he begins by resolving to doubt everything, which is no more than a mere artifice; the defect lies in his resolving to begin by leaving himself out, omitting Descartes, the real man, the man of flesh and blood, the man who does not want to die, so that he can become a mere thinker, that is, an abstraction. But the real man reappears and works his way into the philosophy.

"Le bon sens est la chose du monde la mieux partagée." Thus begins the *Discourse on Method*, and this good sense saved him. He goes on to talk about himself, of the man Descartes, telling us, among other things that he thought highly of eloquence and loved poetry; that above all else he delighted in mathematics, because of the evidence and certainty of its reasons, and that he venerated our theology and strove, as much as any man, to attain Heaven—*et prétendais autant qu'aucun autre à gagner le ciel.* And this attempt—a very laudable one I believe, and very natural—prevented him from drawing all the conclusions from his methodical doubt. The man Descartes attempted, as much as any man, to attain to heaven, "but having realized, for sure, that the way thither is not any the less open to the most ignorant than to the most learned, and that the revealed truths which lead thither are beyond our intelligence, I would not have dared submit them to my feeble reason, and I thought that to undertake to examine them and to succeed therein I would require some extraordinary help from Heaven and need to be more than a man." And here we have the man himself. Here is the man who did not feel obliged, thanks be to God, to make a profession—*métier*—of science by way of improving his fortunes, nor the need to take upon himself the office of cynically denigrating glory. He goes on to tell us of how he was compelled to stay in Germany, and there, shut up in a stove—*poêle*—began to philosophize his method. In Germany, and shut up in a stove! And thus it is that his discourse is a stove-discourse, in a German stove, even though the philosopher shut up inside the stove is a Frenchman who proposed to attain Heaven.

And he comes to the *cogito ergo sum*, which St. Augustine had already anticipated. But the *ego* implied in this enthymeme, *ego cogito, ergo ego sum,* is an unreal, that is, an ideal *ego*, an ideal I, and its *sum*, its existence, something unreal as well. "I think, therefore I am" can only mean, "I think, therefore I am a thinker"; the *being* in the *I am*, derived from *I think*, is no more than a knowing; that *being* is knowledge, not life. The primary reality is not that I think, but that I live, for those who do not think also live, even though that kind of living is not a true life. So many contradictions, dear Lord, when we try to wed life to reason!

The truth is *sum, ergo cogito*—I am, therefore I think, though not everything that is, thinks. Is not consciousness of thought first of all consciousness of being? Is pure thought possible, thought without consciousness of self, without personality? Is pure knowledge possible, knowledge without feeling, without that kind of materiality which feeling lends to it? Is not thought somehow felt, and do we not feel ourselves in the act of knowing and willing? Could not the man in the stove have said: "I feel, therefore I am" or "I will, therefore I am"? And when there is a feeling of self, does not one feel oneself eternal? And in willing oneself, does not one will oneself eternal, that is, will not to die? Is not what the sad Jew of Amsterdam called the essence of a being, its striving to persevere indefinitely in its own being, its self-love, its longing for immortality, perhaps the primary and fundamental condition of all reflective or human knowledge? And is this drive not therefore the true basis, the true point of departure for all philosophy, though philosophers, perverted by intellectualism, do not recognize it?

And, moreover, it was the *cogito* that introduced a distinction which, although fruitful of truths, has also sown confusions, and that is the distinction between the object—*cogito*—and the subject—*sum*. For there is scarcely any distinction which does not also serve to confuse. But we will return to this later.

For the present let us agree on this intense suspicion that the longing not to die, the hunger for personal immortality, the striving to persevere indefinitely in our own being, all of which is, according to the tragic Jew, our very essence, constitutes the affective basis of all knowledge and the personal inner point of departure for any and all human philosophy wrought by man for his fellows. And then we shall see how the solution to this inner affective problem, a solution which may amount to a despairing renunciation of any attempt at solution, is something that colors all the rest of philosophy. Underlying even the so-called problem of knowledge there is nothing more than this human feeling, just as underlying the inquiry into the why, into the cause, there is simply the search for the wherefore, for the end purpose. All the rest is either a self-deception or a wish to deceive others by way of deceiving oneself.

And this personal and affective point of departure for all philosophy and all religion is the tragic sense of life. Let us look into it.

III. The Hunger for Immortality

THOUGH GNOSTICS OR intellectuals may say that what follows is rhetoric and not philosophy, let us nevertheless consider the immortal longing for immortality. The divine Plato himself, discoursing on the immortality of the soul in his *Phaedo*, said that it was right to make legends on the theme: μυθολογεῖν.

First let us recall once again, and it will not be the last time, the saying of Spinoza about every being striving to persevere in itself, that to strive constitutes its very essence and implies indefinite time, and that the soul, in sum, tends to persevere, sometimes with a clear and distinct idea and sometimes confusedly, in its being indefinitely, and that it is aware of its perseverance (*Ethics*, Part III, Propositions VI-X).

In effect it is impossible for us to conceive of ourselves as non-existent. There is no way whatsoever to make consciousness become aware of absolute unconsciousness, aware of its own annihilation. Try, reader, to imagine, when you are wide awake, the state of your soul in deep sleep. Try to flood your consciousness with the image of non-consciousness, and you will see the difficulty. We can not conceive of ourselves as not existing.

The visible Universe, the one created by the instinct of self-preservation, strikes me as too narrow. It is like an over-small cage against whose bars my soul beats its wings. I need more air to breathe: more, more, always more! I want to be myself and, without ceasing to be myself, to be others as well, to encompass the totality of all things visible and invisible, to extend myself to the limitless in space and prolong myself to the endless in time. Not to be everything and not be it forever is the same as not being at all. At least let me be altogether myself and be so forever. And to be altogether myself is to be all others. All or nothing!

All or nothing at all! What other meaning is there in the Shakespearean "To be or not to be," or that passage in *Coriolanus* where it is said of Marcius: "He wants nothing of a god but eternity." Eternity! Eternity! That is the longing. The thirst for eternity is what is called, among men, love, and whoever loves another desires to become eternal in this other. Whatever is not eternal is also not real.

The terrible vision of life flowing away like waves of water has wrung soul-wrenching cries from the poets of all ages, from Pindar and his "dream of a shadow," σχιὰς ὄναρ, to Calderón and his "life is a dream" and Shakespeare and his "We are such stuff as dreams are made on." This last sentence is even more tragic than the Castilian's, for where Calderón merely declares that our life is a dream—our life, but not necessarily we, who are the dreamers of it—the Englishman makes us a dream as well, a dream that dreams.

Love and the vanity of the passing world are the two fundamental and heartfelt notes of true poetry. And they are two notes which can not sound one without the other. The sense of the vanity of the passing world leads us into love, the only feeling which triumphs over the vain and the transitory and which fulfills and eternalizes life—at least apparently, if not in

all reality. Love, especially when it struggles against
destiny, overwhelms us with a sense of the vanity of
this world of appearances and allows us a glimpse of
another world where destiny is overcome and liberty
is law.

Everything passes! That is the refrain of all who
have drunk, lips to the spout, at the fountain of life,
of all who have savored the fruit of the Tree of the
Knowledge of Good and Evil.

To be, to be forever, to be without end! Thirst to
be, thirst to be more! Hunger for God! Thirst for
eternal and eternalizing love! To be forever! To be
God!

"Ye shall be as gods!" the serpent said to the first
pair of lovers, as we know from Genesis (3:5). "If
in this life only we have hope in Christ, we are of all
men most miserable," wrote the Apostle (1 Cor.,
15:19). And all religion has sprung historically from
the cult of the dead, that is to say, from the cult of
immortality.

The tragic Portuguese Jew of Amsterdam wrote
that there is nothing the free man thinks of less than
he does of death. But that sort of free man is no more
than a dead man; he is free only from life's wellspring, lacking in love, a slave to his freedom. The
thought that I must die and the enigma of what will
come afterwards constitutes the very heartbeat of my
consciousness. Whenever I contemplate the green
serenity of the fields or look into the clear eyes from
which a fellow soul is looking, my consciousness
dilates, I feel the diastole of my soul and am bathed
in the flood of life that flows around me, and I believe
in my own future. But at once the voice of the mystery whispers to me: "You will cease to be!" The

wing of the Angel of Death brushes against me, and the systole of my soul inundates the depths of my spirit with the blood of divinity.

Like Pascal, I do not understand anyone who asserts he doesn't give a fig for these considerations. Such indifference "in a matter that concerns themselves, their eternity, their all, exasperates me more than it moves me to compassion; it appalls and terrifies me." And the man who feels in this way is for me, as for Pascal, whose words I have quoted, "a monster."

A thousand times and in a thousand tones of voice it has been said that ancestor worship is generally the starting point of primitive religions, and strictly speaking it may surely be said that what most distinguishes man from other animals is that in one way or another he keeps his dead, refusing to hand them over to the indifference of teeming mother earth. Man is an animal that preserves his dead. And against what does he preserve them? From what does futile man protect them? Unhappy consciousness flees its own annihilation; like an animal spirit whose umbilical cord to the physical world is cut, it finds itself confronted with this alien world and realizes it is a thing apart, and must long then for another life not of this world. For the earth would become a vast cemetery before the dead themselves could die again.

In the days when the living could count on no more than mud huts or straw shelters (which the weather has long ago wiped out), the dead had tumuli raised for them, and stone was employed in sepulchers before it was used for houses. The strong walled houses of the dead are the ones to have outlived the centuries, not the houses of the living: not the inns of passage, but the dwellings of permanence.

This cult, not of death but of immortality, originates and keeps religions. Amidst the delirium of destruction, Robespierre induced the Convention to declare the existence of the Supreme Being and of "the consolatory principle of the immortality of the soul," for the Incorruptible was terrified at the thought that he himself would one day turn to dust.

Is it a disease? Perhaps. But whoever pays no heed to disease is heedless of his health, and man is an animal who is essentially and in substance diseased. Is it a disease? Perhaps it is, as is life, to which it is in thrall, and the only health possible is death. And this disease is the wellspring of all solid health. It is from the depths of this anguish, out of the abyss of the sense of our mortality, that we emerge into the light of another heaven, as Dante emerged from the deep of Hell to behold the stars once again:

> e quindi uscimmo a riveder le stelle.

Though at first blush meditation on our mortality is anguishing, in the end it fortifies us. Withdraw, reader, into yourself, and begin to imagine a slow dissolution of yourself: the light growing dim, things becoming dumb and soundless, silence enveloping you; the objects you handle crumbling between your fingers, the ground slipping from under your feet, your very memory vanishing as if in a swoon, everything melting away into nothingness and you yourself disappearing, not even the consciousness of nothingness remaining by way of grotesque handhold.

I have heard a story told about a poor harvest worker who died in hospital: when the priest went to anoint his hands in extreme unction, the worker refused to open his right hand, in which he was clutching a few grubby coins, unmindful of the fact that

47*

neither his hand nor he himself would soon be his at all. In the same way we close up and clench, not just our hands, but our hearts, seeking to clutch the world.

A friend of mine once confessed to me that foreseeing a violent death within a short time—though he was then in vigorous health—he planned to concentrate all his forces, for the short period he calculated was left to him, on writing a book. Vanity of vanities!

If it is true that on the death of the body that maintains me alive, the body I call mine in order to distinguish it from me myself, which is I, if it is true that my consciousness returns to the absolute unconsciousness whence it sprang, and if a like fate befalls all my brothers in humanity, then our elaborate human lineage is no more than a doomed procession of phantoms trooping from nothingness to nothingness and humanitarianism is the most inhuman notion of all.

The remedy is not to be found in the quatrain that runs

> Every time that I consider
> that I am going to die,
> I spread my cape upon the ground
> And sleep till life is by.

No, not that! The remedy is to consider it face to face, fixing our gaze on the gaze of the Sphinx, for that is the way to break the spell of its evil eye.

If we are all to die altogether—what is the point of everything! Wherefore? It is the Wherefore, the Wherefore of the Sphinx, that corrodes the marrow of our soul and that is the begetter of the anguish which stirs our love of hope.

Among the poetic lamentations of the unhappy Cowper there are some lines written under the weight of delirium, where he exclaims, as he feels himself the mark of divine vengeance,

> Hell might afford my miseries a shelter.

This is a Puritan sentiment, the preoccupation with sin and predestination. Only read the more terrible words of Sénancour, which express Catholic despair, not Protestant, when he makes his Obermann say: "Man is perishable. . . . That may be; but let us perish resisting, and if annihilation must be our portion, let us not make it a just one." For my part I must confess, painful as the confession may be, that even in the days of my youth's simple faith, I never was made to tremble by descriptions of hellfire, no matter how terrible, for I felt, always, that the idea of nothingness was much more terrifying than Hell. Whoever suffers lives, and whoever lives in suffering still loves and hopes, even though over the portal of his abode is written "Abandon all Hope!" And it is better to live in pain than peacefully cease to be at all. The truth is that I could not believe in this atrocious Hell, an eternity of punishment, nor could I imagine a more authentic Hell than that of nothingness and the prospect of it. And I still believe that if we all believed in our salvation from nothingness, we would all be the better for it.

What is this relish for living, *la joie de vivre*, they talk about nowadays? The hunger for God, the thirst for immortality, for survival, will always stifle in us this pitiful pleasure-taking in the life that is fleeting and does not abide. It is the frenzied love of life, the love that would have life be unending, which most often leads us to long for death. "If I am to be altogether annihilated," we say to ourselves, "the world is finished for me, it is over. And why not let it come to an end as soon as possible, so that no new consciousness will have to come into being and suffer the tormenting deceit of a transient and apparential existence? If the illusion of life is destroyed and life for life's sake or for the sake of others who must also die does not satisfy our soul, then what is the point in living? Death is our best release." And so we sing dirges to death, the never-ending respite, simply from fear of it, and call it a liberation.

Leopardi, poet of sorrow and annihilation, having lost the ultimate illusion, that of thinking himself immortal,

> Perì l'inganno estremo
> ch'eterno io mi credei,

spoke to his heart of "the infinite vanity of everything," *l'infinita vanità del tutto*, and saw the close kinship between love and death, and how when "a languid and weary loving affection is born in the depths of the heart, along with it is felt a desire to die." The larger number of those who take their own life are moved by love, by the supreme longing for life, for more life. Led on by the urge to prolong and perpetuate life, they are driven to death once they fully realize the vanity of their longing.

The problem is tragic and eternal, and the more we try to escape it, the more it is thrust upon us. The serene Plato—was he really so serene?—allowed a profound cry to escape from his own soul, twenty-four centuries ago, in his dialogue on the immortality of the soul, where he speaks of the uncertainty of our dream of being immortal, and of the *risk* that it may be vain: "Beautiful risk!"—καλὸς γὰρ ὁ κίνδυνος—. Beautiful the chance that our souls may never die.

And this verdict is the origin of Pascal's famous argument of the wager.

Faced with this risk, I am presented with arguments calculated to eliminate it, arguments to prove the absurdity of a belief in the immortality of the soul. But these ratiocinations do not move me, for they are reasons and no more than reasons, and one does not feed the heart with reasons. I do not want to die. No! I do not want to die, and I do not want to want to die. I want to live always, forever and ever. And *I* want to live, this poor I which I am, the I which I feel myself to be here and now, and for that reason I am tormented by the problem of the duration of my soul, of my own soul.

I am the center of my Universe, the center of the Universe, and in my extreme anguish I cry, along with Michelet: "My I! They are stealing my I!" For "What is a man profited, if he shall gain the whole world, and lose his own soul?" (Matt. 16:26.) Egoism, you say? There is nothing more universal than the individual, for what becomes of one becomes of all. Every man is worth more than all Humanity. Nor is there any point in sacrificing each to all, save in so far as all sacrifice themselves to each. What we call egoism is the principle of psychic gravity, the necessary postulate. "Love thy neighbor as thyself," we were told, on the presupposition that each man loves himself, so that it was not necessary to say: "Love thyself." And yet, we do not know how to love ourselves.

Put aside the perseverance of your own self, and then ponder their platitudes. For example: "Sacrifice yourself for your children!" And you sacrifice yourself for them because they are yours, part and prolongation of yourself, and they in turn will sacrifice

51*

themselves for their children, and these children for theirs, and so it will go on without end, a sterile sacrifice profiting no one. I came into the world to create my self. And what is to become of all our selves? Or: "Live for Truth, Good, Beauty!" We shall see the farfetched insincerity and supreme vanity of this hypocritical posture.

"That art thou!" they tell me with the Upanishads. And I answer: "Yes, I am that, when that is I and all is mine and the totality of things is mine. As mine, I love the all, and I love my neighbor because he lives in me and is part of my consciousness, and because he is like me and is mine."

Oh, to prolong this dulcet moment and fall asleep for all eternity! Here and now, in this mildly diffused light, in this backwater of quietude, when the tempest in the heart is stilled and no echoes of the world reach me! Insatiable desire sleeps and does not even dream; use and wont, blessed use and wont, rule in my eternity; my disillusion has gone with my memory, and my fears have died with my hopes!

They seek to deceive us with the deceit of deceits, telling us that nothing is lost: everything is transformed, they say, everything moves and changes, and not even the smallest dab of matter is annihilated nor is the least impulse of energy altogether dissipated. And there are people who attempt to console us with this theory! A poor consolation indeed! Neither my matter nor my energy causes me any disquiet, for neither of them is mine as long as I myself am not altogether mine, that is, as long as I am not eternal. No, I do not long to be submerged in the great ALL, in infinite and eternal Matter or Energy, or in God. I long to possess God, not be possessed by Him, to become myself God without ceasing to be the I who now speaks to you. Monist tricks are of no use to us. We want the substance, not the shadow, of eternity!

Is this materialism? Doubtless: but either our soul is also some species of matter, or it is nothing. I dread the thought of having to tear myself away from my flesh. I dread still more the idea of having to tear myself away from everything perceptible and material, from everything of substance. If this perhaps merits the name of materialism, and if I cleave to God with all my senses and all my strength, I do so in order that He may carry me in His arms beyond death, and so that when my eyes are closing forever, He may look into them with His glory. Self-delusion? Do not speak to me of delusion, but let me live!

They also call this pride—"stinking pride," Leopardi called it—and they ask us who are we, vile earthworms, to pretend to immortality. "By virtue of what? What for? By what right?" Such are the questions; and I reply: "By virtue of what do we live? What for? And what are we for? By what right? And by what right do we exist at all?" It is just as gratuitous to exist at all as it is to go on existing forever. Let us not speak of the right nor of the wherefore of our longing, which is an end in itself: otherwise we will lose our reason in a vortex of absurdities. I do not claim any right or merit whatever; it is a matter of necessity only: I need my longing in order to live.

"And who are you?" you may well ask me. And along with Obermann I answer: "For the Universe I am nothing. For myself I am everything." Is that pride? Is it pride to want to be immortal? Unhappy mankind! It is a tragic destiny, obviously, to have to base the affirmation of immortality upon the shifting and fragile foundation of a mere desire for immortality. But it would be only will-less and supine to deny our longing for immortality because it appears to have been proved that we can not be immortal—without verifying that proof. I dream, you say? Let me dream. If this dream is my life, do not awaken me from it. I believe in the immortal origin of this longing for immortality, which is the very substance of my soul. But do I really believe . . . ? And you ask: "Why do you want to be immortal?" Why? I do not really understand the question, for it is like asking the reason of the reason, the beginning of the beginning, the end of the end.

All these are points which can not be argued.

The Acts of the Apostles contains an account of how wherever Paul went he stirred up the jealous Jews, who persecuted him. They stoned him in Iconium and Lystra, cities of Lycaonia, despite the wonders he worked; his fellow-Jews scourged him at Philippi in Macedonia, and persecuted him in Thessalonica and Berca. But then he arrived in Athens, the noble city of intellectuals, over which the sublime spirit of Plato kept vigil, the spirit of the man who held that the "risk" of being immortal was a beautiful thing. And there Paul disputed with Epicureans and Stoics: "And some said, What will this babbler (σπερμολόγος) say? other some, He seemeth to be a setter forth of strange gods. . . . And they took him, and brought him unto the Areopagus, saying, May we know what this new doctrine, whereof thou speakest, *is*? For thou bringest certain strange things to our ears: we would know therefore what these things mean." (Acts 17: 18-20.) And then follows that marvelous description of the Athenians of the decadence, those dainty connoisseurs of the curious, "For all the Athenians and strangers which were there spent their time in nothing else, but either to tell or to hear some new thing" (21). An incisive characterization, this, which depicts for us in one stroke the stage of development reached by those Greeks who had learned from the *Odyssey* that the gods weave and accomplish the destruction of mortals in order that their posterity may have something to narrate!

And now we have Paul before the refined Athenians, before the *graeculi*, cultured and tolerant men who admit any doctrine, who study everything and never stone or scourge or imprison any man for professing whatever beliefs he professes. Here he stands, in a place where liberty of conscience is respected and every opinion is heard and listened to. And Paul raises his voice there, in the middle of the Areopagus, and speaks as it was fitting to speak to the cultured citizens of Athens, and all of them listen, anxious to hear the latest novelty. But when he comes to speak to them of the resurrection of the dead, their stock of patience and tolerance comes suddenly to an end, and some of them begin to make mock of him, and others tell him "We will hear about that some other time," intending not to listen to him any more at all. And something similar happened to him at Caesarea, before the Roman praetor Felix, another tolerant and cultured man, who relieved the hardships of his imprisonment and who wanted to hear him, and did listen to him speak of "righteousness," and "temperance"; but when Paul came to speak of the "judgement to come," Felix told him in a fright ($\xi\mu\phi\text{o}\beta\text{o}\varsigma$ $\gamma\epsilon\nu\acute{o}\mu\epsilon\nu\text{o}\varsigma$): "Go thy way for this time; when I have a convenient season, I will call for thee." (Acts 24: 22-25.)

55*

And then when Paul was received in audience by King Agrippa, he spoke of the resurrection of the dead and caused Festus, the governor, to exclaim "Paul, thou art beside thyself; much learning doth make thee mad." (Acts 26:24.)

Whatever the truth of Paul's discourse in the Areopagus—and even if there were none—it is clear that in this admirable narrative we can see just how far Attic tolerance goes and where the patience of the intellectuals ends. Calm and smiling, they all listen to you, and smiling, from time to time urge you on by saying "That's curious!" or "An ingenious thought!" or "Very suggestive!" or "How lovely!" or "Too bad that all that beauty isn't true!" or "That gives one pause!" But then as soon as you mention resurrection and life after death, their patience comes to an end and they cut you off with "Enough of that! We'll discuss it another time." But it is precisely about this matter that I propose to speak to you, my poor Athenians, my intolerant intellectuals, about this matter precisely that I would speak here.

For even if this belief were absurd, why should its exposition be found less tolerable than that of many more absurd beliefs? Why the evident hostility toward this belief? Is it from fear? Is it perhaps from regret at an inability to share the belief?

And sensible men, those who are not about to be put upon, keep dinning into our ears the refrain that it is useless to give way to madness and to butt one's head against a stone wall, for what can not be can not be. "The manly attitude," they say, "is to resign oneself to fate, and, since we are not immortal, not to want to be. Let us bow to reason and not torment ourselves with what is irremediable, and not make life dark and sad. Such an obsession," they add, "is a sickness." Sickness, madness, reason: the same old refrain! Very well then: No! I do not submit to reason and I rebel against it, and I aim to create, by force of faith, my immortalizing God, and I would deflect the course of the stars by the force of my will. For if we had "faith as a grain of mustard seed," we could say to that mountain there "Remove hence to yonder place; and it shall remove"; and nothing would be impossible for us (Matt. 18:20).

There you have that "thief of energies," as Christ was so obtusely called by the man who strove to wed nihilism with the struggle for existence, and who speaks to you of courage. His heart craved the eternal All, while his head showed him nothingness, and, despairing and mad to defend himself against himself, he cursed what he most loved. Because he could not be Christ, he blasphemed against Christ. Full of himself he wished to be unending and dreamed of the "eternal recurrence," a sorry counterfeit of immortality, and, swollen with self-pity, he abominated all other pity. And then there are people who say that his is the philosophy of strong men! No: it is not. My own health and my strength impel me to perpetuate myself. The other is the doctrine of the weak who aspire to be strong, but not of those who really are strong. Only the weak resign themselves to final death and substitute some lesser passion for the longing to survive in personal immortality. Among the strong, the urge toward self-perpetuation overrides the doubtfulness of achieving it, and their overabundance of life overflows the boundaries of death.

Before this terrible mystery of mortality, face to face with the Sphinx, man adopts a variety of attitudes and seeks variously to console himself for having been born. And now it occurs to him to take it all as a great game, and he tells himself, along with Renan, that the Universe is a theatrical performance put on by God for his own benefit, and that we should cooperate with the great Stage Manager and contribute toward making the spectacle as brilliant and varied as possible. And they have made a religion of art as well as a cure for the metaphysical malady, inventing the gibberish about art for art's sake.

And still it is not enough for them. If a man tells you that he writes, paints, sculpts, or sings for his own amusement, and at the same time makes his work public, then he lies: he lies if he puts his signature to his writing, painting, sculpture, or song. He is intent, at the very least, on leaving some shadow of his spirit behind, something to outlive him. If the *Imitation of Christ* is anonymous, it is because its author, seeking eternity of soul, did not seek an eternal name. A man of letters who tells you he scorns glory is a lying rogue. Speaking of Dante, the author of the thirty-three most vigorous verses on the vanity of worldly glory (*Purgatorio*, XI, 85-117), Boccaccio tells us that he enjoyed honors and pomp more than was perhaps consistent with his conspicuous virtue. The most ardent desire of his condemned souls is to be remembered here on Earth and to be spoken of, and it is this consolation which furnishes the principal light in their darkness. Dante himself expounded the concept of Monarchy, not merely for the use of others, but in order to win the palm of glory (*De Monarchia*, I, 1). What more? Even that holy man, of all men the most indifferent, apparently, to human vanity, the Humble One of Assisi, is reported, in the *Legenda trium sociorum*, to have said: "Adhuc adorabor per totum mundum!"—"You will see how I shall yet be adored by the whole world!" (2 Cel. I, i).

58*

And the theologians even say that God Himself created the world as a manifestation of His glory.

Whenever we are invaded by doubt, and our faith in the immortality of the soul becomes clouded over, the longing to perpetuate our name and fame, to grasp even the shadow of immortality, grows more ardent and painfully intense. Hence the tremendous struggle to distinguish oneself, to survive somehow in the memory of others and of posterity. And this struggle is a thousand times more terrifying than the struggle for life. And this struggle gives its tone, color, and character to our society, where the medieval faith in the immortal soul is fading. Every man seeks to affirm himself, even if only in appearance.

Once the demands of hunger are satisfied (and they are soon satisfied), then the vanity, the need—for it is a need—to make an impression and survive in others comes to the fore. Man tends to hand over his life for his purse, but he hands over his purse for his vanity. He is vain, for want of something better, even of his debilities or deficiencies, and is like a child who struts about with a bandaged finger in order to be noticed. And what is vanity but the longing to survive?

The vainglorious man is in the same situation as the miser, who takes the means for the ends, and, forgetting the latter, pursues the means as an end, and goes no farther. Seeming-to-be, en route to being, finally forms our end purpose. We need to have others believe we are superior to them in order to believe the same thing ourselves and to base upon this belief our faith in our own survival, or at least the survival of our fame. We are more gratified at being praised for the talent we show in defending a cause than in having the truth or goodness of the cause itself recognized. A furious mania for originality is rife in the modern intellectual world and characterizes individual endeavor. We would rather err ingeniously than hit the mark through vulgarity. Rousseau said in his *Émile*:

> If the philosophers were in a position to declare the truth, which of them would care to do so? Every one of them knows that his own system rests on no surer foundations than the rest, but he maintains it because it is his own. There is not one of them who, if he chanced to discover the difference between truth and falsehood, would not prefer his own lie to the truth which another had discovered. Where is the philosopher who would not deceive the whole world for his own glory? If he can rise above the crowd, if he can excel his rivals, what more does he want? Among believers he is an atheist; among atheists he would be a believer.

What a deal of fundamental truth there is in these sad confessions by that man of painful sincerity!

Our desperate struggle to perpetuate our name extends backward into the past, just as it pushes forward into the conquest of the future. We battle with the dead, who put the living into the shade. We are envious of past genius, of those whose names, like landmarks in History, loom across the centuries. Fame's heaven is not very extensive, and the greater the number of those who enter, the less the fame of each. The great names of the past rob us of a place: what space they occupy in the memory of nations is space usurped from those of us who aspire to be there too. And so we turn upon them, and hence the bitterness with which the seekers after fame in the field of letters judge those who have already achieved and enjoy such fame. If literature keeps on adding names, there will come a day for sifting, and each man fears he will be left on the meshes of the sieve. In attacking his masters the irreverent youth is only defending himself; the iconoclast, or image-breaker, is a Stylite who erects himself into an image, an *icon*. "Comparisons are odious," runs the familiar adage, and the truth is that we all want to be unique. Do not venture to tell Mr. X that he is one of the most talented of young Spaniards, for though he will affect to be gratified, he will only be annoyed by the supposed eulogy; if you say he is the most talented of Spaniards . . . Well, that's better! . . . But still not good enough. To enjoy one of the world's great reputations would be more to his liking. But he would only be really satisfied to be considered first among all men universally and eternally. The more alone a name stands, the closer it is to apparential immortality, the immortality of the name, for names take away one from the other.

What is the meaning of the irritation which seizes us when we have been robbed of a phrase or an idea or an image which we had thought of as our own; how do we feel, in short, when we are plagiarized? Is it right, though, to speak of robbery? Once made public, are any of these things ours? We are concerned only if they are ours; we are fonder of false coin bearing our stamp than we are of pure gold pieces from which our effigy and device have been effaced. Very often it comes about that a writer most influences the public when his name is no longer spoken, when his spirit has become diffused and disseminated among those who have read him, his authorship having been cited only when his ideas and sayings needed the surety of a name because they went against the current. His thought now belongs to everyone and so he lives in them. But he himself lives sad and dejected in the belief that he has been defeated. He no longer hears the applause or the silent heartbeat of those who continue to read him. Ask any sincere artist his preference: whether he would rather have his work perish and his memory survive, or have his memory perish and his work survive, and just see what he tells you, if he really is sincere. When a man does not work merely to live and get on, he lives to survive beyond life. To work for work's sake is not work at all but play. And play? We shall speak later about play.

The passion to be remembered if possible when oblivion overtakes all others is tremendous. From it flows envy, the cause, according to the biblical narrative, of the crime which began human history: the murder of Abel by his brother Cain. It was not a struggle for bread: it was a struggle to survive in God, in the divine memory. Envy is a thousand times more terrible than physical hunger, for envy is a spiritual hunger. If the so-called problem of life, the basic problem of food, were ever solved, the earth would be turned into a hell, as the struggle for survival would become even more intense.

For the sake of a name, man is prepared to sacrifice not only his life—that goes without saying—but his happiness. "Death to me! Long live my fame!" exclaims Rodrigo Arias in *Las Mocedades del Cid*, as he falls mortally wounded by Don Diego Ordóñez de Lara. One owes oneself to one's name. "Courage, Girolamo! thou wilt long be remembered; death is bitter, but glory is eternal!" exclaimed to himself Girolamo Olgiati, disciple of Cola Montano, and assassin—together with his two fellow conspirators Lampugnani and Visconti—of Galeazzo Sforza, tyrant of Milan. There are men who even covet the gallows as a means to fame, though it be an infamous fame: *avidus malae famae*, as Tacitus said.

And what, basically, is this Erostratism but the longing for immortality, if not for substantial and concrete immortality, at least immortality of name and influence?

And there are degrees in this striving for fame. The man who despises the applause of today's multitude is seeking to live on among generations of ever-new minorities. "Posterity is a superposing of minorities," said Gounod. Man wishes to prolong himself in time more than in space. The idols of the multitude are soon overthrown by the same multitude; the statue lies broken at the foot of the pedestal, disregarded by everyone; while those who win the hearts of the select few go on benefitting from a fervent veneration, in a small and secluded shrine perhaps, but one which protects them from the inroads of oblivion. The artist sacrifices the extent of his fame to its duration: he would rather last forever in his little corner than shine for an instant throughout the entire Universe, rather be an eternal atom conscious of himself than momentarily be the consciousness of the entire Universe. He sacrifices infinity in favor of eternity.

And once again they batter our ears with the cry of "Pride!" "Stinking pride!" But is it pride to want to leave an ineradicable name? Is that pride? That would be like calling the thirst for riches a mere thirst for pleasures: it is not so much a longing for pleasure as terror of poverty that drives us poor men to seek money, just as it was not a desire for glory but terror of Hell which drove men in the Middle Ages into the cloister and its *acedia*. No, it is not pride, but terror of extinction. We aim at being everything because we feel it is the only way to escape being nothing. We wish to preserve our memory, the memory of us, at the very least. How long will it last? At the most, as long as the human race. And what if we saved the memory of us in God?

All these speculative confessions amount to so much wretchedness, I know; but from the depths of wretchedness springs new life, and it is only by draining the dregs of spiritual sorrow that the honey at the bottom of life's cup is tasted. Anguish leads us to consolation.

That thirst for eternal life is quenched by many, especially by simple people, at the fountain of religious faith. But it is not given to everyone to drink there. The institution whose principal objective is to protect this faith in the immortality of the soul is Catholicism. But Catholicism has sought to rationalize this faith by converting religion into theology, proffering a philosophy—and a philosophy of the thirteenth century—as basis for a vital belief. Let us examine the consequences.

IV. The Essence of Catholicism

LET US NOW take up the Catholic, whether Pauline or Athanasian, solution to our inner vital problem, the hunger for immortality.

Christianity sprang from the confluence of two mighty currents of spirituality, the one Jewish and the other Hellenic, each of which had already influenced the other, and Rome gave it all the stamp of practicality and social continuity.

It has been asserted, perhaps somewhat hastily, that primitive Christianity was an-eschatological, that faith in another life after death was not clearly manifested, but that it proclaimed instead an early end of the world and the establishment of the kingdom of God, a belief known as *chiliasm*. But are not these two beliefs one and the same? Faith in the immortality of the soul, the nature of which was not perhaps very precisely defined, may well be said to be a kind of implied understanding, a tacit supposition underlying the whole of the Gospel; and it is only the spiritual outlook of many readers of the Gospel today, an outlook counter to that of the Christians from among whom the Gospel came into being, that prevents them from seeing the obvious. Doubtless all that speculation about the Second Coming of Christ from among the clouds clothed with majesty and great power, to judge the living and the dead, to open the kingdom of heaven to some and to cast others into Gehenna, where there shall be weeping and gnashing of teeth, may all of it be understood in a chiliastic sense. And in the Gospel (Mark 9:1), Christ is made to say: "Verily I say unto you, That there be some of them that stand here, which shall not taste of death, till they have seen the kingdom of God," that is, seen it in their own generation. And in the same chapter, verse 10, it is said of Peter, James, and John, who had gone up the Mount of Transfiguration with Jesus and had heard him speak of rising again from among the dead, that "they kept that saying with themselves, questioning one with another what the rising from the dead should mean." In any event, the Gospel was written when this belief, the basis and *raison d'être* of Christianity, was in process of formation. See Matthew 22:29-32; Mark 12:24-27; Luke 16:22-31, 20:34-37; John 5:24-29; 6:40, 54, 58; 8:51; 11:25, 56; 14:2, 19; and most especially Matthew 27:52, which tells of how, at the resurrection of Christ, "many bodies of the saints which slept arose."

And this was not a natural resurrection. No, the Christian faith was born of the faith that Jesus did not remain dead, but that God raised him up again, and that this resurrection was actually accomplished. And this was no mere immortality of the soul in the philosophic manner (see Harnack, *Dogmengeschichte*, Prolegomena, V, 4). In the eyes of the first Fathers of the Church themselves the immortality of the soul was not something pertaining to the natural order. The teaching of the Divine Scriptures, as Nemesius said, sufficed for its demonstration, and it was, according to Lactantius, a gift—and, as such, gratuitous—of God. But we shall discuss this later.

Christianity sprang, as we have said, from two great spiritual streams, the Judaic and the Hellenic, each of which had reached, on its own account, if not a precise definition of, at least a precise yearning for, another life. Among the Jews, faith in another life was neither general nor clear; but they were led in that direction by their faith in a personal living God, and their entire spiritual history consists of the evolution of this concept.

Yahweh, the Judaic God, was at first merely one god among many others, the god of the people of Israel, revealed amid the tempestuous thunder on Mount Sinai. He was such a jealous god that He required that worship should be paid to Him alone, and it was by way of mono-cultism that the Jews arrived at monotheism. He was worshipped as a living force, not as a metaphysical entity, and He was the god of battles. But this God of social and warlike origin, to whose genesis we shall have to return later, became more intimate and personal in the prophets, and in doing so became more individual and more universal. He is Yahweh, who does not love Israel for being a son, but takes Israel for a son from love (Hosea 11:1). And faith in the personal God, in the Father of men, brings with it faith in the eternalization of the individual man, a faith which already dawned among the Pharisees even before Christ.

Hellenic culture, for its part, finally discovered death, and to discover death is to discover the hunger for immortality. This longing does not appear in the Homeric poems, which are not of an initial nature but of a final one, marking not the start but the close of a civilization. They represent the transition from the old religion of Nature, of Zeus, to the more spiritual religion of Apollo, the religion of redemption. But always persisting underneath was the popular and inner religion of the Eleusinian mysteries, the worship of souls and ancestors. "In so far as it is possible to speak of a 'Theology of Delphi,' the popular belief in the survival of the soul after death and the cult of the disembodied soul formed two of the most important articles in its creed," writes Rohde. Both the Titanic and the Dionysiac existed, and it was the duty of man, according to the Orphic doctrine, to free himself from the fetters of the body, in which the soul was like a prisoner in a jail (cf. Rohde, *Psyche*, "Die Orphiker," 4). The Nietzschean idea of eternal recurrence is an Orphic idea. But the idea of the immortality of the soul was no philosophical principle. The attempt by Empedocles to harmonize a hylozoistic system with spiritualism proved that a philosophical natural science can not by itself corroborate the axiom of the perpetuity of the individual soul; it could only serve as a support for a theological speculation. The first Greek philosophers affirmed immortality by a contradiction, by abandoning natural philosophy and entering into the field of theology, by affirming a Dionysiac and Orphic dogma and not an Apollonian one. But "an immortality of the human soul as such, by virtue of its nature and composition—as the imperishable force of divinity in the mortal body—never became a real part of the belief of the Greek populace." (Rohde, *Psyche*.)

Recall Plato's *Phaedo* and, later, the Neoplatonic lucubrations. The longing for personal immortality is already clear, a longing which, not altogether satisfied by reason, led to Hellenic pessimism. As Pfleiderer so well observes: "No people ever appeared on earth so serene and sunny as the Greeks in the youthful days of their historical existence . . . but no people changed so completely their notion of the value of

life. The Hellenism which ends in the religious speculations of neo-Pythagorism and Neoplatonism came
to view the world, which at one time had seemed to
it so joyful and radiant, as an abode of darkness and
error, and earthly existence as a period of trial never
to be quickly enough traversed." Nirvana is a Hellenic idea.

Thus, Greek and Jew, each in his own way, arrived
at the true discovery of death, a discovery which
causes nations, as it does men, to enter upon spiritual
puberty, the awareness of the tragic sense of life, and
it is then that humanity engenders the living God. It
is the discovery of death that reveals God to us, and
the death of the perfect man, Christ, was the supreme
revelation of death, the death of the man who should
not have died and did die.

Such a discovery, the discovery of immortality,
prepared by Judaic and Hellenic religious developments, was the specifically Christian contribution.
And its achievement was due above all to Paul of
Tarsus, that Hellenized Jewish Pharisee. Paul had
not personally known Jesus, and therefore he revealed
him as Christ. "It may be said that the theology of
the Apostle Paul is, in general, the first Christian theology. For Paul it was a necessity; it was, in a certain
sense, a substitute for his not having known Jesus
personally," as Weizsäcker says. He did not know
Jesus, but he felt Jesus born again in himself, and
thus he could say: "Nevertheless I live; yet not I, but
Christ liveth in me" (Gal. 2:20). And he preached
the Cross, "unto the Jews a stumbling block, and
unto the Greeks foolishness" (1 Cor. 1:23); and the
central doctrine for this convert apostle was the resurrection of Christ. For him the important thing was
that Christ had been made man and had died and had

risen again, and not what He did in life: not His ethical teaching, but His religious and immortalizing work. And it was Paul who wrote those immortal words (1 Cor. 15:12-19):

> Now if Christ be preached that he rose from the dead, how say some among you that there is no resurrection of the dead? But if there be no resurrection of the dead, then is Christ not risen: And if Christ be not risen, then is our preaching vain, and your faith is also vain. . . . Then they also which are fallen asleep in Christ are perished. If in this life only we have hope in Christ, we are of all men most miserable.

And it may be affirmed that thenceforward whoever does not believe in the carnal resurrection of Christ may be a Christ-lover but not strictly speaking a Christian. It is true that Justin Martyr could say that "all those are Christians who live in accordance with reason, even though they be taken for atheists, like Socrates and Heraclitus among the Greeks, and others such"; but is this Martyr a martyr, that is, a witness to Christianity? No, he is not.

And it was around this doctrine, inwardly experienced by Paul, the doctrine of the resurrection and immortality of Christ—which provides assurance for the resurrection and the immortality of each individual believer—that the whole of Christology was formed. The man-God, the Word incarnate, appeared on earth so that in his own way man might become God, that is, immortal. And the Christian God, Father of Christ, a necessarily anthropomorphic God, is the God who created the world for man, for each man— as the catechism of Christian Doctrine that we were made to memorize at school tells us. And the end purpose of redemption, despite all appearances caused by ethical deviations from a dogma rightly religious, was to save us from death rather than from sin, or from sin insofar as sin implies death. And Christ died, or rather rose again, for *me*, for each one of us. And a certain solidarity was established between God and His creature. Malebranche asserted that the first man fell *so that* Christ might redeem us, rather than that Christ redeemed us *because* man had fallen.

After Paul, the years and the generations of Christians followed one another, and they developed the central dogma and its consequences toward assuring faith in the immortality of the individual soul; and then came the Council of Nicaea, and with it the formidable Athanasius, whose name had now become a battle-standard, an incarnation of the faith of the populace. Athanasius was a man of little learning but great faith, of the people's faith above all, and driven by the hunger for immortality. And he stood against Arianism, which like Unitarian and Socinian Protestantism threatened, even though unwittingly, the foundations of his faith. For the Arians, Christ was first and foremost a teacher, a teacher of ethics, the most perfect man and therefore the guarantor that we may all attain to supreme perfection. But Athanasius felt that Christ could not make us as gods if He had not first made Himself God; if His Divinity had been communicated, He could not have communicated it to us. "He was not first man and then became God," he said, "but rather first God and then became man, the better to deify us [θεοποιήσῃ]" (*Orat.* I, 39). It was not the Logos of the philosophers, the cosmological Logos, that Athanasius knew and adored. And thus he established the separation between nature and revelation. The Athanasian or Nicene Christ, who is the Catholic Christ, is not the cosmological, or even,

strictly speaking, the ethical Christ; he is the eternalizing, the deifying, the religious Christ. Of this
Christ, the Christ of Nicene or Catholic Christology,
Harnack says that he is essentially docetic—that is,
apparential—because the process of the divinization
of the man in Christ was made in the interests of
eschatology. But which is the real Christ? Could it
possibly be the so-called historical Christ of rationalist exegesis who is diluted for us in the form of myth
or of a social atom?

This same Harnack, a Protestant rationalist, tells
us that Arianism or Unitarianism would have meant
the death of Christianity, reducing it to cosmology
and ethics, and that it merely served as a bridge to
carry the initiated to Christianity, that is, from reason
to faith. In the eyes of this same learned historian
of dogmas it is a sign of a perverse state of affairs
that a man like Athanasius, who saved Christianity
as the religion of the living communion with God,
should at the same time have effaced the historical
Jesus, Jesus of Nazareth, the one who was personally
unknown to Paul or to Athanasius—or to Harnack,
for that matter. Among Protestants, this historical
Jesus is subject to the scalpel of exegesis; the Catholic Christ, meanwhile, the truly historical one, lives
on, and He is the one who lives through the centuries, guaranteeing faith in personal immortality and
salvation.

Athanasius possessed the supreme audacity of
faith, that of affirming mutually contradictory propositions: "The complete contradiction that exists in the
ὁμοούσιος brought in its train a whole army of contradictions, which multiplied as thought advanced," says
Harnack. Yes, thus it was, and thus it had to be. And
he adds: "Dogma took leave for all time of clear

thinking and tenable concepts, and habituated itself to the contra-rational." What it did in actual fact was to get closer to life, which is contra-rational and opposed to clear thinking. Value judgements are not only never subject to rationalization, they are anti-rational.

At Nicaea then, as later at the Vatican, victory was with the idiots—using this word strictly in its primitive and etymological sense—with the simple-minded, with the unpolished and headstrong bishops, representatives of the authentic spirit of humanity, of the spirit of the people, of the spirit that does not want to die (whatever reason may say) and that seeks a guarantee, the most material guarantee possible, for its desire.

Quid ad aeternitatem? That is the capital question. And the Creed ends with the phrase *resurrectionem mortuorum et vitam venturi saeculi*, the resurrection of the dead and the life to come. In the abandoned cemetery of Mallona, in my native city of Bilbao, there stands a tombstone with the following words engraved:

> Though we lie here turned to dust,
> In you, Our Lord, we place our trust
> That we will live again all clothed
> In the flesh and skin we used to wear.

Or as the catechism has it: "With the same bodies and souls that they had." This feeling is so strong that orthodox Catholic doctrine goes so far as to say that the happiness of the blessed is not altogether perfect until they have recovered their bodies. Fray Pedro Malón de Chaide, of the Order of St. Augustine, a Spaniard and a Basque, tells us that there is "lamentation in heaven, and their lament is due to the fact that they are not altogether whole in heaven, for only their souls are present, and, although they can not suffer pain inasmuch as they see God, in whom they take ineffable delight, nevertheless they seem not entirely satisfied. And they will be so only when they are clothed in their own bodies."

And corresponding to that central dogma of the resurrection in Christ and by Christ is that central sacrament and axis of popular Catholic piety, the sacrament of the Eucharist. In this sacrament, the body of Christ, the bread of immortality, is bestowed.

This sacrament is authentically realistic—*dinglich*, as they say in German and which could be translated without undue violence as "material," "concrete." It is the sacrament most authentically *ex opere operato*, virtuous in itself; something for which the Protestants substitute the idealist sacrament of the Word. It is a matter, in the end—and I say it with all due respect, but without relinquishing the expressiveness of the phrase—of eating and drinking God, the Eternalizer, taking sustenance from Him. Little wonder then if St. Teresa tells us that when she was receiving Communion one day, at the monastery of the Incarnation, during her second year as Prioress, a week after St. Martin's day, the priest, who was St. John of the Cross, broke the Host in two, in order to divide it between Teresa and another nun, and Teresa recalls thinking it was not for lack of Hosts that he did it but only so as to mortify her, "for I had told him how much I delighted in Hosts of a large size, though I knew that even in the smallest piece the Lord is present in His entirety." Here we see how reason goes one way and feeling the other. And, as far as feeling is concerned, what difference does it make that a thousand and one problems arise from reflecting rationally on the mystery of this sacrament? What is a divine body? Was Christ's body, *qua* body, divine? What is an immortal and immortality-making body? What is a substance separated from its accidental properties? What is the substance of a body? Nowadays we have become very subtle in the matter of materiality and substantiality; but even some of the Church Fathers did not find the immateriality of God Himself to be as definite and clear as it is for us. The Sacrament of the Eucharist is the eternal-life-giver *par excellence*, and therefore the axis of the piety of the Catholic populace, and, if it can properly be so stated, the most specifically religious.

The specifically Catholic religious quality is immortalization, and not justification in the Protestant mode. The latter is, strictly speaking, a matter of ethics. It is in Kant—however orthodox Protestants may dislike the notion—that Protestantism reached its penultimate conclusion: religion rests upon morality, and not, as in Catholicism, morality upon religion.

Preoccupation with sin has never been a matter of such anguish, or at least of such apparent anguish, among Catholics. The sacrament of Confession contributes to this situation. And it may be that we conserve, more than they do, the substance of the primitive Judaic and pagan concept of sin as something material and infectious and hereditary, to be cured by baptism and absolution. All of Adam's descendants sinned when Adam sinned, and they sinned almost materially, and his sin was transmitted almost as a material illness is transmitted. Renan, who had a Catholic upbringing, was right therefore when he turned against Amiel, the Protestant, who had charged Renan with not giving due importance to sin. Protestantism, on the other hand, obsessed with the notion of justification—taken more in an ethical

sense than in any other, though the ethics are dressed
out in religious terms—in the end neutralizes and almost obliterates eschatology, and abandons the Nicene
symbology, falls into confessional anarchy, into pure
religious individualism and vague aesthetic, ethical
or cultural religiosity. What we might call "other-
worldliness," *Jenseitigkeit*, gives way to "this-world-
liness," *Diesseitigkeit*. And this happened despite
Kant himself, who wished to preserve "other-world-
liness"—after ruining it. The religious coarseness
of Lutheranism is due to its earthly vocation and
its passive trust in God. It was almost at the point of
expiring in the Age of Enlightenment, the Age of the
Aufklärung, when it was galvanized somewhat by
pietism, which infused into it some of the religious
sap of Catholicism. Thus the appropriateness of
Oliveira Martins in his *History of Iberian Civilization*
(IV, 3), when he writes: "Catholicism produced
heroes. Protestantism produced sensible, happy societies, rich and free in respect to institutions and external economy, but incapable of great actions because
their religion had begun to destroy in the heart of
man that which makes him prone to daring and noble
sacrifice."

Take any of the dogmatic systems that have re-
sulted from the latest Protestant dissolution, that of
Kaftan, the follower of Ritschl, for example, and note
to what extent eschatology is reduced. Ritschl himself
tells us:

> The question regarding the necessity of justification
> or forgiveness can only be solved by conceiving
> eternal life as the direct end and aim of that Divine
> operation. But if the ideal of eternal life be applied
> merely to our state in the next life, then its content,
> too, lies beyond all experience, and cannot form the

basis of knowledge of a scientific kind. Hopes and presentiments, though marked by the strongest subjective certainty, are not any the clearer for that, and contain in themselves no guarantee of the completeness of what one hopes, or has a presentiment of. Clearness and completeness of idea, however, are the conditions of comprehending anything, i.e., of understanding the necessary connection between the various elements of a thing, and between the thing and its given presuppositions. The Evangelical article of belief, therefore, that justification by faith establishes or brings with it assurance of eternal life, is of no use theologically, so long as this purposive aspect of justification cannot be verified in such experience as is possible now.

All this is most rational, but . . .

In the first edition of Melanchthon's *Loci Communes*, 1521, which is the first Lutheran theological work, the author omits all Trinitarian and Christological speculations, the dogmatic basis of eschatology. And Dr. Herrmann, professor at Marburg, the author of a book on the Christian's commerce with God (*Der Verkehr des Christen mit Gott*)—a book whose first chapter deals with the opposition between mysticism and the Christian religion, a book which Harnack feels is the most perfect Lutheran manual— tells us, in another work, with regard to this Christological (or Athanasian) speculation, that "the effective knowledge of God and Christ, wherein faith lives, is something entirely different. Nothing ought to find a place in Christian doctrine that cannot help man to recognize his sins, attain the grace of God and serve Him truly. Until that time [that is, until Luther], a good deal that in no wise could contribute to give man a free heart or a clear conscience had been accepted in the Church as *doctrina sacra*." For my part, I cannot imagine liberty of heart or tranquility of conscience where there is no surety of their continuance after death. "The desire to save one's soul," Herrmann continues, "should finally lead men to know and comprehend the effective doctrine of salvation." And in his book on the Christian's commerce with God this eminent Lutheran doctor repeatedly comes back to talk of trust in God, of peace of conscience, of a certainty of salvation that is not strictly speaking certainty of everlasting life but rather of a remission of sins.

And I have read in a work by a Protestant theologian, Ernst Troeltsch, that the highest reaches attained by Protestantism in the conceptual order have been in the art of music, where Bach has given it its most forceful artistic expression. This, then, is what Protestantism comes down to—*celestial music!* On the other hand we could say that the highest artistic expression of Catholicism, or at least of Spanish Catholicism, is to be found in the most material, tangible, and permanent of arts (for sounds are carried off by the wind), namely, in painting and sculpture, in the *Christ* of Velázquez, that Christ who is always in the death throes and never stops dying—so that we may be given life.

And it is not a question of Catholicism abandoning ethics. Not at all! No modern religion could ignore ethics in any case. But our religion is fundamentally and for the most part a compromise between eschatology and ethics—though the learned doctors may protest—or eschatology put at the service of ethics. What else are those outrageous and eternal pains of Hell which so ill accord with the Pauline apocatastasis? Let us bear in mind the words from the *Theologia Germanica*, the mystic manual that Luther read, which are put in God's mouth: "If I am to reward thee for thy evil and wickedness, I must do it with goodness, for I am and have nothing else." And Christ said: "Father, forgive them, for they know not what they do"; and there is no man who knows what he does. But it has been necessary to turn religion into a kind of police system, for the benefit of the social order, and hence the idea of hell. Oriental or Greek Christianity is predominantly eschatological while Protestantism is predominantly ethical. Catholicism is a compromise between the two, with the stress on the eschatological. The most authentic Catholic morality, monastic asceticism, is an eschatological morality directed toward the salvation of the individual soul rather than toward the maintenance of society. And, may not the cult of virginity conceal a certain obscure notion that the perpetuation of ourselves in others hinders our own personal perpetuation? Ascetic morality is a negative morality. And, strictly speaking, the important thing for a man is not to die, whether he sins or not. There is no need to take literally, but only as a lyrical, or rather rhetorical, effusion of words the famous sonnet which begins

> I am not moved, my Lord, to love Thee,
> by Thy promised heaven. . . .

The real sin—perhaps the sin against the Holy Ghost, for which there is no remission—is the sin of heresy, the sin of thinking for ourselves. We have already heard it said in Spain that to be a liberal, that is, a heretic, is worse than to be an assassin, a thief, or an adulterer. The gravest sin is not to obey the Church, whose infallibility protects us from reason.

Still and all, why should the infallibility of a man,

the Pope, give rise to scandal? What difference does it make whether we say a book—the Bible—is infallible, or a society of men, or the Church, or a single man? Does it in any way change the essence of the rational difficulty? Inasmuch as the infallibility of a book or of a society of men is no more rational than that of a single man, this latter concept, the supreme outrage in the eyes of reason, was bound to be affirmed.

The vital principle asserts itself, and, in asserting itself creates, making use of its enemy rationality, a whole edifice of dogma, and the Church defends it against rationalism, against Protestantism, against Modernism. The Church is defending life. It stood up against Galileo, and it did right, for his discovery, at its inception and until it became assimilated to the economy of human thought, tended to shatter the anthropomorphic belief that the universe was created for man. The Church opposed Darwin, and it did right, for Darwinism tends to shatter our belief that man is an exceptional animal expressly created to be made eternal. Lastly, Pius IX, the first pontiff to be declared infallible, declared himself irreconcilable with modern civilization so-called. And he did right.

Loisy, the ex-Catholic abbé, wrote:

> I simply say that the Church and theology have not favored the scientific movement, but have hindered it rather, insofar as it lay in their power, on certain decisive occasions. Above all else I say that Catholic education has not associated itself with or accommodated itself to this movement. Theology has acted and still acts as if it were in itself in possession of a science of nature and a science of history, together with that general philosophy of nature and history accruing to it as a result of its scientific

knowledge. It might be supposed that the domain of theology and that of science, distinct in principle and even by Vatican Council definition, must not be distinct in practice. Everything goes along almost as if theology had nothing to learn from modern science, whether natural or historical, and as if it was in a position and had the right to exercise a direct and absolute supervision over all the activities of the human spirit.

And thus the Church must be, and thus it does in fact act, in its struggle against the Modernism of which Loisy was the learned leader.

The recent struggle against Kantian and fideist Modernism is a struggle for life. Would it indeed be possible for life, life seeking assurances of survival, to tolerate a Loisy, a Catholic priest, in his assertion that the resurrection of the Savior is not a fact of historical order, demonstrable and demonstrated by the testimony of history alone? And then, on the other hand, if you read an explanation of the central dogma, of the resurrection of Christ, in such a first-rate work as *Dogme et Critique*, by E. Le Roy, where will you find any solid ground upon which to build our hopes? Is it not obvious that the question is not so much the immortal life of Christ, reducible perhaps to one life in the collective Christian consciousness, but rather the guaranteeing of our own personal resurrection in body and soul? This new psychological apologetic appeals to the moral miracle, and we, even as the Jews, seek for a sign, something that can be grasped with all the powers of the soul and all the senses of the body—and with hands and feet and mouth too, if possible.

But, alas, we perceive no sign! Reason attacks, and faith, which does not feel secure without reason, must come to terms with it. And thus appear those tragic contradictions and lacerations of consciousness. We need security, certainty, a sign, and they give us *motiva credibilitatis*—motives for credibility—upon which to build the *rationale obsequium*; and, although, according to St. Augustine, faith precedes reason, *fides praecedit rationem*, that very same doctor of the Church and bishop sought to go from faith to understanding, *per fidem ad intellectum*, and sought to believe in order to understand, *credo ut intelligam*. How far it all is from that superb expression of Tertullian: *et sepultus resurrexit, certum est, quia impossibile est*!: "and he was buried and rose again; it is certain, because it is impossible!"; and his sublime *credo quia absurdum*!: "I believe because it is impossible," an outrage to the rationalists! How far St. Augustine's thought is from Pascal's *il faut s'abêtir* and from Donoso Cortés' "human reason loves the absurd," which he must have learned from the great Joseph de Maistre!

The authority of tradition and the revelation of the word of God was quarried to find a cornerstone, and the principle of unanimous consent was arrived at. *Quod apud multos unum invenitur, non est erratum, sed traditum*, said Tertullian; and Lamennais added, centuries later, that "certitude, the principle of life and intelligence, . . . is, if I may be allowed the expression, a social product." But here, as in so many other instances, the supreme formula was provided by that great Catholic and representative of popular, vital Catholicism, Count Joseph de Maistre, when he wrote: "I do not believe it possible to point to a single universally useful judgement which is not true." Here is the true Catholic norm: the deduction of the truth of a principle from its supreme goodness or utility. And what is of greater, of more sovereign, utility than the immortality of the soul? "Since everything is uncertain, either we must believe all men or none," said Lactantius. But that great mystic and ascetic, Blessed Henry Suso, the Dominican, asked the Eternal Wisdom for a single word to indicate what love was, and when the answer was given: "All creatures proclaim that it is I," Suso, His servant, replied: "Ah, my Lord, that does not suffice a yearning soul." Faith does not feel secure either with consensus or with tradition or with authority. It seeks the support of its enemy, reason.

And thus was scholastic theology wrought, and, with it, its handmaiden—*ancilla theologiae*—scholastic philosophy; and then this handmaiden turned against her mistress and answered back. Scholasticism, a magnificent cathedral, in which all the problems of architectonic mechanics were resolved for all time, but still an adobe cathedral, gradually gave way to so-called natural theology, which is merely Christianity depotentialized. The attempt was made, where possible, to uphold dogmas by the use of reason, to demonstrate at least that though they were superrational they were not contra-rational, and they were furnished with a philosophical foundation of Aristotelian-Neoplatonic thirteenth-century philosophy: such is the Thomism recommended by Leo XIII. It is no longer a question of forcing the acceptance of dogma, but of its medieval and Thomist philosophical interpretation. It is not enough to believe that in receiving the consecrated Host we receive the body and blood of our Lord Jesus Christ; we must also negotiate the difficulties of transubstantiation and of

substance separated from accidents, breaking with
the whole of the modern rational conception of
substantiality.

But over against this stands implicit faith, the
faith of the charcoal burner, the faith of those who,
like St. Teresa (*Life*, Chapter XXV, 2), do not wish
to fall back upon theology. "Do not ask me the reason of that, for I am ignorant; Holy Mother Church
possesses doctors who will know how to answer you,"
as we were made to learn in our catechism. And it
was for this, among other reasons, that the priesthood
was instituted, so that the teaching Church might
be the depository, a "reservoir instead of river," as
Phillips Brooks said, of theological secrets.

"The victory of the Nicene Creed," says Harnack,

> was a victory of the priests over the faith of the
> Christian people. The Logos-doctrine had already
> become unintelligible to those who were not theo-
> logians. The setting up of the Nicene-Cappadocian
> formula as the fundamental Confession of the
> Church, made it perfectly impossible for the Catho-
> lic laity to get an inner comprehension of the Chris-
> tian Faith taking as their guide the form in which
> it was presented in the doctrine of the Church. The
> thought that Christianity is the revelation of some-
> thing incomprehensible became more and more a
> familiar one to men's minds.

And so, in truth, it is.

And why so? Because faith, that is, life, no longer
felt sure of itself. Neither traditionalism nor the theological positivism of Duns Scotus sufficed: it wanted
to rationalize itself. And it sought to establish a foundation, not *against* reason, which is where it stands,
but *upon* reason, that is, within reason itself. The
nominalist or positivist or voluntarist position of

Scotus, which maintains that law and truth depend on the free and inscrutable will of God rather than on any essence, accentuated the supreme irrationality of religion and endangered its position among the majority of believers, who were people endowed with adult reasoning powers rather than with the faith of charcoal burners. And hence came the triumph of Thomist theological rationalism. It is no longer enough to believe in the existence of God; anathema falls on anyone who, though he believe in His existence, does not believe it is demonstrable by rational arguments or believes it has not so far been irrefutably demonstrated by rational arguments. In this connection, however, perhaps we should cite the words of Pohle: "If eternal salvation were to depend on the axioms of mathematics, we should have to expect that the most odious human sophistry would have already attacked their universal validity with the same forcefulness they now use against God, the soul, and Christ."

The fact is that Catholicism oscillates between mysticism and rationalism: mysticism which is the intimate experiencing of the living God in Christ, an untransmissible experience, in which there is a danger, however, of our own personalities' being swallowed in God, thus losing our vital drive, and rationalism, which is its opponent (see Weizsäcker, *op. cit.*); Catholicism oscillates between religionized science and scientificized religion. Apocalyptic enthusiasm gradually changed to Neoplatonic mysticism, which theology then thrust into the background. The Church was apprehensive at the imaginative excesses which were taking the place of faith and creating Gnostic extravagances. But it had to make a kind of pact with Gnosticism and another with rationalism; neither imagination nor reason was easily vanquished.

85*

And thus was Catholic dogma made into a system of more or less harmonized contradictions. The Trinity was a kind of pact between monotheism and polytheism; and in Christ humanity and divinity made a pact, and nature and grace covenanted, and grace and free will, and free will and divine prescience, and so on. And it is perhaps true, as Herrmann says, that "as soon as a religious idea is developed to its logical conclusions, it enters into conflict with other ideas belonging in equal measure to the life of religion." And it is this conflict which lends to Catholicism its deeply vital dialectic. But at what price?

The price paid, it must be said, is the suppression of intellectual demands in believers who possess adult reasoning power. They are required to believe all or nothing, to accept the totality of dogma or face the loss of all merit if the smallest part is rejected. The result, as the great Unitarian preacher Channing pointed out, is that in France and Spain there are many who have passed from rejecting Papism to absolute atheism, because "the fact is, that false and absurd doctrines, when exposed, have a natural tendency to beget scepticism in those who received them without reflection. None are so likely to believe too little as those who have begun by believing too much." Here lies, in all truth, the terrible danger of believing too much! Or no! The terrible danger lies in another quarter: in attempting to believe with one's reason rather than with one's life.

The Catholic solution to our problem, to our unique vital problem, the problem of the immortality and eternal salvation of our own soul, satisfies the will, and, therefore, satisfies life; but, in attempting to give a basis in reason by means of dogmatic theology it fails to satisfy reason. And reason has its own exigencies, as imperious as those of life. There is no use trying to force ourselves to take for super-rational what clearly strikes us as contra-rational, nor is it any good wanting to be a charcoal burner if one is not one. Infallibility, a notion of Hellenic origin, is essentially a rationalist category.

Let us now consider the rationalist or scientific solution—or rather, dissolution—of our problem.

V. The Rational Dissolution

DAVID HUME, the great master of rationalist phenomenalism, begins his essay "On the Immortality of
the Soul," with these decisive words: "By the mere
light of reason it seems difficult to prove the immortality of the soul; the arguments for it are commonly
derived either from metaphysical topics, or moral, or
physical. But in reality it is the gospel, and the gospel alone, that has brought *life and immortality to
light. . . .*" All of which is equivalent to denying any
rationality to the belief that each one of our souls is
immortal.

Kant, who used Hume as point of departure for
his critique, attempted to establish the rationality of
the longing for immortality and the belief that this
longing is of consequence, and therein lies the real
origin, the deep-seated origin, of his *Critique of Practical Reason* and of his categorical imperative and of
his God. Still and all, Hume's sceptical affirmation
holds good, and there is no way of rationally proving
the immortality of the soul. On the contrary, there
are only ways of rationally proving its mortality.

It would be not merely useless but even ridiculous
were we to expatiate here on the extent to which
individual human consciousness is dependent on our
bodily organism, or if we were to trace the manner
in which consciousness slowly emerges in response
to outside stimulus and how it is suspended during
sleep, swooning, and other accidental interruptions,

and how all the evidence points to the rational conclusion that death implies the loss of consciousness. For, just as we did not exist before our birth, nor do we have any personal recollection of that previous time, so shall we not exist after our death. Such is the rational conclusion.

The word "soul" is no more than a term we use to designate the individual consciousness in its integrity and continuity; and the fact that it changes, and that it disintegrates just as it integrates, is self-evident. Aristotle considered the soul the substantial form of the body: the entelechy, but not a substance. And more than one modern has called it an epiphenomenon—an absurd term. It is enough to call it a phenomenon.

Rationalism—and by this term I mean the doctrine which attends only to reason, to objective reality—is necessarily materialist. And let idealists not be scandalized.

In order to make everything clear, we must point out that what we call materialism means no more, in reality, than the doctrine which denies the immortality of the individual soul and the persistence of personal consciousness after death.

In another sense it could be stated that since we can no more say what matter is than we can say what spirit is, and that since matter is for us merely an idea, then materialism is idealism too. In fact, and as far as concerns our problem—the most vital, the only truly vital problem—it is all the same to say that everything is matter as it is to say that everything is idea, or that everything is energy, or is whatever you please. Every monist system will always seem materialist. Only dualist systems preserve the immortality of the soul, only those systems which teach that human consciousness is something substantially distinct and different from other manifestations of phenomena. Reason is, naturally, monist. For it is the function of reason to understand and explain the universe, and in order to understand and explain it there is no need whatsoever for the soul to be an imperishable substance. In order to explain and understand our psychic life, for the purposes of psychology, a hypothetical soul is unnecessary. What used to be called rational psychology, in opposition to empirical psychology, is neither psychology nor rational, but metaphysics, of a particularly obscure variety, and profoundly irrational or, rather, contra-rational.

The so-called rational doctrine of the substantiality and spirituality of the soul, along with all the apparatus accompanying it, is a doctrine born of man's need to base upon reason his undeniable longing for immortality and his consequent belief in this immortality. All the sophistries which aim at proving that the soul is simple and incorruptible substance stem from this source. Further, the very concept of substance itself, as defined and fixed by Scholasticism, a concept which does not bear criticism, is a theological concept specifically designed to sustain faith in the immortality of the soul.

William James, in the third of the lectures he devoted to pragmatism "at the Lowell Institute in Boston, in November and December, 1906, and in January, 1907, at Columbia University, in New York," the weakest of all the writings by the distinguished American thinker—much too weak altogether—says:

> Scholasticism has taken the notion of substance from common sense and made it very technical and articulate. Few things would seem to have fewer pragmatic consequences for us than substances, cut

off as we are from every contact with them. Yet in one case scholasticism has proved the importance of the substance-idea by treating it pragmatically. I refer to certain disputes about the mystery of the Eucharist. Substance here would appear to have momentous pragmatic value. Since the accidents of the wafer don't change in the Lord's supper, and yet it has become the very body of Christ, it must be that the change is in the substance solely. The bread-substance must have been withdrawn, and the divine substance substituted miraculously without altering the immediate sensible properties. But tho these don't alter, a tremendous difference has been made, no less a one than this, that we who take the sacrament, now feed upon the very substance of divinity. The substance-notion breaks into life, then, with tremendous effect, if once you allow that substances can separate from their accidents, and exchange these latter.

This is the only pragmatic application of the substance-idea with which I am acquainted; and it is obvious that it will be treated seriously by those who already believe in the 'real presence' on independent grounds.

Well now, leaving aside the question of whether or not it is sound theology—and I do not say sound reason, for all this lies outside the sphere of reason—to confound the substance of the body, the body and not the soul, of Christ with the very substance of divinity, that is to say, with God Himself, it would appear impossible that one so ardently desirous of the immortality of the soul as William James, a man whose entire philosophy aims at establishing this essence on rational grounds, should not have perceived that the pragmatic application of the concept of substance to the doctrine of Eucharistic transubstantiation is no more than a consequence of its anterior application to the doctrine of the immortality of the soul. As expounded in the preceding chapter, the sacrament of the Eucharist is no more than the reflection of a belief in immortality; for the believer it is a proof, through mystic experience, that the soul is immortal and will enjoy God in eternity. And the concept of substance was born, above all and before all, from the concept of the substantiality of the soul, and the latter was affirmed in order to buttress faith in the soul's persistence after its separation from the body. Such was its first pragmatic application and its origin. And subsequently we have transferred this concept to external objects. It is because I feel myself to be substance, that is to say, permanent in the midst of my changes, that I attribute substantiality to those agents outside me which are permanent in the midst of their changes. It is much the same as when the concept of force—as distinct from movement—arises from my sensation of personal effort in putting something into motion.

Read carefully the first six articles of question LXXV in the First Part of St. Thomas Aquinas' *Summa Theologica*, where he discusses whether the human soul is body, whether it is something self-subsistent, whether the soul of a beast is of the same nature, whether the soul is the man, whether the soul is composed of matter and form, and whether it is incorruptible, and then say whether or not all this is not subtly aimed at buttressing the belief that this incorruptible substantiality of the soul allows it to receive immortality from God, for just as He created the soul when He infused it into the body, according to St. Thomas, He could annihilate it at its separation from the body. As the critique of these proofs has been a hundred times made, there is no sense in repeating it here.

What unprepared reason could conclude that our soul is a substance merely from the fact that consciousness of our identity, and this within very narrow and variable limits, persists throughout all the changes in our body? We might as well speak of the substantial spirit of a ship which sets out from port only to lose on one day a plank (later replaced by another plank of similar shape and size), and a second piece of material later, and thus one part after another, and say that it comes back to port the same ship, in the same shape, as seaworthy as before, and recognizable by all as the same vessel. What unprepared reason could conclude that the soul is simple merely from the fact that we must select and unify our thoughts? Thought is not one, but various, and the soul, as seen from the viewpoint of reason, is nothing but a succession of co-ordinated states of consciousness.

In books of spiritualist psychology it is customary in discussing the existence of the soul as a simple substance separable from the body to begin with a formula in the following manner: "There is in me a principle which thinks, wills, and feels. . . ." Now this implies a begging of the question. For it is far from being an immediate truth that there is in me any such principle; the immediate truth is that *I* think, will, and feel. And I, the I that thinks, wills, and feels, this I immediately constitutes my living body and the states of consciousness which it sustains. It is my living body that thinks, wills, and feels. How? However it may be.

The next move in their argument is to seek to establish the substantiality of the soul, hypostatizing the states of consciousness, and they begin by saying that this substance must be simple, that is, they place thought in opposition to extension, in the manner of Cartesian dualism. Inasmuch as Balmes was one of the spiritualist writers who provided the clearest and most concise form to the argument concerning the simplicity of the soul, I will take the burden of it from him, just as he expounds it in the second chapter of *La Psicología* of his *Curso de filosofía elemental*. "The human soul is simple," he says, and adds:

> Simplicity consists in the absence of parts, and the soul has none. Let us suppose that it had three parts, A, B, C. Then I ask: wherein does thought reside? If in A alone, then B and C are superfluous; and consequently the simple subject A must be the soul. If thought resides in A and B and C, then thought is divided into parts, which is absurd. What kind of a perception would it be, or what kind of comparison, or judgement, or ratiocination that could be distributed among three subjects?

A more obvious begging of the question can not be imagined. From the outset Balmes takes it for granted that the whole, as a whole, is incapable of making a judgement. He continues:

> The unity of consciousness is opposed to the division of the soul. When we think, there is a subject that knows everything that it thinks, and this is impossible if parts are attributed to it. Of the thought that is in A, nothing will be known by B and C, and thus reciprocally. So that there can be no *one* consciousness of the whole thought: each part will have its special consciousness, and there will be within us as many thinking beings as there are parts.

And so the begging of the question continues: it is assumed without any proof that a whole, as a whole, cannot perceive as a unit. Balmes then goes on to ask if these parts A, B, and C are simple or compound, and he repeats his argument until he arrives at the conclusion that the thinking subject must be a part which is not a whole, that is, it must be simple. The argument is based, as can be seen, on the unity of apperception and judgement. Subsequently he endeavors to refute the hypothesis of a communication of the parts among themselves.

Along with all the other *a priori* spiritualists who seek to rationalize faith in the immortality of the soul, Balmes ignores the only rational explanation, which is that apperception and judgement are a resultant, that perceptions or ideas themselves are components which agree. They begin by supposing something external to and distinct from the states of consciousness, something that is not the living body which abides these states, something that is not I but is in me.

The soul is simple, others say, because it reflects upon itself as a complete whole. But no: the state of consciousness A, in which I think of my previous state of consciousness B, is not the same as its predecessor. Or if I think of my soul, I think of an idea distinct from the act by which I think of it. To think only that one thinks, and nothing more, is not to think.

The soul is the principle of life, they say. Yes, and similarly the category of force or energy has been conceived as the principle of movement. But these are concepts, not phenomena, not external realities. Does the principle of motion move? Only that which moves has external reality. Does the principle of life live? Hume was right when he said that he never encountered this idea of himself, but only observed himself desiring or performing or feeling something. The idea of something individual, of this inkstand in front of me, of that horse at my gate, of these two and not any other individual members of their class, constitutes the fact, the phenomenon itself. The idea of myself is myself.

All efforts to make consciousness a substance and make it independent of extension—Descartes, remember, placed thought in opposition to extension—are only sophistical subtleties aimed at establishing the rationality of faith in the immortality of the soul. The attempt is made to give the value of objective reality to what does not possess it, to that whose reality lies only in thought. And the immortality we crave is a phenomenal immortality, the continuation of this present life.

Scientific psychology—the only rational psychology—considers the unity of consciousness no more than a phenomenal unity. No one can say what constitutes a substantial unity. What is more, no one can say what constitutes a substance. For the notion of substance is a non-phenomenal category. It is a noumenon, and it belongs, strictly speaking, to the realm of the unknowable. That is, it depends on its application. But its transcendent application is really inconceivable and, in point of fact, irrational. It is the very concept of substance which an unprepared reason reduces to a use far from the pragmatic application to which William James referred.

And this application is not saved by taking it in an idealistic sense, in accordance with the Berkeleyan principles that to be perceived is to be (*esse est percipi*). To say that everything is idea or that everything is spirit is the same as saying that everything is matter or that everything is energy, for if everything is idea or everything spirit, and if, therefore, this diamond is idea or spirit, just as my consciousness is, it is not clear why the diamond should not endure forever, if my consciousness, because it is idea or spirit, endures forever.

George Berkeley, Anglican Bishop of Cloyne and spiritual brother to the equally Anglican Bishop Joseph Butler, was as anxious as Butler to preserve the belief in the immortality of the soul. From the very first sentence of the Preface to his *Treatise Concerning the Principles of Human Knowledge*, he tells us that he considers his treatise will be useful, "particularly to those who are tainted with scepticism, or want a demonstration of the existence and immateriality of God, or the natural immortality of the soul." In paragraph 140 he states that we have an idea or rather a notion of spirit, and that we know other spirits by means of our own, from which follows, as he roundly asserts in the next paragraph, the natural immortality of the soul. And here he enters upon a series of conclusions arising from the ambiguity with which he invests the term notion. And after having established the immortality of the soul, almost as if it were *per saltum*, on the ground that the soul is not passive like the body, he proceeds to tell us in paragraph 147 that "the existence of God is far more evidently perceived than the existence of men." And still, with all this evidence, there are those who doubt!

The question was made more complicated because consciousness was taken to be a property of the soul, which was something more than consciousness, that is, a substantial form of the body, originator of all the organic functions of the body. The soul not only thinks, feels, and wills, but moves the body and prompts its vital functions; it is in the human soul that the vegetative, animal, and rational functions are united. Such is the doctrine. But separated from the body, the soul can have neither vegetative nor animal functions.

In short, doctrine presents reason with a tissue of confusions.

Following the Renaissance and the restoration of purely rational thought emancipated from all theology, the doctrine of the mortality of the soul was reestablished through the newly unearthed writings of Alexander of Aphrodisias and in the works of Pietro Pomponazzi and others. And, in point of fact, little or nothing can be added to what Pomponazzi wrote in his *Tractatus de immortalitate animae*. He is on the side of reason, and nothing is served by denying it.

There has been no dearth of attempts, nevertheless, to buttress empirically the belief in the immortality of the soul. Among these attempts there is the work of Frederic W. H. Myers on *Human Personality and its Survival of Bodily Death*. No one has ever approached with more eagerness than myself the two thick volumes wherein the man who was the leading spirit of the Society for Psychical Research summarized the formidable mass of data concerning all sorts of psychic presentiments, apparitions of the dead, the phenomena of dreams, telepathy, hypnotism, sensorial automatism, ecstasy, and all the other matter which makes up the spiritualist arsenal. I set about my reading not only without any of the scientific man's prior reservations with respect to this kind of investigation but rather with a predisposition in its favor, like a man in search of confirmation for his most deepseated longings. And for that very reason my disillusion was all the greater. Despite the critical apparatus, all of it in no way differed from medieval miracle-mongering. It entails a fundamental defect of method, an error of logic.

And if the science of the immortality of the soul has been unable to find vindication in rational empiricism, neither is it satisfied by pantheism. To say that everything is God, and that when we die we return to God, or, more accurately, continue in Him, serves our longing not at all. For if such is the case, we were in God before we were born, and if when we die we return to where we were before being born, then the human soul, the individual consciousness, is perishable. And since we know very well that God, the personal and conscious God of Christian monotheism, is nought but the provider and, above all, the guarantor of our immortality, pantheism is said to be, quite rightly said to be, a disguised form of atheism. In my own opinion, it is an undisguised form. And it was right to call Spinoza an atheist, for his pantheism is the most logical and rational. Nor is the longing for immortality assuaged, but rather dissolved and submerged, by agnosticism or the doctrine of the unknowable, which, whenever it professed to be considerate of religious feelings, has always been animated by the most subtle hypocrisy. The entire first part of Spencer's *First Principles*, especially the fifth chapter, entitled "Reconciliation" (reconciliation between reason and faith, between science and religion, it is understood), is a model of British cant, as well as of philosophic superficiality and religious insincerity. The unknowable, if it be something more than the merely hitherto unknown, is but a purely negative concept, a concept of limitation. No human feeling can rise on such a foundation.

*99**

The science of religion, on the other hand, of religion taken as an individual and social psychic phenomenon irrespective of the transcendental objective validity of religious affirmations, is a science which, in explaining the origin of the belief that the soul can live apart from the body, has destroyed the rationality of this belief. The religious man may repeat with Schleiermacher, "Science can teach you nothing. Let it learn from you," but within himself he is bound to feel a reservation.

Whatever the view taken, it always appears that reason confronts our longing for personal immortality and contradicts us. And the truth is that reason is the enemy of life.

Intelligence is a dreadful matter. It tends toward death in the way that memory tends toward stability. That which lives, that which is absolutely unstable, absolutely individual, is, strictly speaking, unintelligible. Logic tends to reduce everything to identities and genera, to a state where each representation has no more than one single selfsame content in whatever place, time, or relation the representation may occur to us. But nothing is the same for two successive moments of its being. My idea of God is different each time I conceive it. Identity, which is death, is precisely what the intellect seeks. The mind seeks what is dead, for the living escapes it. It seeks to congeal the flowing stream into blocks of ice. It seeks to arrest the flow. In order to analyze a body it is first necessary to reduce it or to destroy it. In order to understand anything it must first be killed, laid out rigid in the mind. Science is a cemetery of dead ideas, even though live ideas are born out of it. Worms, also, feed upon corpses. My own thoughts, tumultuous and agitated in the recesses of my mind, once torn up by their roots from my heart, poured out upon this paper and here fixed in unalterable form, are already the cadavers of thought. How, then, is reason to open up to the revelation of life? It is a tragic combat, the very essence of tragedy, this battle of life against reason. And truth? Is it something to be lived or something to be apprehended?

One need only read the appalling *Parmenides* of Plato to agree with his tragic conclusion: "It seems that, whether there is or is not a one, both that one and the others alike are and are not, and appear and do not appear to be." Everything vital is irrational, and everything rational is anti-vital, for reason is essentially sceptical.

The rational, in effect, is no more than the relational; reason limits itself to relating irrational elements. Mathematics is the only perfect science insofar as it adds, subtracts, multiplies, and divides numbers, but not real substantial things, insofar as it is the most formal of the sciences. Who is capable of extracting the cube root of that ash tree there?

Nevertheless, we need logic, that terrible power, to communicate thoughts and perceptions and even to think and perceive, for we think in words and perceive in forms. To think is to converse with oneself, and speech is social, and thought and logic are social. Still, do they not perhaps include an intransmissible and untranslatable individual matter or content? May not their power reside therein?

The fact is that man, the prisoner of logic—without which he cannot think—has always striven to place logic at the service of his desires, most especially of his fundamental desire. He has always sought to hold fast to logic, especially during the Middle Ages, in the interests of theology and jurisprudence, both of which used established authority as their point of departure. It was not until much later that logic took up the problem of knowledge, the question of its own validity, the examination of meta-logical foundations.

"The Western theology," Dean Stanley wrote, "is essentially logical in form, and based on law. The Eastern is rhetorical in form and based on philosophy. The Latin divine succeeded to the Roman advocate. The Oriental divine succeeded to the Grecian sophist."

And all the labored arguments, presuming to be rational or logical in support of our hunger for immortality, are no more than special and sophistical pleading.

The specific characteristic of special pleading, of advocacy, in effect is to put logic at the service of a thesis which is to be defended; the strictly scientific method, on the other hand, proceeds from the facts, from the data presented to us by reality, and then arrives, or does not arrive, at some conclusion. The important consideration is to formulate the problem clearly, whence it follows that progress consists, quite often, in undoing what has been done. Advocacy always involves a *petitio principii*, and its arguments are all *ad probandum*. And the theology which presumes to be rational is no more than advocacy.

Theology proceeds from dogma, and dogma, δόγμα, in its primitive and most direct sense, signifies a decree, something like the Latin *placitum*, that which has seemed to legislative authority most meet to be law. This juridical concept is the starting point for theology. In the eyes of the theologian, as in the eyes of the attorney at law, dogma, the law, is something given, a point of departure not open to discussion except insofar as concerns its applicability and as regards its most exact interpretation. Hence it is that the theological or advocatory spirit is dogmatic on principle, while the strictly scientific and purely rational spirit is sceptical, σκεπτικός, that is, investigative. It is investigative at least in origin, I should add, for scepticism in its other sense, the one most current today, as the term for a system of doubt, suspicion, and uncertainty, arose from the theological or advocatory misuse of reason, from the abuse of dogmatism. The attempt to apply the law, the *placitum*, the dogma, to distinct and sometimes contradictory practical needs has given rise to the scepticism of doubt. It is advocacy, or what amounts to the same thing, theology, which teaches a distrust of reason, and not true science which does so, not investigative science, sceptical in the primitive and direct meaning of the term, science undirected toward any foreseen solution, but rather proceeding only to test a hypothesis.

Take the *Summa Theologica* of St. Thomas, the classical monument of the theology—that is, the advocacy—of Catholicism, and open it wherever you please. First comes the thesis: *utrum* . . . whether such and such be thus or otherwise; then come the objections: *ad primum sic proceditur*; next come the answers to these objections: *sed contra est* . . . or *respondeo dicendum*. All of it special pleading, pure advocacy! And underlying many, perhaps most, of its arguments you will find a logical fallacy which may be expressed *more scholastico* by the following syllogism: "I do not understand this fact save by furnishing it with this explanation; thus it is I must understand it, and therefore that must be its explanation; the alternative would be that I not understand it at all." True science teaches us, above all, to doubt and admit ignorance; advocacy neither doubts nor believes it does not know. Advocacy requires a solution.

The kind of mentality that assumes, more or less consciously, that we must have a solution, also tends to believe in baneful consequences. Take any book of apologetics—that is to say, of theological advocacy—and you will repeatedly meet with the refrain: "The baneful consequences of this doctrine. . . ." Now the baneful consequences of a doctrine may prove, at best, that the doctrine is baneful, but not that it is false, for it has still to be proven that the true is necessarily the best for us. The identification of the true with the good is no more than a pious desire. In his *Études sur Blaise Pascal*, A. Vinet says: "Of the two needs that are continually at work influencing human nature, the need for happiness is not only the more universally felt and the more constantly experienced, it is also the more imperious. And this need is not only sensory, it is also intellectual. Happiness is essential not only for the *soul*, but for the *spirit*. Happiness forms part of the truth." This last proposition—*le bonheur fait partie de la vérité*—is a clear case of special pleading, of advocacy, and has nothing to do either with science or with pure reason. It would be better to say that truth makes part of happiness in a Tertullian-like sense, in the sense of *credo quia absurdum*, which means, strictly speaking, *credo quia consolans*: I believe because it consoles me to do so.

In the eyes of reason, the only truth is that which can be shown to be, to exist, whether or not it offers us any consolation. And reason itself is certainly not a consolatory faculty. That terrifying Latin poet Lucretius, whose apparent serenity and Epicurean *ataraxia* conceal so much despair, said that piety consists in the ability to contemplate all things with a serene soul: *pacata posse mente omnia tueri.* And the same Lucretius wrote that religion can lead us into many evils: *tantum religio potuit suadere malorum.* And of course religion, the Christian religion especially, was, as the Apostle says, a scandal for the Jews and madness for the intellectuals (cf. 1 Cor. 1:23). And Tacitus called the Christian religion, the religion of the immortality of the soul, a pernicious superstition, *exitialis superstitio,* and asserted that it implied a hatred of the human race, *odium generis humani.*

Speaking of the age in which these men lived, the most authentically rationalist age of all, Flaubert addressed the following pregnant words to Madame Roger des Genettes:

> You are right, one must speak respectfully of Lucretius; I cannot see his equal except for Byron, and Byron has not his seriousness nor his genuine sadness. The melancholy of the ancients seems to me deeper than that of the moderns, who all, more or less, assume an immortality on the far side of the "*black pit.*" For the ancients the black pit was infinity itself; their dreams take shape and pass against a background of unchanging ebony. The gods being dead and Christ not yet born, there was between Cicero and Marcus Aurelius one unique moment in which there was nothing but man. I can find no reflection of that great time anywhere. What makes Lucretius intolerable, however, is his physics, which he states as final. He is weak because he did not doubt enough; he wanted to explain, to come to conclusions!

True enough, Lucretius strove to reach conclusions, solutions, and, what is worse, strove to find consolation in reason. For there is also an anti-theological advocacy and an *odium antitheologicum.*

And a great many men of science, the greater number of those who call themselves rationalists, are afflicted by it.

The rationalist acts rationally, that is, he acts within his role, as long as he confines himself to denying that reason satisfies our vital hunger for immortality. But then, possessed by the fury of not being able to believe, he soon becomes enraged by *odium antitheologicum* and cries out with the Pharisees: "This people who knoweth not the law are cursed." There is a good deal of truth in the words of Soloviev: "I have a foreboding of the approach of a time when the Christians will gather again in the Catacombs, because the Faith is persecuted, perhaps in a manner less brutal than in Nero's time, but with a severity no less refined, by lies, mockery, and all manner of hypocrisy."

Anti-theological hate, scientificist (I do not say scientific) fury—hate and fury against faith in another life—is manifest. Consider not the more detached scientific investigators, those who know how to doubt, but the fanatics of rationalism, and observe with what gross brutality they speak of faith. Karl Vogt, for instance, was of the opinion that the cranial structure of the Apostles must have shown marked simian characteristics. There is no point in talking of the indecencies of Haeckel, that master of incomprehension; nor of those of Büchner, either. Even Virchow is not free of these blemishes. And then there are others who tread the same path, only more subtly. There are people who seem scarcely content simply with not believing in another life, or rather in believing that there is none, but who are positively hurt and irritated that others should believe in such a life or even should wish for such a life to exist.

This rationalist attitude is despicable, while the position of the man who strives to believe in another life—because he needs another life—and finds he can not so believe is worthy of respect. But this latter attitude, the most noble, most profound, most human and most fruitful attitude and state of mind, which is that of despair, shall be discussed further on.

And even those rationalists who do not fall prey to anti-theological rage still will insist on convincing mankind that there actually are good reasons for living and a consolation for having been born—even though a time will come, in some tens or hundreds or millions of centuries, when all human consciousness will have disappeared. And these reasons for living and working, all that business known as humanism, are the mooncalf of the affective and emotional emptiness of rationalism and of its stupifying hypocrisy, a hypocrisy bent on sacrificing sincerity to veracity, and on refusing to confess the fact that reason is a disheartening power committed to dissolution.

Is there any need to repeat all that has already been said about forging a culture, about progress, about attaining to the good, the true, and the beautiful, about establishing justice on earth, about making a better life for those who follow us, about serving some destiny or other, all without giving thought to our own ultimate end? Is there any point in speaking of the supreme vacuity of culture, of science, of art, of good, truth, beauty, justice . . . of all those lofty concepts, if, in the end, in four days' time or four million centuries'—either length of time is the same—no human consciousness will exist to receive that culture, science, good, truth, beauty, justice, and all the rest?

Many and varied are the rationalist—more or less

rational—devices by means of which, ever since the days of Epicureans and Stoics, consolation has been sought from rational truth, and the attempt has been made to convince men—though those who tried to do the convincing were not themselves convinced—that there are good reasons for working and inducements to go on living, even though human consciousness was destined one day to disappear.

The Epicurean attitude—the extreme and grossest expression of which is to be found in "Let us eat and drink, for tomorrow we die," or in the Horatian *Carpe diem*, which could be translated as "Live for the day"—does not differ fundamentally from the Stoic position, with its "Do what your conscience dictates, and let what follows follow." Both positions share a common base; and pleasure for pleasure's sake is the same as duty for duty's sake.

Spinoza, the most logical and consistent of atheists—I mean, of those who deny the persistence of individual consciousness through indefinite future time—and at the same time the most pious of atheists, devoted the Fifth, and last, Part of his *Ethics* to elucidating the path which leads to freedom and to delimiting the concept of blessedness. The concept! The concept, and not the sense. For Spinoza—who was an appalling intellectualizer—"blessedness," *beatitudo*, is a concept, and the love of God an intellectual love. In Proposition XXI of this part he establishes that: "The mind can only imagine anything, or remember what is past, while the body endures." This is a denial of the immortality of the soul: for a soul which, separated from the body where it lived, no longer remembers its past is neither immortal nor is it a soul. And in Proposition XXIII, Spinoza then goes on to tell us that: "The human mind cannot be absolutely destroyed with the body, but there remains of it something which is *eternal*"; and this eternity of the mind is a certain mode of thinking. But do not be deceived: there is no eternity of the individual mind. Everything is *sub aeternitatis specie*, that is, a fraud. Nothing could be more dreary, more desolate, more anti-vital than this "blessedness," this Spinozan *beatitudo*, which consists of "The intellectual love of the mind towards God . . . that very love of God whereby God loves himself . . ." (Proposition XXXVI). Our "blessedness," that is, our "freedom," consists in God's constant and eternal love of mankind: so affirms the Note to this Proposition XXXVI. And all this in order to reach the conclusion, the final and crowning proposition of the entire *Ethics*: the statement that: "Blessedness is not the reward of virtue, but virtue itself" (Proposition XLII). The same as always! Or, to put it plainly: we come from God and to God we must return, which, translated into the concrete language of life and feeling, means that my personal consciousness came out of nothingness, from my unconsciousness, and that to nothingness it will return.

And that most mournful and desolate voice of Spinoza is the very voice of reason. And the "freedom" of which he speaks is a terrible freedom. And against Spinoza and his doctrine of "blessedness" there exists only one incontrovertible argument, the argument *ad hominem*. Was the man Baruch Spinoza blessed as, by way of allaying his inner unhappiness, he discoursed on that very blessedness? Was he himself free?

In the Note to Proposition XLI of this same final and most tragic part of that tremendous tragedy of his *Ethics*, the poor desperate Jew of Amsterdam speaks to us of "the general belief of the multitude" regarding the eternal life. Let us attend to what he says:

> They . . . believe that piety, religion, and, generally, all things attributable to firmness of mind, are burdens, which, after death, they hope to lay aside, and to receive the reward for their bondage, that is, for their piety and religion; it is not only by this hope, but also, and chiefly, by the fear of being horribly punished after death, that they are induced to live according to the divine commandments, so far as their feeble and infirm spirit will carry them.
>
> If men had not this hope and this fear, but believed that the mind perishes with the body, and that no hope of prolonged life remains for the wretches who are broken down with the burden of piety, they would return to their own inclinations, controlling everything in accordance with their lusts, and desiring to obey fortune rather than themselves. Such a course appears to me not less absurd than if a man, because he does not believe that he can by wholesome food sustain his body for ever, should wish to cram himself with poisons and deadly fare; or if, because he sees that the mind is not eternal or immortal, he should prefer to be out of his mind altogether, and to live without the use of reason; these ideas are so absurd to be scarcely worth refuting.

When it is said of some assertion that it is "scarcely worth refuting," one may be sure that the assertion is either a piece of egregious foolishness, in which case not even that need be said of it, or the assertion is somehow formidable, the very key to the problem. And so it is in this case. Yes! Poor Portuguese Jew exiled in Holland, yes! Whoever is convinced, beyond a shadow of a doubt, without the slightest ray of redeeming uncertainty, that his soul is not immortal, would surely prefer to have no soul at all, to be without soul, *amens*, irrational, an idiot, and he would

surely prefer not to have been born. And there is
nothing, absolutely nothing, "absurd" about such an
attitude. Was he, poor Jewish intellectualist definer
of intellectual love and of blessedness, was he blessed?
For this, and nothing else, constitutes the problem.
"What good is it to know how to define contrition, if
you don't feel it?" asks Thomas a Kempis. And what
is the use of setting about a definition of blessedness,
if you can not thereby achieve blessedness? Apposite
in this connection is the terrible story told by Diderot
about the eunuch who wished to receive lessons in
aesthetics from a man from Marseille so that he might
better select slave girls for the harem of his master
the Sultan. At the end of the first lesson, a lesson in
physiology—bare, carnal physiology—the eunuch
exclaimed mournfully: "I can see that I shall never
know aesthetics!" And so it is: eunuchs will never
know aesthetics as applied to the selection of lovely
women, and pure rationalists will never know ethics
or be able to define blessedness, which is something
lived and felt and not something thought out and
defined.

Then we have that other rationalist—one not resigned and sad like Spinoza, but rebellious and feign-
ing a hypocritical joyousness, though he was no less
in despair—Nietzsche, who *mathematically* (!!!) invented that counterfeit of the immortality of the soul
called "the eternal recurrence," a most formidable
tragi-comedy or comi-tragedy. Since the number of
atoms or irreducible primary elements is finite, he
presumes that, in an eternal universe, a combination
identical with the present one must occur, and that
what happens now must be repeated an endless number of times. Of course! And so, just as I will again
live the life I am now living, I have already lived it an

infinite number of times, for there is an eternity that stretches into the past, *a parte ante*, just as there will be one into the future, *a parte post*. But the sad fact is that I can not remember any of my previous existences, assuming that it would be possible for me to remember any such thing, inasmuch as two things that are absolutely and totally identical are no more than one and the same. Instead of supposing that we live in a finite universe composed of a finite number of irreducible primary elements, let us suppose that we live in an infinite universe, without limits in space— a concrete infinity is no less inconceivable than a concrete eternity in time—and then it would follow that this our system, with its Milky Way and all, is repeated an infinite number of times in the infinity of space, and that I am living an infinite number of lives, all of them exactly identical. It's a joke, you see, and no less comic—that is, no less tragic—than Nietzsche's jest, the one about the laughing lion. And what makes the lion laugh? Rage, I think, because he can not console himself with the thought that he has already been the same lion before and will be the same lion still again.

But if Spinoza as well as Nietzsche were both of them rationalists, each in his own way, they were neither of them spiritual eunuchs; they had hearts, feeling, and, above all, a hunger, a mad hunger for eternity, for immortality. The physical eunuch does not feel the need to reproduce carnally, in body, and the spiritual eunuch does not feel the hunger for self-perpetuation.

It is certainly true that there are people who assert that reason alone suffices for them and who advise us to desist from seeking to penetrate the impenetrable. But I do not know what to think of those others who claim they need no faith whatever in an eternal personal life by way of incentive to go on living and working. Someone blind from birth may assure us that he feels no great desire to enjoy the world of sight, nor great anguish at having missed it, and we must believe him, for there can be no desire felt for something totally unknown—*nihil volitum quin praecognitum*: it is not possible to care for anything except something already known. But I can not believe that anyone who has once, either in his youth or some other period, harbored a faith in the immortality of the soul will ever be able to rest easy without that faith. As regards congenital blindness, moreover, there are few instances of it among us, unless it be as the result of an exotic aberration. And the man who is merely and exclusively rational is also an aberration and nothing else.

More sincere, much more sincere, are those who say: "We must not talk about all that, for it is a waste of time and leads to an enervation of the will. Let us do our duty here, and then let come what may." And yet this sincerity masks a deeper insincerity. For is it possible by the mere repetition of the phrase "We must not talk about it," to forget the matter? Our will is enervated, they say? . . . And what of it? We are rendered incapable of some human action? And what of that? It is too easy to tell someone condemned to an early death by a fatal disease, and who knows it, that he should not think about it.

> Meglio oprando oblïar, senza indagarlo,
> questo enorme mister de l'universo!

"Better to work and forget and not delve too deeply into the vast mystery of the universe!" says Carducci in his *Idillio maremmano*. And the same Carducci, in

113*

his ode *Su Monte Mario*, speaks to us of how the earth, mother of the fugitive soul, revolves its glory and sorrow round the sun:

> until, withered at Equator
> beneath the insistence of a terminal heat,
> the faded lineages produce one last
> man, one woman,
>   standing alone amid rent cliffs,
> dead woods, ash-colored and their eyes
> glazed, watching the sun go down
> across the immense ice.

But is it possible to devote oneself to any serious and lasting work and forget about the vast mystery of the universe, refusing always to delve more deeply? Is it possible to contemplate the universe with a serene soul, in the spirit of Lucretian piety, conscious all the while that one day this universe will no longer be reflected in any human consciousness?

Cain, in Byron's poem of the same name, asks Lucifer, the prince of the intellectuals: "Are ye happy?" And Lucifer replies: "We are mighty." Cain repeats: "Are ye happy?" And the Great Intellectual retorts: "No: art thou?" And further on, Lucifer tells Adah, Cain's sister and wife: "Choose betwixt Love and Knowledge—since there is no other choice." And in this same marvelous poem, when Cain says that the Tree of the Knowledge of Good and Evil was a *lying tree*, for "we *know* nothing. At least it *promised knowledge* at the *price* of death," Lucifer answers him: "It may be death leads to the *highest* knowledge"—that is, to nothingness.

Byron's "Knowledge"—Spanish *ciencia*, French *science*, German *Wissenschaft*—is often placed in opposition to wisdom—Spanish *sabiduría*, French *sagesse*, German *Weisheit*.

> Knowledge comes, but Wisdom lingers,
>   and he bears a laden breast,
> Full of sad experience, moving towards
>   the stillness of his rest,

says another Lord, Tennyson, in his *Locksley Hall*. And what is "wisdom," that we must look for it in the poets mainly, leaving "knowledge" to one side? It is all very well to say with Matthew Arnold—in his Preface to Wordsworth's poems—that "Poetry is the reality, philosophy the illusion"; but reason is always reason, and reality is always reality, that which can be proved to exist outside ourselves, whether it affords us any consolation or causes us to despair.

I do not know why so many people were scandalized, or pretended to be scandalized, when Brunetière proclaimed, once again, the bankruptcy of science. For science as a substitute for religion and reason as a substitute for faith have always come to nought. Science may satisfy, and in point of fact does increasingly satisfy, our increasingly logical or intellectual needs, our desire to know and understand the truth; but science does not satisfy the needs of our feeling or of our will, and far from satisfying our hunger for immortality, it contradicts it. Rational truth stands in opposition to life. And is there any other truth but rational truth?

It should be admitted, then, that reason, human reason, within its own limits, not only does not prove rationally that the soul is immortal or that the human consciousness will be indestructible through time to come, but rather proves, within its limits, I repeat, that individual consciousness cannot persist after the death of the physical organism upon which it depends. And these limits, the limits within which human reason proves what I say above, are the limits of rationality, of what we know from proof. Outside these limits lies the irrational or the contra-rational; outside these limits is Tertullian's absurdity, the impossibility of the *certum est, quia impossibile est*. And this absurdity can rest only upon the most absolute uncertainty.

The rational dissolution ends by dissolving reason itself into the most absolute scepticism, into the phenomenalism of Hume, or into the doctrine of absolute contingencies of men like John Stuart Mill, the most consistent and logical of the positivists. The supreme triumph of reason, which is analytical, that is, destructive and dissolvent, is to cast doubt upon its own validity. A stomach ulcer ends by causing the stomach to digest itself, and reason ends by destroying the immediate and absolute validity of the concept of truth and of the concept of necessity. Both concepts are relative: there is no absolute truth, no absolute necessity. We call true that concept which agrees with the general system of all our concepts; and we call true that perception which does not contradict the system of our perceptions; truth, then, is coherence, connection. And as regards the system as a whole, an aggregate: inasmuch as there exists nothing outside it known to us, it is unacceptable to say it is true or otherwise. It is conceivable that the universe, in itself and outside ourselves, may be quite different from what it seems to us, though such a supposition is lacking in all rational meaning. And as regards necessity: is there an absolute necessity? By necessary we mean nothing more than what is and insofar as it is; for in another, more transcendent sense, what absolute necessity, what logical necessity independent of the fact that the universe exists, is there for a universe, or anything else, to exist at all?

Absolute relativism, which is nothing more or less than scepticism—in the most modern sense of that term—is the supreme triumph of ratiocinating reason.

Sentiment cannot turn consolation into truth, and reason cannot turn truth into consolation. And yet reason, proceeding on the basis of truth itself, on the basis of the very concept of reality, plunges into the depths of scepticism. And in the abyss, rational scepticism comes face to face with sentiment's despair, and the encounter gives us a basis—a terrible basis!—for consolation. Let us examine it.

VI. In the Depths of the Abyss

Parce unicae spei totius orbis.

Tertullian, *Adversus Marcionem*, 5

AND SO, NEITHER the vital longing for human immortality can count on any rational confirmation nor can reason supply us with any incentive or consolation in life or any true end purpose for it. And yet, here in the depths of the abyss, the despair of the will and of the heart meets rational scepticism and in the encounter they embrace like brothers. And from this embrace, this tragic embrace, that is, this intimately loving embrace, will surge a wellspring of life, a life both true and terrible. It is scepticism, uncertainty, the final position reached by reason in its exercise of self-analysis, the analysis of its own validity, that provides a foundation upon which the heart's despair must build its hope.

We had to abandon in disillusionment the position of those who seek to turn consolation into rational and logical truth by attempting to prove its rationality or at least its non-irrationality, and we had also to abandon the position of those who seek to turn rational truth into consolation and endow it with a reason for life. Neither the one nor the other of these positions could satisfy us. The first is at odds with our reason, the other with our senses. Any peace between these two powers is impossible, and we must live from their warfare. And we must make this warfare, make war itself, the condition of our spiritual life.

There is no room in this connection for that repugnant and vulgar makeshift, the expedient of politicians—more or less parliamentary politicians—known as a "working agreement," in which there are neither victors nor vanquished. There is no room here for compromise. A degenerate and cowardly reason might perhaps concoct some formula for an arrangement—after all, reason lives on formulas. But life, which does not submit to formulas, life, which lives and seeks always to live, does not accept formulas. Its only formula is: all or nothing. Feeling does not compromise with middle terms.

Initium sapientiae timor Domini was perhaps meant to mean *timor mortis*, or perhaps *timor vitae*, which is the same. It is always true that the beginning of wisdom lies in some fear or other.

And, as for this saving scepticism of which I shall now speak, can it be said to be doubt? Yes, it is doubt, and it is much more than doubt. Doubt is often very cold, a not very vitalizing force, and, above all, rather artificial, especially ever since Descartes degraded it to the function of method. The conflict between reason and life is something more than doubt. For doubt is easily reduced to a comic element.

Descartes's methodical doubt is a comic doubt, a purely theoretic and provisional doubt; that is, it is the doubt of a man who plays at doubting without really being in doubt. It is a hothouse doubt, and so the man who concluded that he existed because he thought, this man did not approve of "those turbulent [*brouillonnes*] and restless persons who, being called neither by birth nor by fortune to the management of public affairs, are perpetually devising some new reforms," and he was pained to think that there might be some of this element in his own writing. No, this man, Descartes, proposed only to reform his own thoughts and to build upon ground that was wholly his. And he resolved not to accept anything as true which he did not manifestly know to be such, and to destroy all prejudices and received ideas so that he might construct for himself anew an intellectual habitation. But "as it is not enough, before beginning to rebuild one's dwelling-house, to pull it down and to furnish the materials and architects, or to study architecture oneself . . . but it is also necessary to be provided with some other wherein to lodge conveniently while the work is in progress," he framed for himself a provisional ethic—*une morale de provision*—whose first law was to follow the customs of his country and keep the religion in which, by the grace of God, he had been instructed since childhood, guiding himself in all matters in accordance with the most moderate opinion. In other words, a provisional religion and even a provisional God! And he chose the most moderate opinion, as being "the most convenient in practice." But it will be best not to follow him further.

This methodical or theoretical Cartesian doubt, this philosophico-hothouse doubt, is not the doubt, the scepticism, the uncertainty of which I speak, and nothing like it. The doubt I mean is a passionate doubt, the eternal conflict between reason and feeling, between science and life, between the logical and the biotic. For science destroys the concept of personality, reducing it to a complex in continual state of momentary flux, that is, it destroys the very foundation of the spiritual and emotional life, which, since it never gives up, turns against reason.

And this kind of doubt can not avail itself of any provisional ethic, but must establish its own ethic, as we shall see, on conflict itself, so that it becomes a battle ethic, and upon this ethic it will build the foundation of religion. And it inhabits a house in process of continuous demolition and in continuous need of rebuilding. The will, the will not ever to die, the refusal to resign oneself to death, ceaselessly builds the house of life while the keen blasts and icy winds of reason unceasingly batter at the structure and beat it down.

Moreover, as regards the concrete life-problem in question, reason takes no position whatever. The truth is that reason goes even further than to deny the immortality of the soul, which would be one solution, for it refuses to recognize the problem in the form in which our life's desire presents it. In the rational and logical sense of the term "problem," there is no such problem. The question of the immortality of the soul, of the persistence of individual consciousness, is not a rational concern, it falls outside the scope of reason. As a problem—whatever solution is assumed—it is irrational. Rationally, even the stating of the problem lacks sense. The immortality of the soul is as inconceivable as, strictly speaking, its absolute mortality would be. For purposes of explaining the world and existence—and such is the task of reason—there is no need to suppose that our soul is either mortal or immortal. The very statement of the supposed problem, then, is irrational.

Let us listen to brother Kierkegaard, who tells us:

> This questionable character of abstract thought becomes apparent especially in connection with all existential problems, where abstract thought gets rid of the difficulty by leaving it out, and then proceeds to boast of having explained everything. It explains immortality in general, and all goes quite smoothly, in that immortality is identified with eternity, with

the eternity which is essentially the medium of all thought. But whether an existing individual human being is immortal, which is the difficulty, abstract thought does not trouble to inquire. It is disinterested; but the difficulty inherent in existence constitutes the interest of the existing individual, who is infinitely interested in existing. Abstract thought thus helps me with respect to my immortality by first annihilating me as a particular existing individual and then making me immortal, about as when the doctor in Holberg killed the patient with his medicine—but also expelled the fever. Such an abstract thinker, one who neglects to take into account the relationship between his abstract thought and his own existence as an individual, not careful to clarify this relationship to himself, makes a comical impression upon the mind even if he is ever so distinguished, because he is in process of ceasing to be a human being. While a genuine human being, as a synthesis of the finite and the infinite, finds his reality in holding these two factors together, infinitely interested in existing—such an abstract thinker is a duplex being: a fantastic creature who moves in the pure being of abstract thought, and on the other hand, a sometimes pitiful professorial figure which the former deposits, about as when one sets down a walking stick. When one reads the story of such a thinker's life (for his writings are perhaps excellent), one trembles to think of what it means to be a man. And when you read in his writings that thought and being are one, it is impossible not to think, in view of his own life and mode of existence, that the being which is thus identical with thought can scarcely be the being of a man.

What intense passion, that is, what truth, lies in this bitter invective directed against Hegel, the prototype of the rationalist, who relieves us of our fever by relieving us of our life and promises us, in place of concrete immortality an abstract immortality—as if our ravening hunger for immortality were abstract and not concrete!

It can of course be said that "once the dog is dead there's an end to the rabies," and that once I'm dead I'll no longer be tormented by this rage to live beyond death, and that the fear of death, or more properly, of nothingness, is an irrational fear, but . . . yes, but . . . *Eppur si muove*! And it will go on moving. For it is the source of all movement!

And yet, I do not believe that brother Kierkegaard is altogether in the right, for that very same abstract thinker, or thinker in abstractions, Hegel, thinks *so that* he may exist, so as not to cease existing, or perhaps so as to forget that he will have to cease existing. Such is the basis for the passion toward abstract thought. And it may be that Hegel was as infinitely interested as Kierkegaard in his own concrete singular existence, even if the professional decorum incumbent on an official State-philosopher compelled him to conceal the fact: such are the demands of office.

Faith in immortality is irrational. Nevertheless, faith and life and reason are mutually in need of each other. This vital longing is not properly speaking a problem, it can not be given any logical status, it can not be formulated in propositions rationally disputable; but it poses itself as a problem the way hunger poses itself as a problem. Likewise the wolf, when it hurls itself upon its prey to devour it or upon a she-wolf to impregnate it, can not state rationally, or logically pose, the "problem" of its impulse. Reason and faith are enemies of each other and can not either of them maintain itself without the other. The irrational seeks to be made rational, and reason can operate only on the basis of the irrational. They must rely on each other and associate—but associate in battle, for battle is a form of association.

In the world of the living the struggle for life establishes an association, an association of the closest kind, not merely of the type that unites allies in combating a foe, but an association between those that combat each other. Could any association be more intimate than that between a beast of prey and its prey, between the devourer and the devoured? And if this relationship is clear in the struggle for survival among individuals, it is even clearer among nations. War has ever been the most effective factor in progress, more so even than commerce. It is through war that victors and vanquished learn to know each other and, in consequence, to love each other.

Christianity, "the madness of the Cross," the irrational faith that Christ rose from the dead in order to raise us also, was saved by rationalistic Hellenic culture just as the latter was saved by Christianity. Without Christianity the Renaissance would have been impossible. Without the Gospel, without St. Paul, the nations who had lived through the Middle Ages would have understood neither Plato nor Aristotle. A purely rationalist tradition is as impossible as a purely religious tradition. It is frequently debated whether the Reformation was a child born of the Renaissance or in protest against it, and it would be possible to say that it was both, for a child is always born in protest against the father. It is also said that the revival of the Greek classics led men like Erasmus back to St. Paul and to primitive Christianity, its most irrational form. But it may be retorted that it was St. Paul, that it was the Christian irrationality underlying his Catholic theology, that led them back to the classics. "Christianity is what it has come to be," it is said, "only through its alliance with antiquity, while among the Copts and the Ethiopians it is merely a kind of buffoonery. Islam evolved under the influence of Persian and Greek culture; under the influence of the Turks it has been transformed into destructive barbarism."

We emerge from the Middle Ages and its faith, a faith as ardent as it is basically despairing and not without deep-seated uncertainties, and we enter the age of rationalism, also not free of uncertainty. Faith in reason is prone to the same rational indefensibility as any other faith. And we may well say with Robert Browning

> All we have gained, then, by our unbelief
> Is a life of doubt diversified by faith
> For one of faith diversified by doubt.

And if, as I have said, faith—life—can sustain itself only by depending upon reason, which will make it transmissible—transmissible, especially, from me to myself; that is, reflective and conscious—then, by the same token, reason can sustain itself only upon faith, upon life, even if it is merely upon faith in reason, upon faith which is good for something more than knowledge, upon faith which is good for living. And yet, faith is not transmissible or rational, and neither is reason vital.

Will and intelligence have need of one another, and that old aphorism *nihil volitum quin praecognitum*, nothing is willed but what is previously known, can be inverted without being as paradoxical as may seem at first sight: *nihil cognitum quin praevolitum*, nothing is known but what is previously willed. Vinet, in considering Cousin's book on Pascal's *Pensées*, writes: "Spiritual knowledge itself has need of the heart.

Without a desire to see, there is no seeing. When life and thought are altogether materialized, there is no believing in the things of the spirit." We shall see that believing is, in the first instance, wanting to believe.

Will and intelligence seek opposite ends. Our will seeks to absorb the world to ourselves, to appropriate it; our intelligence wants us to be absorbed in the world. Are these opposite ends? Are they not rather one and the same? No, they are not, although they may seem to be. Intelligence is monist or pantheist; will is monotheist or egoist. Intelligence has no need to act upon anything outside itself, it is fused with ideas themselves; while will requires matter. To know something is to make myself into the thing I know; but in order for me to make use of it, for me to dominate it, it must remain distinct from me.

Philosophy and religion are enemies, and, because they are enemies, they need each other. There is no religion without some philosophic basis, nor is there any philosophy without religious roots: each lives off its opposite. Strictly speaking, the history of religion is the history of philosophy. And the attacks directed against religion from a presumably scientific or philosophic point of view are merely attacks from another, opposite, but religious point of view. "Thus the opposition which professedly exists between natural science and Christianity really exists between an impulse derived from natural religion blended with the scientific investigation of nature, and the validity of the Christian view of the world, which assures to spirit its pre-eminence over the entire world of nature," says Ritschl (*Rechtfertigung und Versöhnung*, III, Ch. IV, para. 28). Now this instinct is the very same as the instinct toward rationality. And Kant's critical idealism has a religious origin; it was to save religion that Kant enlarged the limits of reason after having first in a certain sense dissolved it in scepticism. The system of antithesis, contradictions, and antimonies, upon which Hegel constructed his absolute idealism, has its root and germ in Kant himself, and this root is an irrational root.

Further on we shall see, as we consider faith, that faith is in essence no more than a matter of will, not one of reason, just as to believe is to want to believe, and that to believe in God is to wish, above all and before all, that there may be a God. In the same way, to believe in the immortality of the soul is to want the soul to be immortal, and to want it so strongly that the wish rides roughshod over reason. But reason will have its revenge.

The instinct to know and the instinct to live (or rather, to survive) come into conflict with each other. In his work on *The Analysis of Sensations, and the Relation of the Physical to the Psychical*, Dr. Ernst Mach tells us that the scientific investigator, too, the research worker, *der Forscher*, fights in the battle for existence; that the ways of science still lead to the mouth; and that the pure instinct to know, *der reine Erkenntnisstrieb*, is still merely an ideal, given our present social conditions. And thus it will always be. *Primum vivere, deinde philosophari*, or perhaps better, *primum supervivere*, or *superesse*.

Every position of permanent accord and harmony between reason and life, between philosophy and religion, is rendered impossible. And the tragic history of human thought is simply one of struggle between reason and life—reason bent on rationalizing life and forcing it to submit to the inevitable, to mortality; life bent on vitalizing reason and forcing it to serve as a support for its own vital desires. This is the history of philosophy, and it is inseparable from the history of religion.

Our sense of the world, of objective reality, is necessarily subjective, human, anthropomorphic. And vitalism will always rise up to assert itself in the face of rationalism, reason always be confronted by will. Hence the rhythm of the history of philosophy and the alternation of periods in which life imposes itself and gives birth to spiritual forms, with periods in which reason imposes itself and gives birth to materialist forms, though both classes of belief, both forms, be disguised under other names. Neither reason nor life ever acknowledges its own defeat. We will return to this matter in the next chapter.

The vital consequence of rationalism would be suicide. Kierkegaard puts it very well: "For suicide is the only tolerable existential consequence of pure thought. . . . This is not to praise the suicide, but to respect the passion. Nowadays a thinker is a curious creature who during certain hours of the day exhibits a very remarkable ingenuity, but has otherwise nothing in common with a human being."

Inasmuch as the thinker remains, despite everything, a man, he places reason at the service of life, whether or not he knows it. Life deceives reason, and reason deceives life. Scholastic-Aristotelian philosophy forged, in the interests of life, a teleological-evolutionist system of metaphysics, rational in appearance, to serve as support for our vital longing. This philosophy, the basis of orthodox Christian supernaturalism, whether Catholic or Protestant, was essentially no more than a bit of cunning on the part of life to oblige reason to lend life its support. But the weight of reason's support was such that in the end it pulverized life.

I have read that the ex-Carmelite Hyacinthe Loyson declared that he would be able to present himself before God in all tranquillity, for he was at peace with his conscience and with his reason. With what conscience was that? With his religious conscience, was it? In that case I fail to understand him. The truth is that no man can serve two masters, least of all when the two masters, though they may affix their signatures to truces and armistices and compromise-agreements, are enemies because of opposing interests.

Someone will surely object that life ought to submit to reason; to which we will reply that no one should do what he can not do, and that life can not submit to reason. "It ought, therefore it can," some Kantian or other will retort. And to that we shall counter-retort: "It can not, therefore it ought not." And life can not because the end purpose of life is to live, and not to understand.

And then there are those who speak of the religious duty of resigning oneself to mortality. This is truly the height of aberration and insincerity. But of course someone is sure to counterpose veracity to our sincerity. So be it; but both concepts may very well be reconciled. Veracity, the respect I owe to what I believe to be rational, to what logically we call truth, moves me in this instance to affirm that the immortality of the individual soul is a contradiction in terms, that it is not only irrational, but even contra-rational; but sincerity also leads me to affirm that I do not resign myself to the previous affirmation and that I protest against its validity. Truth is whatever I feel to be truth, and it is a truth at least as true as what I see,

*129**

touch, hear, or what is demonstrated to me—even more of a truth, I believe—and sincerity obliges me not to hide what I feel.

And life, quick to defend itself, seeks out the chink in reason's armor, and finds it in its scepticism, and attacks reason at this weak point, striving to save itself by this tactic. It depends on the weakness of its adversary.

Nothing is secure, everything remains up in the air. And so Lamennais, in an outburst of passion, cries out:

> What! Shall we, losing all hope, shut our eyes and plunge into the voiceless depths of universal scepticism? Shall we doubt that we think, that we feel, that we are? Nature will not allow us; she forces us to believe even when our reason is not convinced. Absolute certainty and absolute doubt are both equally beyond us. We hover in a vague mean between these two extremes, as between being and nothingness, for complete scepticism would mean the extinction of the intelligence and the total death of man. But man is not given to annihilation; there is something in him which invincibly resists destruction, some vital faith, indomitable even by his will. Whether he wants to or not, he must believe, because he must act, he must maintain himself. His reason, which teaches him to doubt everything, even itself, would, if he listened exclusively to it, reduce him to a state of absolute inaction; he would perish before he had been able even to prove to himself that he existed at all.

Reason does not, strictly speaking, lead us to absolute scepticism. No! Reason does not lead me nor can it lead me to doubt that I exist. Reason leads me, more precisely, to vital scepticism, or better still, to vital negation: leads me, not to doubt, but to deny that my consciousness may survive my death. Vital scepticism is brought about by the clash between reason and desire. And from this clash, from this embrace between despair and scepticism, is born uncertainty, holy, sweet, saving uncertainty, our supreme consolation.

The absolute certainty that death is a complete and definitive and irrevocable annihilation of personal consciousness, a certainty of the same order as our certainty that the three angles of a triangle are equal to two right angles, or, contrariwise, the absolute certainty that our personal consciousness continues beyond death in whatever condition (including in such a concept the strange and adventitious additional notion of eternal reward or punishment)—either of these certainties would make our life equally impossible. In the most secret recess of the spirit of the man who believes that death will put an end to his personal consciousness and even to his memory forever, in that inner recess, even without his knowing it perhaps, a shadow hovers, a vague shadow lurks, a shadow of the shadow of uncertainty, and, while he tells himself: "There's nothing for it but to live this passing life, for there is no other!" at the same time he hears, in this most secret recess, his own doubt murmur: "Who knows? . . ." He is not sure he hears aright, but he hears. Likewise, in some recess of the soul of the true believer who has faith in a future life, a muffled voice, the voice of uncertainty, murmurs in his spirit's ear: "Who knows? . . ." Perhaps these voices are no louder than the buzzing of mosquitoes when the wind roars through the trees in the woods; we scarcely make out the humming, and yet, mingled in the uproar of the storm, it can be heard. How, without this uncertainty, could we ever live?

The foundations of our inner life are formed by these very questions: "And suppose there is . . . ?"

"Suppose there is not . . . ?" Some rationalist may exist who has never wavered in his conviction that the soul is mortal, and some vitalist who has not faltered in his faith in immortality; but that would only prove that, just as there are monsters in nature, so there are people defective in feeling, whatever their intelligence may be, and people defective in intellect, whatever their other virtues. But, in normal people, I can not believe anyone who says that he has never, not even for the briefest moment, not even in moments of intense loneliness or tribulation, felt the breath of the voice of uncertainty. I do not understand a man who tells me that he has never been tormented by the prospect beyond the grave nor disturbed by the thought of his own annihilation. For my part I do not want to make peace between my heart and my head, between my faith and my reason; I prefer that they be at war.

In the ninth chapter of the Gospel according to Mark, we are told of a man who brought his son before Jesus, for the boy was possessed of "a dumb spirit; And wheresoever he taketh him, he teareth him: and he foameth, and gnasheth with his teeth, and pineth away" (9:17-18), and so he wanted to present him to Jesus, so that he might be cured. And the Master, impatient with men who looked only for miracles and signs, exclaimed: "O faithless generation, how long shall I be with you? how long shall I suffer you? bring him unto me" (9:19). And they brought the lad. And when the Master saw him wallowing and foaming on the ground, He asked the father how long the son had been in that condition, and the father answered that ever since he was a child. And Jesus said: "If thou canst believe, all things are possible to him that believeth" (9:23). And then the father of the epileptic or possessed boy uttered those supremely meaningful, immortal words: "Lord, I believe; help thou mine unbelief": "Πιστεύω, βοήθει μοῦ τῇ ἀπιστίᾳ."

Lord, I believe; succor me from unbelief! An apparent contradiction, it would seem, for if he believes, if he has faith, why does he ask the Lord to succor him from his lack of trust? And yet, this contradiction is precisely what lends the profoundest human value to the cry from the heart of the possessed boy's father. His faith is a faith based on uncertainty. Because he believes—that is, because he wants to believe, because he wants his son to be cured—he asks the Lord to help his unbelief, to succor him from his doubt that such a cure will be effected. Such is human faith; such was the heroic faith which Sancho Panza had in his master, the knight Don Quijote de la Mancha, as I think I have shown in my *Life of Don Quixote and Sancho*, a faith based on uncertainty, on doubt. And the point is that Sancho Panza was a man, a whole man, a true man, and he was no defective, for if he had been a defective he would have believed, without a shadow of a doubt, in the extravagances of his master. And neither did Don Quixote believe in them without a shadow of doubt, for neither was he, though a madman, a defective man. He was, at heart, a man in despair, as I believe I have shown in the work just mentioned. And because he was a man of heroic despair, a hero of inner, resigned despair, he stands as the eternal model of every man whose soul is a battlefield between reason and immortal desire. Our Lord Don Quixote is the prototype of the vitalist whose faith is founded on uncertainty, and Sancho is the prototype of the rationalist who doubts his own reason.

Tortured by the torment of his doubt, August Hermann Francke resolved to call upon God, a God in whom he no longer believed, or rather in whom he believed he did not believe, imploring Him to take pity on him, the poor pietist Francke, if by any chance He actually existed. And a similar state of mind inspired the sonnet titled "The Atheist's Prayer," which is included in my *Rosary of Lyric Sonnets* and which concludes thus:

> I suffer because of Thee,
> Thou non-existent God, for if Thou didst exist,
> I should certainly exist too.

Yes, if God the guarantor of our personal immortality existed, then we ourselves should certainly exist. And if not, not!

The terrible secret, the hidden will of God which is translated by the term "predestination," an idea which led Luther to his *servum arbitrium* and which gives Calvinism its tragic sense, the doubt in one's own salvation, all of it is in essence nothing but the same uncertainty, which, in league with despair, forms the basis of faith. Faith, for some people, consists of not thinking of faith, of handing themselves over confidentially into the arms of God, the secrets of whose providence are inscrutable. True enough, but lack of faith, too, consists of not thinking about faith. That absurd faith, that faith without a shadow of a doubt, the faith of the limited charcoal burner, joins hands with an absurd non-belief, a non-belief without the shadow of a doubt, the non-belief of the intellectuals who are prey to defective emotion: both agree not to think about faith.

And what was that abyss, that terrible *gouffre* before which Pascal trembled, what was it but uncertainty, doubt, the voice of reason? And it was doubt that led Pascal to pronounce his terrible sentence, *il faut s'abêtir*: we must stupefy ourselves.

All of Jansenism, the Catholic adaptation of Calvinism, bears the same stamp. Port-Royal, which owed its existence to a Basque, the Abbé de Saint-Cyran, a man of the same race as Iñigo de Loyola and as the writer of the present lines, always had in its depths the lees of religious despair, of the suicide of reason. Loyola, too, drowned his reason in obedience.

Affirmation is reached through despair, negation is reached through despair, and despair also causes us to refrain from either affirming or denying. Observe the majority of atheists and you will notice that they are atheists from rage, rage at not being able to believe that there is a God. They are personal enemies of God. They have invested Nothingness with substance and personality, and their No-God is an Anti-God.

We will have nothing to say concerning that abject and ignoble phrase "If God did not exist, it would be necessary to invent Him." This sentence is an expression of the obscene scepticism of those conservatives who look upon religion merely as an instrument of government and who hope for a hell into which they may consign whoever opposes their own worldly interests in this life. That repugnant and Sadducean phrase is worthy of the incredulous adulator of the powerful to whom it is attributed.

None of this has anything to do with the profound vital sense. It is not a matter of a transcendental police force, nor of maintaining order—some order!—on earth by means of threats of punishment or the cajolery of offering eternal rewards after death. All this is of a quite base nature; it is no more than politics, or, at best, ethics. The real point is to live.

The surest basis for doubt, what shakes us in our vital desire, what most intensifies the dissolving power of reason, is our attempt to consider the life of the soul after death. For, even if we overcome reason by a powerful effort of faith, even if we overcome that reasoning which tells us and shows us that the soul is only a function of the physical organism, we must still wonder what an immortal and eternal life of the soul may be. Such wondering involves a series of contradictions and absurdities, leading, as it does in Kierkegaard, to the conclusion that if the mortality of the soul is terrifying, its immortality is no less so.

But once we have overcome the first and only real difficulty, once we have overcome the difficulty posed by reason, once we have achieved faith, however painful and shrouded in uncertainty that faith may be, once we believe that our personal consciousness will survive death, what obstacle or impediment lies in the way of our conceiving such survival in a measure consonant with our desire? Of course we can imagine our survival as a kind of eternal rejuvenescence, as an eternal growth and advance toward God, toward the Universal Consciousness, without ever reaching that goal, and we can imagine it some other way. . . . Once the rational bond is broken, there is no end to our imagining. . . .

I realize the argument is becoming heavy-handed, annoying, perhaps tedious, but there is no help for it. And I must repeat that we are not concerned with some transcendental police system, nor with considering God as Great Judge or Civil Guard, that is, we are not concerned with heaven and hell as devices to shore up our paltry mundane morality, and neither is it a purely egotistic and personal matter. Not only I, but the entire human race is in the balance, as is the ultimate end of all our culture. I am one man, and each man is an I.

Let us recall the final part of the "Song of the Wild Cock" which the despairing poet Leopardi, a victim of reason who never succeeded in achieving belief, set down in prose. "The time will come," he says, "when this universe, and Nature herself, will be no more. And in the same way as of great kingdoms and empires of mankind, and their wondrous works, far-famed in other ages, there is now no sign nor any name; so of the whole world, and of the infinite vicissitudes and calamities of created things, no vestige will remain; but a bare silence, and a deepest stillness, will pervade the immensity of space. Thus this dread and wondrous mystery of universal life, before it has been declared or understood, will vanish and be lost."

This eventuality they now label, using a scientific and most rationalist term, "entropy." That's a pretty word now, isn't it? Spencer invented the concept of a primordial homogeneity, from which it is impossible to conceive how any heterogeneity could have originated. Very well then, this entropy is a kind of ultimate homogeneity, a state of perfect equilibrium. For a soul avid for life, it is the closest to nothingness that can be imagined.

*   *   *

So far, then, have we come, the reader and I, the reader who has had the patience to follow me through a series of painful reflections; for my part I have endeavored always to give reason its due and to give feeling its portion also. I have not kept silent on matters where others have done so; I have striven to bare, not only my own soul, but the human soul, whatever its nature may be and whether or not it be destined to disappear. And now we have reached the very depths of the abyss: the irreconcilable conflict between reason and vital feeling. I have already said that this conflict must be accepted for what it is, and that we must live by it. It remains to explain how—according to my way of feeling, and even to my way of thinking—this despair can be the basis of a vigorous life, of an effective activity, of a system of ethics, of aesthetics, of a religion, and even of a logic. But, in what follows, there will be as much imagination as ratiocination, or in point of fact, much more.

I have no wish to deceive, or to offer up as philosophy something which may be but poetry or phantasy, mythology in any case. The divine Plato, after discussing in his *Phaedo* the immortality of the soul—an ideal immortality, that is to say, a deceptive immortality—embarked on an exposition of the myths concerning the other life, remarking that it was also necessary to mythologize. Let us, then, mythologize.

The man who looks for reasons, what we call reasons *sensu stricto*, for scientific theses, for technically logical considerations, is free to cease following my thought. Throughout the remainder of these reflections upon the tragic sense I am going to fish for the attention of the reader with a bare, unbaited hook. Let him who will, bite; I will deceive no one. Not until the end do I plan to gather everything together and maintain that this religious despair I have been talking about and which is nothing other than the tragic sense of life itself is, though more or less veiled, the very basis of the conscience of civilized individuals and peoples today; that is, of those individuals and peoples who do not suffer from either deficiency of intellect or deficiency of feeling.

And this tragic sense is the wellspring of heroic achievement.

If in what follows you meet with arbitrary apothegms, brusque transitions, inconsequent solutions, with veritable somersaults of thought, do not cry Fraud! We are about to enter, if you care to accompany me, into a field of contradictions, contradictions between feeling and reasoning, and we must have recourse to one and the other.

The following thoughts are not the products of reason but of life, although in order to transmit them I must rationalize, after a fashion. Most of my message can not be reduced to a theory or a logical system. Like Walt Whitman, the magnificent Yankee poet,

> I charge that there be no theory or school founded
> out of me.

Nor are the phantasies that follow altogether mine. They also belong to other men, if not exactly other thinkers, who have preceded me in this vale of tears and have revealed their life to us and given it expression. Their life, I say, not their thought, except insofar as their thought was inspired by life, thought with roots in irrationality.

Does this mean that what we are to examine, the struggle of the irrational to express itself, is totally lacking in rationality, in all objective value? No: the absolutely, irrevocably irrational is inexpressible, intransmissible. But the contra-rational is not inexpressible. Perhaps there is no way of rationalizing the irrational; but there is a way of rationalizing the contra-rational, and that is by trying to expound it. Since only the rational is intelligible, truly intelligible, and since the absurd, being devoid of sense, is condemned to incommunicability, it becomes obvious that whenever it is possible to express anything apparently irrational or absurd and give it meaning, it is invariably by resolving it into something rational, even though it be into the negation of what is affirmed.

The maddest dreams of phantasy contain some ground of reason, and who knows if everything the imagination of man may conceive has not already happened some time, or is not now happening, or will not happen some time in the future in this world or another? The possible combinations are perhaps infinite. It only remains to ascertain if everything imaginable is possible.

It may also be said, justifiably, that much of what I am about to set forth is merely a repetition of ideas expounded a hundred times before and already refuted a hundred times; but the repetition of an idea once again indicates that it was never really refuted. I do not pretend that most of these fancies are new, and neither do I pretend—of course not!—that other voices have not before me launched the same lament on the winds. But the fact that the same eternal lament can be voiced yet again means that the sorrow has not been allayed.

And it is right to repeat once again the same eternal lamentations, those that were already old in the days of Job and Ecclesiastes, and even to repeat them in the same words, so that the progressives may see that this is something that never dies. Whoever, making it his own, repeats the "Vanity of vanities" of Ecclesiastes or the complaints of Job, even in the very same words, carries out an admonitory task. One must continually go on repeating *memento mori*.

"To what end?" you may ask. Even if it be only to irritate certain people and show them that these things are not dead, that these things, so long as man exists, can not die, and to convince them that in this the twentieth century all past centuries still live on. Whenever a supposed error reappears, it is because, believe me, it has not ceased to have some truth to it, in the same way that resurrection implies that death was not total.

Yes, I know well enough that others before me have felt what I feel and express, and that many another feels so today, albeit in silence. And why do I not remain silent too? Well, for the very reason that the majority of those who feel as I feel do remain silent; even though silent, however, they heed that visceral voice. I do not keep silent precisely because for many people all this is exactly what must not be stated, the unmentionable abomination—*infandum*—and I believe that the unmentionable should be mentioned time and again. But suppose it leads to nothing? Even if it only led to irritating the progressives, those who believe that truth is consolation, it would be quite enough for me. It would be no small matter merely to arouse them into saying: "Poor man! If he would only apply his mind to a better purpose!" And somebody might be led to exclaim that I do not know what I am saying, and I will agree that perhaps he is right—to be right is such a trifling matter!—but I will add that I feel what I say and know what I feel, and that's enough for me. It is better to be short on reason than to be long on it.

Whoever perseveres and reads on will see how, out

of this abyss of despair, hope may emanate, and how this crucial point may serve as source for human, profoundly human, effort and action, may serve the cause of solidarity and even of progress. The reader who perseveres and reads on will discover a pragmatic justification. And he will see that to work and be morally effective there is no need to count on either of the two opposed certitudes, no need to depend on the certainty of faith or the certainty of reason, and even less need to evade—ever—the problem of the immortality of the soul, or to distort it idealistically, that is, hypocritically. The reader will see that this uncertainty, the suffering, and the fruitless struggle to escape uncertainty, can be and are a basis for action and a foundation for morals.

And the fact that the sense of uncertainty, and the inner struggle of reason against both faith and the passionate longing for eternal life, together serve as a basis for action and a foundation for morals, this fact would, in the eyes of a pragmatist, justify the sense of uncertainty. But I must make clear that I do not seek out such a practical consequence in order to justify this uncertainty; it is simply that I encounter it in my inner experience. Nor do I wish nor would I wish to seek any justification for this state of inner struggle and uncertainty and longing: it is a fact, and that suffices. And if any man, finding himself in the depths of the abyss, fails to find there motives and incentives for life and action, and thereupon commits bodily or spiritual suicide, either by self-destruction or by renouncing any effort at human solidarity, I will not be the one to cast the first stone. And apart from the fact that the evil consequences, or those we call evil, of any doctrine merely go to prove, I repeat, that the doctrine is evil vis-à-vis our desires, but not that it is false, the consequences themselves depend not so much upon the doctrine as upon the one who deduces them. One and the same principle provides one man with grounds for action and another with grounds for abstaining from action; the same principle may lead this man to act in one way and that man to act in a contrary manner. The truth is that our doctrines tend to be no more than a justification *a posteriori* of our conduct, or else they are the manner in which we attempt to explain that conduct to ourselves.

Man is unwilling, in effect, to remain in ignorance of the motives for his own conduct. And, just as a man who has been mesmerized into a certain course of action will later invent reasons to justify it and make it appear logical in his own eyes and those of others, unaware the while of the true cause of his action, so will everyman, too—for every man is mesmerized, in the sense that "life is a dream"—look for suitable reasons for his conduct. And if chess pieces possessed consciousness, they might well ascribe their moves to free will, that is, claim for them a finalist rationality. And thus it is that every philosophic system serves to explain and justify an ethic, a doctrine of conduct, which in reality has its origin in the inner moral sense of the author of the theoretical system. But the real reason or cause of this sense may not be clearly present in the consciousness of its possessor.

Consequently I believe I may assume that if my reason, which in a certain sense forms part of the reason of my brothers in humanity in time and space, teaches me this absolute scepticism as regards the longing for never-ending life, then my sense of life, the very essence of life itself, my own vitality, my unbounded appetite for life and abhorrence of death, my refusal to resign myself to dying, are the very things that suggest to me the doctrines with which I attempt to counteract the effect of reason. "Have these doctrines any objective value?" someone may ask. And I will reply that I do not understand what is meant by the "objective value" of a doctrine. I will not claim that the more or less poetical and unphilosophical doctrines I am intent on expounding are the ones which give me life. But I will venture to say that my longing to live, and to live forever, inspires these doctrines in me. And if these doctrines strengthen and sustain the same longing in another, when perhaps it was languishing, I will have accomplished something of human worth, and, above all, I shall have lived. In a word: with reason, without reason, or against reason, I do not want to die. And when at last I do die, if I die altogether, it will not be I who will have died, that is, I will not have let myself die, but will have been killed by man's fate. Unless I lose my mind, or rather my heart, I will not resign from life; I must be dismissed.

Nothing is to be gained by bringing forth those ambiguous words "optimism" or "pessimism," words which often come to mean the opposite of what their user intends. To label a doctrine as "pessimistic" does not denigrate its validity, and neither are "optimistic" doctrines more effective for action. I believe, on the contrary, that many of the greatest heroes, perhaps the very greatest, have been despairing men and that they carried out their feats from desperation. These considerations apart, and accepting the terms—ambiguous and all as they are—of optimism and pessimism, there is a certain transcendent pessimism which engenders a temporal and earthly optimism, and I propose to develop this theme in the following part of this treatise.

Very different, and well I know it, is the position of our progressives, the partisans of "the central current of contemporary European thought"; but I can not bring myself to accept the way in which these fellows deliberately close their eyes to the great problem, and essentially live a lie by attempting to stifle the tragic sense of life.

These last considerations are in the nature of a practical résumé of the critical matter developed in the first six chapters of this book, a manner of establishing the practical position to which such criticism may lead anyone who does not care to renounce life and who does not care to renounce reason either and who must, consequently, live and act between these two facing millstones which grind our souls; the reader who follows me further will know that I am leading on into a region of phantasy, but phantasy not devoid of reason—for nothing subsists without reason—phantasy founded on sensibility. And as regards the truth of it all, true truth, truth independent of ourselves, beyond our logical and cardiacal truth, as regards that truth—*¿quién sabe?*

VII. Love, Pain, Compassion, and Personality

> *Cain*: Let me, or happy or unhappy, learn
>   To anticipate my immortality.
> *Lucifer*: Thou didst before I came upon thee.
> *Cain*:   How?
> *Lucifer*: By suffering.
> > Byron: *Cain*, Act II, Scene I.

LOVE, MY READERS and brothers, is, in the world and in life, the most tragic thing there is. Love is the child of illusion and the parent of disillusion. Love is consolation in desolation, it is the only remedy against death, since it is death's sister.

> Brothers, fate engendered, at the same time,
> Love and Death,

as Leopardi sang.

Love seeks, in a fury, in the person of the beloved, for something beyond the beloved, and, since it does not find it, despairs.

Whenever we speak of love it is sexual love we have in mind, the love between man and woman leading to the perpetuation of the human race upon the earth. Hence it is that we never succeed in reducing love either to a purely intellectual or a purely volitional element, leaving aside the emotional, or, if you will, the sensory aspects of it. For, in its essence, love is neither idea nor volition; it is, rather, desire, emotion; it is, even in its spiritual side, a carnal thing.

*146**

Thanks to love we can feel whatever is flesh in the spirit.

Sexual love is the generative type of all other love. We seek to perpetuate ourselves in love and through love, and we perpetuate ourselves on earth only by dying, by yielding our lives to others. The humblest forms of animal life, the lowest of living beings, multiply by dividing themselves, splitting up, ceasing to be what they formerly were.

But when at last the vitality of the being that multiplies itself by division is exhausted, the species must renew the source of life from time to time by the union of two declining individuals, by means of what is called "conjugation" in protozoaria. They unite in order to begin dividing again with more *brio*. And every act of generation is a ceasing to be, either in part or as a whole, whatever one was; it is a splitting up, a partial death. To live is to give oneself, perpetuate oneself, and to perpetuate oneself, to give oneself, is to die. Perhaps the supreme delight of procreation is nothing other than a foretasting or savoring of death, the spilling of one's own vital essence. We unite with another, but it is to divide ourselves: that most intimate embrace is nought but a most intimate uprooting. In essence, the delight of sexual love, the genetic spasm, is a sensation of resurrection, of resuscitation in another, for only in others can we resuscitate and perpetuate ourselves.

Without much doubt there is something tragically destructive in love's essence, as it appears in its primitive animal form, in the invincible instinct driving a male and a female to entangle their essences in the grip of fury. The same impulse that joins their bodies separates their souls, in a certain sense. In their embrace they hate as much as they love, and above all, they fight each other, they fight for a third being, one as yet without life. Love is a battle, and there are species of animals in which the male abuses the female during union, and others in which the female devours the male after he has fertilized her.

Love has been called mutual egotism. And in truth each lover seeks to possess the other, and, even without being conscious of it or purposing it at the time, seeks self-pleasure in seeking self-perpetuation in and through the other. Each of the lovers is, for the other, an immediate instrument of enjoyment and a mediate instrument of perpetuation. And thus they are both tyrants and slaves, each one a tyrant over and a slave to the other simultaneously.

Is there really anything strange in the fact that the deepest religious sense has condemned carnal love and exalted virginity? The love of money, said the Apostle, is the root of all evil, and that is because it takes riches for an end, when they are only a means. And the essence of sin is precisely that it takes means for ends, that it does not recognize or that it despises the end purpose. And what is carnal love if not avarice, since it takes pleasure for its end, when pleasure is only a means, instead of taking it as an instrument of self-perpetuation, which is its true end. And some people may prefer to preserve their virginity the better to perpetuate themselves: to perpetuate something more human than their flesh.

Lovers, on earth, perpetuate suffering flesh: they perpetuate sorrow and death. Love is at one and the same time the brother, son, and father of death; of death, which is the sister, mother, and daughter of love. And thus in the depths of love lies a profundity of eternal despair, from which hope and consolation spring. And from the carnal and primitive love of which I speak, the love of the whole body with all its senses, the animal origin of human society, from this love and its lovemaking, arises spiritual, sorrowful love.

This spiritual love is born of sorrow, from the death of carnal love. It is also born of the compassionate sense of protection which parents feel for helpless children. Lovers do not love each other with true self-abandon, with a true fusion of souls—and not just of bodies—until the heavy pestle of sorrow has ground down their hearts by crushing them in a mortar of mutual suffering. Sensual love joins their bodies but separates their souls, keeps them strangers to one another; but this love produces a fruit of their flesh, a child. And then let us say that this child, engendered out of death, falls sick and dies. And it comes about that over the dead body of their carnal fusion— but simultaneous spiritual separation and mutual estrangement—their bodies grow cool and estranged from each other as well, but their spirits join in sorrow, and then the lovers, now parents, embrace, and from the death of their child of the flesh there is now born a true spiritual love. Or perhaps, once the bond of flesh which united them is broken, they merely sigh with relief. For in truth, human beings love each other spiritually only when they have suffered the same sorrow, when they have long plowed the stony earth, joined together by the mutual yoke of a common grief. It is then that they know one another and feel for and feel with one another in their common anguish, and pity one another and love one another. For to love means to pity, and, though their bodies are united by pleasure, their souls are united by pain.

All this is felt more clearly and strongly whenever one of those tragic loves takes seed, grows roots, and

flowers, although doomed to contend with the ada-
mantine laws of Fate; one of those loves which are
born out of due time or season, before or after the
right moment, or outside the norm in which the
world—which is custom—would have been willing
to welcome them. The more barriers that Fate and
the world with its law interpose between lovers, the
stronger they feel impelled toward one another, and
their pleasure in loving turns bitter, and the sorrow
of not being able to love each other openly and freely
increases, and they pity one another from the bottom
of their hearts; and this mutual pity, which constitutes their common misery and their common felicity,
provides fire and fuel for their love. And they suffer
their joy in the enjoyment of their suffering. And
they place their love outside the confines of this world,
and the force of this poor love as it suffers beneath
the yoke of Fate inspires them to intuit another world
where there is no law above the liberty of love, another world where there are no barriers—because
there is no flesh. For nothing inspires in us more hope
or faith in another world than the impossibility of our
love truly coming to flower in this world of flesh and
appearances.

And what is maternal love but compassion for the
weak, the stricken, the helpless child in need of
milk and a mother's lap? And in woman all love is
maternal.

To love spiritually is to feel compassion, and whoever feels most compassionate loves most. Men aflame
with a burning charity for their fellowmen feel as they
do because they have plumbed the depths of their own
misery, of their own apparential insubstantiality, their
own nothingness, and then, after turning their newly
opened eyes upon their fellows, they have seen them

equally wretched, apparential, subject to annihilation, and they have felt compassion and love for them.

Man yearns for love, or, what amounts to the same, for compassion. Man wants others to feel and share his hardships and his sorrows. The roadside beggar's exhibition of his sores or gangrened stump to the passer-by is something more than a stratagem to extract alms. Alms, more than any real alleviation of the travails of life, is compassion. The beggar is not gratified by alms given him by one who averts his face to avoid seeing him and gives merely to be rid of a nuisance; he is more gratified by a person who condoles with him and does not alleviate than by one who alleviates but does not condole, though he may well prefer the latter practically. Observe with what satisfaction he relates his woes to whoever is moved by the narrative. He wants to gain compassion, love.

Woman's love is, I was saying, above all essentially compassionate, maternal. A woman yields herself to her lover because she feels he is suffering with desire. Isabel had compassion upon Lorenzo, Juliet upon Romeo, Francesca upon Paolo. Woman seems to say: "Come, don't suffer for my sake!" And thus her love is more loving and purer than man's, more valiant and longer lasting as well.

Inverting the terms of the adage *nihil volitum quin praecognitum* we said that *nihil cognitum quin praevolitum*, we know nothing save what we have previously desired in one way or another, and we would be justified in adding that we can not know, to any great degree, anything we have not loved, anything for which we have not felt compassion.

As love grows, the ardent longing to reach the uttermost, the innermost of all things, is extended to everything in sight, and compassion is felt for all. As one delves within oneself, the deeper one goes the more one discovers one's inanity, the truth that one is not altogether oneself, not what one wants to be, and, in short, that one is nothing. When you reach your own nothingness, when you can not find an unshifting ground within yourself, when you can not discover your own infinity, let alone your own eternity, you will feel wholehearted compassion for your own fate, and you will burn with a sorrowful love for yourself, extinguishing so-called self-love, which is merely a kind of sensual self-delectation, a self-gratification, as it were, on the part of your own soul's flesh.

Spiritual love for oneself, the compassion one feels for oneself, may perhaps be called egotism, but nothing could be more opposed to common ordinary egoism. For from this love or compassion for yourself, from this intense despair, from the knowledge that just as before you were born you did not exist so after you die you will be no more, you go on to feel compassion for—that is, to love—all your fellow beings and brothers in this world of appearance, those wretched shadows who file by, going from nothingness to nothingness, mere sparks of consciousness shining for a moment in the infinite and eternal darkness. And from feeling compassion for other men, for those akin to you, beginning with those most akin to you, for those you live among, you go on to feel compassion for everyone alive, and perhaps even for that which does not live but merely exists. That distant star shining up there in the night will one day be extinguished and turn to dust and cease shining and existing. And as with the one star, so it will be with the whole of the starry sky. Poor sky!

And if it is painful to have to cease to be one day,

perhaps it would be even more painful to be oneself for all time and no more than oneself, never being able at the same time to be someone else, never being everything else as well, unable to be everything.

If you look at the universe as closely and as inwardly as you can, that is, within yourself, if you sense, and not merely contemplate, everything in your consciousness, where all things have left their painful imprint, then you will plumb the depths of tedium, not only the tedium of life, but of something more: the tedium of existence, the bottomless well of the vanity of vanities. And thus you will come to feel compassion for all things: you will feel universal love.

In order to love everything, in order to feel compassion for all things, human and extra-human, living and not living, you must feel everything within yourself, you must personalize everything. For love personalizes everything it loves, everything it pities. We pity, that is, we love, only that which is like us, and thus our compassion grows, and with it our love for things in the measure to which they are discovered to be in our likeness. If I am moved to pity and love the luckless star which will one day vanish from the sky, it is because love, compassion, makes me feel that it possesses a consciousness, more or less obscure, which causes it to suffer because it is no more than a star doomed to cease being itself one day. For all consciousness is an awareness of death and suffering.

Consciousness, *conscientia*, is participated knowledge, and it is co-feeling, and co-feeling is compassion.

Love personalizes whatever it loves. We need only personalize an idea to fall in love with it. And when love is so great and vital, so strong and overflowing, that it loves everything, then it personalizes everything and discovers that the total Whole, the Universe, is also a Person with a Consciousness, a Consciousness which suffers, pities and loves, and is therefore consciousness. And this Consciousness of the Universe, which love discovers by personalizing whatever it loves, is what we call God. And thus our soul feels compassion for God and feels pitied by Him, loves Him and feels loved by Him, sheltering its wretchedness in the bosom of eternal and infinite wretchedness, which, in making itself eternal and infinite, constitutes supreme happiness itself.

God, then, is the personalization of the Whole, the eternal and infinite Consciousness of the Universe, a Consciousness in thrall to matter and struggling to free itself from it. We personalize the Whole in order to save ourselves from Nothingness, and the only truly mysterious mystery is the mystery of suffering.

Suffering is the way of consciousness, and it is through suffering that living beings achieve self-consciousness. To possess consciousness of oneself, to have personality, is to know and feel oneself distinct from other beings. And this feeling of distinctiveness is reached only through a collision, through more or less severe suffering, through a sense of one's own limits. Consciousness of oneself is simply consciousness of one's own limitation. I feel that I am myself when I feel that I am not others; to know and feel the extent of my being is to know where I cease being, the point beyond which I no longer am.

How would one know one existed unless one suffered in some measure? How turn inward, achieve reflective consciousness, unless it be through suffering? In pleasure one forgets oneself, forgets that one exists, passes into someone else, into an alien being, becomes alien-ated. And one turns inward, returns to oneself, becomes oneself again only in suffering.

> Nessun maggior dolore
> che ricordarsi del tempo felice
> nella miseria,

as Dante has Francesca da Rimini say in the *Inferno*; but if there is no greater sorrow than the remembrance in adversity of past happiness, there is no pleasure, either, in remembering adversity in present prosperity.

"Verily 'tis the sorest of all human ills, to abound in knowledge and yet have no power over action" ("πολλὰ φρονέοντα μηδενὸς κρατέειν"), as a Persian said to a Theban at a banquet, according to Herodotus (IX, 16). And so it is. With knowledge and desire we can encompass everything, or almost everything; with will, nothing, or almost nothing. And contemplation is not happiness—no!; not if contemplation means impotence. And from the clash between our knowing and our ability to achieve comes compassion.

We feel compassion for what is like ourselves, and the more or the stronger we feel the likeness, the more we feel compassion. And if we can say that this likeness arouses our compassion, it may also be maintained that our reserves of compassion, ready to flow over everything, cause us to discover the likeness of things to ourselves and see the common bond that unites us with them in suffering.

Our own struggle to acquire, preserve, and enlarge our own consciousness causes us to notice, in the strivings and movements and revolutions of all things, the struggle to acquire, preserve, and enlarge consciousness to which everything tends. Underlying the actions of those most akin to myself, my fellow men, I sense—or, rather, I con-sense—a state of consciousness similar to that which underlies my own actions. My brother's cry of pain provokes my own pain into crying out in the depths of my consciousness. I feel the pain of animals in the same way, and the pain of a tree when one of its branches is torn off, especially when my imagination is aroused, imagination being the faculty of intuition, of in-sight.

Descending from ourselves as point of departure, from our own human consciousness, which is the only consciousness we feel within us and in which feeling is identical with being, we attribute some sort of consciousness, more or less obscure, to all living beings, and even to the stones themselves, for they also live. And the evolution of organic beings is simply a struggle to realize the fullness of consciousness through suffering, a constant aspiration to be others without ceasing to be themselves, to break the limits by limitation.

And this process of personalization or subjectivization of everything phenomenally or objectively external constitutes the vital process itself of philosophy in the struggle of life against reason and of reason against life. There was an indication of this fact in the preceding chapter, and here it will be confirmed by further development of the theme.

Giambattista Vico, who possessed a profound aesthetic understanding of the soul of antiquity, saw that the spontaneous philosophy of man, impelled by an *istinto d'animazione*, led him to make himself the measure of the universe. Language, necessarily anthropomorphic, mythopeic, generates thought:

> Hence poetic wisdom, the first wisdom of the gentile world, must have begun with a metaphysic not rational and abstract like that of learned men now,

but felt and imagined as that of these first men must have been. . . . This metaphysic was their poetry, a faculty born with them (for they were furnished by nature with these senses and imaginations); born of their ignorance of causes, for ignorance, the mother of wonder, made everything wonderful to men who were ignorant of everything. . . . Their poetry was at first divine, because they imagined the causes of the things they felt and wondered at [*sic*] to be gods. . . .

In such fashion the first men of the gentile nations, children of nascent mankind . . . created things according to their own ideas. . . . Of this nature of human things there came an eternal property, expressed in a noble phrase of Tacitus: that frightened men vainly "no sooner feign than they believe." (*fingunt simul creduntque*)

And then Vico, passing from the age of imagination, proceeds to show us the age of reason, this age of ours in which our civilized minds, even those of "the vulgar," are too much detached from the senses, "by abstractions corresponding to all the abstract terms our languages abound in," so that it is "naturally beyond our power to form the vast image of this mistress called 'Sympathetic Nature.' Men shape the phrase with their lips but have nothing in their minds; for what they have in mind is falsehood, which is nothing." And now, adds Vico, it is naturally "beyond our power to enter into the vast imagination of those first men." And yet, is this altogether true? Do we not continue to live by the creations of their imagination, embodied forever in the language in which we think, or rather, which thinks in us?

It was useless for Comte to declare that human thought had already emerged from the age of theology and was now emerging from the age of metaphysics into the age of positivism. The three ages actually coexist and, though antagonistic, mutually support one another. Flamboyant positivism is nothing but metaphysics whenever it leaves off denying and asserts anything, whenever it becomes really positivism, and metaphysics is always essentially theology, and theology is born of imagination enlisted in the service of life, which craves to be immortal.

Our sense of the world, upon which we base our understanding of it, is necessarily anthropomorphic and mythopeic. When rationalism dawned with Thales of Miletus, this philosopher abandoned Oceanus and Thetis, gods and the progenitors of gods, and he attributed the origin of everything to water, but this water was a god in disguise. Underlying Nature, φύσις, and the World, κόσμος, there throbbed mythic, anthropomorphic creations. Language itself bore them along. Xenophon tells us (*Memorabilia*, *I*, i., 6-9) that among phenomena Socrates distinguished between those which were within the scope of human learning and those which the gods had reserved for themselves, and that he execrated the attempt by Anaxagoras to explain everything rationally. His contemporary, Hippocrates, regarded all disease as of divine origin, and Plato believed that the sun and the stars were animated gods and had their own souls (*Philebus*, 16, *Laws*, X), and he allowed for astronomical investigation only in so far as it did not constitute blasphemy against the gods. And Aristotle in his *Physics* tells us that Zeus sends rain, not to make wheat grow, but out of necessity, ἐξ ἀνάγκης. An attempt was made to mechanize and rationalize God, but God rebelled against them.

And what is the concept of God, a concept continually renewed, since it springs from the eternal sense of God within man, but the eternal protest of life against reason, the unconquerable instinct for personalization? And what is the very notion of substance but the objectivization of what is most subjective, that is, of the will, of consciousness? For consciousness, even before it recognizes itself in reason, senses itself, is palpable to itself, is itself most especially in the form of will—the will not to die. Hence the aforementioned rhythm in the history of thought. Positivism brought us an age of rationalism, that is, of materialism, mechanism, or mortalism; and thus it is that now vitalism, spiritualism, return to the scene. What did pragmatism attempt but to restore faith in a human finality of the universe? What did Bergson, for example, attempt, especially in his work on creative evolution, but to restore a personal God and an eternal consciousness? The truth is that life will not surrender.

And it is no good trying to suppress this mythopeic or anthropomorphic process and rationalizing our thought, as if we thought merely for the sake of thinking and knowing rather than for the sake of living. Language itself, with which we think, prevents us. Language, the substance of thought, is a system of metaphors with a mythic and anthropomorphic base. And to construct a purely rational philosophy we would need to use algebraic formulas, or specifically create a new language, an inhuman language, that is, one unsuitable to the needs of life, as, indeed, was attempted by Dr. Richard Avenarius, professor of philosophy at Zürich, in his *Critique of Pure Experience* (*Kritik der reinen Erfahrung*), with a view to avoiding preconceptions. And this zealous attempt by Avenarius, headman of the "Empiriocriticists," leads only to pure scepticism. He himself tells us, at the end of the Prologue to the aforementioned work: "The infantile belief that we are endowed with the faculty for discovering truth has long since been discarded. As we advance we become more aware of the difficulties and correspondingly of the limitations of our powers. And the end-purpose? So long as we achieve an insight and see clearly into ourselves . . . !"

See clearly! . . . See clearly! Only a pure thinker would see clearly, and he would use algebra instead of language and would be able to divest himself of his own humanity; that is to say, he would be an insubstantial, merely objective being—a non-being, in short. However hard it may be for reason to accept the fact, thought must work with life, and however hard it may be for life, thought must work with reason.

This animation, this personification is interwoven with our very perception of things. "Who is raining? Who thunders?" old Strepsiades asks of Socrates in *The Clouds* of Aristophanes; and the philosopher retorts "It's not Zeus, but the clouds." "But," says Strepsiades, "who if not Zeus makes them move?" And Socrates: "Not at all. It's done by ethereal vortex." "By Vortex is it? I didn't know. . . . So it's not Zeus, then, but Vortex who reigns now in his stead." And the poor old man goes on personifying and animating Vortex, who reigns like a king, not unaware of his regal dignity. And we all do the same, whenever we exchange any Zeus whatever for any Vortex whatever, as, for example, when we exchange God for matter. And that is because philosophy does not work from the objective reality available to our senses, but from a complex of ideas, images, notions, perceptions, and so on, embodied in the language and transmitted to us by our forebears. The world, what we call the world, the "objective" world, is a social tradition. It has been given us ready made.

Man, in his consciousness, does not resign himself to being alone in the universe, or to being merely one more objective phenomenon. He wants to preserve his vital or passional subjectivity by making the entire universe alive, personal, and animated. For this purpose he has discovered God and substance, and God and substance keep reappearing in his thought in one disguise or another. Because we are conscious we feel that we exist, which is quite different from knowing we exist, and we want to feel that everything else also exists and that every other individual entity is also an "I."

The most consistent—though also the most incongruous and unstable—idealism, that of Berkeley, which denied the existence of matter, of anything inert, extensive, and passive, and of the possibility of its giving rise to our sensations and serving as substratum for external phenomena, this idealism is not, in its essential nature, other than an absolute spiritualism, or dynamism, a supposition that every sensation comes to us, causatively, from another spirit, that is, from another consciousness. And Berkeley's doctrine shows a certain affinity with those of Schopenhauer and Hartmann. The former's doctrine of the Will and the latter's doctrine of the Unconscious are already adumbrated in the Berkeleyan theory that to be is to be perceived; to which must be added: and cause another to perceive the one who is. And thus the old adage *operari sequitur esse*, action follows being, must be modified by saying that to be is to act, and that only whatever acts, what is active, exists, and only insofar as it acts.

*161**

And as regards Schopenhauer, it is not necessary to prove the point that Will, which he posits as the essence of things, arises out of Consciousness. It is enough to read his book *On the Will in Nature* to see how he attributed a certain spirit and even a certain personality to the very plants. And his doctrine led him logically to pessimism, for the most natural and most essential tendency of the will is to suffer. Will is a force which feels, that is, which suffers. "And which feels pleasure, too," someone will add. But the capacity for pleasure is impossible without the capacity for suffering, and the faculty for pleasure is the same as the faculty for pain. He who does not suffer does not enjoy, just as he who does not perceive cold does not perceive heat either.

It is also quite logical that Schopenhauer, who deduced a pessimism from the voluntarist doctrine or the doctrine of universal personalization, should also have deduced from these two doctrines that the foundation of morality is compassion. Only, his lack of a social and historical sense, his inability to feel that humanity is also a person, though a collective one, in short, his egotism, prevented him from feeling God, prevented him from individualizing and personalizing the total collective Will—the Will of the Universe.

On the other hand, it is easy to understand his aversion to purely empirical evolutionist or transformist doctrines and to such as he saw expounded by Lamarck and Darwin. Judging Darwin's theory solely on the basis of a lengthy extract in the London *Times*, he characterized it as "insipid empiricism" (*platter Empirismus*), in a letter to Adam Louis von Doss (of March 1, 1860). For a voluntarist like Schopenhauer, in effect, a theory so sanely and cautiously empirical and so rational as that of Darwin left out of account the inner force, the essential motive behind evolution. For what, after all, is the occult force, the ultimate agent, which impels organisms to perpetuate themselves, to fight to persevere and propagate? Selection, adaptation, heredity, are all merely external conditions. The inner, essential force has been called will, on the supposition that other beings feel what we feel as a sense of will, the impulse to be everything, to be all others as well as ourselves, without ceasing to be what we are. And it can be said that this force is the divine in us, that it is God in us, working in us because He suffers in us.

And it is sympathy which leads us to discover this force, this aspiration toward consciousness, and to discover it in all things. This aspiration moves and activates the most minute living creatures; possibly it moves and activates the very cells of our own corporal organism, which is a more or less integrated federation of lives; it moves the very globules of our blood. Our life is composed of many lives, our vital aspiration is composed of aspirations existing perhaps in the limbo of subconsciousness. To fancy that our cells, our globules, should possess a kind of consciousness, or the beginnings of a rudimentary, cellular, globular consciousness, is no more farfetched than many fancies which pass for valid theories; and neither is it any more fanciful to imagine that they might come to have such consciousness. And now that we are being fanciful, let us imagine that these cells communicate with each other and that one of them would express its belief that it formed part of some superior organism endowed with a personal collective consciousness. And more than once in the history of human feeling this fancy has been expressed in some philosopher's or poet's conjecture that we are a species of globules in the blood of a Supreme Being who possesses his own personal collective consciousness, the consciousness of the Universe.

Perhaps the infinite Milky Way we see in the sky on clear nights, that enormous encircling ring in which our planetary system is itself but a molecule, is in turn a cell in the Universe, the Body of God. All the cells of our body combine and concur in their activity in maintaining and arousing our consciousness, our soul; and if the consciousness or the souls of these cells penetrated into our consciousness, into the composite whole, if I possessed consciousness of all that happens in my bodily organism, I should feel the universe happening within myself, and then perhaps the painful sense of my limitation would be erased. And if all the consciousnesses of all beings wholly concur in the universal consciousness, then this consciousness, that is, God, is all.

Obscure and varied consciousnesses, elemental souls, are born and die within us at every turn, and their birth and death constitute our life. And their sudden death, by violence, in collision with each other, goes to form our pain. And in a like manner, a varied consciousness lives and dies—does it, do they, really die?—in the heart of God, and the varied births and deaths constitute His life.

If there is a Universal and Supreme Consciousness, I am an idea within it; and is it possible for any idea whatsoever in this Supreme Consciousness to die out? After I have died God will go on remembering me, and to be remembered by God, to have my consciousness maintained by the Supreme Consciousness, is not that, perhaps, to be?

And if anyone should say that God has made the Universe, we may rejoin that so also our soul has

made our body as much as, if not more than, the soul
has been made by the body. If, indeed, there be a
soul.

When compassion—when love—reveals to us the
entire Universe striving to gain and preserve and
enlarge its consciousness, striving more and more to
intensify this consciousness, meanwhile feeling the
pain of the discrepancies that appear, compassion, I
say, reveals the likeness of the whole universe to ourselves, reveals that it is human, and leads us therein
to discover our Father, of whose flesh we are flesh;
love leads us to personalize the whole, of which we
form a part.

Fundamentally, to say that God is eternally producing things is the same as to say that things are
eternally producing God. And the belief in a personal
and spiritual God is based on the belief in our own
personality and spirituality. Because we feel ourselves
to be in consciousness, we feel that God is consciousness, that is, a person, and because we long to have
our consciousness live and be independent of the body,
we believe that the divine person lives and exists independently of the universe and that His state of consciousness is *ad extra*.

No doubt logicians will come forward with all the
obvious rational difficulties which are bound to occur:
we have already pointed out that the content here,
though it be presented in rational forms, is not, strictly speaking, rational. Any rational conception of God
is in itself contradictory. Faith in God is born of love
for God: we believe that God exists because we want
Him to exist, and perhaps it is born also of God's
love for us. Reason does not prove to us that God
exists, but neither does it prove that He cannot exist.

We shall have more to say farther on about this

conception of the faith in God as the personalization of the Universe.

And using what was said in another part of this work as point of departure, we may go on to say that material things, in so far as they are known to us, come into our knowledge through hunger, and out of hunger arises the material world of the senses in which we agglomerate these things, and further, that ideal things issue out of love and out of love comes God, in whom we concentrate these ideal things as the Consciousness of the Universe. Social consciousness, which is the offspring of love, of the instinct of self-perpetuation, leads us to general socialization, to see society everywhere, and ultimately makes us aware how truly all of Nature is an infinite society. For my own part, hundreds of times I have felt, as I walked in the woods, possessed by a sense of solidarity with the oaks—which in an obscure way seemed to sense my own presence—that Nature was indeed a society.

Imagination, which is the social sense, animates the inanimate and anthropomorphizes everything; it humanizes everything, and even makes it like man. And man's task is to supernaturalize Nature, that is, to make it divine by humanizing it, by making it human, by helping it assume consciousness, in short. Reason, on the other hand, mechanizes or materializes everything.

And thus, just as a fruitful union is consummated between the individual (who is, in a certain sense, society) and society (which is also an individual), the two being so inseparable from each other that it is impossible to say where the one begins and the other ends, for they are rather the two aspects of a single essence, so also does spirit (the social element, which makes us conscious by relating us to every-

thing else) unite with matter (the individual individualizing element). And similarly, reason and intelligence and imagination join in a mutually fruitful
union, and the Universe and God become one.

* * *

Is all this the truth? "And what is truth?" I will ask
with Pilate. But I will not turn away and wash my
hands without staying for an answer.

Does truth lie in reason, or above reason, or beneath reason, or outside reason in some fortuitous
manner? Is only the rational true? May there not exist
a reality unavailable by its very nature to reason, and
also, perhaps, by its very nature opposed to reason?
And how to know *this* reality if we "know" only
through reason?

Our desire to live, our need for life, would like
truth to be that which is conducive to our self-preservation and self-perpetuation, that which sustains man
and society; it would like true water to be that liquid
which when drunk quenches our thirst, true because
it quenches the thirst, and would like true bread to
be that bread which slakes our hunger and true because it does so.

Our senses subserve the instinct of self-preservation, and whatever satisfies this need for self-preservation, even when it does not directly involve the
senses, represents a kind of deep incursion of reality
into us. Is the process of assimilating nutriment any
less real than the process of knowing about the nutriment? It may be objected that to eat a loaf of bread
is not the same as to see, touch, or taste it; that in the
first case it enters our body but not necessarily our
consciousness. Is this true? Does not the bread I have
converted into my own flesh and blood enter more

fully into my consciousness than that other loaf which I see and touch and of which I say "This is mine"? And am I to refuse objective reality to the bread I have converted into my own flesh and blood and made my own, refuse it the reality I grant to the bread which I merely touch?

Some people live on air without knowing it. In the same way we may live by and in God, in God the spirit and consciousness of society and of the entire Universe, insofar as the Universe is also society.

God is felt only insofar as He is lived; and man does not live by bread alone, but by every word that proceedeth out of the mouth of God (Matt. 4:4, Deut. 8:3).

And this personalization of the All, of the Universe, to which we are led by love, by compassion, is the personalization of a person who encompasses and encloses within himself all the other persons which go to compose his own person.

The only way to assign a finality to the Universe is to give it a consciousness. For where there is no consciousness, there is no finality presupposing a purpose. And faith in God, as we shall see, is quite simply based upon the vital need to endow existence with a finality, to make it answer to a purpose. We need God, not in order to understand the *why*, but in order to feel and assert the ultimate *wherefore*, to give meaning to the Universe.

We ought not be surprised, either, by the assertion that the consciousness of the Universe is composed of and integrated by the consciousness of all the beings that form the Universe, by the consciousness of all beings, and that at the same time it is a personal consciousness distinct from those which compose it. Only thus is it possible to understand how "in God

we live, move, and have our being." That great visionary Emanuel Swedenborg saw—or descried—this
in his book on Heaven and Hell (*De Coelo et Inferno*,
52), where he tells us:

> . . . an entire angelic society sometimes appears in
> the form of a single angel, as I have been permitted
> by the Lord to see. When the Lord Himself appears
> in the midst of angels, He does not appear encom-
> passed by a multitude but as One Being in an angelic
> form. Hence it is that the Lord in the Word is called
> an angel and also that an entire society is so called.
> Michael, Gabriel, and Raphael are only angelic so-
> cieties so named from the functions they perform.

May we not perhaps live and love, that is, suffer
and feel compassion, in this all-enveloping Supreme
Person, all of us who suffer and feel compassion, all
beings who struggle to achieve personality, to acquire
consciousness of their suffering and limitations? And
are we not, perhaps, ideas of this total Supreme Consciousness, which, by thinking of us as existing,
makes us exist? Does not our existence consist in being perceived and felt by God? And this same visionary tells us, farther on, in his image-making manner,
that each angel, each society of angels, and the whole
of heaven contemplated as a single whole, appear in
human form, and by virtue of this human form the
Lord rules as if over a single man.

"God does not think, He creates; God does not
exist, He is eternal," wrote Kierkegaard (*Afslutende
uvidenskabelige Efterskrift*); but perhaps it is more
exact to say with Mazzini, that mystic of Italian unification, "God is great because His thought is action"
("Ai giovani d'Italia"), for in Him to think is to create and to give existence to that which He makes exist
merely by thinking it. And is not the impossible that

which is unthinkable to God? Does not the Scripture tell us that God creates by His word, that is, by His thought, and that by His Word everything in existence was made? And does God forget whatever He once thought? Do not all the thoughts that have ever been thought in the Supreme Consciousness perhaps remain there? In Him who is eternal is not all existence eternalized?

So great is our longing to preserve our consciousness, to assign a personal and human finality to the Universe and to existence, that even in the crux of a supreme, most painful, and heartrending sacrifice we would still be able to hearken to the message that if our soul is to evanesce, it does so in order to enrich the infinite and eternal Consciousness, and in order that our souls may serve to nourish the Universal Soul. I enrich God, yes, because before I existed He did not think of me as existing, and because I am one more, one more though it be among an infinite number, who, as a result of having really lived, suffered, and loved, abide in His bosom. It is the furious longing to assign finality to the Universe, to make it conscious and personal, which has led us to believe in God, to want God to be—in a word, which has led us to create God. Yes, to create Him! And this statement should not scandalize even the most devout theist. For to believe in God is, in a certain sense, to create Him, even though He creates us beforehand. It is He who is continually creating Himself in us.

We have created God in order to preserve the Universe from Nothingness, for all that is not consciousness, eternal consciousness, conscious of its eternity and eternally conscious, is no more than appearance. There is nothing truly real save that which feels, suffers, pities, loves, and desires—save consciousness.

There is nothing substantial save consciousness. And we need God in order to preserve consciousness; not in order to think existence, but to live it; not in order to know the why and how of it, but to feel the wherefore of it. If there is no God, love is a contradiction.

Let us go on to consider the idea of God, of the logical God or Supreme Reason, and of the biotical or vital God or Supreme Love.

VIII. From God to God

To ASSERT THAT the religious sense is a sense of divinity, and to hold that it is impossible—without a violation of current human speech—to speak of an atheistic religion, is not, I think, a distortion of the truth. Though clearly it all depends on the concept we form of God, a concept which depends in turn on our concept of divinity.

It will be best to begin with the simple sense of divinity, before we give it an initial capital and a definite article and change it into "the Divinity," that is, into God. For man has reached God through divinity rather than deduced divinity from God.

I have already alluded, in the course of these somewhat wandering but at the same time urgent reflections upon the tragic sense of life, to the *timor fecit deos* of Statius with the intention of limiting and correcting it. And it is not my intention to trace yet once again the historical processes by which peoples have arrived at the consciousness and concept of a personal God like the God of Christianity. And I say peoples and not isolated individuals, for if there is any feeling or concept that is truly collective and social it is the sense and concept of God, even though the individual subsequently individualizes it. Philosophy may, and in fact does, boast an individual origin; theology is necessarily collective.

Schleiermacher's theory, which attributes the origin, or rather the essence, of the religious sense to the

immediate and simple feeling of dependency, seems
to be the most profound and exact explanation. Primitive man living in society feels himself dependent on
the mysterious forces invisibly surrounding him; he
feels that he is in social communion, not only with
other men, his fellow beings, but with all of Nature,
animate and inanimate, which is only to say that he
personalizes everything. Not only is he conscious of
the world, but he imagines that the world possesses
a like consciousness. Just as a child talks to his doll
or his dog as if they understood him, the savage believes that his fetish or that the storm-cloud is aware
of him and pursues him. And the fact is that the
spirit of natural primitive man has not yet cut itself
off from the placenta of Nature, nor has it set the
boundary between waking and dreaming, nor the
limits between reality and imagination.

The divine, therefore, was not originally something
objective, but was rather the subjectivity of consciousness projected outwardly, the personalization of the
world. The concept of divinity arose out of the sense
of divinity, and the sense of divinity is nought but the
dim and nascent sense of personality turned upon the
outer world. Strictly speaking, it is not possible to
speak of outside and inside, objective and subjective,
when no such distinction was actually felt; indeed it
is precisely from the lack of distinction that the feeling and concept of divinity come. The clearer our
consciousness of the distinction between the objective
and subjective, the more obscure is the sense of divinity in us.

It has been said, and very justly so, that Hellenic
paganism was not so much polytheistic as pantheistic.
I do not know if the belief in many gods, taking the
concept of God in the sense in which we understand

it today, has ever really existed in any human mind. And if pantheism is taken to mean the doctrine not that all and everything is God—a proposition I find unthinkable—but that everything is divine, then it is possible to say, without forcing the language, that paganism was pantheistic. Its gods not only moved among men, they also mingled with them. The gods begat gods with mortal women, and mortal men begat demigods with goddesses. And if there were demigods, that is, demi-men, it is merely because the divine and the human were facets of the same reality. The divinization of everything was no more than its humanization. To say that the sun was a god was equivalent to saying that it was a man, a human consciousness, more or less aggrandized and sublimated. And this is true of all beliefs from fetishism to Hellenic paganism.

The real distinction between gods and men lay in the fact that the former were immortal. A god came to be an immortal man; and to deify a man, to consider him to be like a god, was to decide that at his death he had not really died. Certain heroes were thought to have gone, still alive, into the kingdom of the dead. And this point is most important in estimating the value of what is divine.

In the republic of gods there was always some maximum god, some true monarch. It was this divine monarchy with its monocultism that led primitive peoples into monotheism. Monarchy and monotheism are twin phenomena. Zeus, Jupiter, was in process of being converted into a single god, just as Yahweh, originally one god among so many others, came to be considered one god, first of the people of Israel, then of humanity, and finally of the entire universe.

Like monarchy, monotheism had a warlike origin.

"It is only on the march and in time of war," says Robertson Smith in *The Prophets of Israel*,

> that a nomad people feels any urgent need of a central authority, and so it came about that in the first beginnings of national organization, centering in the sanctuary of the ark, Israel was thought of mainly as the host of Jehovah. The very name of Israel is martial, and means "God (*El*) fighteth," and Jehovah in the Old Testament is Iahwĕ Çebāôth—the Jehovah of the armies of Israel. It was on the battlefield that Jehovah's presence was most clearly realized; but in primitive nations the leader in time of war is also the natural judge in time of peace.

God, the one God, issued, then, from man's sense of divinity, as a warlike, monarchical, and social God. He revealed himself to the people as a whole, not to each individual. He was the God of a people and He jealously exacted worship for Himself alone. The transition from this monocultism to monotheism was effected largely by individual action, more philosophical perhaps than theological, on the part of the prophets. In short, it was the individual activity of the prophets which individualized divinity—above all, by giving divinity an ethical base.

Reason—that is, philosophy—subsequently took over this God who had emerged into human consciousness as a result of a sense of divinity in man, and then tended to define Him and convert Him into an idea. To define something is to idea-lize it, for which purpose its incommensurable or irrational element, its vital essence, must first be put aside. And thus the God who is felt, the divinity sensed as a unique person and consciousness outside ourselves—though at the same time enveloping and sustaining us—was converted into the idea of God.

The logical, rational God, the *ens summum*, the

primum movens, the Supreme Being of theological philosophy, the God who is attained by the three famous ways of negation, eminence, and causality, *via negationis*, *eminentiae*, *causalitatis*, is no more than an idea of God, a dead something. The traditional and much debated proofs of His existence are, basically, no more than a vain attempt to determine His essence: as Vinet very well noted, existence derives from essence, and to say that God exists, without saying what God is and what His nature is, is as good as saying nothing at all.

And this God, arrived at by the methods of eminence and negation or the putting aside of finite qualities, becomes finally an unthinkable God, a pure idea, a God of whom, by the very fact of His ideal excellence, we can say that He is nothing, as indeed He has been defined by Scotus Erigena: *Deus propter excellentiam non inmerito nihil vocatur*. Or in the words of the pseudo-Dionysius, Dionysius the Areopagite, in his Fifth Epistle: "The divine darkness is the inaccessible light in which God is said to dwell." The anthropomorphic God, the God who is sensed, is purified of human attributes—finite, relative, and temporal attributes—and evanesces into the God of deism or of pantheism.

The classic supposed proofs of the existence of God all refer to this God-Idea, to this logical God, this God by elimination, and hence they really prove nothing, or rather, they prove no more than the existence of this idea of God.

In my early youth, when first I became disquieted by these eternal problems, I read a book, whose author's name I do not care to recall, and found this sentence: "God is the great X at the ultimate limit of human knowledge; in the measure that science advances, the limit recedes." And I made a marginal note: "On this side of the barrier everything is understandable without need of Him; on the other side, nothing is understandable, either with or without Him; God is therefore superfluous." And as regards the God-Idea, the God of the proofs, I continue to hold the same view. Laplace is credited with a phrase to the effect that he had not found any need for the hypothesis of God in order to construct his own system to explain the origin of the Universe. And so it is. The idea of God serves us in no way to understand better the existence, the essence, or the finality of the Universe.

That there should be a Supreme Being, infinite, absolute, and eternal, whose existence is unknown to us and who has created the Universe, is no more conceivable to us than that the material basis of the Universe itself, matter itself, is eternal and infinite and absolute. We do not understand the existence of the world one bit better by telling ourselves that God created it. We are merely begging the question or supplying a purely verbal solution in order to conceal our ignorance. Strictly speaking, we infer the existence of the Creator from the fact that whatever has been created actually exists, and His own existence is not rationally justified: necessity cannot be inferred from a fact, or else everything is necessary.

And if from the nature of the Universe we pass to what is called its order, and which we must assume requires an Ordainer, we must then admit that whatever is constitutes order, and we do not then conceive of any other. This inference of God's existence from the order of the Universe implies a transition from the ideal to the real order, an outward projection of our mind, a supposition that the rational explanation of a thing produces the thing itself. Human art, instructed by Nature, possesses a conscious creative faculty by means of which it apprehends the process of creation, and we proceed to transfer this deliberate and artistic faculty to the consciousness of an artist, but from Whom and what nature He in His turn learnt His art we cannot tell.

The traditional analogy of the watch and the watchmaker is inapplicable to an absolute, infinite and eternal, Being. It is, moreover, a way of explaining nothing. For to say that the world is the way it is and not otherwise because God made it so, while at the same time we admit that we do not know why He made it so, is the same as saying nothing. And if we knew the reason why God made it as it is, then God is superfluous and the reason is sufficient in itself. If everything were a question of mathematics, if there were no irrational element present, then we should not have had recourse to the explanatory theory of a Supreme Ordainer, who is nothing more than reason in unreason, reason in the irrational, and thus merely another cloak for our ignorance. And let us not discuss here that absurd proposition that if all the type in a printing press were printed up at random, the result could not possibly be the book *Don Quixote*. Something else would result which would become a *Don Quixote* for those who would be forced to depend or rely upon it, and they would be formed by it and would form part of it.

This traditionally supposed proof of God's existence resolves itself into hypostatizing or substantivating the explanation or reason for some phenomenon; it amounts to saying that Mechanics is the cause of movement, Biology the cause of life, Philology the cause of language, Chemistry the cause of bodies; all we need do is to give an initial capital to the science in question and convert it into a force different from the phenomena out of which we derive it, and distinct from our mind, which effects the derivation. But the God thus deduced, a God who is no more than reason hypostatized and projected into infinity, cannot possibly be taken and felt as something alive and real, nor even be imagined except as a mere idea which will die with us.

The question arises, on the other hand, whether anything imaginable, but not in existence, does not exist because God wills that it should not exist, or whether God does not will it to exist because it does not actually exist; and, as regards the impossible, whether a thing is impossible because God wills it so, or whether God so wills it because, by reason of its innate absurdity, it cannot be. God must submit to the organic law of contradiction, and He cannot, according to the theologians, cause two plus two to be any more or less than four. The law of necessity bears upon Him, or He Himself is the law of necessity. And in the moral order the question arises whether falsehood, or homicide, or adultery, is wrong because He has so decreed it, or whether He has decreed it so because they are wrong in themselves. If the former is the case, then God is an absurd and capricious God who decrees a certain law when He might just as well have decreed another; either that, or He acts in accord with a nature and essence inherent in the things themselves and independent of Him, that is, independent of His sovereign will; and if such is the case, if He acts in accord with the *raison d'être* of things, and this *raison* would suffice us without any further need of God, if we but knew it, then, since we do not know it, even "God" explains nothing. This *raison*, this reason would bear upon God, would be above him. And it is of no avail to say that this reason is God Himself, the supreme reason for things. A reason of this kind, a necessitous reason, is not personal. Only will imparts personality. And it is this problem of the relation between God's reason, necessitously necessary, and His will, necessarily free, that forever makes the logical or Aristotelian God a contradictory God.

The scholastic theologians never succeeded in disentangling themselves from the difficulties in which they found themselves when they attempted to reconcile human liberty with divine prescience and with God's knowledge of the free and contingent future; the cause of their difficulty is that, strictly speaking, the rational God is wholly irreconcilable with contingency, for the notion of contingency is fundamentally the same as the notion of irrationality. The rational God is forcibly necessary as regards His being and His action, and He cannot do other than follow the best course in every instance, but a number of different things cannot all be the best equally, for among infinite possibilities there is only one that is best suited to its end, just as among the infinite number of lines that can be drawn from one point to another, there is only the one straight line. And the rational God, the God of Reason, cannot but follow in every instance the straight line, the line which leads most directly to the end proposed, a necessary end, just as the only straight course to Him is necessary. And thus God's necessity is substituted for His divinity. And God's free will, that is, His conscious personality, gives way to His necessity. The God we desire, the God who will save our soul from nothingness, the immortalizing God, must needs be an arbitrary God.

God is not God because He thinks, but because of what He has wrought, because of what He creates. He is not a meditative but an active God. A God-Reason, a theoretical or meditative God, such as this God of theological rationalism, is a God evanescing in His own meditation. This sort of God corresponds, as we shall see, to the beatific vision as the supreme expression of eternal felicity. This is a quietist God, in short, just as reason, by its very essence, is quietist.

Then there is the other famous proof of God's existence: that of the supposed unanimous consent to believe in Him among all mankind. But this proof is not strictly rational, nor is it an argument in favor of the rational God who would explain the Universe, but rather an argument in favor of the God of the heart, who makes us live. We would be justified in calling it rational proof only if we were to believe that reason is the consent, more or less unanimous, of mankind, a universal suffrage, in which we gave credence to the *vox populi*, which is said to be *vox Dei*.

Such, indeed, was the belief of Lamennais, that tragic and ardent spirit, who asserted that life and truth were essentially one and the same—would that they were!—and who declared that reason is like Religion: one, universal, everlasting, and holy. Lamennais invokes the "we must believe them all or believe none of them at all," "aut omnibus credendum est aut nemini," of Lactantius and the saying of Heraclitus that every individual opinion is fallible, and cites Aristotle's notion that the strongest proof consists in the general agreement of mankind, and he emphasizes Pliny's thought that one man cannot deceive all men or be deceived by all, *nemo omnes, neminem omnes fefellerunt*. Would that it were so! And he concludes with Cicero's dictum that we "must believe the word of our ancestors, even without proof," "maioribus autem nostris etiam nulla ratione reddita credere."

Let us assume, then, that this belief of the ancients in the divine interpenetration of the whole of Nature is universal and constant, and that it is, as Aristotle calls it, an ancestral dogma, πάτριος ζόξα; this would only go to prove that there is a motive impelling nations and individuals—either all of them, or almost all of them, or many of them—to believe in a God. But are there not illusions and fallacies rooted in human nature itself? Do not all nations begin by believing that the sun turns around the world? And do we not all of us naturally incline to believe in whatever appeases our longing? Shall we say with Herrmann that "if there is a God, He has not left us without some indication of Himself, and it is His will that we should find Him"?

Herrmann's thought is a pious desire, no doubt, but we cannot call it a reason, strictly speaking, unless we relate it to the Augustinian sentence—but which again is not a reason—"Since thou seekest Me, it must be that thou hast found Me," the underlying belief being that God is the cause of our seeking Him.

This famous argument from the supposed unanimity of mankind's belief in God, the argument which the ancients, with sure instinct, most made use of, is in essence identical with the so-called moral proof which Kant employed in his *Critique of Practical Reason*, transposing its application from mankind collectively to the individual; Kant derives his proof from our conscience, or rather, from our feeling of divinity. This proof of Kant's is not strictly or specifically rational, but vital; it cannot be applied to the logical God, the *ens summum*, the quintessentially simple and abstract Being, the immobile and impassible prime mover, in short, the God-Reason, the God who neither suffers nor desires, but instead to the biotic God, quintessentially complex and concrete, to the consenting God who suffers and desires in us and with us, to the Father of Christ, who cannot be attained except through man, through His Son (John 14:6), and whose revelation is historical, or, if one prefers, anecdotical, but not philosophical or categorical.

The unanimous consent of mankind (let us assume it is unanimous), or the universal longing of all human souls who have achieved consciousness of their humanity, a consciousness which longs to be the end and meaning of the Universe, a longing which is the very quintessence of the soul striving to persist eternally and without a break in the continuity of consciousness, this consciousness leads us to the human, anthropomorphic God, a projection of our consciousness upon the Consciousness of the Universe; it leads us to the God who endows the Universe with a human meaning and finality. This God is not the *ens summum*, the *primum movens*, nor the Creator of the Universe, and not the Idea-God; He is the living God, the subjective God—He is, in short, subjectivity objectified, or personality universalized. He is more than a mere idea: He is will rather than reason. God is Love—that is, He is Will. Reason, the Word, derives from Him, but He, the Father, is, above all else, Will.

"There can be no doubt whatever," Ritschl writes,

that a very imperfect view was taken of God's spiritual personality in the older theology, when the functions of knowing and willing alone were employed to illustrate it. Religious thought cannot but ascribe to God the attributes of spiritual feeling as well. The older theology, however, labored under the impression that feeling and emotion were characteristic only of limited and created personality; it transformed, for example, the religious idea of the Divine blessedness into eternal self-knowledge, and that of the Divine wrath into a fixed purpose to punish sin.

Yes, this logical God, arrived at by the *via negationis*, was a God who, strictly speaking, neither loved nor hated, because He neither enjoyed nor suffered, an inhuman God without pain or glory, and His justice was a rational or mathematical justice—that is, an injustice.

The attributes of the living God, of the Father of Christ, must be deduced from His historical revelation in the Gospel and in the conscience of every Christian believer, and not from metaphysical reasonings which lead only to the Nothing-God of Scotus Erigena, to the rational or pantheistic God, to the atheist God, in short, to the depersonalized Divinity.

We attain to the living God, the human God, not through reason, but only through love and suffering. Reason rather separates us from Him. We cannot first know Him so that then we may love Him; we must begin by loving Him, longing for Him, hungering after Him, before we can know Him. The knowledge of God proceeds from the love of God, and this knowledge has little or nothing of the rational in it. For God is indefinable. To seek to define Him is to seek to confine Him within the limits of our mind—that is, to kill Him. Whenever we try to define Him, we come face to face with Nothingness.

The idea of God postulated by rational theodicy is no more than a hypothesis, like the hypothesis of ether, for example.

Ether is merely, in effect, a hypothetical entity, useful only insofar as it explains whatever we endeavor to explain by means of it—light, electricity, or universal gravitation—and only to the degree that these phenomena cannot be explained in any other way. In like manner the idea of God is also a hypothesis, useful only insofar as it helps explain whatever we are endeavoring to explain to ourselves—the essence and existence of the Universe—and useful only so long as we cannot explain these things better in another way. Since in reality we can explain the Universe neither better nor worse with this idea than without it, the idea of God—that supreme *petitio principii*—is useless.

If ether is nothing but a hypothesis to explain light, we have, on the other hand, a direct experience of air; even if it did not help us to explain the phenomenon of sound, we would nevertheless always be directly aware of air, and even more so, of the lack of it, in a moment of suffocation or air-hunger. In the same way God Himself, not the idea of God, may become a reality that is directly felt; and even though the idea of Him does not help us to explain either the existence or essence of the Universe, we have at times an immediate feeling of God, above all in moments of spiritual suffocation. And this feeling—mark it well, mark it for all that which makes it tragic, and for the fact that the tragic sense of life itself springs from it—is a feeling of hunger for God, a lack of God. To believe in God is, in the first place, as we shall see, to wish for God to exist and to be unable to live without Him.

So long as I was a pilgrim in the fields of reason in search of God, I could not find Him, for I was not deluded by the idea of God and neither could I accept an idea as being God, and then, as I wandered among the wastes of rationalism, I told myself that we ought not to seek any consolation other than the truth—as I then called reason—and I found no satisfaction in that consolation. But as I sank deeper and deeper into rational scepticism on the one hand and into emotional despair on the other, the hunger for God was aroused in me and the suffocation of spirit made me feel His reality precisely in my want of Him. And I wished there were a God, and that God existed. And God does not exist, but rather super-exists, and He is sustaining our existence by existing us, making us exist.

God, who is Love, the Father of Love, is in us the son of love. Certain facile and superficial men, slaves to reason, to that reason which externalizes us, think they have said something meaningful when they say that far from God's having made man in His image and likeness it is man who has made his gods or his God in his own image and likeness. So superficial are these men that they do not pause to consider that if the latter proposition is true, which it is, it is true because the first proposition is no less true. God and man mutually create one another, in effect. God creates or reveals Himself in man, and man creates himself in God. God is His own maker—*Deus ipse se fecit*, says Lactantius—and we may say that He is continually creating Himself in man and being created by man. And if each one of us, impelled by love, by a hunger for divinity, creates for himself an image of God according to his own measure, and if according to His measure God creates Himself for each man, then there is a collective, social, human God, the re-

sult of all the human imaginations that imagine Him.
For God is, and God reveals Himself, in our collectivity; at the same time, He is the most ample and
the most personal of all human conceptions.

The Master of divinity has bidden us to be perfect
as our Father who is in heaven is perfect (Matt.
5:48), and in the sphere of thought and feeling our
perfection consists in the zeal with which we strive
to harmonize our imagination with the total imagination of the humanity of which, in God, we form part.

The logical theory of the opposition between the
extension of a concept and the comprehension of a
concept—the one increasing in the ratio in which the
other diminishes—is well known. The concept which
is most extensive and at the same time least comprehensive is that of the thing or being which includes
everything in existence and possesses no other sign
than that of being, while the concept that is most
comprehensive and least extensive is that of the Universe, which is only applicable to itself and which
comprehends all existing signs. And the logical or rational God, the God obtained by way of negation,
the absolute entity, merges, like reality itself, into
nothingness; for as Hegel pointed out, pure being
and pure nothingness are identical. And the God of
the heart, the God who is felt, the God of living
humanity, is the Universe itself conceived as personality, it is the consciousness of the Universe: a universal and personal God, totally different from the
individual God of rigid metaphysical monotheism.

I should once again allude to the manner in which
I oppose individuality to personality, even though one
needs the other. Individuality is, if I may so put it,
the container, while personality is the contents; or I

might also say that my personality is in a certain sense my comprehension, that which I comprehend or contain within myself—which is, in a manner of speaking, the entire Universe—and that my individuality is my extension; the one is my infinite, the other my finite. A hundred jars of hard earthenware may be highly individualized, but it is possible for them to be all equally empty or all equally full of the same homogeneous liquid, whereas two bladders, delicate of membrane and allowing the action of osmosis and exosmosis, may be radically different and be full of complex liquids. And thus a man, insofar as he is an individual, may be very far removed from other men, be a sort of spiritual crustacean, and yet be lacking in differential content. Further, the more personality a man possesses and the greater his inner amplitude, the more he forms a society within himself, the less sharply is he divided from his fellows. In the same way, the rigid God of deism, of Aristotelian monotheism, the *ens summum*, is a being in whom individuality, or rather simplicity, stifles personality. Definition kills him, for to define is to impose boundaries, to limit—and it is impossible to define the absolutely indefinable. This God is lacking in inner amplitude; he does not form a society within himself. This lack was superseded by the vital revelation and belief in the Trinity, which makes God a society and even a family in Himself, and no longer a pure individual. The God of Faith is personal; He is a person because He includes three persons; and personality does not feel itself isolated. An isolated person ceases to be a person—for whom should he love? If he does not love, he is not a person. Nor can a simple or single being love himself without his love expanding into a compound being.

It was the sense of God as Father that brought with it the idea of the Trinity. For a Father-God could not be a single, that is, a solitary, God. A father is always father of a family. And the sense of God as Father acted as a constant incentive to conceive Him not merely anthropomorphically, that is, as a man, ἄνθρωπος, but andromorphically, as a male, ἀνήρ. In the Christian folk imagination, in fact, God the Father is naturally thought of as a male. And the reason is that man, *homo*, ἄνθρωπος, as we know him, is necessarily either a male, *vir*, ἀνήρ, or a female, *mulier*, γυνή. And to these may be added the child, who is neuter. And thus, to satisfy imaginatively this need to feel God as a perfect man, that is, as a family, arose the cult of the God-Mother, the Virgin Mary, and the cult of the Child Jesus.

The cult of the Virgin—Mariolatry, in short—which came about by the gradual exaltation of the divine quality in the Virgin, until she was just short of deification, answers the need to feel that God should be a perfect man, that God should include in His nature the feminine element. From calling her Mother of God, θεοτόκος, *deipara*, Catholic piety has gone on exalting the Virgin Mary to the point where she is called co-redeemer and to the dogmatic declaration of her conception without stain of original sin. Hence she now occupies a place between Humanity and Divinity—and a bit closer to Divinity than to Humanity. And it has been surmised that in due course she may perhaps even come to be looked upon as yet another divinity.

Such an exaltation would not necessarily convert the Trinity into a Quaternity. If πνεῦμα, *pneuma*, the Greek for spirit, instead of being neuter had been feminine, who can say that the Virgin Mary might not already have become an incarnation or humanization of the Holy Spirit? Luke's narrative of the Annunciation, where the angel Gabriel hails Mary with the words "The Holy Spirit shall come upon thee," "πνεῦμα ἅγιον ἐπελεύσεται ἐπὶ σε" (Luke, 1:35), could have served as sufficient warranty for the fervent piety which always knows how to mold theological speculation to its own desires. And a dogmatic development would have taken place parallel to that which saw Jesus, the Son, made divine and identified with the Word.

In any case, the cult of the Virgin, of the eternal feminine, of the divine maternity, helps to complete the personalization of God by constituting Him a family.

In one of my books (*The Life of Don Quixote and Sancho*, Part II, Chapter 67) I have said that

God was and remains masculine in our minds. His manner of judging and condemning men has been a man's way, not that of a human being independent of sex; it has been the way of a Father. To compensate, the Mother was needed; the Mother who always pardons, the Mother who always opens her arms to her child, when the child flees the raised hand or frowning brow of the vexed Father, the Mother in whose lap one seeks the consolation of an obscure recollection, the memory of the warm peace of the unconscious which was the dawning of birth, and the taste of that milk which sweetened our dreams of innocence, the Mother who knows no other justice but pardon nor any law but love. Maternal tears blot out the tables of the Decalogue. Our poor and imperfect concept of a male God, of a God with long beard and thunderous voice, of a God imposing precepts and pronouncing sentences, of a God who is the Master, a Roman Paterfamilias, such a God needed compensation and a complement; and

since we really cannot conceive of a live, personal
God beyond human characteristics, even beyond
male qualities, and even less of a neuter or hermaph-
roditic God, we resort to a complementary female
God. Next to God the Father we place a Mother
Goddess, who always forgives because, since she regards everything with blind love, she always under-
stands the basis of sin and sees in it its own reasons
for forgiveness, the unique justice of pardon.

And to this I must now add that not only are we
unable to conceive of the full and living God merely
as masculine, but we are unable to conceive of Him
merely as an individual, merely as a projection of a
solitary I, an asocial I, as an abstract I, in reality.
My living I is an I that is in reality a We; my living
personal I lives only in others, from other and by other
I's; I am sprung from a multitude of ancestors, I
carry them within me in extract, and at the same time
I carry within me, potentially, a multitude of descendants, and God, the projection of my I into the infinite—or rather, I, the projection of God into the
finite—must also be multitude. Hence, the need for
faith, that is, for sense and imagination to conceive
of Him and feel Him to be a certain internal multi-
plicity, and thus save the personality of God, save
the living God.

The pagan sense of living divinity obviated this
need by polytheism. It is the complex of its gods, the
republic of them, which really constitutes their divinity. The true God of Hellenic paganism is not so much
Father Zeus, Jupiter, but rather the entire society of
all the gods and demigods. Hence the solemnity of
the invocation by Demosthenes when he invoked all
the gods and all the goddesses: "Τοῖς θεοῖς εὔχομαι πᾶσι
καὶ πάσαις." And when the rationalizers converted the

term god, θεός, which is properly an adjective, a quality predicated of each one of the gods, into a substantive, and added the definite article to it, they produced *the* god, ὁ θεός, the dead and abstract god of philosophical rationalism, a substantivized quality and therefore void of personality. For the masculine "god" [*el dios*] is no more than the neuter [*lo divino*] "that which is divine." Now the transition from sensing divinity in all things to making it substantive and converting the Divinity into God cannot be achieved without a certain risk to the former. And the Aristotelian God, the God of logical proofs, is nought but Divinity, a concept and not a live person or one that can be sensed, not one that can speak to man through love. This God is merely a substantivized adjective, a constitutional God who reigns but does not govern, and Science is His constitutional charter.

Even in Greco-Latin paganism itself the tendency toward a living monotheism is apparent in the fact that Zeus was conceived of and felt to be a father, Ζεὺς πατήρ, as Homer calls him, the *Ju-piter* or *Jupater* of the Latins, and as a father of a widely extended family of gods and goddesses who together with him constituted the Divinity.

The conjunction of pagan polytheism with Judaic monotheism, which had endeavored by other means to preserve the personality of God, gave us the sense of the Catholic God, who is a society, as the pagan God of whom I have spoken was a society, and who at the same time is one, just as the God of Israel eventually became one. Such is the Christian Trinity, whose deepest meaning was scarcely ever understood by rationalistic deism, that deism which though more or less impregnated with Christianity always remained Unitarian or Socinian.

And the fact is that we sense God less as a super-human consciousness than as the actual consciousness of the human race, past, present, and future, as the collective consciousness of the whole human race, and still more, as the total and infinite consciousness, which embraces and sustains all consciousness, infra-human, human, and perhaps super-human. The divinity which permeates everything, from the lowest of living forms, that is, of the least conscious, to the highest, including our own human consciousness, this divinity is felt by us to be personalized, conscious of itself in God. And this gradation of consciousness, this sense of the gulf between our human consciousness and the fully divine, universal consciousness, finds its correspondence in the belief in angels with their different hierarchies, as intermediaries between our human consciousness and that of God. And a faith consistent with itself must believe these gradations to be infinite, for only through an infinite number of degrees is it possible to pass from the finite to the infinite.

Deistic rationalism conceives God as the Reason of the Universe, but its logic compels it to conceive Him as an impersonal reason, that is, as an idea, while deistic vitalism senses and imagines God as Consciousness, and therefore as a person, or rather as a society of persons. The consciousness of each one of us is, in effect, a society of persons; in me there are various I's and even the I's of those among whom I live, live in me.

The God of deistic rationalism, in effect the God of the logical proofs of His existence, the *ens realissimum* and immobile prime mover, is nought but a Supreme Reason, but in the same sense in which we can call the universal law of gravity the reason for

193

falling bodies, when the law is merely the explanation. But will anyone hold that what we call the universal law of gravity, or that any other law or mathematical principle, is in itself an independent reality, that it is an angel, that it is something possessing consciousness of itself and others, that it is a person? No, it is nothing but an idea with no reality outside the mind of its conceiver. And thus this God-Reason either possesses consciousness of himself or he possesses no reality outside the mind of the conceiver. And if he is conscious of himself, he is already a personal reason and all the value of the traditional reasons disappears, for these proofs only proved a reason and not a supreme consciousness. Mathematics prove an order, a constancy, a reason in the series of mechanical phenomena, but they do not prove that this reason is conscious of itself. This reason is a logical reason, but logical necessity does not prove teleological or final necessity. And where there is no finality there is no personality, there is no consciousness.

The rational God, therefore—that is, the God who is no more than the Reason of the Universe—is destroyed in our mind insofar as he is such a God, and is only born again in us when we feel him in our heart as a living person, as Consciousness, and no longer merely as the impersonal and objective Reason of the Universe. If we wish for rational explanation of the construction of a machine, all that we need to know is the mechanical science of its builder; but if we want to understand why such a machine exists, then, since it is the work not of Nature but of man, we must suppose a conscious, constructive being. But the second part of this reasoning is not applicable to God, even though it be said that in Him the mechanical science and the mechanism of the machine are

one and the same thing. This identification is rationally no more than a begging of the question. And
thus it is that reason destroys this Supreme Reason,
insofar as the latter is a person.

Human reason, in point of fact, is reason based on
the irrational, upon the total vital consciousness, upon
will and feeling. Our human reason is not one which
can prove to us the existence of a Supreme Reason,
which in turn would have to be based upon the Supreme Irrational, upon the Universal Consciousness.
And the revelation in our feeling and imagination,
brought about by love, by faith, by the process of
personalization of this Supreme Consciousness, is that
which leads us to believe in the living God.

And this God, the living God, your God, our God,
is in me, is in you, lives in us, and we live and move
and have our being in Him. And He is in us by virtue
of the hunger, the longing we have for Him, and He
makes Himself desired. And He is the God of the
humble, for in the words of the Apostle, God "hath
chosen the foolish things of the world to confound the
wise: and God hath chosen the weak things of the
world to confound the things which are mighty"
(1 Cor. 1:27). And God is in each one of us in the
measure in which each one feels and loves Him. "If
of two men," says Kierkegaard, "one prays to the true
God without sincerity of heart, and the other prays
to an idol with all the passion of an infinite yearning,
it is the first who really prays to an idol, while the
second really prays to God." It might be better to say
that the true God is He to whom man truly prays and
whom man truly desires. And there may even be a
truer revelation in superstition itself than in theology.
The venerable Father of the long beard and white
locks who appears among the clouds carrying the

globe of the world in His hand is more alive and more real than the *ens realissimum* of theodicy.

Reason is an analytical, that is, a dissolving force, whenever it transfers its activity from the form of intuitions, whether those of the individual instinct of preservation or those of the social instinct of perpetuation, and applies it to the basis and very matter of them. Reason provides order to the perceptions of the senses given us by the material world; but when its analysis is applied to the reality of the perceptions themselves, it dissolves them and plunges us into a world of appearances, a world of insubstantial shadows, for reason outside formal bounds is nihilist, annihilating. And it performs that same terrible office when we withdraw it from its proper domain and apply it to the scrutiny of the imaginative intuitions given us by the spiritual world. For reason annihilates, and imagination *completes*, integrates, or totalizes; reason by itself alone kills; only imagination gives life. If it is true that imagination by itself alone, in giving us life without limitation, leads us to lose our identity in the All and also kills us as individuals, it does so by excess of life. Reason, the head, pronounces a dread "Nothing!" Imagination, the heart, speaks to us and says "All!" And thus between nothingness and the All, in the fusion in us of the All and the Nothing, we live in God, who is All, and God lives in us, and without Him we are Nothing. Reason reiterates: "Vanity of vanities, all is vanity!" And imagination answers "Plenitude of plenitudes, all is plenitude!" And so we live the vanity of plenitude or the plenitude of vanity.

And so deeply rooted in the depths of man's being is this vital need to create and act in an illogical, irrational, personal, or divine world, that those who do

not believe in God, or who believe they do not believe
in Him, believe nonetheless in some godlet or other,
or in some little demon, or in an omen, or in a horse-
shoe which they may perchance have found in the
roadway and carried about to bring them good luck
and protect them from that very reason whose loyal
and devoted partisans they believe themselves to be.

The God for whom we hunger is the God to whom
we pray, the God of the *Pater Noster,* the God of the
Lord's Prayer; the God whom we beseech, before all
and above all—whether or not we are aware of it—
to instill faith into us to make us believe in Him, to
create Himself in us, the God to whom we pray that
His name may be hallowed and that His will be
done—His will, and not His reason—on earth as it
is in heaven, all the while sensing that His will cannot be other than the essence of our will, the desire
to persist eternally.

And such is the God of Love. The *how* of why He
is such is of no avail to question; rather let each one
ask his heart and allow his fancy to imagine Him in
the remoteness of the Universe, gazing down with
the myriad eyes of the nighttime heavens. He in
whom you believe, reader, He is your God, He who
has lived with you and within you, who was born
with you, who was a child when you were a child,
who became a man as you became a man, who will
vanish when you yourself vanish, and who is your
principle of continuity in the spirit, because he is the
principle of solidarity among all men and in each man
and between men and the Universe, and who is, like
you, a person. And if you believe in God, God believes in you, and by believing in you He ceaselessly
creates you. For in your essence you are nought but
the idea God has of you, but a living idea, as from a

living God conscious of Himself, a God-Consciousness, and, apart from what you are in the society of God, you are nothing.

How to define God? Yes, that is what we long to do; it was Jacob's longing when, a man wrestling all night until dawn with a divine force, he said: "Tell me, I pray thee, thy name!" (Gen. 32:29). And listen to the words of that great Christian preacher, Frederick William Robertson, in a sermon preached in Trinity Chapel, Brighton, on June 10, 1849:

> And this is our struggle—*the* struggle. Let any true man go down into the deeps of his own being, and answer us,—what is the cry that comes from the most real part of his nature? Is it the cry for daily bread? Jacob asked for that in his *first* communing with God—preservation, safety. Is it even this,—to be forgiven our sins? Jacob had a sin to be forgiven, and in that most solemn moment of his existence he did not say a syllable about it. Or is it this—"Hallowed be Thy name"? No, my brethren. Out of our frail and yet sublime humanity, the demand that rises in the earthlier hours of our religion may be this—"Save my soul"; but in the most unearthly movements it is this—"Tell me thy Name." We move through a world of mystery; and the deepest question is, What is the being that is ever near, sometimes felt, never seen,—That which has haunted us from childhood with a dream of something surpassingly fair, which has never yet been realized—That which sweeps through the soul at times as a desolation, like the blast from the wings of the Angel of Death, leaving us stricken and silent in our loneliness—That which has touched us in our tenderest point, and the flesh has quivered with agony, and our mortal affections have shrivelled up with pain—That which comes to us in aspirations of nobleness and conceptions of superhuman excellence? Shall we say It or He? What is it? Who is He? Those anticipations of Immortality and God—what are they? Are they the mere throbbings of my

own heart, heard and mistaken for a living something beside me? Are they the sound of my own
wishes, echoing through the vast void of Nothingness? or shall I call them God, Father, Spirit, Love?
A living Being within me or outside me? Tell me
Thy name, thou awful mystery of Loveliness! This
is the struggle of all earnest life.

Thus far Robertson. And I would add that "Tell me
thy name!" is essentially the same as "Save my Soul!"
We ask Him His name so that He may save our soul,
so that He may save the human soul, so that He may
save a human finality for the Universe. And if we
are told that God is called He, or that He is the *ens
realissimum* or Supreme Being, or given any other
metaphysical name, we are not satisfied, for we know
that any metaphysical name is an X, and we go on
asking for His name. And there is only one name that
satisfies our longing, and it is the name Saviour,
Jesus. God is the love that saves:

> For the loving worm within its clod,
> Were diviner than a loveless God
> Amid his worlds, I will dare to say

as Browning wrote in his "Christmas Eve and Easter
Day." The essence of divinity is love, personalizing
and eternalizing will, which hungers for eternity and
infinity.

It is ourselves, our eternity that we seek in God;
we seek to be made divine. Browning, again, wrote,
in *Saul*

> " 'Tis the weakness in strength that I cry for!
> my flesh, that I seek
> In the Godhead! . . ."

But this God who saves us, this personal God, the
Consciousness of the Universe who envelops and sustains our consciousness, this God who gives human

finality to the whole creation—does He exist? Have
we proofs of His existence?

The question leads in the first place to an inquiry
into the meaning of this notion of existence. What is
it to exist and in what sense do we speak of things
as not existing?

In an etymological sense to exist means to be outside ourselves, outside of our mind, *ex-sistere*. But is
there anything outside our mind, outside our consciousness, which embraces the sum of the known?
Doubtless there is. The matter of knowledge comes
to us from outside. And what is the nature of this
matter? It is impossible for us to know, for to know
is to give form to matter, and thus there is no possibility of knowing the formless *qua* formless. To do
so would be equivalent to bringing order into chaos.

This problem of the existence of God, a problem
that is rationally insoluble, is really identical with the
problem of consciousness, of the *ex-sistentia* and not
of the *in-sistentia* of consciousness; it is the problem
of the substantial existence of the soul, the problem of
the perpetuity of the human soul, the problem of the
human finality of the Universe itself. To believe in a
living and personal God, in an eternal and universal
consciousness that knows and loves us, is to believe
that the Universe exists *for* man: for man or for a
consciousness of the same order as the human consciousness, of the same nature, though sublimated,
of a consciousness which is capable of knowing us
and in whose memory we are able to live forever.

Perhaps by a supreme and desperate effort of resignation we might succeed, as I have already said, in
sacrificing our own personality if we knew that at our
death it went to enhance a Personality, a Supreme

Consciousness; and provided we knew that the Universal Soul was nourished by our souls and had need of them. We might perhaps meet death with a desperate resignation or with a resigned despair, delivering up our soul to the soul of Humanity, bequeathing to it our work, that bears the imprint of our person, if it were certain that this humanity were destined to bequeath its soul in its turn to another soul, when at long last consciousness will have become extinct upon this anguished Earth. But—what if such should not be the case?

And if the soul of humanity is eternal, if the human collective consciousness is eternal, if there is a Consciousness of the Universe, and if this Consciousness is eternal, why should our own individual consciousness, yours, reader, and mine, not be eternal?

In the entire vast Universe could there be such a contradiction: a consciousness that knows itself, loves itself, and feels itself, arbitrarily joined to an organism which can only live within such and such degrees of heat, and is thus merely a transitory phenomenon? No, it is not mere curiosity that inspires the wish to know whether or not the stars are inhabited by living, animated organisms, by consciousness akin to our own; there is a profound longing in the dream of the transmigration of our souls through the stars inhabiting the vast reaches of the sky. The sense of the divine makes us wish and believe that everything is animate, that consciousness, in a greater or lesser degree, extends through everything. We wish to save not only ourselves but the world itself from nothingness. And God is our medium. Thus do we sense His finality.

What would a universe be without any consciousness capable of reflecting it and knowing it? What would objectified reason be without will and feeling? For us it would be equivalent to nothingness, a thousand times more dreadful than nothing.

If such a supposition is indeed the reality, our lives lack all sense and value.

It is not, therefore, rational necessity, but vital anguish which drives us to believe in God. And to believe in God is, I repeat, first and foremost to hunger for Him, hunger for divinity, to feel His absence and the void, to want God to exist. And it is to want to give a human finality to the Universe. For we might even come to resign ourselves to being absorbed by God if our consciousness were to be assimilated into a Consciousness, if consciousness is the end of the Universe.

"The wicked man hath said in his heart, There is no God." And it is because he speaks from the heart that he is wicked. For the just man may say in his head "God does not exist!" But it is only the wicked man who can say so in his heart. Not to believe that there is a God or to believe that there is not a God, is one thing; to resign oneself to there not being a God is still another matter, albeit a terrible and inhuman position; but not to want a God to exist is to exceed any other moral monstrosity whatsoever. In point of fact, however, those who deny God deny Him out of despair at not finding Him.

Reason now confronts us once more with its Sphinx-like question—the Sphinx is, in effect, reason—does God exist? This eternal and eternalizing person who gives meaning—and I need not add human meaning, for there is no other—to the Universe, is it a substantial something, existing outside our consciousness, outside our longing? Here we come up against the insoluble, and it is best that it remain so.

It is enough that reason cannot prove the impossibility of His existence.

To believe in God is to long for His existence, and, furthermore, to act as if God did exist; it is to live by this longing and to make it the inner wellspring of our action. This longing or hunger for divinity begets hope; hope begets faith, and faith and hope together beget charity. Out of this longing is born our sense of beauty, finality, goodness.

Let us see how this may come about.

IX. Faith, Hope, and Charity

. . . sanctiusque ac reverentius visum de
actis deorum credere quam scire.

Tacitus, *Germania*, 34

THE GOD OF THE HEART, the living God is reached
by way of faith and not by way of rational or mathematical conviction, and faith leads us back to Him,
when we have left Him to stray after the lifeless God
of logic.

And what is faith?

That is the question put to us in the catechism of
Christian Doctrine in school, and the answer used to
run: "Faith is to believe what we have not seen."

To which answer I added an amendment (in an
essay a dozen years ago): "Not believe what we have
not seen, but create what we do not see!" And I have
already said to you that to believe, in the first instance
at least, is to want God to be, to long for His
existence.

The theological virtue of faith, according to the
Apostle Paul, whose definition serves as the basis of
the traditional Christian disquisitions upon it, is "the
substance of things hoped for, the evidence of things
not seen": "ἐλπιζομένων ὑπόστασις, πραγμάτων ἔλεγχος οὐ
βλεπομένων" (Heb. 11:1).

Faith is the substance, or rather the support or
basis, for hope, the guarantee of it. It is that which
connects, and, more than connects, subordinates, faith
to hope. And in fact we do not hope because we be-

lieve, but rather we believe because we hope. It is hope in God, the ardent longing for a God to be, to vouch for the eternity of consciousness, which leads us to believe in Him.

But faith, which in the last analysis is a compound of elements, among them a cognitive, logical, or rational element, along with an affective, biotic, or pathetic—strictly speaking, irrational—element, appears to us in the form of knowledge. Hence the insuperable difficulty in separating it from some dogma or other. Pure faith, free from dogmas, concerning which I wrote so much once upon a time, is a phantom. Not even the invention of that formula of "faith in faith itself" overcomes the difficulty. Faith requires matter to work upon.

Believing is a form of knowing, even if it be no more than a knowing—and even a formulating—of our vital longing. In ordinary language the term "believing," however, is used in a double and even contradictory sense: meaning, on the one hand, the highest degree of the mind's conviction of the truth of something understood, and, on the other hand, a dubious and vacillating conviction. For if in one sense believing expresses the strongest conviction possible, the expression "I believe that is so, though I am not sure of it," is common parlance.

All of which corresponds with what we have said about uncertainty as the basis of faith. The most robust faith, insofar as it is distinct from all other knowledge that is not *pistic* or of faith—faithful, we might say—is based on uncertainty. And this is so because faith, which vouches for what we hope for, is not so much a rational conviction of a theoretical principle as trust in a person who assures us of something. Faith assumes an objective personal element.

We do not so much believe something as we believe someone who gives assurances or promises something or other. We believe in a person, or in God as person and personalization of the Universe.

This personal, or religious, element in faith is self-evident. Faith, it is often said, is not in itself either theoretical knowledge or a rational conviction in a truth, nor is its essence sufficiently explained as trust in God. Seeberg says of faith that it is "the inner submission to the spiritual authority of God, close obedience. And insofar as this obedience is a means of achieving a rational principle, faith is a personal conviction."

The faith defined by St. Paul, the πίστις, the Greek *pistis*, is best translated as trust. The word *pistis* is derived in effect from the verb πείθω, *peitho*, which in its active voice means to persuade and in its middle voice means to trust in someone, to pay him heed, believe in him, to obey. And to trust in, *fidare se*, is derived from the stem *fid*—whence *fides*, faith, and also trust. The Greek stem πιθ—*pith*—and the Latin *fid*, are as alike as brothers. In short, the very word faith itself implies in its origin the sense of trust, of yielding to the will of another, to a person. We trust only in persons. We trust in Providence, which we conceive to be something personal and conscious, not in Fate which is something impersonal. And thus we believe in whoever tells us the truth, in whoever gives us hope, and not directly and immediately in the Truth itself, in Hope itself.

And this personal or rather personifying sense of faith reveals itself even in its lowest forms, for it is this sense which produces faith in divine afflatus, in inspiration, in the miraculous. There is the well-known story of the Parisian doctor who, when he found that a quack in his quarter was taking away his clientele, removed himself to another quarter, as far away as possible, where he was known to no one, and there set up as a quack, claiming to be one and acting like one; when he was accused of illegally practicing medicine, he produced his medical license, and explained himself more or less as follows: "I am a medical man, but if I had asserted myself as one, I would not have obtained the practice I have built up as a quack; and now that my patients know that I am a properly qualified doctor, they will desert me for some healer who can assure them he has not devoted himself to study, but cures by inspiration alone." For a doctor is discredited when he is found never to have studied medicine and possesses no license, and the quack is discredited when he is found to have studied and to be a qualified practitioner. For some believe in science and in study, and others believe in the person, in inspiration, and even in ignorance.

There is one distinction in the world's geography which comes immediately to our minds when we thus state the different thoughts and desires of men concerning their religion. We remember how the whole world is in general divided into two hemispheres upon this matter. One half of the world, the great dim East, is mystic. It insists upon not seeing anything too clearly. Make any one of the great ideas of life distinct and clear, and immediately it seems to the Oriental to be untrue. He has an instinct which tells him that the vastest thoughts are too vast for the human mind, and that if they are made to present themselves in forms of statement which the human mind can comprehend, their nature is violated and their strength is lost.

On the other hand, the Occidental, the man of the

West, demands clearness and is impatient with mystery. He loves a definite statement as much as his brother of the East dislikes it. He insists on knowing what the eternal and infinite forces mean to his personal life, how they will make him personally happier and better, almost how they will build the house over his head, and cook the dinner on his hearth. This is the difference between the East and the West, between man on the banks of the Ganges and man on the banks of the Mississippi. Plenty of exceptions, of course, there are—mystics in Boston and St. Louis, hard-headed men of facts in Bombay and Calcutta. The two great dispositions cannot be shut off from one another by an ocean or a range of mountains. In some nations and places, as for instance among the Jews and in our own New England, they notably commingle. But in general they thus divide the world between them. The East lives in the moonlight of mystery, the West in the sunlight of scientific fact. The East cries out to the Eternal for vague impulses. The West seizes the present with light hands, and will not let it go till it has furnished it with reasonable, intelligible motives. Each misunderstands, distrusts, and in large degree despises the other. But the two hemispheres together, and not either one by itself, make up the total world.

Thus spoke the eminent preacher Phillips Brooks in one of his sermons.

It might be better to say, rather, that throughout the whole world, in the East as well as the West, rationalists seek definition and believe in the concept, while vitalists seek inspiration and believe in the person. The rationalists plumb the Universe in order to wrest its secrets from it; the vitalists address the Consciousness of the Universe, striving to come into direct relation with the Soul of the World, with God, so that they may thus find a warranty or substance in what they hope, which is not to die, and to find evidence for what they do not see.

And inasmuch as a person is a will, and will always has reference to the future, whoever believes, believes in what is to come—that is, in what he hopes. We do not believe, strictly speaking, in what is or what was, except as warranty for and as substance of what is to be. For the Christian to believe in the resurrection of Christ, that is, to believe in tradition and the Gospel— and both of these authorities are personal—which tell him that Christ rose, is to believe that he himself will one day rise again by the grace of Christ. And even scientific faith—for there is such a thing—has reference to the future and is an act of trust. The man of science believes that at a certain date in the future an eclipse of the sun will take place: he believes that the laws which have governed the world in the past will continue to govern it.

To believe, I repeat, is to place confidence in some-one, and that someone is a person. I say that I know that there is an animal called a horse, and that it pos-sesses certain characteristics, because I have seen it; and I say that I believe in the existence of the giraffe or the ornitho-rhynchus, and that they possess certain characteristics, because I believe those who assure me that they have seen them. But herein lies the ele-ment of uncertainty which faith bears with it, for a person can be deceived or he may deceive us.

On the other hand, however, this personal element in belief lends it an affective and loving character, and above all, as concerns religious faith, makes it refer to what is hoped. No one is likely to sacrifice his life to maintain that the three angles of a triangle are equal to two right angles, for such a truth does not require the sacrifice of anyone's life; but many have sacrificed their lives for the sake of their religious faith, and in fact martyrs create faith more than faith creates martyrs. For faith is not the mere adherence of the intellect to an abstract principle, it is not the recognition of a theoretical truth, a process wherein the will merely moves us to believe; faith is an act of the will, it is a movement of the spirit toward a practical truth, toward a person, toward something which makes us not merely understand life but also makes us live it.

Faith makes us live by showing us that life, though dependent on reason, has its wellspring and source of power outside itself, in something supernatural and miraculous. The mathematician Cournot, a singularly well-balanced man of science, wrote that it is the impetus toward the super-natural and the miraculous which animates us, and that wherever this drive is lacking, all of reason's speculations lead to nothing but affliction of spirit. The truth is that we want to live.

Moreover, though we have said that faith is a matter of will, we might perhaps better say it is will itself, the will not to die, or better still, it is some other psychic force distinct from intelligence, from will, and from feeling. Faith would then include feeling, knowing, willing, believing, that is, creating. For neither feeling alone, nor intelligence, nor will creates; they work upon material supplied them, given them in advance by faith. Faith is the creative power in man. But since it bears a more intimate relation with the will than with any other of his faculties, we conceive it in the form of volition. It should be borne in mind, however, that to want to believe, that is, to want to create, is not precisely the same as to believe or to create, though it is the point of departure.

Faith, then, if not a creative faculty, is the flowering of the will and its work is to create. In a certain sense, faith creates its object. And faith in God consists in creating God, and, since it is God who gives us faith in Him, God is continually creating Himself in us. So that St. Augustine could say: "I shall look for you, Lord, by praying to you and as I pray I shall believe in you. . . . It is my faith that calls to you, Lord, the faith which you gave me and made to live in me through the merits of your Son, who became man, and through the ministry of your preacher." The power of creating God in our own image and likeness, of personalizing the Universe, simply means that we carry God within us, as substance of that for which we hope, and that God is continuously creating us in His own image and likeness.

And we create God, that is, God creates Himself in us, by compassion, by love. To believe in God is to love Him and to fear Him with love, and we begin by loving Him even before knowing Him, and by loving Him we come at last to see and discover Him in all things.

Those who say they believe in God and neither love nor fear Him, do not believe in Him, but believe rather in those who have taught them that God exists, and these in their turn often enough do not believe in Him either. Whoever believes he believes in God, but believes without passion, without anguish, without uncertainty, without doubt, without despair-in-consolation, believes only in the God-Idea, not in God Himself. And just as belief is born of love, so can it be born of fear, and even of hate, as it was in the thief Vanni Fucci, whom Dante depicts in Hell insulting God with obscene gestures. For even demons believe in God, as do many atheists.

Is it not perhaps a way of believing in God that those who do not want God to exist, because they cannot believe in Him, should so ferociously deny and even insult Him? Like believers, they would wish He did exist; but being weak-minded or ill-willed men, in whom reason counts for more than will, they are overthrown by reason, in their own despite, and they despair and deny out of despair, and in denying they testify to a belief in what they deny, and God is revealed in them, Himself affirmed by their denial of Him.

It may be objected that to demonstrate that faith creates its own object is to demonstrate that this object is an object good for faith alone, and that outside the realm of faith it has no objective reality; just as, on the other hand, to maintain that faith is necessary to contain the masses or console them is to declare that the object of faith is illusory. And the truth is that to believe in God today, as far as intellectual believers is concerned, is to want God to exist.

To want God to exist means also to act and feel as if He did exist. And by desiring that God should exist and acting in conformity with this desire we create God; that is to say, just as God creates Himself in us, just as God makes Himself manifest in us, in the same way so does He open out in us and reveal Himself. For God goes to encounter whoever seeks Him with love and through love, and evades whoever inquires after Him with cold, loveless reason. God wills surcease for the heart but no surcease for the head; in the physical world the head finds rest and surcease at times, while the heart suffers travail. Pure knowledge without love separates us from God, while love, even without knowledge, and perhaps better without it, brings us to God, and through God, to wisdom. Blessed are the pure in heart, for they shall see God!

If I should be asked how I believe in God, that is, why I believe that God creates Himself and reveals Himself in me, I shall perchance scandalize my interlocutor, or make him smile, or laugh outright.

I believe in God as I believe in a friend, because I feel the breath of His affection and feel His invisible and intangible hand, drawing me, leading me, pressing my hand; I believe because I have an inner consciousness of a particular providence and of a universal mind which traces the course of my own destiny. But the concept of the law—nothing but a concept after all!—tells me nothing and teaches me nothing.

Several times in my life I have found myself on the edge of the abyss; several times I have found myself at a crossroads, confronted with a choice of ways and aware that in choosing one I would be renouncing all the others, for there is no turning back along the road of life, and each time in these unique moments I have felt the thrust of a conscious, sovereign, loving power. And then the way to the Lord opens before one.

A man can feel the Universe calling out to him and guiding him as one person does another, hear within him its voice speaking without words but saying: "Go ye therefore and teach all nations!" How do you know that the man you see before you possesses a consciousness like you, and that, more or less obscurely, so does an animal, while a stone does not? Because the man responds to you in a human way, in your own image, while the stone does not respond to you but merely endures your action. And thus do I conceive the Universe to possess a consciousness somewhat like my own, because it acts toward me in a human way, and I feel it environing me in a personal way.

Behold a formless mass; it seems a species of animal; I cannot make out any of its members; I see only two eyes, eyes that look at me with a human look, the look of a fellow being, a look which asks for compassion, and I hear a breathing. And I conclude that in this formless mass there is a consciousness. In just such a way and no other do the starry heavens look down upon the believer, with a superhuman, divine look, which asks him for supreme compassion and supreme love, and in the serenity of the night the believer hears the breathing of God, and he hears it in his heart of hearts, and God is revealed. It is the Universe living, suffering, loving, and asking for love.

From loving ephemeral matter which comes to us as it goes, without taking root, we come to love the more lasting things, the things we cannot grasp in our hands; from loving goods we come to love the Good; from beautiful objects to loving Beauty; from the true to loving Truth; from loving pleasure to loving Happiness; and finally we come to loving Love. We come out of ourselves in order to penetrate farther into our supreme I; individual consciousness emerges in order to submerge itself in the total Consciousness of which we form part, but it does so without dissolving itself. And God is nought but Love emanating from universal suffering and becoming consciousness.

But all this, we will be told, is merely to revolve

inside an iron ring, and we will also be told that such a God is not objective. At this point it would be well to grant reason its due and examine what it means for something to exist, to be objective.

What, in effect, does it mean to exist, and when can we say that something exists? Something exists when it is so placed outside ourselves that it precedes our perception of it and can subsist apart from us when we shall perish. But am I at all sure that anything preceded me or that anything will outlive me? Can my consciousness know that there is anything outside it? Whenever I know or can know anything, it is already in my consciousness. Let us not become ensnared, therefore, in the insoluble problem of another objectivity outside our perceptions; something exists when it acts, and to exist is to act.

But once again it will be said that it is not God, but the idea of God, which acts in us. And we shall reply that it is sometimes God as idea and rather very often directly as Himself that he acts in us. And the retort will be to demand proofs of the objective truth of the existence of God, since we ask for signs. And then we shall have to ask with Pilate: "What is truth?"

So he asked, in effect, and then, without waiting for an answer, he washed his hands of the matter to vindicate his having allowed Christ to be condemned to death. And many there are who ask, "What is truth?" And they have no intention of waiting for an answer, and ask only in order meanwhile to wash their hands of the crime of having contributed to killing God in their own consciousness or in those of others.

What is truth? There are two classes of truth, the logical or objective, whose opposite is error, and the

moral or subjective, the opposite of which is falsehood. In a previous essay I have endeavored to show
that error is the fruit of falsehood.

Moral truth, the road to the other truth—which is
also moral—teaches us to cultivate science, which
above all else is a school of sincerity and humility.
Science shows us, in effect, to submit our reason to
truth and to know and judge things as they are: that
is, as they choose to be, and not as we want them to
be. In any religiously scientific investigation, it is the
data of reality themselves, the perceptions we receive
from the outer world, which formulate themselves in
our minds as laws, and it is not we who formulate
them. It is the numbers themselves which in us are
translated into mathematics. And science is the most
exclusive school for resignation and humility, since it
teaches us to bow before the facts, however insignificant the facts may seem. And it is the portico, the
gateway to religion; but within the temple itself its
function ends.

And just as there is a logical truth to which error
is the opposite, and a moral truth to which falsehood
is the opposite, so there is also aesthetic truth or verisimilitude to which extravagance is the opposite, and
a religious truth or hope to which the disquiet of
absolute despair is the opposite. For neither aesthetic
verisimilitude, the truth which is demonstrated by
reason, nor religious truth, the truth of faith, the substance of what is hoped for, is equivalent to moral
truth, but moral truth is superimposed upon them.
Whoever affirms his faith upon a basis of uncertainty
does not and cannot lie.

And not only does one not believe with reason nor
above reason nor beneath reason—but one believes
against reason. Religious faith, it needs to be re-

peated once again, is not only irrational, it is contra-rational. Kierkegaard puts it thus:

> Poesy is the illusion which precedes the under-standing; religiosity, the illusion which comes after the understanding. Between poesy and religiosity, worldly wisdom presents its vaudeville perform-ance. Every individual who does not live either poet-ically or religiously is stupid.

The same writer tells us that Christianity is a "desperate way out." And so it is, but only through the desperation of this way out can we win through to hope, to that hope whose vitalizing illusion is more forceful than all rational knowledge and which assures us that there is always something irreducible to reason. The same thing may be said of reason as was said of Christ: he who is not with it is against it. Whatever is not rational is contra-rational. And such is hope.

By this circuitous route we always come, in the end, to hope.

The mystery of love, which is the mystery of suffering, is enveloped in a mysterious form, which is that of time. We join yesterday and today with links of anguish; "now" is not, strictly speaking, anything but "before" striving to be "after"; the present is noth-ing but the determination of the past to become the future. "Now" is a point which, if not sharply articu-lated, vanishes; and, nevertheless, all eternity, the substance of time, is contained in this point.

Whatever has been can now be only as it was, and what it is cannot be but what it is; the possible re-mains forever relegated to the future, the sole domain of liberty, where the imagination, the creative and liberating power, the flesh of faith, roams at will.

Love always looks and tends to the future, for its

role is to effect our perpetuation; the nature of love is to hope, and it nourishes itself solely on hope. And thus once love achieves its desire, its grows melancholy, for it thereupon finds that what it desired is not its true end but only what God had placed before it as a lure to impel it into action; it discovers that its end lies farther on, and it sets out again on its travail, on its whirling course of illusions and disillusions through life. And continually it builds up a store of memories from its truncated hopes, and from these memories draws fresh hopes. The quarry from which we extract the visions of our future is in the subterranean layers of memory; our imagination forges our hopes from our memories. And Humanity is like a young girl abounding with longing, hungering for life, and thirsting for love, a girl weaving her days out of dreams; and she waits and hopes ceaselessly for the eternal lover, predestined for her from before time, from long before her remotest memories, from the past before her cradle, for the day when he shall live with her and for her until beyond the beyond, beyond the stretch of her farthest imaginings, until beyond the tomb and its future. And for poor love-lorn humanity, as for the girl ever awaiting her lover, there is no more charitable a wish than that the green hopes of springtime be converted in the winter of life into even greener memories capable of engendering new hopes. In the winter days of our shorter sunlight, what a savor of calm felicity, of resignation to destiny, should flow from our recollection of hopes never yet realized and conserving thus the purity of the unrealized!

Love hopes, waits and hopes without wearying ever of hoping, and the love of God, our faith in God, is before all else hope in Him. For God does not die, and whoever waits and hopes in God shall live forever. And our fundamental hope, the root and stem of all our hopes, is the hope of eternal life.

And if faith is the substance of hope, hope is in turn the form of faith. Faith, before it gives us hope, is a formless faith, vague, chaotic, potential, no more than the possibility of believing, a longing to believe. But we must believe in something, and we believe in what we hope, we believe in hope. We remember the past, we know the present, we believe only in the future. To believe in what we have not seen is to believe in what we will see. Faith, then, I repeat, is faith in hope; we believe in what we hope.

Love impels us to believe in God, in whom we hope, and from whom we hope for a future life; love causes us to believe in what the dreams of hope have engendered in us.

Faith is our longing for the eternal, for God, and hope is the longing of God in us, of the eternal in us, of the divine in us which joins to meet our faith and to raise us above ourselves. Man aspires to God through faith and cries out: "Lord, I believe; give me the something to believe in!" And God, the divinity in man, sends him hope in another life so that he may believe in that. Hope is the reward of faith. Only the man who believes truly hopes, and only whoever truly hopes believes. We only believe what we hope, and we only hope what we believe.

It was hope which gave God the name of Father, and it is hope which still gives Him that consoling and mysterious name. Our father gave us life and the substance to maintain us, and we ask that our father continue to sustain us. And if it was Christ who with the fullest heart and the purest mouth called by the name of Father His Father and ours, if Christianity is heightened by the feeling of the Fatherhood of God, it is because in Christ the human race sublimated its hunger for eternity.

It may perhaps be said that this longing of faith, this hope, is more than anything else an aesthetic feeling. Doubtless aesthetics enters into the matter, but it does not fully satisfy the impulse.

We do, in effect, seek for an image of eternalization in art. If our spirit finds quiet and surcease for the moment in beauty, though its longing is not thereby assuaged, it is because beauty is a revelation of the eternal, of the divinity in things, and simply a perpetuation of momentaneity. Just as truth is the goal of rational knowledge, so beauty is the goal of hope, perhaps irrational in its essence.

Nothing is lost, nothing wholly passes away, for in some way or another everything is perpetuated; and everything, after passing through time, returns to eternity. The temporal world has its roots in eternity, and there, in eternity, yesterday is joined to today and tomorrow. Scenes pass before our eyes as in a cinema, but there is an integral film beyond time.

Physicists affirm that not a particle of matter nor a tremor of energy is lost, but that each is transformed and transmitted and persists. And can any form whatsoever, however ephemeral it may be, be lost? We must believe—believe and hope!—that it is not, but that somewhere it remains and is perpetuated, and that there is a mirror of eternity in which, clear and sharp, all the images passing through time are reflected. Every impression which impinges on me remains stored in my brain even though it may be so deep or so weak that it be buried in the depths of my subconsciousness; still, from there it animates my life; and if the whole of my spirit, the total content of my soul, were to awake to full consciousness, all these dimly perceived and forgotten fugitive impressions would come to life again, including those of which I had never been aware. I carry within me everything that has passed before me and I perpetuate it all in myself, and perhaps it is carried in my germ plasm, and perhaps my ancestors live undiminished in me and will continue to live on, and they will live on, together with me, in my descendants. And perhaps I, the whole of me, with all this universe of mine, go into each of my actions, or, at least, the essential part of me, the essence which makes me be myself, my individual essence, goes into each action.

And how is this individual essence of each thing, that which makes it itself and not another, revealed to us save as beauty? What is the beauty of anything but its eternal essence, that which unites its past with its future, that element of it which remains and abides in the matrix of history? Or, rather, what is beauty in anything but the revelation of its divinity?

And this beauty, which is the root of eternity, is revealed to us by love; it is the supreme revelation of the love of God and the sign of our ultimate victory over time. It is love which reveals to us the eternal in ourselves and in our fellows.

Is it the beautiful, the eternal in things, which awakens and kindles our love for them, or is it our love for things which reveals to us the beautiful, the eternal, in them? Is not beauty perhaps a creation of love, in the same way and in the same sense that the sensible world is a creation of the instinct for preservation and the supersensible world a creation of the instinct for perpetuation? Is not beauty and eternity, too, a creation of love? "Though our outward man perish," says the Apostle, "yet the inward man is renewed day by day" (2 Cor. 4:16). The man of passing appearances is consumed and passes with them; but the man of true reality remains and grows. "For our light affliction, which is but for a moment, worketh for us a far more exceeding and eternal weight of glory" (17). Our suffering causes us anguish, and this anguish, bursting from fullness, comes to us as a consolation. "While we look not at the things which are seen, but at the things which are not seen: for the things which are seen are temporal; but the things which are not seen are eternal" (18).

This suffering yields up hope, which is the beautiful in life, the supreme beauty, or the supreme consolation. And since love is full of suffering, it is compassion and pity, and beauty springs from compassion and is simply the temporal consolation that compassion seeks. A tragic consolation! And the supreme beauty is that of tragedy. In our anguish at the knowledge that everything passes away, that we ourselves pass away, and that everything which surrounds us passes away, we find that anguish itself reveals to us the consolation of what does not pass away: the eternal, the beautiful.

And the beauty thus revealed, the perpetuation of momentaneity, only realizes itself in practice, only lives through the workings of charity. Hope in action is charity, and beauty in action is goodness.

*   *   *

Charity, which eternalizes everything it loves and brings to light its hidden beauty, proffering thus its good, has its root in the love of God, or, if you like, in charity toward God, pity for God. Love, compassion, personalizes everything, we have said; in its discovery of the suffering inherent in all and in personalizing everything, love personalizes the Universe itself as well, for the Universe also suffers, and love discovers God in us. For God is revealed to us because He suffers and because we suffer; because He suffers he requires our love, and because we suffer He gives us His love, and He envelops our anguish with the eternal and infinite anguish.

All this constituted the scandal of Christianity among the Jews and Greeks, among the Pharisees and the Stoics, and this ancient scandal, the scandal of the Cross, is still its scandal and will continue to be so, even among Christians: the scandal of a God who becomes man in order that He may suffer and die, and rise again because He has suffered and died, the scandal of a God who suffers and dies. And this truth, the truth that God suffers, a truth which appalls the mind of man, is the revelation emerging from the very matrix and mystery of the Universe, revealed to us when God sent His Son so that He might redeem us by suffering and dying. It was the revelation of the divinity of suffering, for only that which suffers is divine.

And men made a god of Christ, who suffered, and through Him they discovered the eternal essence of a living, human God, that is, of a God who suffers— only what is dead, inhuman, does not suffer—a God who loves, who thirsts for love and compassion, and who is a person. Whoever does not know the Son will never know the Father, and the Father is known only through His Son. Whoever does not know the Son of man, the Son who suffers blood anguish and heart torment, who lives with a sadness of soul until death, who suffers the pain which kills and brings back to life, will never know the Father, nor will know forbearing God.

The God who does not suffer, and does not suffer because he does not live, is the logical and frozen *ens realissimum*, the *primum movens*, that impassive entity, which because of its impassivity is nothing but a pure idea. The category does not suffer, but neither does it live or exist as a person. And how is the world to derive its origin and life from an impassive idea? Such a world would merely be the idea of a world. But the world suffers, and suffering means to sense the flesh of reality; it is to sense the mass and substance of the spirit; it is to palpate oneself; it is immediate reality.

Suffering is the substance of life and the root of personality, for only suffering makes us persons. And suffering is universal; all living beings are united by suffering, the universal or divine blood which flows through us all. Will, what we call will, what is it but suffering?

And suffering has its degrees, in accord with its depth: from the suffering which floats upon the sea of appearances to the eternal anguish, the source of the tragic sense of life, which comes to rest in the depths of the eternal and there arouses consolation; from the physical suffering which racks our body to the religious anguish which throws us upon the bosom of God, there to be restored by the water of His divine tears.

Anguish is something far deeper, more intimate and more spiritual than suffering. We often feel the touch of anguish even in the midst of what we call happiness, and even because of this happiness itself, to which we cannot quite resign ourselves and before which we tremble. Those happy men who yield to their apparent good luck, an ephemeral good fortune, seem like men without any substance, or, at least, men who have not found their own essence, who have not palpated it. Such men are usually incapable of loving or of being loved, and they go through life without any inner meaning.

True love does not exist apart from suffering, and in this world we must choose either love, which is suffering, or happiness. And love leads us to no happiness apart from love itself and its tragic consolation in uncertain hope. The moment love is equated with happiness, it is satisfied—and is no longer love. The satisfied, the happy ones, do not love; they fall asleep in habit, near neighbor to annihilation. To fall into habit is to begin to cease to be. Man is all the more man, that is, all the more divine, the greater his capacity for suffering, or better, for anguish.

In this world we are given the choice between love and happiness, and—poor fools!—we want both: the happiness of loving and the love of happiness. But we should ask for love rather than happiness, for the latter allows us to doze off into habit, and then we may fall asleep altogether and, without ever waking, lose consciousness forever. We should ask God to make us conscious of ourselves in ourselves, in our suffering.

What is Fate, what is Fatality, but the brotherhood of love and suffering? What is it but the terrible mystery wherein love dies as soon as it touches the very happiness toward which it reaches and wherein true happiness dies then too? Love and suffering mutually engender one another; and love is charity and compassion, and love that is not charitable and complaisant is not love. Love, in short, is resigned despair.

What mathematicians call the problem of maxima and minima, also called the law of economy, is the formula for all existential, that is, passional, activity. In material mechanics and in social mechanics, in industry and in political economy, the problem as a whole reduces itself to an attempt to obtain the greatest possible useful result with the least possible effort, the greatest income with the least expenditure, the most pleasure with the least pain. And the terrible and tragic formula of the inner, spiritual life is to obtain either the most happiness with the least love or the most love with the least happiness. And a choice must be made between the one and the other. And it must be clear that whoever approaches the infinite of love, the love which is infinite, approaches the zero of happiness, the supreme anguish. And in reaching this zero, he puts himself beyond the wretchedness which kills. "Be nought, and thou shalt be more than aught that is," said Fray Juan de los Angeles in one of his *Diálogos de la conquista del reino de Dios.*

And there is something still more anguished than suffering.

There was a man awaiting a much dreaded attack, which he expected would fell him with pain, and when the blow came he scarcely felt it; but later, when he came to his senses and felt nothing, he was overcome with terror, and cried out, choking with anguish: "Do I exist at all?" What would terrify you most: to feel pain which would deprive you of your senses as a white-hot iron pierced you, or to find yourself pierced and feel no pain whatever? Have you never felt the fright, the terrible fright, of finding yourself incapable of tears and suffering? Suffering tells us we exist; suffering tells us those who love exist; suffering tells us the world we live in exists, and suffering tells us that God exists and suffers; and this is the suffering of anguish, the anguish to survive and be eternal. It is anguish which reveals God to us and makes us place our love in Him.

To believe in God means to love Him, and to love Him is to sense His suffering and have compassion for Him.

It may perhaps appear blasphemous to say that God suffers, for suffering implies limitation. Nevertheless, God, the Conscience and Consciousness of the Universe, is limited by brute matter around Him, by the unconscious, from which He seeks to liberate Himself and to liberate us. And we, in turn, must seek to liberate Him. God suffers in each and all of us, in each and every consciousness imprisoned in ephemeral matter, and we all suffer in Him. Religious anguish is nought but divine suffering, the feeling that God suffers in me and that I suffer in Him.

Universal suffering is the anguish of all, seeking to be all else, fruitlessly, the anguish of each to be himself and at the same time to be all that he is not, and to be all forever. The essence of a being is not only the endeavor to persist forever, as Spinoza taught us, but also the endeavor to become universal; it is a hunger and thirst for eternity and for infinity. Every created being tends not only to preserve itself in itself, but to perpetuate itself, and, moreover, to encroach upon all else, to be all others without ceasing to be itself, to extend its limits to infinity, but yet without breaking them down. It does not wish to demolish its walls, and thus lay everything flat, communal, defenseless, confounding and losing its own identity, but wishes to push its walls to the extreme limits of creation and to encompass everything within them. It seeks the maximum of individuality with the maximum also of personality; it aspires to identify itself with the Universe, it aspires to God.

And this vast I, within which each individual I seeks to situate the Universe—what is it but God? And because I aspire to God, I love Him, and my aspiration toward God is my love for Him, and just as I suffer because I am He, He also suffers because He is I and each one of us.

I am well aware that despite my warning that I am attempting here to give a logical form to a system of a-logical feelings, that I shall be scandalizing not a few readers in speaking of a forbearing God who suffers, and in applying to God Himself, *qua* God, the passion of Christ. The God of so-called rational theology in effect excludes all suffering. And the reader will no doubt think that this idea of suffering can have only a metaphorical value when applied to God, similar to that supposed to attach to those passages in the Old Testament which describe the human passions of the God of Israel. Anger, wrath, vengeance are impossible without suffering. And as regards the idea of God suffering through being bound by matter, I shall be told that, in the words of Plotinus: "The Soul of the Universe cannot be in bond to what [bodies or matter] itself has bound."

Herein is involved the whole problem of the origin of evil, the evil of sin no less than the evil of pain, for if God does not suffer, He causes suffering, and if His life—for God lives—is not a process of realizing in Himself a total consciousness continually becoming fuller, that is, continually becoming more and more God, then it is a process of drawing all things toward Himself, of imparting Himself to all, of causing the consciousness of each part to enter into the consciousness of the all, which is He Himself, until at last He comes to be all in all, πάντα ἐν πᾶσι, according to the expression of St. Paul, the first Christian. We will discuss this question more fully in the next chapter, in dealing with the *apocatastasis*, or beatific union.

For the present let us say that a vast current of suffering impels living beings toward one another and binds them to love each other and seek each other out and strive to complete each other, each one remaining an individual and all others at the same time. In God everything lives, and in His suffering everything suffers, and in loving God we love all creatures in Him, just as in loving and pitying all creatures we love and pity God in them. The soul of each one of us will not be free so long as anything is enslaved in God's world; neither can God Himself, who lives in the soul of each one of us, be free so long as our soul is not free.

My most immediate feeling is to sense and love my own wretchedness and bane; to feel compassion for myself, and to hold to my love of myself. And when this compassion is vital and overflowing, it flows from me to others, and out of the excess of my own self-compassion, I feel compassion for my fellows. My own bane is so great that the compassion rising in me soon goes beyond me and reveals to me the universal woe.

And what is charity but an overflow of compassion? What is it but reflected sorrow, which brims over and pours itself out in a flood of compassion for the woe of others and in the exercise of charity?

When the force of our compassion drives us to a

consciousness of God within ourselves, we are so anguished by the divine woefulness of all life that we
must pour forth our feeling, and do so in the form
of charity. And thus we find surcease and the sweet
sorrow of the good. Teresa of Jesus, the mystical doctor, called it "sweet-tasting dolor," and she knew the
nature of dolorous love. Similarly, when we regard
something beautiful, we are possessed with a desire
to share the experience with others. For the creative
impulse, which is also a matter of charity, is the work
of dolorous love.

In effect, we feel satisfaction in good works when
the good abounds in us to superfluity, when we
abound in charity; and we abound in charity when
God, surfeiting our souls, imparts the dolorous sensation of universal life, of the universal longing for the
eternally divine. For we are not merely placed side
by side with others in the world, without common
root, nor is their lot a matter of indifference to us,
but rather the fact is that their pain hurts us, their
anguish moves us to anguish, and we feel our community of origin and of sorrow even without knowing it. Suffering and the compassion born of it reveal
to us the fellowship of all living beings possessing
some degree of consciousness. St. Francis of Assisi
addressed the poor wolf painfully hungering after
sheep, and, perhaps also painfully anticipating having to eat them, by the name "Brother Wolf"; and
this fellowship reveals the fatherhood of God, reveals
that God is Father and as such exists; and as Father
He shelters us in our common woe.

Charity, then, is the impulse to liberate myself and
all my fellows from suffering and to liberate God,
who embraces us all.

Suffering is a spiritual matter and the most immediate revelation of consciousness, and it may be that our body was not given us except as a means to suffering. Whoever had never suffered, much or little, would have no consciousness of himself. The first cry of man, at birth, is when the air floods into his chest, limiting him, and it seems to say: "You will have to breathe me in order to live!"

We must believe with faith, whatever reason teaches, that the material or sensible world created for us by the senses exists solely to embody and sustain the other world, the spiritual or imaginable world which the imagination creates for us. Consciousness tends to be ever more conscious, to intensify its consciousness, to acquire full consciousness of its complete self, of its whole content. We must believe with faith, whatever reason teaches, that in the depths of our own bodies, in animals, in plants, in rocks, in everything alive, in the entire Universe, there is a spirit that strives to know itself, to acquire consciousness of itself, to be itself—for to be oneself is to know oneself—and thus to be pure spirit; and since it can only achieve its goal by means of the body, by means of matter, it creates and makes use of matter while at the same time it remains its prisoner. One sees one's face only as outlined in a mirror; but in order to see oneself one is a prisoner of the mirror in which one sees oneself, and one sees oneself in the measure of the mirror's distortion; and if the mirror breaks, the image is broken, and if the mirror clouds over, one's image is clouded.

Spirit finds itself limited by the matter in which it must live and acquire consciousness of itself, just as thought is limited by the word, which is its social embodiment. Without matter there is no spirit, but matter limits spirit and causes it to suffer. And suffering is simply the obstacle which matter opposes to spirit; it is the clash of the conscious with the unconscious.

Suffering, in effect, is the barrier which unconsciousness, that is, matter, sets up against consciousness, against the spirit; it is the resistance to will, the limit which the visible universe sets to God, it is the wall up against which consciousness runs whenever it strives to impose itself upon unconsciousness, it is the resistance which unconsciousness offers to its being brought into consciousness.

Although we may accept the fact from superior authority, we do not really know we possess a heart, stomach, or lungs until they pain us, or oppress us, or cause us anguish. It is physical suffering, or even discomfort, which reveals the existence of our inner being. And the same is true of spiritual suffering and anguish, for we do not realize we possess a soul until we feel its hurt.

Anguish causes consciousness to turn back to itself. A man without anguish may know what he does and what he thinks, but he does not really know that he does it or that he thinks it. He thinks, but he does not think he thinks, and his thoughts are as if they were not his own. And he himself does not belong to himself. For it is only anguish, only the passionate longing never to die, which makes a human spirit master of itself.

Suffering, which is a form of dissolution, causes us to discover our inner being; and in the supreme dissolution, which is death, we shall, through the suffering of annihilation, reach the core of our temporal matrix, which is God, whom we breathe and learn to love in our spiritual anguish.

Thus must we believe, with faith, whatever reason teaches.

The origin of evil, as many men discovered of old, is nothing but what is also called the inertia of matter, or, as applied to the spirit, sloth. And it was well said that sloth is the mother of all vice. Nor should we forget that the supreme sloth consists in failing to long madly for immortality.

Consciousness, the appetite for more and more, always more, the hunger for eternity and the thirst for infinity, the craving for God—none of these is ever satisfied. Each consciousness seeks to be itself and to be all others as well without ceasing to be itself: it seeks to be God. And matter, unconsciousness, tends to become less and less, tends toward nothingness, its thirst being for a state of rest. Spirit exclaims: "I want to be!"; matter answers: "I want not to be!"

And in the order of human life, the individual, moved by the mere instinct of preservation, which is the creator of the material world, would find himself heading toward destruction, toward nothingness, if it were not for society, which, instilling him with the instinct of perpetuation, which is the creator of the spiritual world, carries and impels him toward the All, toward self-immortalization. And everything man does as an individual, in confrontation with society, for the sake of his own preservation even at the expense of society, is bad; and everything he does as a social person, for the sake of the society of which he is part, for the sake of its perpetuation and for his own preservation in it, is good. And many of those who seem great egoists, trampling everything underfoot to reach self-achievement, are in reality ardent souls aflame with charity, highly endowed with it, since they subordinate and subject their petty I to the social I which has a mission to achieve.

Whoever links the workings of love, of spirituality, of liberation, to ephemeral and individual forms, crucifies God in matter; whoever makes the ideal serve his temporal interests or worldly glory crucifies God in matter. And such a person is a deicide.

The workings of charity, of the love of God, is to endeavor to liberate God from brute matter, to endeavor to spiritualize and universalize everything, to make it conscious; it is to dream that rocks will come to speak and to act in accord with this dream; it is to dream that everything in existence shall become conscious, to dream that the word may come alive.

We need only observe the instance of the Eucharist. There the Word has been imprisoned in a piece of material bread, and it has been imprisoned so that we may eat it, and in eating make it our own, part of this our body in which the spirit dwells, and thus beat in our heart and think in our brain and become consciousness. It has been imprisoned in this bread so that, buried in our body, it may resurrect in our spirit.

The fact is we must spiritualize everything. And we do this by giving our spirit, which grows the more it gives, to all men and all things. And to give the spirit means to invade the spirits of others and become their proprietor.

And all this we must believe with faith, whatever reason teaches.

*   *   *

And now we shall go on to see the practical consequences of all these more or less imaginative doctrines in relation to logic, aesthetics, and, above all, ethics, their religious concretion. And perhaps then my words will find more justification in the eyes of whoever has been seeking in these pages, despite my warnings, for a scientific or even philosophical development of an irrational system.

I think it may not be inappropriate to refer the reader, once again, to my conclusions at the end of Chapter VI, "In the Depths of the Abyss." And now we are approaching the practical or pragmatic part of this treatise. But first we must examine how the religious sense may find a concrete objectivation in the vision of hope in another life.

X. Religion, *Mythology of the Beyond, and Apocatastasis*

Καὶ γὰρ ἴσως καὶ μάλιστα πρέπει μέλλοντα ἔχεισε
ἀποδημεῖν διασκοπεῖν τε καὶ μυθολογεῖν περὶ τῆς
ἔχει, ποίαν τινὰ αὐτὴν οἰόμεθα εἶναι.

"I suppose that for one who is soon to leave
this world there is no more suitable occupation
than inquiring into our views about the future
life, and trying to imagine what it is like."

Plato, *Phaedo*

RELIGION IS FOUNDED on the sense of divinity and
of God, and on the faith, hope and charity in turn
founded on this sense. Faith in man is born of faith
in God, hope in men from hope in God, and charity
toward men from charity or piety toward God: as
Cicero said, *Est enim pietas iustitia adversum deos*,
"Piety is justice toward the gods." God is the sum not
only of Humanity, but of the whole Universe, the
Universe spiritualized and interpenetrated; Christian
faith tells us that God shall at last be all in all. St.
Teresa said, and Miguel de Molinos more stridently
and despairingly repeated: the soul must realize that
nothing exists but itself and God.

And this relation with God, this more or less close
union with Him, we call religion.

Yet what is religion? How does it differ from the
religious sense and how are the two related? Every
man's definition of religion is based on his own inner
experience of it rather than upon his observation of

it in others, and it is impossible to define it without in one way or another experiencing it. Tacitus, speaking of the Jews, said that they regarded everything the Romans held sacred to be profane and that what they considered sacred was to the Romans profane: *Profana illic omnis quae apud nos sacra, rursum concessa apud illos quae nobis incesta.* And thus it was that he, the Roman, should speak of the Jews as people given to superstition and refractory to religion: *gens superstitioni obnoxia, religionibus adversa,* and when he comes to consider Christianity, which he knew poorly and which he scarcely differentiated from Judaism, he deemed it a most mischievous superstition, *exitiabilis superstitio,* stemming from a hatred for the human race, *odium generis humani.* Thus Tacitus, and thus many like him. But where does religion end and superstition begin, or, perhaps better, where does superstition end and religion begin? What criterion should we use to distinguish between them?

It would be of little profit to recapitulate, even summarily, the main definitions given, in accord with the feelings of each definer, of what constitutes religion. Religion is better described than defined, and better sensed than described. But if any one definition has latterly obtained some currency it has been Schleiermacher's, to the effect that religion consists in the simple sense of a dependent relationship upon something superior to us and of a desire to establish relations with this mysterious power. And Herrmann's statement (in the work already cited) that the religious longing of man is a desire for the truth about his human existence. To cut short these extraneous testimonials, I will end with a citation from the judicious and perspicacious Cournot: "Religious manifestations

237*

are the necessary consequence of man's predisposition to believe in the existence of an invisible, supernatural, and miraculous world, a predisposition which it has been possible to consider sometimes as a reminiscence of a previous state, sometimes as an intimation of a future destiny." And now we come to the problem of human destiny, of eternal life, that is, of the human finality of the Universe or of God. We come to this point by all the highways of religion, for it is the very essence of all religion.

Beginning with the savage's personalization of the entire Universe by means of his fetish, religion has its roots in the vital necessity of investing the Universe, God, with a human finality, and this necessity involves attributing a consciousness of self and of finality to the Universe, to God. And we may possibly say that religion is nought but union with God, with God sensed in the manner that each man senses Him. God lends a transcendent meaning and finality to life; but He gives it in relation to each one who believes in Him. And thus God is for man as much as man is for God, since God gave Himself to man in becoming man, in making Himself human for love of man.

And the religious longing for union with God is a longing not consummated either through science or through art, but through life. "Whoever has science and art has religion; whoever has neither—let him have religion," said Goethe in one of his frequent accesses of paganism. And yet, whatever he said, what of Goethe, the man?

And to wish to be united with God is not to wish to be lost and submerged in Him; for this loss and submersion of self ends in complete dissolution in the dreamless sleep of Nirvana; it is a wish to possess

Him rather than to be possessed by Him. When the disciples of Jesus heard how it was humanly impossible for a rich man to enter the kingdom of heaven, they asked who then could be saved, and the Master replied that it was impossible for men but not for God. And Peter said: "Behold we have forsaken all and followed thee; what shall we have therefore?" And Jesus replied, not that they would be absorbed in the Father, but that they should sit upon twelve thrones, judging the twelve tribes of Israel (Matt. 19:23-28).

It was a Spaniard, very much a Spaniard, Miguel de Molinos, who said in his *Guía espiritual*, that "Whoever would attain to the mystical science must abandon and be detached from five things. First, from creatures; second, from temporal things; third, from the very grace of the Holy Spirit; fourth, from himself; and fifth, he must be detached even from God Himself." And he adds that "the last is the most perfect, for the soul which thus knows how to detach itself is the one which attains to being lost in God, and only the soul which succeeds in losing itself succeeds in finding itself." Molinos was, indeed, very Spanish, and so was his paradoxical expression of quietism or rather of nihilism—for he himself speaks elsewhere of annihilation—but no less Spanish, and perhaps even more Spanish, were the Jesuits who opposed him, when they upheld the prerogatives of All against Nothingness. For religion is not the longing for self-annihilation, but for completion, a longing for life and not for death. The "eternal religion of man's essence . . . the individual dream of the heart, is the worship of his own being, the adoration of life," as the tortured Flaubert sensed.

When at the beginning of the so-called Modern

Age, at the Renaissance, the pagan sense of religion
came to life again, it took concrete form in the knightly ideal with its codes of love and honor. But it was
a Christianized paganism, a paganism baptized.

> Woman was the divinity of the rough hearts of
> that age. If we look among the contemporary rec-
> ords we find this ideal in its purity and its omnip-
> otence: the universe was Woman. The same ideal
> prevailed in the beginnings of modern society in
> Germany, France, Provence, Spain, and Italy. And
> history too was made of knightly images: Trojans
> and Romans were wandering knights, together with
> Arabs, Saracens, Turks, the Sultan, and Saladin. . . .
> In the same fraternity were put angels, saints, mira-
> cles, and Paradise, all strangely intermixed with the
> fantastic and voluptuous world of the East, and all
> baptized with the same name of "chivalry."

Thus in his *Storia della letteratura italiana*, writes
Francesco de Sanctis, who in an earlier passage tells
us that "Even in Paradise a lover's joy is the contemplation of his lady; if she be absent, 'non vi vorria
gire' ('he would not care to walk in it')." What, in
effect, was Chivalry—which Cervantes, intending to
laugh it away, went on to purify and Christianize in
Don Quixote—but a truly prodigious religion, a hy-
brid of paganism and Christianity, whose Gospel was
perhaps the legend of Tristan and Iseult? And did not
even the Christianity of the mystics—those knights-
errant of the spirit—possibly culminate in the cult of
the divine woman, the cult of the Virgin Mother?
What else was the Mariolatry of a St. Bonaventura,
the troubadour of Mary? And this inspiration was
love for the source of life, which saves us from death.

But as the Renaissance advanced, men turned from
the religion of women to the religion of science; desire, which is essentially a matter of curiosity, was

reduced to its essence, to the longing to taste of the fruit of the Tree of Good and Evil. All Europe converged on the University of Bologna in search of learning. Chivalry was followed by Platonism. Men sought to discover the mystery of the world and of life. But it was really in order to save life, which they had also sought to save in the worship of woman. Human consciousness sought to penetrate the Universal Consciousness, but its real object, whether it was aware of it or not, was to save itself.

For the truth is that we do not feel or imagine Universal Consciousness—and this feeling and imagination constitute religiosity—except as a way of saving our own individual consciousness. How?

Again I am forced to repeat that the longing for the soul's immortality, for the permanence in one form or another of our personal and individual consciousness, is as much of the essence of religion as is the longing that God may exist. The one emotion does not exist apart from the other, and that is because they are one and the same thing. But as soon as we strive to give a concrete and rational form to this basic longing, to define it for ourselves, we encounter even more difficulties than we encountered in attempting to rationalize God.

Universal consensus has been invoked to justify to our own feeble reason this immortal longing for immortality: "Permanere animos arbitramur consensu nationum omnium," said Cicero, echoing the opinion of the ancients. But this same observer of his own feelings confessed that although while he was reading the arguments in favor of the immortality of the soul in Plato's *Phaedo* he assented to them, as soon as he put down the book and began to consider the problem in his mind, all his acquiescence vanished: *assentio*

241*

omnis illa illabitur. And just as with Cicero, so with the rest of us; and so it was with Swedenborg, that most intrepid visionary of the other world. Swedenborg confessed that whoever speaks of life after death without learned cogitations about the soul or its mode of reunion with the body must be a person disposed to believe that after death he will live on in grand fruition and vision, a man among angels; but as soon as such a person begins to reflect upon the doctrine of the reunion of the soul with the body, or upon theories about the soul, doubts arise about its nature, and when this happens, his former idea is dissipated. "Because," as Cournot says, "what affects me, what disquiets me, what consoles me, what moves me to self-sacrifice and abnegation, is the kind of destiny which awaits me, *me* or *my person*, whatever may be the origin, the nature, the essence of that imperceptible bond, without which the philosophers are pleased to decide that my person will evanesce."

Must we then accept the pure and naked truth in an eternal life without attempting to represent it to ourselves? Such a course is impossible; it is not acceptable to us. And yet there are those who call themselves Christians and leave this attempt at representation to one side. Pick up any book or other of the most enlightened Protestantism, that is, of the most rationalistic and liberal nature; examine, for instance, the *Dogmatik* of Dr. Julius Kaftan, a book in whose 668 pages (in the 1909 Sixth Edition) only one page, the last, is concerned with this question. And in this page, after the affirmation is made that Christ is more or less the beginning and middle and also the end-purpose of History, and that those who are in Christ will attain to the life of plenitude, the eternal life of those who are in Christ, there is not a single word concerning what that life may be. There are a half-dozen words at most about eternal death, that is about hell, "for its existence is demanded by the moral character of faith and of Christian hope." Its moral character, now, is it? Not its religious character, for as far as I am aware the latter knows no such exigency. The whole attitude is one of prudent agnostic parsimony.

Yes, the prudent, the rational, and, some will say, the pious attitude is not to seek to penetrate into mysteries veiled to our knowledge, is not to insist upon shaping a plastic representation of eternal glory such as that of a *Divina Commedia*. True faith, true Christian piety, we shall be told, consists in having confidence that God, by the grace of Christ, will, in some way or another, make us live in Him, in His Son; and that, inasmuch as our destiny lies in His almighty hands, we should deliver ourselves into His hands in the assurance that He will do with us whatever is best for the ultimate purpose of life, of the spirit and of the Universe. Such is the teaching that has come down through the centuries, and most especially from the period between Luther and Kant.

Nevertheless, men have not ceased endeavoring to imagine to themselves what this eternal life may be, nor will they cease in their endeavors so long as they are men and not merely thinking machines. There are books of theology—or of whatever it may be called—full of disquisitions upon the conditions in which the blessed live in paradise, upon the manner of their bliss, and upon the properties of the glorious body. In short, it is impossible to conceive of the soul without some form of body.

The indestructible vitality of doctrines such as spiritualism, metempsychosis, the transmigration of souls through the stars, and other such beliefs, must reflect in large measure this very necessity, a real necessity to create for ourselves a concrete representation of what the other life might be like. These doctrines, however often they may be pronounced defunct and superseded, continually recur in other more or less new forms. And it would be notably inattentive to overlook such doctrines and not to seek their permanent substance. Man will never willingly renounce his attempt to create a concrete representation of the other life.

But is an eternal and endless life after death perhaps even thinkable? What can the life of a disembodied spirit be like? How can we conceive of such a spirit? How can we conceive of a pure consciousness without a corporal organism? Descartes divided the world into thought and extension, a dualism which was imposed upon him by the Christian dogma of the immortality of the soul. But: is it extension, matter, which thinks and is spiritualized, or is it thought which is extended and materialized? The gravest questions of metaphysics arise practically out of our desire to arrive at an understanding of the possibility of our immortality—and because of this fact they derive their value and cease merely to be the idle discussions of fruitless curiosity. For the truth is that metaphysics has no value save insofar as it attempts to explain how our vital longing can or cannot be satisfied. And thus it is that there is and always will be a rational metaphysic and a vital metaphysic, in perennial conflict with each other, the one with the notion of cause as point of departure, the other departing from the notion of substance.

And even if we were to succeed in imagining personal immortality, might we not possibly feel it to be something no less terrible than its negation? "The grief of Calypso for the departure of Ulysses would admit of no comfort; and she regretted her immortality," writes the gentle, the mystical Fénelon at the beginning of his *Télémaque*. Did not the damnation of the ancient gods, as well as that of the demons, consist in their inability to commit suicide?

When Jesus took Peter and James and John up into a high mountain and was transfigured before them, his raiment shining as white as snow, and Moses and Elias appeared and talked to him, Peter said to Him: "Master, it is good for us to be here; and let us make three tabernacles; one for thee and one for Moses and one for Elias," for he wished to eternalize the moment. And as they came down from the mountain, Jesus charged them that they should tell no man what they had seen until the Son of Man was risen from the dead. "And they kept that saying with themselves, questioning one with another what the rising from the dead should mean" (Mark 9:10), like men who do not understand. And a little later Jesus met the man whose son was possessed by "a dumb spirit," and the father cried out "Lord, I believe; help thou mine unbelief" (9:24).

Those three apostles did not understand the meaning of rising from the dead. And neither did those Sadducees who asked, speaking of a woman who had seven brothers for husband, "In the resurrection whose wife shall she be of the seven? for they all had her" (Matt. 22:28); whereupon Jesus told them that "God is not the God of the dead, but of the living" (22:32). And the other life is not, in fact, thinkable for us except in the same forms as those of this earthly and transitory life. Nor is the mystery at all clarified by the metaphor of the grain and the wheat which it bears, which was Paul's answer to the question "How are the dead raised up, and with what body do they come?" (1 Cor. 15:35).

How can a human soul live and enjoy God eternally without losing its individual personality, that is, without losing itself? What is the enjoyment of God? What is eternity as opposed to time? Does the soul change or does it not change in the other life? If it does not change, how does it live? And if it changes, how does it preserve its individuality through so vast a period of time? For though the other life may exclude space, it cannot exclude time, as Cournot observes in the work quoted above.

If there is life in heaven, there is change. Swedenborg observed that the angels change, because the delight of the celestial life would gradually lose its value if they always enjoyed it in its fullness, and because angels, like men, love themselves, and he who loves himself experiences changes of state; and he adds that at times the angels are sad, and that he, Swedenborg, conversed with some of them when they were sad. In any case, it is impossible for us to conceive of life without change, change as growth or as decline, as sadness or as joy, as love or as hate.

An eternal life is unthinkable; an eternal life of absolute felicity, of beatific vision, is more unthinkable still.

And what precisely is this beatific vision? In the first place, we must note that it is called vision and not action, assuming thus something passive. And does not this beatific vision presuppose loss of personal consciousness? A saint in heaven, says Bossuet, is a being who is scarcely sensible of himself, so completely is he possessed by God and immersed in His glory. . . . One cannot keep one's attention fixed upon him, for he is only to be found outside himself and

subject to an immutable love for the source of his being and his felicity. And all these are the words of
Bossuet, the anti-quietist. This loving vision of God
supposes an absorption in Him. He who in a state of
beatitude enjoys God in His fullness must perforce
not think of himself, not remember himself, nor have
any consciousness of himself, but be in a perpetual
ecstasy—ἔκστασις—outside himself, in a condition of
alienation. And the ecstasy that the mystics describe
is a prelude to this vision.

He who sees God shall die, say the Scriptures
(Judg. 13:22); and may not the eternal vision of
God be an eternal death, an evanescence of the personality? Yet St. Teresa, in her description of the last
state of prayer, the rapture, transport, flight or ecstasy
of the soul, tells us that the soul is borne as upon a
cloud or a powerful eagle, and "you see yourself carried away, knowing not whither," borne away "with
delight," and, "if you do not resist, the senses are not
lost, at least I was so much myself as to be able to
realize I was taken": that is, she did not suffer loss
of consciousness. And God "appears not to be content
merely to carry off the soul so thoroughly to Himself,
but wants the body, even though it be mortal and of
such rude earth." "Often the soul is absorbed, or, to
say it better, the Lord absorbs it to Himself; and when
He has held it thus for a time, He holds the will
alone"—not the intelligence alone. We see, thus, that
it is not a matter of vision, but a volitive union; and
meanwhile, "the understanding and the memory are
distraught . . . like a person who has slept long and
dreamt and still does not quite wake." It is "a soft
flight, a delight-filled flight, a flight without sound."
And in this delight-filled flight the consciousness of
self is preserved, as is the awareness of distinction

from God with whom the person is united. And this rapture is achieved, in the eyes of the mystical Spanish doctor, by contemplating the Humanity of Christ, that is, of a concrete, human entity, the vision of the living God, not of the idea of God. And later in the same book, her *Life*, she tells us that "though there were nothing else to delight the sight in heaven but the great beauty of the glorified bodies, that is a most grand glory, most especially to see the Humanity of Jesus Christ our Lord. . . ." "This vision," she adds, "though it be imaginary, I never did see with the eyes of my head, or any other eyes, but only with the eyes of my soul." So that it would appear that in Heaven the soul does not see God alone, but everything in God, or rather, it sees everything as God, since He embraces all. And this idea is even more emphasized by Jakob Böhme. For her part, St. Teresa tells us in the *Moradas sétimas* that "this secret union takes place in the innermost centre of the soul, where God Himself must dwell." And then, she says that "the soul, I mean the spirit of the soul, remains one with God . . ."; and it is "as if two wax tapers were to fuse so closely that there was no distinguishing but the one light, or that the wick, the wax, the light, form one, only that later the one taper can be separated from the other and the two tapers remain separate, or the wick be separate from the wax." But there is another more intimate union, and this is "like rain falling from heaven into a river or stream where all becomes the one water so that the river and rainwater cannot be separated, or as if a flash-river flowed to the sea so that there was no manner of separation, or like a room where bright light enters by two windows and though divided forms one light." And what difference between this kind of thought and that of

Miguel de Molinos, his internal and mystical silence, of which the third and most perfect degree is the silence of thought? Are we not close here to his view that nothingness is the way to reach the high state of a re-formed mind? How remarkable that Amiel, in his *Journal intime*, should twice make use of the Spanish word *nada*, nothing or nothingness! Doubtless he did so because he found no word in any other language quite so precisely expressive. And still, if one reads carefully in our mystical doctor Teresa, it will be seen that the sensory element of delight, that is, of consciousness, is never outside her sphere. The soul allows itself to be absorbed in God in order that it may absorb Him, in order that it may achieve consciousness of its own divinity.

A beatific vision, a loving contemplation in which the soul is absorbed in God and, as it were, lost in Him, appears, to our inherent sensibilities, either as an annihilation of self or as a prolonged tedium. And hence there is that certain feeling which we not infrequently observe and which has often been expressed satirically, not altogether free of irreverence or perhaps even impiety, to the effect that the heaven of eternal glory is a place of eternal boredom. And there is no use disdaining such sentiments, so spontaneous and altogether natural, or attempting to denigrate them.

It is clear enough that those people who feel in such wise have failed to realize that man's highest pleasure consists in achieving and intensifying consciousness: not so much the pleasure of knowing, but that of learning. In knowing something we tend to forget it, to make the knowing of it unconscious, so to say. Man's pleasure, his purest delight, is allied to the act of learning, of becoming aware of acquiring differentiated knowledge. There is the well-known story told of the old Spaniard accompanying Vasco Núñez de Balboa to the peak in Darién from which both oceans could be seen, and who there fell upon his knees and exclaimed: "Thank you, Lord, that you did not let me die without seeing so fantastic a sight!" But if the old man had stayed on there, the wonder of it all would soon have ceased, and with it his amazed delight. His joy was the joy of discovery. And perhaps the joy of the beatific vision may be, not precisely the contemplation of the supreme Truth, whole and entire, for no soul could endure so much, but rather the continuous discovery of it all, the ceaseless learning through an effort which maintains the sense of personal consciousness forever active.

It is difficult to imagine a beatific vision of mental quietude, of full knowledge rather than of gradual perception, as in any way different from a kind of Nirvana, a kind of spiritual diffusion, a kind of dissipation of energy in the essence of God, a return to the unconscious through lack of tension, lack of differentiation, in short, of a lack of activity.

Might it not be that the very condition which makes it possible for us to think of a union with God also destroys our longing? What difference is there between our being absorbed by God and absorbing Him in ourself? Is it the stream that is lost in the sea or the sea that is lost in the stream? It makes no difference.

Our fundamental feeling is our longing not to lose the sense of the continuity of our consciousness, not to break the linkage of our memories, the sense of our own concrete identity, even though we may gradually be absorbed into Him, thus enhancing Him. Who, as a man of eighty, remembers the child he was at eight, though he feels the link between them both? And it may be said that the question of feeling is basically a matter of whether there is a God, a human finality to the Universe. And yet: what is a finality? For just as it is always possible to ask the why of every why, so it is also possible to ask the wherefore of every wherefore. Assuming there is a God, wherefore God? "For His own purpose," it may be said. And someone else may retort: "And what difference is there between this kind of consciousness and no-consciousness?" But it will always be true, as Plotinus said, that to ask why God made the world is the same as to ask why there is a soul. Or rather: not why, but wherefore— διὰ τί.

For whoever places himself outside himself, in a hypothetically objective position—which is the same as saying in an inhuman position—the ultimate wherefore is as much beyond his reach, and strictly speaking, as absurd, as the ultimate why. What difference does it make, in effect, that there is not any finality? What logical contradiction is there in the Universe not being destined to any finality, either human or superhuman? What objection is there to the argument that there is no finality to the sum of things other than that they exist and happen, as they do exist and happen? None: such is the answer for the man who places himself outside himself. But for whoever lives and suffers and longs within himself—for him it is a matter of life and death.

Seek, therefore, thyself! But in finding oneself, does not one find one's own nothingness? "Having become a sinner in seeking himself, man has become wretched in finding himself," said Bossuet. "Seek thyself!" begins with "Know thyself!" To which Carlyle answers: "The latest Gospel in this world is, Know thy work and do it. 'Know thyself': long enough has that poor 'self' of thine tormented thee; thou wilt never get to 'know' it, I believe! Think it not thy business, this of knowing thyself; thou art an unknowable individual: know what thou canst work at; and work at it, like a Hercules! That will be thy better plan." Yes, but what I work at, will not that too be lost in the end? And if it be lost, wherefore should I work at it? Yes, yes, it may be that to accomplish my work—and what is my work?—without thinking about myself is to love God. And what is it to love God?

And on the other hand, in loving God in myself, am I not loving myself more than God, am I not loving myself in God?

What we really long for after death is to go on living this life, this same mortal life, but without its evils, without its tedium—and without death. This longing was given expression by Seneca, the Spaniard, in his *De Consolatione ad Marciam*: What he desired was to live this life again, *ista moliri*. And what Job asked for was to see God in the flesh, not in the spirit. And what else is the meaning of that comical notion of the *eternal recurrence* which issued from the tragic inner voice of poor Nietzsche, in his hunger for a concrete, temporal immortality?

And how can this beatific vision, which is the primary Catholic solution, be realized—I ask again—without annihilation of the consciousness of self? Will it not be like a sleep in which we dream without knowing what we dream? Who would care for an eternal life of that nature? To think without knowing we think is the same as not sensing ourselves and the same as not being ourselves. But is not eternal life perhaps rather eternal consciousness, not merely a matter of seeing God, but seeing that we see Him,

252*

seeing ourselves at the same time that we see ourselves as beings distinct from Him? A man asleep is
living but is not conscious of himself. Could anyone
wish for an eternal sleep? When Circe advised Ulysses
to descend to the abode of the dead in order to consult the soothsayer Tiresias, she told him that Tiresias
alone among the shades of the dead was possessed of
understanding, for all the others flitted about like
shadows. Tiresias apart, then, can it be said that the
others had overcome death? Is death really overcome
by flitting about like shadows without understanding?

May we not, rather, perhaps imagine that this
earthly life of ours is to the other life what sleep is
to waking? May not our entire life be a dream and
death an awakening? But an awakening to what? And
what if everything were but a dream of God and God
were to wake some day? Would He recall His own
dream?

Aristotle, the rationalist, tells us in his *Ethics* of
the higher felicity of the contemplative life, βίος
θεωρητικός, and all rationalists are given to identifying
well-being with knowledge. And the concept of eternal felicity, of the enjoyment of God, as a beatific
vision, as knowledge and comprehension of God, is of
rationalist origin, the kind of felicity which corresponds with the ideal God of Aristotelianism. But the
truth is that, in addition to vision, felicity implies delight, and delight is not a very rational matter and is
only to be attained when one feels oneself distinct
from God.

St. Thomas Aquinas, our Aristotelian Catholic
theologian, who attempted to rationalize Catholic
feeling, tells us in his *Summa* that "delight is necessary for happiness. For it is caused by the appetite
being at rest in the good attained. Wherefore, since

happiness is nothing else but the attainment of the Sovereign Good, it cannot be without concomitant delight." But where is the delight for him who rests? Is it not true that to rest, *requiescere*, is to sleep without even the consciousness that one is resting? "The very sight of God causes delight," the theologian continues. But does the soul feel itself distinct from God? "Delight that is attendant upon the operation of the intellect does not hinder it, rather does it perfect it," he says later. Of course! Otherwise, what kind of delight would it be? And in order to assure delectation, delight, pleasure, which—like pain—always preserves something material about it, and which we conceive of only as existing in a soul incarnate in a body, it was necessary to imagine that the soul in a state of blessedness should be united with its body. Without some kind of body, how would delight be possible? Without some kind of body or spirit-cover, the immortality of the pure soul is not true immortality. In the end, what we long for is a prolongation of this life, of this life and no other, this life of flesh and suffering, this life which we abominate at times precisely because it comes to an end. The majority of suicides would never take place if the self-immolators were sure they would never die on this earth. The self-slayer kills himself to avoid waiting for death.

When Dante relates how he attained to the vision of God, he tells us that it was in the manner of a man perceiving something in his sleep, but who, after his dream, retains only the vivid impression of a passion stamped on his mind: so it was with him, for as the vision all but evanesced, the sweetness that came with it is distilled in his heart:

> Cotal son io chè quasi tutta cessa
> mia visione, ed ancor mi distilla
> nel cuor lo dolce che nacque da essa.

like snow that melts in the sun

          Così la neve al sol si disigilla.

That is to say, the vision, the intellectual content, evanesces, and what remains is the delight, the *passione impressa*, the emotive, the irrational, in short, the corporeal.

What we desire is not merely spiritual felicity, not merely vision, but delight, corporal felicity. That other felicity, the rationalist *beatitude*, the happiness of being submerged in understanding can only . . . but no, I will not say satisfy or deceive, because I do not believe it ever satisfied or deceived even a Spinoza. At the conclusion of his *Ethics*, Spinoza affirms that "God loves himself with an infinite intellectual love." And that: "The intellectual love of the mind towards God is that very love of God whereby God loves himself, not in so far as he is infinite, but in so far as he can be explained through the essence of the human mind regarded under the form of eternity; in other words, the intellectual love of the mind towards God is part of the infinite love wherewith God loves himself." And after these tragic, these desolating propositions, he tells us at the end of the book, in the last proposition, which closes and crowns this tremendous tragedy of the *Ethics*: "Blessedness is not the reward of virtue, but virtue itself; neither do we rejoice therein, because we control our lusts, but, contrariwise, because we rejoice therein, we are able to control our lusts." Intellectual love! Intellectual love! What does it mean? It is something in the nature of a crimson flavor, or a bitter sound, an aromatic color, or rather, something like a love-stricken triangle or an enraged ellipse—pure metaphor, but a tragic metaphor. A metaphor which tragically corresponds with the saying that the heart also has its reasons. Reasons of the heart! Loves of the head! Delightful intellections! Intellective delights! Tragedy, tragedy, tragedy!

And nevertheless, there is something which can be called intellectual love, and it is the love of understanding, Aristotle's contemplative life: for comprehension involves something active and amorous in the act of understanding, and the beatific vision is a vision of the total truth. Is there not perhaps something of curiosity at the root of all passion? Did not our first parents, according to the Bible story, fall from grace because of their eagerness to taste of the fruit of the Tree of the Knowledge of Good and Evil, and to be like gods, knowers of that knowledge? The vision of God, that is, of the Universe itself, of its very soul, its very essence, would not that appease all our longing? And such a prospect would fail to satisfy only men of gross sensibilities who do not perceive that the greatest joy of man is to be more quintessentially man, that is, to be more God-like, and he is more God-like the greater his consciousness.

And this intellectual love, which is none other than so-called Platonic love, is a means to dominion and possession. There is not, in effect, any more perfect dominion than knowledge: whoever knows something, possesses it. Knowledge unites the knower with the known. "I contemplate thee and in contemplating thee I make thee mine": such is the formula. And to know God: what does it mean but to possess Him? Whoever knows God is already himself God.

In *La Dégradation de l'énergie*, B. Brunhes relates a story told him by Monsieur Sarrau, who had it from Père Gratry: Gratry was strolling in the Luxembourg Gardens conversing with the renowned mathematician and well-known Catholic, Cauchy, and they spoke of the felicity of the elect at knowing fully and endlessly, at last, the truths which had been so long and laboriously pursued on this earth. And Père Gratry, alluding to the studies Cauchy had made on the mechanistic theory of the reflection of light, suggested that one of the finest intellectual joys in the next world for the geometrician himself would be to penetrate into the mystery of light; to which Cauchy replied that it did not seem to him possible to know more than he already knew, nor could he imagine that the most perfect intelligence could comprehend the mystery of reflection better than he, Cauchy, had comprehended and expressed it, for he had already furnished a mechanical theory for the phenomenon. "His piety," Brunhes adds, "did not go so far as to believe that anything different or better could be achieved."

From this narrative two points of interest emerge. The first is the meaning of contemplation, intellectual love, or beatific vision as expressed by men of a superior order, men whose ruling passion is knowledge; and the second is the faith shown in the mechanistic explanation of the world.

This mechanistic disposition of the intellect coheres with the well-known formula, "Nothing is created, nothing is lost, everything is transformed," a formula by means of which the attempt has been made to interpret the ambiguous principle of the conservation of energy, in forgetfulness of the fact that, practically speaking, for us, for men, energy is utilizable energy, and that this energy is being continually lost, dissipated through the diffusion of heat, debased, so that its tendency is one of leveling and homogeneity. What has value for us, and even more, reality for us, is the differential, which is the qualitative; pure, undifferentiated quantity is something that might as well not exist as far as we are concerned, for it does not act.

And the material Universe, the body of the Universe, would appear to be gradually proceeding—unaffected by the retarding action of living organisms or even by the conscious action of man—toward a state of perfect stability, of homogeneity, as Brunhes points out in the above-mentioned book. For, if spirit tends toward concentration, material energy tends toward diffusion.

And may not this fact bear an intimate relation with our problem? May there not exist a connection between this conclusion of scientific philosophy as to a final state of stability and homogeneity and the mystical dream of the apocatastasis? May not this death of the body of the Universe be the final triumph of its spirit, of God?

There is manifestly an intimate relation between the religious need for an eternal life after death and the conclusions—always provisional—at which scientific philosophy arrives with respect to the probable future of the material or sensible Universe. And the fact is that just as there are theologians of God and the immortality of the soul, so there are those whom Brunhes calls theologians of monism, who might better be called atheologians, people who pertinaciously adhere to the spirit of *a priori* affirmation; and they are intolerable, he adds, when they harbor the pretension of disdaining theology. Haeckel is a notable type of this kind of gentleman—he has succeeded in dissipating the enigmas of Nature.

These atheologians have seized upon the principle of the conservation of energy, the formula of "Nothing is created, nothing is lost, everything is transformed," which has a theological origin, to be seen in Descartes, and they have made use of it all as a way for us to dispense with God. "The world built to last, without any wear or tear, or rather, which itself repairs whatever rents may appear in it—what a splendid theme for oratorical amplifications! But these very amplifications, which in the seventeenth century served to prove the wisdom of the Creator, have in our own day served as arguments to buttress those who would do without Him," as Brunhes puts it. It is the same old story: so-called scientific philosophy, whose origin and inspiration is basically theological or religious, put to the service of atheology or irreligion, which is itself nothing but a theology and a religion. Let us here recall the comments of Ritschl on this head, as cited before.

Nowadays, the last word of science, more than that of scientific philosophy even, appears to be that the material world of the senses is on the way to an ultimate leveling, a kind of final homogeneity, because of the debasement of energy, the predominance of irreversible phenomena. And this calls to mind the hypothesis of a primordial homogeneity so ubiquitous, in use and abuse, in the thought of Spencer, and of the fantastic instability of the homogeneous: an instability required by the atheological agnosticism of Spencer to serve by way of explaining the inexplicable transition from the homogeneous to the heterogeneous. For how can any heterogeneity whatever emerge from perfect and absolute homogeneity, without external action? But since every form of creation must be dismissed, "the unemployed engineer turned metaphysician," as Papini called him, invented the theory of the instability of the homogeneous, which is more—how shall I say it?—more mystical and even more mythological, if you like, than the creative action of God.

The Italian positivist Roberto Ardigò was on the right track when, objecting to Spencer's theory, he retorted that the most natural assumption was that, as is true today, there always have been worlds in process of formation, in a nebulous stage, worlds totally formed and worlds in process of dissolution; in short, that heterogeneity is eternal. And this constitutes another way of not solving the riddle.

Or is this perhaps the solution? But then in that case the Universe would be infinite, and in all truth we cannot conceive of a Universe both eternal and limited like the one that served Nietzsche as basis for his theory of eternal recurrence. If the Universe must be eternal, if periods of movement toward homogeneity, of degradation of energy, must be followed, in each of the component worlds, by periods of movement toward heterogeneity, then it is necessary that the Universe should be infinite and that there should be scope, always and in each of the worlds, for some action from outside. And in fact, the body of God cannot be other than eternal and infinite.

But as far as our own world is concerned, its gradual leveling, or, as we might say, its death, seems certain. And how will this process affect the fate of our spirit? Will it wane with the diminution of the energy of our world and return to unconsciousness, or will it rather grow according to the waning of the utilizable energy and by virtue of the very efforts it makes to retard this diminution and to dominate Nature? For it is this action of the spirit that constitutes its life. Are consciousness and its extended support two separate powers in contraposition, the one growing at the expense of the other?

The fact is that the best of our scientific work, as well as the best of our industry, that is, that part of it—and it is a great part—which does not conspire for destruction, is directed toward retarding this fatal process of the diminution of energy. And organic life itself, substance of our consciousness, constitutes an effort to avoid, insofar as possible, the fateful outcome, or at least to stretch it out.

There is no sense in seeking to deceive ourselves with pagan paeans to Nature, for as Leopardi, that Christian atheist, said in his splendid song to the broom shrub, "La Ginestra," Nature "is our mother by birth, but our stepmother by feeling." The origin of human companionship itself was a form of opposition to Nature: a terrified reaction to ruthless Nature first linked men together in a social bond. Human society is, in effect, the source of reflective consciousness and of the craving for immortality, and it is human society which sets the seal of grace upon the state of Nature: and man, by humanizing and spiritualizing Nature through his industry, supernaturalizes her.

In two superb sonnets which he called "Redemption," the tragic Portuguese poet Antero de Quental dreamed of a spirit imprisoned, not in atoms or ions or crystals, but—as would naturally occur to a poet— in the sea, in trees, in the forest, in the mountains, in the wind, in all material individualities and forms; and he imagines a day to come when all these captive souls, as yet in the limbo of existence, will awaken to consciousness, and, emerging as pure thought from the forms that imprisoned them, they will perceive these forms, creatures of illusion, fall apart like a vague dream. This poem is a magnificent vision of the coming of consciousness to quicken all things.

May it not be that the Universe, this our Universe—and who knows if there are any others?— began with a zero of spirit (and zero is not the same as nothing) and an infinitude of matter, and that its progress is toward an infinitude of spirit and a zero of matter? Dreams!

May it not be that everything has a soul and that this soul seeks to be freed?

> O land of Alvargonzález,
> In the heart of Spain:
> Poor land, and land,
> So sad it has a soul!

sings our poet Antonio Machado in his *Campos de Castilla.* Is the sadness of the land in the land itself, or in those of us who look upon it? Do they not, truly, suffer? And yet, what can an individual soul in a world of matter actually be? Is a rock or a mountain individual? Is a tree?

Nevertheless the fact remains that spirit and matter are in constant strife. The poet Espronceda expressed the thought:

> To live a life of peace on earth,
> either soul or matter is of extra worth.

And is there not in the history of thought, or of human imagination, if you prefer, something that corresponds to this process of the reduction of matter, in the sense of a reduction of everything to consciousness?

Yes, there is, and the author of this idea is the first Christian mystic, St. Paul of Ephesus, the Apostle to the Gentiles, who, because he had never with the carnal eye of his face looked upon the face of the carnal, mortal Christ, the ethical Christ, created within himself an immortal and religious Christ, and who was caught up into the third heaven and there heard secret and unspeakable words (2 Cor. 12). And this first Christian mystic dreamed also of a final triumph of spirit, of consciousness, and it is this which in theology is technically called the apocatastasis or restitution.

In verses 26 through 28 of chapter 15 of the First Epistle to the Corinthians, Paul tells us: "The last enemy that shall be destroyed is death. For he hath put all things under his feet. But when he saith, all things are put under him, it is manifest that he is excepted, which did put all things under him. And when all things shall be subdued unto him, then shall the Son also himself be subject unto him that put all things under him, that God may be all in all" "ἵνα ᾗ ὁ θεὸς πάντα ἐν πᾶσιν." That is, in the end, God, Consciousness, will become the all in all.

This doctrine is completed by Paul's teaching, in his Epistle to the Ephesians, concerning the end of the whole history of the world. In this epistle, as we all know, he represents Christ—by whom "were all things created, that are in heaven and that are in earth, visible and invisible" (Col. 1:16)—as the head over all things (Eph. 1:22), and in him, in this head, we shall all be raised up that we may live in the communion of saints and that we "may be able to comprehend with all saints what is the breadth, and length, and depth, and height, and to know the love of Christ, which passeth knowledge" (Eph. 3:18-19). And this gathering together of us in Christ, who is the head and, as it were, the compendium of Humanity, is what the Apostle calls the gathering or collecting together or recapitulating of all things in Christ: ἀνακεφαλαιώσασθαι τὰ πάντα ἐν Χριστῷ. And this recapitulation—ἀνακεφαλαίωσις, anacephalaeosis—the end of the world's history and of the human race, is merely another aspect of the apocatastasis. The apocatastasis, God's coming to be all in all, thus resolves itself into the anacephalaeosis, the gathering together of all things in Christ, in Humanity, so that Humanity is therefore the end of creation. And does not this apocatastasis, this humanization or divinization of all things, do away with matter? But if matter, which is the principle of individuation, the scholastic *principium individuationis*, is once done away with, does not everything return to pure consciousness, which, in its pure purity, neither knows itself nor is it anything that can be conceived or felt? And if matter be abolished, what support is there left for spirit?

Thus, the same difficulties, the same unthinkable quandaries are encountered even in this other quarter.

It may be said, on the other hand, that the apocatastasis, God's coming to be all in all, presupposes that there was a time when He was not the all in all. The supposition that all beings shall attain to the enjoyment of God implies that God shall attain to the enjoyment of all beings, for the beatific vision is mutual, and God is perfected in being better known, and His being is sustained and enhanced by souls.

Along this road of mad dreams we might imagine an unconscious God, slumbering in matter until He becomes a God conscious of all, conscious of His own divinity. We might imagine the entire Universe becoming conscious of itself as a whole and becoming conscious of each constituent consciousness and becoming God. But in that case, how did this unconscious God begin? Is He not matter itself? God would thus be the end rather than the beginning of the Universe. But can something which was not a beginning be an end? Or can it be that outside time, in eternity, there is a difference between beginning and end? "The Soul of the Universe cannot be in bond to what"—that is, matter—"itself has bound," as Plotinus says. Or is it not rather the Consciousness of the Whole which strives to become the consciousness of each part and to make each partial consciousness conscious of itself, that is, of the total consciousness? Is not this universal soul a monotheist or solitary God who is in the process of becoming a pantheist God? And if it is not so, if matter and pain are alien to God, why then, it will be asked, did God create the world? For what purpose did He make matter and introduce pain? Would it not have been better if He had not made anything? What added glory does He gain by the creation of angels or of men who fall and whom He must punish with eternal torment? Did He perhaps create evil so that He might alleviate it? Or was redemption His design, complete and absolute redemption, redemption of all things and all men? Such a hypothesis is neither more rational nor more pious than the other.

Insofar as we attempt to represent eternal happiness to ourselves, we are confronted with a series of questions to which there is no satisfactory, that is, rational, answer, whether or not we start from a monotheist, or pantheist, or even panentheist point of departure.

Let us return to the Pauline apocatastasis.

Is it not possible that by becoming all in all God completes Himself, that He finishes being God, infinite consciousness who encompasses all and each consciousness? And what is an infinite consciousness? Since consciousness supposes limitation, or rather since consciousness is a consciousness of limitation, of distinction, does it not thereby exclude infinitude? What value has the notion of infinitude applied to consciousness? What is a consciousness which is all consciousness, with nothing outside itself that is not consciousness? In such a case, of what is consciousness the consciousness? Of its content? Or may it not be truer to say that, starting from chaos, from absolute unconsciousness, in the eternity of the past, we continually approach the apocatastasis or final apotheosis without ever reaching it?

May not this apocatastasis, this return of all things to God, be rather an ideal finality which we ceaselessly approach—some of us faster than others—but which we never reach? May not the absolute and perfect happiness be an eternal hope, which would die if it were ever realized? Is it possible to find happiness without hope? And once possession is achieved, there is no question of hope, for possession does away with hope, does away with desire. May it not be, I say, that all souls grow ceaselessly, some in greater measure than others, but all of them having, at some point, to go through the same degree, whatever it may be, of growth, without ever arriving at the infinite, at God, whom they continually approach? Is not eternal happiness an eternal hope, with its eternal nucleus of sorrow, so that thus happiness shall not be swallowed in nothingness?

The questions without answer follow one another.

"He shall be all in all," says the Apostle. But will He be the same in all, or in each one different? Will not God be entire in one of the damned? Is He not in the soul of a damned man? Is He not in what is called Hell? And in what mode is He there?

Whence arise new problems, those relating to the opposition between heaven and hell, between eternal happiness and eternal unhappiness.

In the end, may it not be the case that all shall be saved, including Cain and Judas, and Satan himself, as Origen hoped when he developed upon the Pauline concept of apocatastasis?

When our Catholic theologians seek to justify rationally—that is, ethically—the dogma of the eternity of the pains of hell, they adduce reasons so specious, so ridiculous and infantile, that it seems incredible they should ever have gained credence. For to say that since God is infinite any offense against Him is infinite also and therefore requires an eternal punishment is, apart from the inconceivability of an infinite offense, to be unaware that in the realm of human morality, if not in the sphere of the terrestrial police, the gravity of the offense is measured more by the intention of the offender than by the dignity of the offended person, and that the idea of an infinite intention to offend is a piece of nonsense, and nothing else. In this connection it would be most apropos to cite the words which Christ addressed to His Father: "Father, forgive them, for they know not what they do"; for no man who offends God or his neighbor knows what he does. In the realm of human ethics, or in that of the terrestrial police, if you like—in what is called penal law, in short, and which is anything but law—the concept of eternal punishment is meaningless.

"God is just and punishes us; that is all we need to know; as far as we are concerned the rest is pure curiosity." Such was the conclusion reached by Lamennais, and he was not alone in his conclusions. Calvin thought the same. But is there really anyone who could be content with this view? Pure curiosity! Imagine calling that which makes our soul writhe a matter of pure curiosity!

May not the truth be that the damned man is condemned because he longs for annihilation, or that, because he was a damned soul he did not sufficiently desire to become eternal? May we not say that it is not the belief in another life that makes a man blest, but rather that because he is blest he believes in it?

And what is being blest or being damned? The state of being good or being bad belongs to the domain of ethics, not of religion: or, rather, does not doing good though being evil belong to the sphere of ethics, and being good though committing evil belong to the sphere of religion?

Shall we not be told, though, that if the sinner suffers an eternal punishment, it is because he ceaselessly sins, for the damned do not cease to sin? But the problem is not thereby resolved, and its absurdity is all derived from the concept that punishment is a matter of vindictiveness or vengeance and not a corrective; in short, from conceiving of it in the manner of barbarians. In the same way hell has been conceived as a police institution, to inspire fear in this world. But the worst of it all is that it no longer frightens anyone, and therefore it will have to be closed down.

Still, from a religious point of view and within the domain of mystery, why should there not be an eternity of suffering—even though the idea violates our sentiments? Why should there not be a God who battens on our sufferings? Is our happiness, perchance, the end-purpose of the Universe? Or do we not perhaps sustain some alien wellbeing with our suffering? Let us read again in the *Eumenides*, by that powerful tragedian Aeschylus, the choruses in which the Furies curse the new gods for overturning the ancient laws and snatching Orestes from their hands: impassioned invectives against the Apollonian redemption. Does not redemption snatch from the hands of the gods their captive plaything, man, whose suffering provides them with play and amusement, as tormenting a beetle does for children, as the tragic poet tells us? And let us also recall the cry: "My God, my God, why hast thou forsaken me?"

Yes, why should there not be an eternity of suffering? Hell is an eternalization of the soul, even though it be an eternity of pain. Is not pain an essential to life?

Men continue to invent theories to explain what they call the origin of evil. And why not the origin of good? Why assume that the good is the positive and original, while evil is the negative and derivative? "Everything that is, insofar as it is, is good," St. Augustine affirmed. But why? What does "being good" mean? The good is good for something, conducive to some end, and to say that everything is good is the same as saying that everything is en route toward its end. But what is its end? Our desire is to make ourselves eternal, to persist, and whatever conspires to this end we call good, and evil is whatever tends to lessen or annihilate our consciousness. We assume that human consciousness is an end and not a means to something else that may not be consciousness, either human or superhuman.

All metaphysical optimism, such as that of Leibnitz, and all metaphysical pessimism, such as that of Schopenhauer, have no foundation other than the above assumption. For Leibnitz, this world is the best because it works to perpetuate consciousness and its accompanying will, because intelligence increases will and perfects it, because the end-purpose of man is the contemplation of God; while for Schopenhauer, this world is the worst of all possible worlds, because it conspires to destroy will, because intelligence, representation, nullifies the will which begot it.

And similarly Franklin, who believed in another life, asserted that he was willing to live this life over again, the life he had actually lived, "from its beginning to the end"; while Leopardi, who did not believe in another life, was sure that no one would want to live over again the life he himself had lived. These two attitudes are not merely ethical but religious as well; likewise the sense of moral good, insofar as it has a teleological value, is of religious origin also.

And one returns to the question: shall we not all be saved, all be made eternal, and eternal no longer in suffering, but in blessedness, all alike, those we call good as well as those we call evil?

In the matter of good and evil, does not the malice of whoever makes the judgment play a part? Does the evil lie in the intention of the perpetrator of the deed or does it not lie rather in the intention of the judge of its evil? The terrible fact is that man sets himself up as his own judge, and judges himself!

Who then shall be saved? And now the imagination suggests another possibility—neither more nor less rational than those possibilities interrogatively offered—and that is the thought that only those are saved who longed to be saved, that only those are made eternal who lived consumed by a terrible hunger for eternity and a need to be made eternal. Whoever longs never to die and who believes he will never die in spirit, desires it because he deserves it, or better, whoever longs for personal eternity does so because he already bears his immortality within him. Only the man who does not long, always and passionately, with a passion overwhelming all reason, for his own personal immortality does not deserve it, and, because he does not deserve it, does not desire it. And there is no injustice in not giving a man something he does not know enough to desire: "Ask, and it shall be given you." Perhaps each is given what he desires. And perhaps the sin against the Holy Ghost, for which, according to the Gospel, there is no remission, is none other than that of not desiring God, that of not longing to be made eternal.

> As is your sort of mind,
> So is your sort of search: you'll find
> What you desire, and that's to be
> A Christian.

said Robert Browning in "Christmas Eve and Easter Day."

Dante condemns the Epicureans, who did not believe in another life, to his *Inferno*, and he condemns them to a fate worse than not having another life, and that is to a consciousness of their not having it, and he does so vividly, immuring and sealing them in their tombs throughout eternity without light, without air, without movement, without life.

What cruelty is there in denying a man something he never desired nor could desire? In the Sixth Book of his *Aeneid*, the gentle Virgil makes us hear the plaintive wailing of the infants at the threshold of Hades

> Continuo auditae voces, vagitus et ingens,
> Infantumque animae flentes in limine primo,

unhappy in that they had scarcely entered upon life and never known its pleasures, before they were torn away, one dark day, from their mothers' breasts, to be plunged in bitter gloom:

> Quos dulcis vitae exsortes et ab ubere raptos
> Abstulit atra dies et funere mersit acerbo.

But what life did they lose, if they never knew nor longed for it? Or did they not in reality long for it?

It could be said that others craved immortality for them; that their progenitors wished them eternal, so they might enjoy them later in eternity. And here a new field is opened to the imagination: that of the solidarity and the representativeness of eternal salvation.

Many, in truth, think of the human race as one being, a collective individuality bound by solidarity, in which each member may represent or comes to represent the total collectivity, and they think of salvation also as collective. Thus virtue and vice are collective, and so is redemption. Either everyone is saved, or no one is saved, according to this line of feeling and imagining; redemption is total and mutual; each man is his neighbor's Christ.

And is there not perhaps a hint of all this in the popular Catholic belief concerning the blessed souls in Purgatory and of the intercessory prayers offered for them by the living, praying for their own dead, accumulating merits for them through prayer? This sense of the transmission of accumulated merits both to the living and to the dead is widespread in popular Catholic piety.

Nor should it be forgotten that in the history of man's religious thought the idea of an immortality restricted to a choice number of the elect, of spirits representing all others and in a certain manner including them all, has often recurred. This idea is of a pagan derivation, for the elect are analogous to the heroes and demigods, and sometimes this attitude lies behind the use of the phrase "many are called but few are chosen" (Matt. 22:14).

In these very days, while I was engaged upon this essay, a book came into my hands, the third edition of the *Dialogue sur la vie et sur la mort*, by Charles Bonnefon, a book in which musings analogous to those I have been setting forth are succinctly and suggestively expressed. The soul, says Bonnefon, cannot live without the body, nor the body without the soul, so that in reality there is no death nor birth, nor, strictly speaking, either body, or soul, or birth, or death, for all these are abstract terms or apparential matters: there is only a thinking life, of which we form part and which can neither be born nor die. Thus Bonnefon is led to deny human individuality and to assert that no one can say, "I am," but rather only "We are," or, even more correctly "It is in us." It is humanity, the species, which thinks and loves in us. And just as bodies are transmitted, just so are souls. "The living thought or the thinking life which we are will re-integrate immediately in a form analogous to that of our origin and corresponding to our being when it was in the quickened womb of a woman." Each one of us, then, has lived before and will live again, though unaware of the process. "If humanity gradually raises itself above itself, then when the last man, who will contain all humanity, comes to die, can we deny that humanity at that stage may have reached the highest point possible anywhere, even heaven? . . . Bound together we shall all, bit by bit, garner the fruits of our travail." It follows, according to this line of imagining and feeling, that since nobody is born, nobody dies: no soul has ever ceased its travail but has often been submerged in the human struggle "ever since the type of embryo corresponding with the same consciousness was represented in the succession of human phenomena." Since Bonnefon begins by denying personal individuality, he clearly leaves out of account our real longing, which is to save our own individuality; but since he, Bonnefon, is a personal individual and feels this longing, he falls back upon the distinction between the called and the chosen, and has recourse to the idea of representative spirits, and he endows a certain number of men with this representative individual immortality. Of these elect he says that "they will be somewhat more necessary to God than we ourselves are." And he brings this grandiose dream to an end by supposing that "it is not impossible that we shall reach supreme bliss by a series of ascensions, and that our life shall be merged in the perfect Life, like a drop of water in the sea. Then we shall understand," he continues, "that everything was necessary, that every philosophy and every religion had its hour of truth, and that in all our wanderings and errors and in the darkest moments of our history we discerned the light of the distant beacon, and that we were all predestined to share the Eternal Light. And if the God we shall find again should possess a body—and we cannot conceive a living God without a body—we shall be one of His conscious cells, along with those of the myriads of races brought into being by myriads of suns. If this dream should be fulfilled, an ocean of love would beat upon our shores, and the end of every life would be to add a drop of water to its infinity." But what is this cosmic dream of Bonnefon's but a literary representation of the Pauline apocatastasis?

Yes, this dream, of ancient Christian antecedents, is fundamentally nothing other than the Pauline anacephalaeosis, the fusion of all men in Man, the whole of Humanity embodied in a Person, who is Christ, the fusion of all and the subjection of all to God, so that God, who is Consciousness, may be all in all. This concept supposes a collective redemption and a society beyond the grave.

In the middle of the eighteenth century, two pietists of Protestant origin, Johann Jakob Moser and

Friedrich Christoph Oetinger, added new force and value to the Pauline anacephalaeosis. Moser "declared that his religion consisted not in holding certain doctrines to be true and in living a virtuous life conformably therewith, but in being reunited to God through Christ. But this demands the thorough knowledge—a knowledge that goes on increasing until the end of life—of one's own sins and also of the mercy and patience of God, the transformation of all natural feelings, the appropriation of the atonement wrought by the death of Christ, the enjoyment of peace with God in the permanent witness of the Holy Spirit to the remission of sins, the ordering of life according to the pattern of Christ, which is the fruit of faith alone, the drawing near to God and the intercourse of the soul with Him, the disposition to die in grace and the joyful expectation of the Judgement which will bestow blessedness in the more intimate enjoyment of God and in the *commerce with all the saints*": the commerce with all the saints, that is, with the eternal human society. And Oetinger, for his part, considers eternal felicity to be, not in the contemplation of God in His infinitude, but, taking the Epistle to the Ephesians as his authority, the contemplation of God in the harmony of the creature with Christ. The commerce with all the saints was, according to him, essential to the content of eternal felicity. It was the realization of the kingdom of God, which proves thus to be the kingdom of Man. And in his exposition of these two pietists, Ritschl confesses that both witnesses have with these doctrines contributed to Protestantism something as valuable as Spener, another pietist, contributed with his theological method.

We see, therefore, how the mystical Christian inner longing, ever since St. Paul, has been to give human, that is, divine finality to the Universe, to save human consciousness, and to save it by converting all humanity into a person. This longing is expressed in the anacephalaeosis, the recapitulation of all things, all things on earth and in heaven, the visible and the invisible, in Christ, and also in the apocatastasis, the return of all things to God, to consciousness, so that God may be all in all. And does not God's being all in all mean that everything that has happened will come to life again, and that everything that has existed in time will become eternal? And within the all, each individual consciousness, all those that have been, those that are, and those that will be, will exist in social solidarity just as they were, as they are, and will be.

But does not this return to consciousness of all that ever was necessarily involve a fusion of the identical, an amalgamation of like things? In this conversion of the human race into a true society in Christ, a communion of saints, a kingdom of God, will not deceptive and even iniquitous individual differences be obliterated, so that in the perfect society all that will remain of each man will be his essence? Thus, according to Bonnefon's assumption, would not the consciousness which lived in this particular corner of the earth in the twentieth century end by feeling itself to be the same as other entities of consciousness which lived in other centuries and perhaps in other earths?

And what possibilities are suggested by a true, effective union, a substantial and intimate union of soul with soul, among all those who have existed!

> If any two creatures grew into one
> They would do more than the world has done,

Browning pronounced in "The Flight of the Duchess"; and Christ has left for us the message that where two or three are gathered together in His name, He is among them.

Paradise, then, according to many, is society, a more perfect society than that of this world; it is human society made into a person. And there are people who believe that all human progress tends to make our species into one collective being with a true consciousness: is not an individual human organism perhaps a kind of confederation of cells? And they also believe that when this collective being has achieved full consciousness, then all who have ever existed will come alive again in it.

In the eyes of many, heaven is society. Just as no one can live in isolation, so no one can survive in isolation. No one who beholds his brother suffering in hell can rejoice in God, for the fault and the merit were common to both. We think the thoughts of others and we feel with their feelings. To see God when He shall be all in all is to see all in God and to live in God with all.

This grand dream of the final solidarity of mankind is the Pauline anacephalaeosis and apocatastasis. We Christians, said the Apostle, are "the body of Christ, and members in particular" (1 Cor. 12:27); "we are members of his body, of his flesh, and of his bones" (Eph. 5:30); we are vine-shoots of the vine.

But in this final solidarity, this true and supreme *Christianation* of all creatures, what becomes of each individual consciousness? What becomes of me, of this poor tenuous I, this I that is the slave of time and space, this I which reason tells me is no more than an ephemeral accident, but for the saving of which I live and suffer and hope and believe? Supposing the human finality of the Universe is secured, if it is finally secured, supposing consciousness is achieved, would I even so resign myself to sacrifice this poor I of mine, through which and by which alone I am to know of this finality and this consciousness?

And here, at the height of the tragedy, we come face to face with the supreme religious sacrifice, the very heart of it, the sacrifice of our own individual consciousness on the altar of the perfected Human Consciousness, the Divine Consciousness.

But is there really such a tragedy? If we were to attain a clear vision of this anacephalaeosis, if we were to understand and feel that we were going to enhance Christ, would we hesitate for a moment in handing ourselves altogether over to Him? Would the stream that flows into the sea and tastes the bitter salt of the ocean seeping into the sweetness of its waters care to flow back to its source? Would it wish to return to the cloud sprung from the sea? Is not its fulfillment to feel itself absorbed?

And yet . . .

Yes, despite everything, here lies the heart of the tragedy.

And the soul, my soul at least, longs for something more: not absorption, not quiescence, not peace, not extinguishment, it longs for an eternal approach without any arrival; its longing is interminable, an unending hope eternally renewed and never fulfilled or obliterated. Along with this longing, my soul feels an eternal lack and an eternal sorrow. This sorrow, this pain, allows it ceaselessly to expand in consciousness and in longing. Do not inscribe upon the gate of Paradise what Dante did on the gate of Hell: *Lasciate ogni speranza!* Do not kill time! Our life is hope continually changing into memory which in turn again engenders hope. Let us live! An eternity which would be like an eternal present, without memory or hope, would be death. Ideas are like that; but men do not

live like that. Ideas about the God-Idea are like that;
but men cannot live that way in the living God, in
the God Man.

My soul longs, then, for an eternal Purgatory perhaps, rather than for a Paradise: it seeks eternal
ascension. If there were an end to all suffering, however pure and spiritualized we may suppose such a
condition to be, an end to all desire, what would make
the blessed go on living? If they did not suffer for
God, in what manner do they love Him? And if even
there, in Paradise, beholding God ever closer without ever quite attaining Him, they are left without
something further to know and desire, if there is no
wellspring of doubt left them, how could they avoid
falling asleep?

In sum, if nothing is left in Paradise of the innermost tragedy of the soul, what kind of life is left?
Is there any greater joy possible than to recall grief—
and to remember is to feel it—in time of felicity?
Does not the freed prisoner feel nostalgia for his
prison? Does he not miss his former dreams of
freedom?

*   *   *

"Mythological fantasies!" someone will cry. We have
not suggested that they are anything else. Does not
the mythological dream contain its own truth? Are
not dream and myth perhaps revelations of an ineffable truth, an irrational truth, of a truth which cannot
be proved?

Mythology! Perhaps. But we need to mythologize
as much now as in Plato's day whenever we deal with
the afterlife. We have just seen that whenever we
try to give concrete, conceivable—that is, irrational—
form to our primary, primordial, fundamental longing

*279**

for an eternal life conscious of itself and of its personal individuality, then the aesthetic, logical, and ethical absurdities begin to multiply and there is no way to conceive of the beatific vision and the apocatastasis without contradictions and inconsistencies.

And nevertheless . . .

Yes, nevertheless, we must long for it, no matter how absurd it all seems; nay, more, we must also believe in it, in one way or another, in order to live at all. In order that we may live, I say, not in order that we may understand the Universe. We must believe, and to believe is to be religious. Christianity, the only religion we Europeans of the twentieth century can truly feel, is a desperate way out, as Kierkegaard said, a way out which can prove successful only through the martyrdom of faith, which in turn, according to this same tragic thinker, amounts to the crucifixion of reason.

No wonder that a man entitled to make the statement spoke of the madness of the Cross. Madness, without a doubt, madness. And the Yankee humorist, Oliver Wendell Holmes, was not altogether wide of the mark when he made one of the characters in his ingenious conversations say that he thought better of "persons in insane hospitals, sent there in consequence of what are called *religious* mental disturbances . . . than of many who hold the same notions, and keep their wits and appear to enjoy life very well, outside of the asylums." But are not the latter also, thanks be to God, living in madness as well? Are there not also tractable forms of madness, which not only allow us to mingle with our neighbors without detriment to society, but which rather help us to do so, inasmuch as our madness supplies us a meaning and an end-purpose for life and for society itself?

And after all, what is madness and how are we to distinguish it from reason, unless we place ourselves outside the one and the other—an impossible maneuver for us?

Perhaps it is madness, a great madness, for us to try to penetrate the mysteries beyond the tomb; madness to want to superimpose the self-contradictory dreams of our imagination upon the dictates of sound reason. And sound reason tells us that nothing should be erected without foundations, and that it is not only a useless but a self-destructive activity to fill the void of the unknown with fantasies. And yet . . .

We must believe in the other life, in the eternal life beyond the tomb, and in an individual and personal life, a life in which each one of us senses his own consciousness and senses that it is joined, without being confounded, with all others in their consciousness within the Supreme Consciousness, in God; we must believe in that other life in order to live this life and endure it and endow it with meaning and finality. And perhaps we must believe in that other life in order to deserve it, to attain it, for perhaps whoever does not desire it above reason and, if need be, against reason, neither deserves it nor attains it.

And above all, we must feel and act as if an endless continuation of our earthly life were reserved for us after death; and if nothingness is our fate instead, let us not make it a just fate, to echo the cry in *Obermann*.

This thought leads us, as if by the hand, to examine the practical or ethical aspect of our unique problem.

XI. The Practical Problem

L'homme est périssable.—Il se peut; mais périssons en résistant, et, si le néant nous est réservé, ne faisons pas que ce soit une justice.
Sénancour, *Obermann*, lettre XC

SEVERAL TIMES in the wandering course of these observations I have been bold enough to define, in spite of my horror of definitions, my own position vis-à-vis the problem I have been examining. But I know there is bound to be some dissatisfied reader, indoctrinated in some dogmatism or other, who will say: "This man cannot make up his mind; he vacillates; first he seems to assert one proposition, then he maintains the opposite; he is full of contradictions; it is impossible to place him. What is he?" There you have me: a man who affirms opposites, a man of contradiction and quarrel, as Jeremiah said of himself; a man who says one thing with his heart and the opposite with his head, and for whom this strife is the stuff of life. It is a clear-cut case, as clear as the water which flows from the melted snow upon the mountain tops.

I shall be told that mine is an untenable position, that a foundation is needed upon which to build our actions and our works, that it is impossible to live by contradictions, that unity and clarity are essential conditions for life and thought, and that it is imperative to unify the latter. And so we are back where we started from. For it is precisely this inner contradiction which unifies my life and gives it a practical purpose.

Or, rather, it is the conflict itself, this selfsame passionate uncertainty which unifies my action and causes me to live and work.

We think in order that we may live, I have said, but perhaps it would be more correct to say that we think because we live, and that the form of our thought corresponds to the form of our life. Once more I must point out that our ethical and philosophical doctrines in general are no more than *a posteriori* justifications of our conduct, of our actions. Our doctrines are usually the means by which we seek to explain and justify to others and to ourselves our own mode of action—to ourselves, be it noted, as well as to others. The man who does not really know why he acts as he does, and not otherwise, feels the need to explain to himself his reason for so acting, and so he manufactures a motive. What we believe to be the motives for our conduct are usually mere pretexts. The reason which impels one man carefully to preserve his life is the same reason given by another man for shooting himself in the head.

Nevertheless it cannot be denied that reasons, ideas, exert an influence on human actions, and sometimes even determine them by a process analogous to that of suggestion in the case of a hypnotized person, and this is due to the tendency of all ideas to resolve themselves in action—for an idea in itself is but an inchoate or aborted act. It was this tendency which suggested to Fouillée his theory of idea forces. But ordinarily ideas are forces which we reconcile with other deeper and much less conscious forces.

But leaving all this to one side for a moment, I should like to establish the fact that uncertainty, doubt, the perpetual wrestling with the mystery of our final destiny, the consequent mental despair, and the lack of any solid or stable dogmatic foundation, may all serve as basis for an ethic.

Whoever bases or thinks he bases his conduct—his inner or outward conduct, his feeling or his action—on a dogma or theoretical principle which he deems incontrovertible, runs the risk of becoming a fanatic; moreover, the moment this dogma shows any fissure or even any weakness, he finds the morality based on it giving way. If the ground he thought firm begins to rock, he himself trembles in the earthquake, for we are not all like the ideal Stoic who remains undaunted among the ruins of a world shattered to pieces. Luckily, the matter which underlies his ideas will tend to save him. For if a man should tell you that he does not defraud or cuckold his best friend because he fears hellfire, you may depend upon it that he would not do so even if he stopped believing in hell, but would instead invent some other excuse for not transgressing. And this truth is to the honor of the human race.

But whoever is convinced that he is sailing, perhaps without a set course, on an unstable or sinkable craft, will not be daunted if he finds the deck giving way beneath his feet and threatening to sink. For this type of man acts as he does, not because he believes his theory of action to be true, but because he believes that by acting thus he will make it true, prove it true, and that by thus acting he will create his spiritual world.

My conduct must be the best proof, the moral proof, of my supreme desire; and if I do not finally convince myself, within the limits of the ultimate and irremediable uncertainty, of the truth of what I hope for, it is because my conduct is not sufficiently pure. Virtue, therefore, is not based upon dogma, but dogma upon virtue, and it is not faith which creates martyrs but rather martyrs who create faith. There is no security or repose—so far as security and repose are attainable in this life which is essentially insecure and lacking in repose—save in passionately good conduct.

Conduct, which is practice, is the proof of doctrine, which is theory. "If any man will do his will," the will of Him who sent Jesus, "he shall know of the doctrine, whether it be of God, or whether I speak of myself," said Jesus (John 7:17). And there is a well-known saying of Pascal: "Begin by taking holy water and you will end by becoming a believer." And pursuing a similar line of thought, Johann Jakob Moser, the pietist, concluded that no atheist or naturalist has the right to regard the Christian religion as devoid of truth so long as he has never tried keeping its precepts and commandments.

What is the anti-rational truth of our heart? It is the immortality of the human soul, the truth of the persistence of our consciousness without any termination whatever, the human finality of the Universe. And what is its moral proof? We may formulate it thus: Act so that in your own judgement and in the judgement of others you may deserve eternity, act so that you may be irreplaceable, act so that you do not deserve death. Or perhaps thus: Act as if you were to die tomorrow, but only in order to survive and become eternal. The end-purpose of morality is to give personal, human finality to the Universe; to discover the finality it possesses—if it does in fact possess any—and discover it by acting.

More than a century ago, in 1804, the deepest and

most intense of the spiritual sons of the patriarch Rousseau, most tragic of French men of feeling (not excluding Pascal), Sénancour, in Letter XC of that series which constitutes the immense monody of his *Obermann*, wrote the words which I have placed as epigraph to this chapter: "Man is perishable. . . . That may be; but let us perish resisting, and if annihilation must be our portion, let us not make it a just one." If you change this sentence from a negative to a positive form—"And if annihilation must be our portion, let us make it an unjust reward."—you get the firmest basis for action by the man who cannot or will not be a dogmatist.

The pessimism which Goethe puts into the mouth of Mephistopheles when he makes him say "Whatever has achieved existence deserves to be destroyed" ("denn alles was entsteht/Ist wert, dass es zugrunde geht"), is a pessimism which is irreligious and demoniacal, which incapacitates us for action and leaves us without any ideal defense against our own penchant for evil. It is this pessimism which we know as evil, rather than the pessimism which consists in deploring and fighting the fear that everything is doomed to annihilation in the end. Mephistopheles asserts that whatever has achieved existence deserves to be destroyed, annihilated, but not that it will be destroyed or annihilated: and we assert that whatever exists deserves to be exalted and made eternal, even if no such destiny is achieved. The moral attitude is altogether different.

Yes, everything deserves to be eternalized, absolutely everything, even evil itself, for what we call evil would lose its malignancy in being made eternal and thereby losing its temporal nature. For the essence of evil consists in its temporal nature, in the fact that it is not directed toward any ultimate and permanent end.

And it might not be superfluous here to say something about the difference between what is called pessimism and what is called optimism——one of the most confusing of differences, not less than the confusion between individualism and socialism. In all truth, it is scarcely possible to say what pessimism really is.

Just today I read in *The Nation* an article entitled "A Dramatic Inferno," which deals with a translation into English of the works of Strindberg, and it begins with the following judicious observation:

> If there were in the world a sincere and total pessimism, it would of necessity be silent. The despair which finds a voice is a social mood, it is the cry of misery which brother utters to brother when both are stumbling through a valley of shadows which is peopled with comrades. In its anguish it bears witness to something that is good in life, for it presupposes sympathy. . . . The real gloom, the sincere despair, is dumb and blind; it writes no books, and feels no impulse to burden an intolerable universe with a monument more lasting than brass.

This judgement doubtless conceals some sophistry, for a man really in pain cries out, even if he is alone and there is no one to hear him, thus alleviating his pain, though his reaction may be conditioned by social custom. Does not the lion, alone in the desert, roar if he has an aching tooth? But apart from this qualification, there is no denying the substance of truth underlying the quoted observation. Pessimism which protests and defends itself cannot truly be said to be pessimism. And, strictly speaking, it is not pessimism at all to hold that nothing ought to perish, while it is pessimism to affirm that, though nothing may perish, everything ought to.

Pessimism, moreover, may possess different values. Eudaemonistic or economic pessimism denies happiness; ethical pessimism denies the triumph of moral good; religious pessimism despairs of the human finality of the Universe and of the eternal salvation of the individual soul.

All men deserve to be saved, but, as I have said in the previous chapter, whoever desires immortality with a passion and even against all reason deserves it most of all. The writer H. G. Wells, who has given himself over to prophecy (not an uncommon phenomenon in his country), tells us in his *Anticipations* that "Active and capable men of all forms of religious profession today tend in practice to disregard the question of immortality altogether." And this is so because the religious professions of these active and capable men of whom Wells speaks are usually no more than a lie, and their lives are a lie, too, if they pretend to base them upon religion. But perhaps what Wells tells us is not basically as true as he and others like him imagine. Those active and capable men live in the midst of a society imbued with Christian principles, surrounded by institutions and social reactions produced by Christianity, so that a belief in the immortality of the soul runs deep in their own souls like a subterranean river, neither seen nor heard, but watering the roots of their deeds and their motives.

In all truth it must be admitted that there exists no more solid foundation for morality than the foundation provided by the Catholic ethic. Man's end-purpose is eternal happiness, which consists in the vision and enjoyment of God *in saecula saeculorum*. Where that ethic errs, however, is in the choice of means conducive to this end; for to make the attainment of eternal happiness dependent upon believing or not believing that the Holy Ghost proceeds from the Father and the Son and not from the Father alone, or in the divinity of Jesus, or in the theory of the hypostatic union, or even in the existence of God is nothing less than monstrous, as a moment's reflection will show. A human God—and we can conceive of no other—would never reject whoever could not believe in Him with his head; it is not in his head but in his heart that the wicked man says there is no God, that is: he does not *want* God to exist. If any belief could be linked with the attainment of eternal happiness it would be the belief in this happiness itself and in the possibility of attaining it.

And what shall we say of that other notion of the emperor of pedants, to the effect that we have not come into the world to be happy but to fulfill our duty ("Wir sind nicht auf der Welt, um glücklich zu sein, sondern um unsere Schuldigkeit zu tun")? If we are in this world *for something* (*um etwas*), whence can this *for* be derived but from the very essence of our own will, which asks for happiness and not duty as ultimate end? And if we were to attempt to attribute some other value to this *for*, an "objective value," as some Sadducean pedant might say, then we would have to recognize that this objective reality—the reality which would remain though humanity should disappear—is as indifferent to our duty as to our happiness, as little concerned with our morality as with our felicity. I am not aware that Jupiter, Uranus, or Sirius would allow their courses to be affected because we do or do not fulfill our duty any more than because we are or are not happy.

These reflections must appear ridiculously vulgar and superficial, the reflections of a dilettante. (The intellectual world is divided into two classes: dilettanti on the one hand, pedants on the other.) What can we do about it? Modern man resigns himself to the truth, and to not knowing the complex of culture: witness Windelband's testimony on this head in his study of Hölderlin's fate. Yes, the cultured are resigned, leaving a few poor savages like ourselves for whom resignation is impossible. We do not resign ourselves to the idea of having to disappear some day, and the great pedant's critique does not console us.

The epitome of everything sensible was expressed by Galileo Galilei: "Some perhaps will say that the bitterest pain is the loss of life, but I say that there are others more bitter; for whoever relinquishes life loses at the same time the power to lament this loss or any other." Whether Galileo was conscious or not of the humor in this sentence I do not know, but in any case the humor is tragic.

But, to turn back, I repeat that if any belief could be linked with the attainment of eternal happiness, it would be the belief in the possibility of its realization. And yet, strictly speaking, not even this will do. The reasonable man says in his head "There is no other life after this one"; but only the wicked man says it in his heart. Yet, since the wicked man himself may be no more than a man in despair, a desperado, can a human God condemn him because of his despair? Despair alone is misfortune enough.

In any event, let us adopt the formula of Calderón in *Life is a Dream*:

> I am dreaming and would
> do and act well, for not even
> in dreams are good works lost.

But are good works not really lost? Did Calderón really know? He went on to add:

> Let us attend on eternity
> which is truly living fame
> wherein good fortune never wanes
> nor glory ever quiet stay.

Is that really true? Did Calderón know?

Calderón had faith, a robust Catholic faith; but for whoever cannot have faith, for whoever cannot believe what Don Pedro Calderón de la Barca believed, there always remains the attitude of *Obermann*.

If annihilation must be our portion, let us act in such a way that we make it an unjust portion; let us fight against destiny, even without hope of victory; let us fight quixotically.

We fight against death not only by longing for the irrational, but also by acting in such wise that we become irreplaceable, impressing our seal upon others, working upon our fellow men and dominating them, giving ourselves to them and making ourselves eternal through them insofar as possible.

Our greatest effort must be the endeavor to make ourselves irreplaceable, to make a practical truth of the theoretical fact (if the term "theoretical fact" does not involve a contradiction in terms) that each one of us is unique and irreplaceable, and that no one else can fill the gap left by our death.

In all truth every man is unique and irreplaceable: another I is inconceivable; each one of us—our soul, not our life—is worth the whole Universe. I say our soul and not our life deliberately, for I am thinking of those who assign a ridiculously excessive value to life: they do not really believe in the spirit, that is, in their own personal immortality, and so they inveigh against war and the death penalty, for example, precisely because they do not really believe in the spirit, in whose service life should be, and thus they overvalue life. But life is of use only insofar as it serves its lord and master, spirit, and if the master perishes along with the servant, then neither the one nor the other is of any great value.

And to act in such a way as to make our annihilation unjustified, in such a way as to make our brothers and sisters, our children and their children, and the children of these children, all feel that we ought not to have died is something within the reach of all men.

The doctrine of the Christian redemption is based on the fact that the unique man, Man, the Son of Man, that is, the Son of God, suffered passion and death, when He, given His sinless condition, did not deserve to die; and that this propitiatory and divine victim died in order to rise again and to raise us from the dead, thus delivering us from death by virtue of applying His merits to us and by showing us the way of life. And the Christ who gave Himself entirely to His brothers in humanity with total self-abnegation is the model for our action.

All of us, each one of us, can and ought to resolve to give as much of himself as he can, and even more than he can, exceeding himself, going beyond himself, making himself irreplaceable, giving himself to all others so that they may give him back himself in them. And each one of us starts from his civil calling or office as point of departure: the word office, *officium*, means obligation, debt, in a concrete sense, and that is what it always ought to mean in practice. We ought not so much try to seek the particular vocation or calling we think most suitable for ourselves as to make a vocation of the employment in which luck or Providence or our own will has placed us.

Perhaps Luther rendered no greater service to Christian civilization than that of establishing the religious value of the civil professions as such, thus revoking the monastic and medieval idea of the religious vocation, an idea which was enveloped in the mist of extravagant and imaginative passions and which gave rise to terrible human tragedies. If we could only enter a cloister and scrutinize the religious vocation of the poor men whom the selfishness of their parents forced as children into a novice's cell and who suddenly awake, if they ever do awake at all, to the worldly life! Or if we could examine the careers of those whom their own autosuggestion had deceived! Luther, who saw the life of the cloister at close quarters and endured it himself, was able to understand and sense the religious value of the civil professions, to which no man is bound by perpetual vows.

Everything the Apostle said in the fourth chapter of his Epistle to the Ephesians with regard to the Christian vocation should be applied to civil life, inasmuch as today among ourselves the Christian— whether he know it or not, whether he like it or not —is the citizen. And just as the Apostle exclaimed, "I am a Roman citizen!" each one of us, even the atheist, may exclaim, "I am a Christian!" And this sentiment implies the *civilizing* of Christianity—in the sense of making it civil, or dis-ecclesiasticizing it. And that was Luther's task, though he himself later founded a Church.

"The right man in the right place" is an English expression. And in Spain, we, too, use the phrase "Cobbler, stick to thy last!" Who knows what position suits him best and for which he is most fitted? Does a man himself know it better than others, or do they know it better than he? Who can measure capacities and aptitudes? The religious attitude, undoubtedly, is to make whatever occupation we happen to pursue the right one, and only as a last resort to change it for another.

This question of a proper vocation is possibly the gravest and most deepseated of social problems, the basis of all other questions. The quintessential so-called "social question" is perhaps not so much a problem of the distribution of wealth, that is, of the products of labor, as a problem of the distribution of vocations, that is, of the modes of production. It is not a question of aptitude—something impossible to ascertain without first putting aptitude to the test, and not clearly indicated in any man, since a man is not born, but made, for the majority of vocations—it is not a question of any special aptitude, but of social, political, and customary considerations which determine a man's occupation. At certain times and in certain countries it is a matter of caste and heredity; at other times and in other places, it is the guild or corporation; in later times, the machine; in almost all cases it is a matter of necessity, almost never of free choice. The tragedy of it all culminates in those meretricious occupations in which a living is earned by selling one's soul, where the workman works in the knowledge that his work is not only superfluous but also a perversion of social values, for he may be producing a venom designed to annihilate him, an artifact which will perhaps be used to murder his children. Herein lies the fundamental problem, and it is not a matter of wages.

I shall never forget a scene to which I was witness on the banks of the estuary of Bilbao, my native city. A workman in a shipyard was hammering away at something or other, quite obviously in a listless fashion, going through the motions of earning his wage without any energy, when suddenly a woman's cry rent the air calling "Help!" A child had fallen into the water. The listless worker was instantly transformed and, in an access of energy, speed, and cold-blooded decision, threw off his clothes and plunged into the water to rescue the drowning child.

Possibly the reason why there is comparatively less ferocity behind the socialist agrarian movement is that though the field worker does not earn more or live better than the industrial worker or the miner, he does have a clearer notion of the social value of his work. Sowing grain is a different matter from extracting diamonds from the earth.

Perhaps the greatest social progress consists in a certain undifferentiation of labor, in the facility for leaving one form of work to take up another, not necessarily a more lucrative form but simply a nobler form of work—for there are definite degrees of nobility in labor. But unhappily it is only too seldom that a man who keeps to one occupation without changing it does so from any attempt to make a "religious" endeavor of it, or that the man who changes his occupation for another does so from any religiosity of motive.

And of course we all know of cases where a man evades the strict performance of his duty, justifying his attitude on the ground that the professional entity of which he forms part is poorly organized and does not function as it should, and that he therefore is fulfilling a higher duty by not serving. Such people call the literal carrying-out of duties routine disciplinarianism; and they speak of bureaucracy and the Pharisaism of public functionaries. All this is as if an intelligent and perspicacious military officer, realizing the deficiencies in his country's military organization, were to denounce them to his superiors and perhaps even to the public—thus doing his "higher duty"—

and then, in the field, were to refuse to carry out an operation assigned to him, because he believed its success was a minimal possibility, or even that defeat was certain while those deficiencies went uncorrected. He would of course deserve to be shot. And as regards the question of Pharisaism . . .

And there is always a way of obeying an order while yet retaining command, a way of carrying out an order one deems to be absurd, while remedying its absurdity, even if it be by one's own death. When in the course of my own official bureaucratic capacity I have chanced upon some legislative measure which, by reason of its manifest absurdity, has fallen into disuse, I have nevertheless always endeavored to apply it. There is nothing worse than a loaded pistol left lying idle in some corner: a child comes along, gets to playing with it, and shoots his father. Laws fallen into desuetude are the most terrible of laws, especially when the cause of the desuetude is that the law is a bad one.

And these are not vague suppositions, least of all in our country. For while certain people go about on some mission or other, fulfilling some ideal duties or responsibilities—that is to say fictitious ones—they themselves do not put their whole souls into the immediate and concrete endeavors upon which they live, and the rest—the vast majority—perform their functions merely to "do their duty" as the vulgar and terribly immoral phrase puts it, in order to get out of a fix, going through the motions, getting the job done, paying lip-service rather than doing it justice, for the sake of the emolument, whether it be money or something else.

Here behold one type of shoemaker, living off making shoes, but doing it with the minimum workmanship needed to keep his clientele. Then you have this other shoemaker, living on a rather different spiritual plane, for he is possessed by the instinct of workmanship, and out of pride of self or as a point of honor works to earn the reputation as best shoemaker in town, or in Christendom, even if this renown will not earn him any more money or more clientele, but only more renown and prestige. But there is a still higher degree of moral perfection as concerns the office of shoemaker, and that is for the shoemaker to work in order to become for his fellow townsmen the one and only shoemaker, the one who makes their footwear so well that they will miss him when he "dies on them," and not merely "dies," and they will all feel that he ought not to have died at all; and this will come about because he made their footwear in the thought of sparing them from thinking of their feet when they could be thinking of higher things, of the highest truths; in short, he made their footwear with love in his heart for them and for God in them—he made their footwear religiously.

This pedestrian example I have chosen deliberately, for the ethical sense, let alone the religious one, is very low in our cobblers' shops.

Workers form associations, cooperatives, and unions for defense, they fight very justly and nobly for the betterment of their class, but it is not at all obvious that these associations make for a better instinct of workmanship. They have succeeded in forcing the employers to hire the workers the unions designate— and not others. But they have not noticeably concerned themselves with the technical fitness of the workers hired. On occasion, the employer cannot easily dismiss an inept worker, for his fellows back him up. And on the job itself they may merely go through the motions, for the sake of the wage, and will go so far as to do the work badly to get back at the boss.

An apparent justification for this state of things lies in the fact that the employers are a hundred times more culpable than the workers: damned if they'll bother to give better pay to the worker who does better work, nor will they bother about their worker's general and technical education, and even less with assuring the intrinsic goodness of the product under production. The improvement of the product, which should result from natural industrial and mercantile competition, which should also benefit the consumers, and which should, even if only for charity's sake, be the chief end of the industry, is not so considered by either workers or employers, and that is so because neither side looks upon its social role religiously. Neither the one nor the other strives to be irreplaceable. The evil is aggravated with the appearance of the corporations or limited companies, which in Spain we call anonymous societies, for with the loss of the individual's signature, the vanity which seeks to accredit the signature, and which stands for the longing for eternity, disappears too; along with the disappearance of concrete individuality, the basis of all religion, the religiosity of the personal role disappears as well.

And everything that has been said of workers and employers applies even more to members of the liberal professions and to public functionaries. There scarcely exists a public servant who feels any religious commitment to his public office. Nothing is more dubious or confused than the feeling among us concerning our duty toward the State, a feeling further confounded by the Catholic Church, which, in strict truth, adopts a truly anarchist position. It is not uncommon to find priests defending smuggling and contraband as licit, as if the smuggler or the contrabandist did not disobey the legally constituted authority which prohibits it and thus offends against the Fourth Commandment of the law of God, which in commanding us to honor our mother and father commands us to obey lawful authority whenever it is not contrary—as it is not in the imposition of customs tribute—to the law of God.

Because of the stricture which says that "in the sweat of thy face shalt thou eat bread," many people regard work as a punishment and do not show any regard for civil employment beyond its economico-political, or, at best, its aesthetic value. For such people—chief among them the Jesuits—there are two distinct enterprises: the inferior, ephemeral one of earning a living, of earning our bread, for ourselves and our children, in an honorable manner (though the elasticity of honor is well known), and the grand enterprise of our salvation, of winning eternal glory. The inferior or worldly enterprise is to be undertaken not only insofar as it allows us, without deceit and without detriment to our fellows, to live decently and in accord with our social position, but also in a manner to afford us the greatest possible amount of time to attend to the other, grander, enterprise. And there are those who, rising a bit above this concept, a concept more economic than ethical, of our civil employment, attain to an aesthetic concept and aesthetic sense of it, and they set themselves the task of acquiring distinction and renown in their occupation, even to the point of making out of it an art for art's sake, an art for beauty's sake. But it is imperative to rise still higher than this, to attain to an ethical sense of our civil employment, a sense deriving from our religious feeling, from our hunger for eternity. To work, each one of us, at our own civil occupation, with our eyes fixed on God, to work for the love of God—which is equivalent to saying for the love of our eternalization—is to make of this work a religious one.

The text from Genesis "In the sweat of thy face shalt thou eat bread," does not mean that God condemned man to work, but simply condemned him to the painful awareness of it. Man could not be condemned to work itself, inasmuch as work is the only practical consolation for having been born. The proof that man was not "condemned" to work in itself lies, for a Christian, in the Book of Genesis (2:15), where it is stated that when man was put into the Garden of Eden he was "to dress it and keep it." And how, in fact, would man have passed his time in the Garden if he did not work it? And may not the beatific vision itself perhaps be a kind of work?

And even if work were our allotted punishment, we should strive to make of it, of our very punishment, our consolation and redemption; and if we are to embrace some cross there is none better for each one of us than the cross of his work at his own daily civil employment. For Christ did not say "Take up my cross and follow me," but "Take up thy cross and follow me": every man bearing his own cross, for only the Saviour can carry His cross. The imitation of Christ, therefore, does not consist in the monastic ideal which glows from the book ordinarily associated with Thomas a Kempis, an ideal only applicable to a very limited number of persons and, therefore, anti-Christian. To imitate Christ is to take up each one his own cross, the cross of his own civil occupation, as Christ took up His own cross, the cross of one's calling, civil as well as religious, and to embrace and carry it, one's eyes fixed on God and striving to make

300

each act of one's own calling into a true prayer. By making shoes, and precisely because one makes them, one can gain the kingdom of heaven, providing that as shoemaker one strives to be perfect, just as our Father in heaven is perfect.

Fourier, the socialist dreamer, already dreamed of making work attractive in his phalansteries by the free choice of vocations, and in other similar ways. But the only true way is that of liberty. Wherein lies the enchantment inherent in the play of chance, which is a kind of work, a working-out, but in voluntary submission to free Nature, that is, to chance? But let us not lose ourselves in comparing work and play.

And the drive to make ourselves irreplaceable, the impulse to refuse to deserve death, the striving to make our annihilation—if annihilation be our portion—an act of injustice, should lead us not only to carry out our own civil office religiously, from love of God and love of our own eternity and our being made immortal, but also to perform our office passionately, tragically if you prefer. It should impel us to endeavor to leave the stamp of our seal upon others, to perpetuate ourselves in them and in their children, by superior force, to leave on all things the imperishable sign of our impress. For the most fruitful ethic is the ethic of mutual imposition.

Above all, we must recast in a positive form the negative commandments inherited from the Ancient Law. Thus, for the textual "Thou shalt not lie!" let us understand "Thou shalt always speak the truth, in season and out of season!" Though it is we ourselves, and not others, who are judges in each instance of its seasonableness. And for "Thou shalt not kill!" let us understand "Thou shalt give life and increase it!" And let us assume that "Thou shalt not steal!" means

"Thou shalt increase the general wealth!" And for "Thou shalt not commit adultery!" let us read "Thou shalt give to heaven and thy country children who are healthy and strong and good!" And so on with all the other commandments.

He who does not lose his life shall not find it. Give yourself then to others, but in order to give yourself to them, first master them. For it is not possible to master without being mastered. Everyone nourishes himself upon the flesh he devours. In order to master your neighbor you must know him and love him. By attempting to impose my ideas upon him I become the recipient of his. To love my neighbor is to wish he may be like me, that he may be another I: that is to say, it is to wish I may be he, it is to wish to obliterate the division between him and me, to suppress its evil. My endeavor to impose myself upon another, to be and live in him and by him, to make him mine, which is the same as making my self his, is what gives religious meaning to our collectivity, to human solidarity.

The feeling of solidarity originates in myself; since I am a society, I feel the need of making myself master of human society; since I am a product of this society, I must socialize myself, and from myself I proceed to God—who is I projected to the All—and from God to each of my fellows.

My first impulse is to protest against the inquisitor and to prefer the merchant who comes to offer me his wares. But when I withdraw and think the matter over, I begin to see that the inquisitor, when he is well intentioned, treats me like a man, an end in myself, for if he interferes with me, he does so from a charitable desire to save my soul, while the merchant merely treats me as one more client, as a means to an end, and his indulgence and tolerance is basically no more than a supreme indifference to my destiny. The inquisitor has much more humanity about him.

By the same token there is more humanity to war than there is to peace. Resistance to evil implies an equal resistance to good, and even more than the defensive position, the offensive is perhaps the most divine attitude possible to humanity. War is a school for fraternity. It is a bond of love. Through mutual aggression and collision, war has brought entire nations into touch and contact, has caused them to know and love one another. Human love's purest and most fruitful embrace is the one between victor and vanquished on the battlefield. Even the purified hatred that flowers from warfare is fruitful. In its strictest sense, war is the sanctification of homicide: Cain is redeemed by being made general of the armies. And if Cain had not killed his brother Abel, he might have died at Abel's hands. God has revealed Himself, above all, in warfare. He began by being God of Hosts. And one of the greatest uses of the Cross is that, in the form of a sword-hilt, it protects the hand which wields the sword.

Enemies of the State say that Cain, the fratricide, was the founder of the State. And we must accept that such is the fact, and turn this fact to the glory of the State, the child of war. Civilization began upon the day that one man, subjecting another to his will and compelling him to do the work for both of them, was enabled to devote himself to contemplation of the world, and thereafter put his captive to the creation of lavish works. Slavery allowed Plato to speculate upon the ideal republic, and it was war which brought about slavery. It is for no idle reason that Athena is

303

the goddess of warfare and of science. But is there any real need to reiterate these obvious truths, so often forgotten only to be so many times recalled?

The highest precept which arises from the love of God, and the basis for all morality, is this: yield yourself up entirely, hand over your spirit so that it may be saved, so that it may be made eternal. Such is the meaningful sacrifice of life.

And yielding oneself assumes, I repeat, an imposition of oneself. True religious morality is essentially aggressive, ever ready to launch an invasion.

The individual *qua* individual, the wretched individual who lives a prey to the senses and to the instinct of self-preservation, cares only about preserving himself, and his sole concern is to keep others from forcing their way into his sphere, to keep them from disturbing him, from interrupting his idleness; and in return for their abstention, or for the sake of example, he refrains from forcing himself upon them, from interrupting their idleness, from disturbing them, from taking possession of them. "Do not do unto others what you would not have them do unto you," he translates as: "I do not interfere with others. Let them not interfere with me." And he shrinks back, and pines and perishes in this rut of spiritual avarice, in the slough of the repellent ethic of anarchic individualism, of each one for himself. And inasmuch as each one is not himself alone, he can scarcely live for himself alone.

But as soon as the individual senses that he is a member of society, he feels himself with God, and, moved by the instinct for self-preservation, he is imbued with love of God, and with overmastering charity he seeks to perpetuate himself in others, make himself perennial in spirit, make himself eternal, make God manifest, and his sole desire is to leave his spiritual seal upon the souls of others and to receive their seal in return. He has, then, shaken off the yoke of spiritual sloth and avarice.

Sloth, it is said, is the mother of all vices; and in truth sloth does engender two vices—avarice and envy, which in their turn are the source of all the rest. Sloth is the weight of matter, in itself inert, inside us, and this sloth, while it professes to preserve us by economizing our forces, in reality works toward lessening us and reducing us to nothing.

Man is possessed either of an excess of matter or an excess of spirit, or to put it better, either he feels a spiritual hunger, that is, a hunger for eternity, or he feels a material hunger, that is, a hunger to submit to annihilation. When spirit is in excess and man feels a hunger for yet more of it, he pours his own spirit out and spreads it abroad, and as it pours out it grows by contact with the spirits of others; when, on the other hand, avarice takes hold, man withdraws into himself, thinking thus to better preserve himself, and ends by losing everything, like the man who was endowed with a single talent and buried it so as not to lose it, only to find himself without it altogether. For, to him that has shall be given more, and from him that has but little shall be taken even that little.

Be ye therefore perfect even as your Father which is in heaven is perfect, we are bidden, and this terrible precept—terrible because for us the infinite perfection of the Father is unattainable—must be our supreme rule of conduct. Unless a man aspires to the impossible, the possible that he achieves will scarcely be worth the trouble of his achieving it.

We should aspire to the impossible, to absolute and infinite perfection, and say to the Father: "Lord, I cannot; help Thou my impotence!" And He will achieve it in us.

And to be perfect is to be all; it is to be I and to be all others as well; it is to be humanity, to be the universe. And there is no other way of being all else but by giving oneself to all, and when all shall be all in all, all will be in each one of us. The apocatastasis is more than a mystical dream: it is a norm of action, it is a beacon for high deeds.

And from here springs the invasive, overmastering, aggressive, inquisitorial ethic, if you will. For true charity is a species of invasion: it consists in forcing my spirit upon other spirits, in offering them my suffering as nutriment and consolation for their own sufferings, in arousing their unrest, in whetting their hunger for God by my hunger for God. It is not charity to rock and lull our fellow men to sleep in the inertia and heaviness of matter, but rather to arouse them to the anguish and torment of spirit.

To the fourteen works of mercy we learned in the Catechism of Christian Doctrine there should be added yet another: that of awakening the sleeper, sometimes at least, and most certainly on occasion, as when the sleeper is asleep on the brink of a precipice; for to awaken him is much more merciful than to bury him after he is dead. Let the dead bury the dead. It has been very well said that "Whoever loves you deeply will make you weep," and charity often causes weeping. "The love that does not mortify does not deserve so divine a name," said the ardent Portuguese apostle, Fray Thomé de Jesus, who also exclaimed: "O infinite fire, O eternal love, who weepest when thou hast nought to embrace and feed upon and many hearts to burn!" He who loves his neighbor burns his heart, and the heart, like green wood, groans when it burns, and distills itself in tears.

And this act is one of generosity, one of the two mother virtues which are born when inertia and sloth are overcome. Most of our miseries come from spiritual avarice.

Suffering—which comes from the collision between consciousness and unconsciousness, as we said—is cured, not by submerging oneself in the unconscious, but by raising oneself to the highest consciousness and thus suffering more. The evil of suffering is cured by more suffering, by higher suffering. There is no point in taking opium; it is better to put salt and vinegar in the soul's wound, for if you fall asleep and no longer feel the pain, then you no longer exist. And the point is to exist. Do not, then, close your eyes before the overawing Sphinx, but gaze on her face to face, and let her take you in her mouth and chew you with her hundred thousand poisonous teeth and swallow you up. And when she has swallowed you, you will know the sweet taste of suffering.

And the ethic of mutual imposition is the practical way to this end. All men should strive to impose themselves upon one another, to give their spirits up to one another, to leave their seals on one another's souls.

It gives one pause to recall the argument that Christian morality is the morality of slaves. Who said so? The anarchists! It is anarchism itself, indeed, which is the morality of slaves: only the slave hymns anarchic liberty. *Anarchism*: *No*! Panarchism: *Yes*! In short: No! to the creed of "Neither God nor Master!" Yes! to the creed of "Everyone a God! Everyone a Master!": all men striving to become gods, all striving to become immortal, and doing so by mastering all others.

And there are so many ways of acting the master! At times, even an apparently passive way of domination fulfills this law of life. Adaptation to environment, imitation, putting oneself in another's place, in a word, sympathy, besides being a manifestation of the unity of the species, is a way of self-expansion, a way of being someone else. To be overcome, or at least to appear to be overcome, is often a way of overcoming another. To take something belonging to someone else is a way of living in that other person.

When I speak of mastering or overcoming, I don't mean in the manner of a tiger. The fox also overcomes, by cunning, and the hare by flight, and the viper by poison, and the mosquito by its minuteness, and the squid by the inky discharge which clouds the sea and allows it to flee. And no one is outraged at these phenomena, for the Father of us all, the same Father who provided the tiger with its fierceness, talons, and jaws, gave the fox cunning, the hare speed, the viper poison, the mosquito minuteness, and the squid ink. Nobility or ignobility does not consist in the weapons used—for each species and even each individual is possessed of its own—but rather in the way they are used, and above all in the cause in which they are wielded.

Among the weapons of conquest must be included the weapon of impassioned patience and resignation, informed by inner action and longing. Recall the splendid sonnet by Milton, that grand fighter and profound Puritan disturber of the peace, the follower of Cromwell and hymnist of Satan, who, when he found himself blind, considered how his light was spent,

"And that one Talent which is death to hide," lodged with him useless, and heard the voice of Patience say:

> God doth not need
> Either man's work or his own gifts, who best
> Bear his milde yoak, they serve him best, his State
> Is Kingly. Thousands at his bidding speed
> And post o'er Land and Ocean without rest:
> They also serve who only stand and waite.

"They also serve who only stand and wait."—Yes, but only when they wait passionately, with a hunger and a longing to live on in Him.

And so we must impose ourselves, even though it be only by our patience. "My cup is small, but I drink out of my cup," wrote an egotistical poet of an avaricious people. No! Out of my cup let all men drink. I want all men to drink with me: I proffer my cup to all, and it increases in size as the number of drinkers increases, and all of them, in putting their lips to the cup, leave something of their spirit. And while they drink from my cup, I drink from theirs. For the more I am my own man, and the more I am myself, the more I belong to others; out of the plenitude of myself I pour upon my brothers, and as I pour upon them, they pour upon me.

"Be ye therefore perfect even as your Father which is in heaven is perfect," we are bidden, and our Father is perfect because He is Himself and because He is each one of His children who live and move and have their being in Him. And the end-purpose of perfection is to make us all one (John 17:21), all one body in Christ (Rom. 12:5), and, at the last, when all things are subject to the Son, the Son himself may be subject to Him who made everything subject so that God may be all in all. And thus will the Universe be made consciousness, and Nature made a society, a human society. And then shall we be able fully to call God Father.

I am well aware that those who say ethics is a science will say that all this commentary of mine on this head is nothing but rhetoric. Each of us has his own language and his own passion: at least the passionate man does, and if a man does not have passion, science is of little avail to him.

The passion which finds its expression in this rhetoric is called egotism by the "ethical scientists." But this *egotism* is the only true cure for *egoism* or spiritual avarice, the vice of keeping and saving oneself for oneself rather than striving to make oneself eternal by giving oneself.

"Be nought, and thou shalt be more than aught that is," said Fray Juan de los Angeles in one of his *Dialogues*. But what does it mean to "Be nought!"? May it not paradoxically mean, as sometimes happens with the mystics, the opposite of what it seems literally to mean? Is not the entire ethic of submission and quietism an immense paradox, or rather, a great tragic contradiction? Is not the monastic ethic, the purely monastic ethic, an absurdity? And I mean here, when I speak of the monastic ethic, the ethic of the solitary Carthusian, that of the hermit, who flees the world— perhaps taking it with him nonetheless—so that he may live alone, by himself in the company of a God who is as alone and solitary as himself. I do not mean the ethic of the Dominican inquisitor who scoured Provence in search of Albigensian hearts to burn.

"Let God do it all," some reader may exclaim. But if a man folds his arms, God will go to sleep.

It is this Carthusian ethic, and the scientific ethic which derived from ethical science, which may well be a matter of egoism and coldness of heart. O ethics as science! Rational and rationalistic ethics! Pedantry of pedantries, all is pedantry!

There are those who say they retreat to God the better to gain their salvation, their redemption. But redemption must be collective since guilt is collective. "Religiosity is a total decision, and everything else is a delusion of the senses, and so the greatest criminal is fundamentally an innocent man of good will, a saint," as Kierkegaard wrote in his *Concluding Unscientific Postscript*.

Are we to understand, on the other hand, that men would want to gain the other, the eternal, life by renouncing this temporal life? If the other life is anything, it must be a continuation of this life, and only as a continuation of this life, more or less purified, is it imagined by our longing. And if such is the case, then eternal life will be a continuation of this temporal life of ours.

"This world and the other world are like the two wives of one and the same husband: if you please one, you make the other envious," says an Arab thinker quoted by Windelband. But such a thought could only have occurred to someone who had failed to resolve the tragic conflict between his spirit and the world: failed to resolve it and convert it into a fruitful struggle, into a practical contradiction. "Thy kingdom come," is the imperative Christ taught us to address to His father, not "Let us go to Thy kingdom." And according to primitive Christian belief, eternal life was to be realized on the earth itself, as a continuation of this earthly life. We were created men and not angels so that we might seek our fortune by means of this life, and the Christ of the Christian faith became a human being, not an angel, and redeemed us by assuming a real and true body, not an apparential one. According to this same primitive Christianity, even the highest in the angelic hierarchy venerate the Virgin, the supreme symbol of earthly Humanity. The angelic ideal is not, therefore, a Christian ideal, and still less is it the human ideal, nor can it be. An angel, moreover, is a neutral being, without sex and without a country.

We are unable to conceive of the other life, the eternal life—as I have repeatedly said—as a life of angelic contemplation. It must be a life of action. Goethe said that "man should believe in immortality; he has a right to this belief." And he added: "To me, the eternal existence of my soul is proved from my idea of activity; if I work on incessantly until my death, nature is bound [*so ist die Natur verpflichtet*] to give me another form of existence when the present one can no longer sustain my spirit." Change "Nature" for "God," and you have a thought which remains Christian in character, for the first Fathers of the Church did not believe that the immortality of the soul was a natural gift—that is, a rational thing—but rather a divine gift of grace. And whatever pertains to grace, basically pertains also to justice, inasmuch as justice is divine and gratuitous, not natural. And Goethe went on to say: "I would not know how to launch myself upon any enterprise if I were confronted solely with eternal happiness before me, and unless new tasks and difficulties were given me to overcome." And so it is: contemplative idleness is no gift.

But may not some justification exist for the morality of the hermit, of the Carthusian, some justification for the ethic of the Thebaid? May we not perhaps contend that it is necessary for these exceptional types to exist as an eternal pattern for mankind? Do not men breed racehorses, useless for any practical work but preserving the purity of the breed and siring splendid hackneys and hunters? Can we not perhaps afford a de luxe ethic as well as any other luxury? And yet, in the end, is not this kind of ethics really aesthetics rather than morality, and even less religion? Is not the medieval ideal of monastic contemplation rather a matter of aesthetics and not of religion at all, not even of ethics? In short, those seekers of solitude who have told us of their conversations with God have performed a labor tending to make us eternal, for they have imposed themselves upon the souls of others. And by this alone, by the fact that the monastic orders have given us mystics, is the cloister justified: for it has given us an Eckhart, a Suso, a Tauler, a Ruysbroeck, a John of the Cross, a Catherine of Siena, an Angela of Foligno, a Teresa of Jesus.

But among our Spanish orders the principal ones are, above all, the Order of Preachers, otherwise known as the Dominicans or Black Friars, founded by Domingo de Guzmán for the aggressive task of extirpating heresy; the Society of Jesus, a militia "in the midst of the world," a phrase which explains all; the Piarists, or Clerks Regular of the Religious Schools, also dedicated to the equally invasive labor of education. . . . And someone is bound to remind me that the reform of the contemplative order of Carmelites undertaken by Teresa of Jesus was a Spanish endeavor. Yes, it was indeed Spanish, and it was a search for liberty.

It was, in fact, a yearning for liberty, inner liberty, which, in the troubled days of the Inquisition, led many choice spirits to the cloister. They imprisoned themselves so that they might be freer. "Is it not a funny thing that a poor little nun of St. Joseph's should attain mastery over the whole earth and all the elements?" exclaimed St. Teresa. These people were moved by the Pauline yearning for liberty, the longing to shake off the bondage of the external law, which was then very severe, and, as Maestro Fray Luis de León said, good and stubborn.

But did they actually find liberty in the cloister? It is quite doubtful that they did; today it would be impossible. For true liberty is not a matter of ridding oneself of external law; liberty is consciousness of the law. The free man is not the one who has rid himself of the law, but the one who has made himself master of it. Liberty must be sought in the midst of the world, which is the domain of the law, and of transgression, offspring of the law. It is guilt, transgression, from which we must be freed, and guilt is collective.

Instead of renouncing the world in order to dominate it (who can be unaware of the collective instinct toward domination shown by those religious orders whose members renounce the world?), what we should do is dominate the world in order to be able to renounce it. Rather than seek poverty and submission, we should seek wealth and power, and use it to expand human consciousness.

It is curious that friars and anarchists should fight each other, when fundamentally they both profess the same ethics and are so closely related to each other. Anarchism tends to be a kind of atheistic monkhood and more of a religious than an ethical or socio-economic doctrine. The friars start from the assumption that man is by nature evil, born in original sin, and that it is grace which makes him good, if indeed he ever does become good; and the anarchists start from the assumption that man is naturally good and is subsequently perverted by society. In the end, one theory is the same as the other: in both cases the individual is opposed to society, as if the individual had preceded society and therefore were destined to survive it. And both sets of ethics are the ethics of the cloister.

And the fact that guilt is collective must not serve as an excuse for me to shed my own guilt upon others, but rather to take upon myself the burden of the guilt of others, the guilt of all men; not to merge and drown my guilt in the total guilt, but instead to make this total guilt my own; not to alienate my own guilt, but rather to take upon myself, to appropriate and be utterly possessed by the guilt of all men. And everyman ought to do his part to expiate the guilt of all, some men having to expiate for others. The truth that society is guilty aggravates the guilt of each member of it. " 'Some one ought to do it, but why should I?' is the ever re-echoed phrase of weak-kneed amiability. 'Someone ought to do it, so why *not* I?' is the cry of some earnest servants of man, eagerly forward springing to face some perilous duty. Between those two sentences lie whole centuries of moral evolution." So spoke Annie Besant in her autobiography. Thus spoke theosophy.

The fact that society is guilty aggravates the guilt of each one, and he is most guilty who most feels the guilt. The innocent Christ, since He felt the intensity of the guilt most, was in a certain sense the most guilty. In Him the culpability of humanity, together with its divinity, reached full consciousness of itself. Many people are readily amused when they read how, because of the most trifling faults, faults at which a man of the world would merely smile, the greatest saints counted themselves the greatest of sinners. But the intensity of the fault is not to be measured by the external act, but by consciousness of it, and a deed for which the conscience of one man suffers acutely may scarcely stir the conscience of another. And in a saint, conscience may be developed so fully and to such a degree of sensitivity that the slightest fault may cause him more remorse than the foulest crime causes a great criminal. And guilt stems from consciousness of it; it lies in the judge of it and to the extent that he makes a judgement. Whenever a man commits a vicious deed, believing in good faith that he is doing something virtuous, we cannot hold him morally reprehensible; while if another man believes that some quite unimportant, or even possibly meritorious, deed was actually evil, then that man is culpable. The deed evanesces, the intention remains, and the evil in an evil deed consists in its corruption of intention; if evil is done with malice aforethought, one's conscience becomes beclouded and there is a predisposition to more wrongdoing. Doing evil is not the same as being evil. Evil beclouds the conscience, and not only the moral conscience but the general, physical consciousness. And whatever depresses or diminishes consciousness is bad, while whatever exalts and expands consciousness is good.

And here we might pose the question which, according to Plato, was posed by Socrates, and that is whether or not virtue is knowledge, a question which is equivalent to asking whether or not virtue is rational.

The ethicists—those who maintain that ethics is a science, those whom the reading of these digressions will provoke to exclaim "Rhetoric, rhetoric, rhetoric!"—they will believe, I suppose, that virtue is attained through science, through rational study, and

even that mathematics help us be better men. I do
not know if they are right, but it seems to me that
virtue, like religion, like the longing never to die—
and all three are fundamentally the same—are the
fruit of passion.

"But what then is passion?" I shall be asked. I do
not know; or rather, I know full well, because I feel
it, and since I feel it there is no need for me to define
it to myself. Nay, more: I fear that if I were to arrive at a definition of it, I should cease to feel and
to possess it. Passion is like suffering, and like suffering it creates its object. It is easier to find fuel for
the fire than to find fire for the fuel.

And this, I know well enough, may seem like so
much empty sophistry. And I shall also be told that
there is a knowledge of passion and a passion of
knowledge, and that in the moral sphere reason and
life unite.

I do not know, I do not know, I do not know. . . .
And perhaps what I am saying, though I say it somewhat more obscurely, is essentially the same as what
my imaginary adversaries, whom I imagine in order
to have someone to oppose, say in their turn, only
they say it more clearly, more definitely, and more
rationally. I do not know, I do not know. . . . But
only, the things they say leave me cold and strike me
as being emotionally empty.

But returning to our former question: is virtue a
matter of knowledge? Is knowledge virtue? Here we
have two separate questions in reality. Virtue may be
knowledge, the knowledge of how to conduct oneself
well, without all other aspects of knowledge being a
matter of virtue. Machiavelli's virtue is knowledge,
but it cannot be said that his *virtù*, his artistic excellence, is always a moral virtue. It is well known,

moreover, that the most intelligent or the most learned men are not necessarily the best men.

No, no, no! Physiology does not teach us how to digest, nor logic how to reflect, nor aesthetics how to feel beauty or express it, nor ethics how to be good. And we are lucky if these sciences do not teach us to be hypocrites, for pedantry, whether the pedantry of logic, or of aesthetics, or of ethics, is essentially nothing but hypocrisy.

Reason may perhaps teach us certain bourgeois virtues, but it does not produce either saints or heroes. For the saint is one who does good not for the sake of the good, but for the sake of God, for the sake of becoming eternal.

Perhaps, on the other hand, culture, that is, Culture—O Culture!—the work, primarily, of philosophers and men of science, was not made by either heroes or saints! For saints have concerned themselves very little with the progress of human culture; they have concerned themselves rather with the salvation of individual souls, the souls of those individuals among whom they lived. Compared to Descartes, of what account is St. John of the Cross, that incandescent little friar, as he has been culturally—but perhaps not in a cultured manner—described?

What have all the saints, burning with religious charity toward their fellows, hungering to have themselves and their neighbors made eternal, longing to set fire to the hearts of others, what have they done to advance the progress of science or of ethics? Did any one of them perchance invent the categorical imperative, as did the old bachelor of Königsberg, who if he was not a saint deserved to be one?

One day, the son of a grand professor of ethics, a professor who scarcely ever allowed that imperative to leave his lips, complained to me that his life was a barren sterility of spirit and that he lived in an inner vacuum. And I was forced to tell him:

"The fact is, my friend, that your father could count on an underground river, a ready current of ancient belief from his childhood and of hopes in the beyond. And while he thought he was nourishing his soul on that imperative or on something of a like nature, he was in reality drinking the waters of his beginnings. And he has perhaps given you the flower of his spirit, that is, his rational doctrines regarding ethics, but he has not given you the root, not the subterranean source, not the irrational substratum."

Why did Krausism happen to take root here in Spain, rather than the doctrines of Hegel or Kant, which are rationally and philosophically much more profound than Krausism? Because Krausism was brought here with its roots intact. The philosophical thought of a nation or of an epoch is, so to say, its flower, the part which is external and above ground. But this flower, or if you wish, this fruit, draws its juice from the roots of the plant, and these roots, which are in and under the earth, are its religious sense. Kant's philosophical thought, the ultimate flower of the mental evolution of the Germanic people, has its roots in Luther's religious sense, and it is not possible for Kantianism, especially the practical part of it, to take root and bring forth flower and fruit in nations which have not experienced the Reformation and which perhaps were not capable of undergoing the experience. Kantianism is Protestant, and we Spanish are fundamentally Catholic. And if Krause put down some roots here—more than is commonly supposed and less ephemeral than is imagined—it is because Krause had his roots in pietism.

And pietism, as Ritschl demonstrated in his history of that tendency, *Geschichte des Pietismus*, possesses specifically Catholic roots and signifies the permeation, or rather the persistence, of Catholic mysticism within the heart of Protestant rationalism. And this explains why not a few Catholic thinkers in Spain were touched by Krausist doctrine.

And since the Spanish are Catholics, whether we know it or not, or whether we like it or not, and although some of us may presume to be rationalists or atheists, it may be that the greatest service we can render to the cause of culture, and of religiosity, which is of more worth than culture—unless indeed culture and religiosity are the same thing—is in endeavoring to realize and clarify this subconscious, social, or popular Catholicism. And that has been the work in hand in this study.

What I have called the tragic sense of life in men and in nations is at any rate the Spanish tragic sense of life, that of Spanish people and of the Spanish nation, as it is reflected in my consciousness, which is a Spanish consciousness, made in Spain. And this tragic sense of life is essentially the Catholic sense of it, for Catholicism, above all popular Catholicism, is tragic. The people abominate comedy. When Pilate, the epitome of the refined gentleman, the superior person, the aesthete—the rationalist if you like—proposes to give the people comedy and mockingly presents Christ to them, saying "Behold the man!," the people go mad and cry out "Crucify him! Crucify him!" They do not want comedy, but tragedy. And the work which Dante, that great Catholic, called the *Divine Comedy* is the most tragic work ever written.

In these essays I have endeavored to reveal the soul of a Spaniard, and therewith the Spanish soul as such, and in the course of so doing I have advisedly curtailed the number of quotations from Spanish sources and, perhaps excessively, scattered citations from non-Spanish sources. For the fact is that all human souls are brother souls.

There is one figure, a comically tragic figure, a figure in which is revealed all that is profoundly tragic in the human comedy, the figure of Our Lord Don Quixote, the Spanish Christ, in whom is resumed and enclosed the immortal soul of my people. Perhaps the passion and death of the Knight of the Sorrowful Countenance is the passion and death of the Spanish people, its death and resurrection. And there exists a Quixotic philosophy and even a Quixotic metaphysics, and also a Quixotic logic and a Quixotic sense of religion. This philosophy, this logic, this ethics, this religious sense is what I have tried to outline, to suggest rather than to develop, in the present work; not to develop rationally, of course, for Quixotic madness does not admit of scientific logic.

And now, before concluding my work and taking leave of my readers, it remains for me to speak of the role reserved for Don Quixote in the modern European tragi-comedy.

Let us see, in one final essay, what it may be.

XII. Don Quixote in the Contemporary European Tragicomedy

"A voice crying in the wilderness!"

Isaiah 40:3

FORCIBLY must I bring to an end, for the time being at least, this series of essays which threaten to turn into a tale without end. They have gone from my hands direct to the printer in a kind of improvised commentary upon notes gathered over a period of years, so that I have not had before me, as I wrote each essay, those that preceded it. And thus they go forth full of quintessential contradictions—apparent contradictions, at any rate—like life and like myself.

My fault, if one is to be picked out, has been to interlard an excess of remote citations, many of which will appear to have been dragged in with a certain degree of force. I will explain some other time.

A few short years after Our Lord Don Quixote went riding through Spain, Jacob Böhme told us, in his *Aurora*, that he was not writing a story related to him by others, but was himself forced to take part in the battle, fighting furiously, and often beaten down, like all other men: and he added, farther on in his text: "Although I must become a spectacle of scorn to the world and the devil, yet my hope is in God concerning the life to come; in Him will I venture to hazard all and not resist or strive against the Spirit. Amen."

*322**

And like this Quixote of the German world of thought, neither will I resist the Spirit.

And I therefore raise my voice, to clamor in the wilderness, and I raise my voice from here, from the University of Salamanca, which had the arrogance to style itself *Omnium scientiarum princeps*, and which Carlyle called a Fortress of Ignorance, and which a Frenchman of letters recently labeled a phantom university; I raise my voice from out of Spain, "the land of dreams which become realities; the defender of Europe, the home of the ideal of chivalry" (to quote from a letter sent me the other day by Archer M. Huntington, the Hispanist); from this Spain which was the head and font of the Counter-Reformation in the sixteenth century. And Spain is still paying the price!

In the fourth of these essays I spoke of the essence of Catholicism. And in *de-essentializing* it—that is, de-Catholicizing Europe—the chief agents have been the Renaissance, the Reformation, and the Revolution, as they substituted the ideal of progress, reason, and science, or rather, of Science with a capital S, for the ideal of an eternal ultra-terrestrial life. Now, for the moment, the latest, most popular notion is that of Culture.

In the second half of the nineteenth century, an age essentially unphilosophical and given to technique, dominated by a myopic specialization and historical materialism, this scientific ideal took a practical form, not so much of the popularization, as of the vulgarization of science—or rather of pseudo-science—and expressed itself in a proliferation of democratic sets of cheap popular and propagandist literature. Science was thus thought to be achieving popularity, as if it were its function to lower itself to the level of the people and serve their passions, and not the duty of the people to rise to science and through science rise to higher levels still, to new and profounder aspirations.

These developments led Brunetière to proclaim the bankruptcy of science, and this science, or whatever it was, did in effect become bankrupt. And as it failed to give satisfaction, men continued their search for felicity, but it was not found, either in wealth, or in knowledge, or in power, or in pleasure, or in resignation, or in a good moral conscience, or in culture. And the result was an access of pessimism.

The Gospel of Progress did not satisfy either. Why progress? Man refused to be satisfied with rationalism; the *Kulturkampf* did not suffice; so men sought to lend life a final finality, that final finality which is the real ὄντως ὄν. And the famous *mal du siècle*, whose note was sounded in Rousseau and was echoed more clearly than anywhere in Sénancour's *Obermann*, was in reality nought but the loss of faith in the immortality of the soul, in the human end-purpose of the Universe.

Its symbol, its true symbol is a fictional creation, Dr. Faustus.

This immortal Dr. Faustus, product of the Renaissance and the Reformation, first comes into our ken at the beginning of the seventeenth century, when, in 1604, he is introduced to us by Christopher Marlowe. This is the same Faust whom Goethe will rediscover two centuries later, although in certain respects the earlier is the fresher and more spontaneous. And side by side with him appears Mephistophilis, to whom Faust puts the question: "Stay, Mephistophilis, and tell me, what good will my soul do thy lord?" To

which Mephistophilis replies: "Enlarge his kingdom."
And the Doctor again asks: "Is that the reason why
he tempts us thus?" Whereupon the evil spirit answers: "Solamen miseris socios habuisse doloris," a
sentence which, mistranslated into the vernacular,
yields our common proverb: "The misfortune of many
is the consolation of fools." Mephistophilis adds to his
part of the dialogue: "In one self place; for where we
are is hell,/And where hell is, there must we ever be."
And then Faust says that he believes that Hell is a
fable, and asks Mephistophilis who made the world.
This tragic Doctor, tortured by our selfsame torture,
in the end finds Helen, who is none other—though
Marlowe perhaps never suspected the truth—than
renascent Culture. And here in Marlowe's *Faust* there
is a scene worth the whole of the Second Part of the
Faust of Goethe: Faust says to Helen "Sweet Helen,
make me immortal with a kiss"—and he kisses her:

> Her lips suck forth my soul: see, where it flies!—
> Come, Helen, come, give me my soul again.
> Here will I dwell, for Helen is in these lips,
> And all is dross that is not Helena.

". . . give me my soul again." Such is the cry of
Faust the Doctor, when, after kissing Helen, he goes
to his perdition. For there is no ingenuous Margaret
at all to save him. The idea of Faust's salvation was
Goethe's invention. And who does not know this Faust
of Goethe's, our Faust, who studied Philosophy, Jurisprudence, Medicine, and even Theology, only to find
we cannot know anything, and who sought a way out
into the open country (*hinaus ins weite Land*) and
there encountered Mephistopheles, the embodiment of
that force which, ever willing evil, achieves good in
spite of itself; and Mephistopheles led him to the arms

of Margaret, child of the simplehearted people, whom the wise Faust had lost; and thanks to her, who gave herself to him, Faust is saved, redeemed by the people which believes with a simple faith. But there was that second part, for the other Faust was the anecdotic Faust and not the categorical one of Goethe, and he gave himself over again to Culture, to Helen, and begot Euphorion with her, and so everything ends among mystical choruses with the discovery of the eternal feminine. Poor Euphorion!

This Helen is the spouse of the fair Menelaus, the Helen whom Paris bore away, who was the cause of the Trojan War, and of whom the ancient Trojans said that it was not unseemly that men should fight over a woman who in her countenance bore such an awesome likeness to the immortal gods. But I rather think that Faust's Helen was really the one who accompanied Simon Magus, and whom he declared to be the divine intelligence. And Faust could say to her: ". . . give me my soul again."

For Helen with her kisses sucks away our soul. And what we need and want is soul, a soul with some substance.

But the Renaissance, the Reformation, and the Revolution came, bringing Helen with them; or rather these phenomena were brought upon us by Helen. And now they talk to us of Culture and of Europe.

Europe! The primitively and immediately geographic idea of Europe has been transformed for us, as if by magic, into an almost metaphysical category. Who can say today (at least in Spain) what Europe is? I know only that it is a shibboleth, or *schibolet* as I have called it elsewhere. And when I proceed to examine what our Europeanizers mean by "Europe," it often strikes me that they leave out a good deal of the periphery: Spain of course, but also England, Italy, Scandinavia, Russia. Thus Europe is reduced to the central core: Franco-Germany and its annexes and dependencies.

And this state of things is the consequence of the Renaissance and the Reformation, which were twin brothers, though they lived in an apparent state of internecine war. The Italians of the Renaissance were all of them Socinians. The humanists, with Erasmus at their head, considered Luther, the German monk, a barbarian—Luther, who derived his strength from the cloister, as did Bruno and Campanella. But the barbarian was their twin brother: while he fought them, he fought alongside them against the common enemy. The Renaissance and the Reformation, I say, along with their daughter the Revolution, have brought us all these things, and they have also brought us a new Inquisition: that of science and culture, which turns its weapons of ridicule and contempt against whoever does not submit to its orthodoxy.

When Galileo sent his treatise on the earth's motion to the Grand Duke of Tuscany, he wrote him that it was only proper to obey and believe in the decisions of one's superiors, and that he, Galileo, considered his own treatise to be "like poetry or a dream and as such I desire your highness to accept it." And at other times he calls it a "chimera" or a "mathematical caprice." And in the same way, in these essays, from fear also—why not confess it?—of the Inquisition, but of today's Inquisition, the scientific Inquisition, I proffer what springs from the deepest part of me as poetry, dream, chimera, or mystical caprice. And I say with Galileo, "Eppur si muove!" And yet, is it solely fear that moves me to subterfuge? Ah, no!

There exists another, more tragic Inquisition, I mean the Inquisition that the modern man, the man of culture, the European man—which is what I am, whether I want to be one or not—carries within him. There exists a more terrible ridicule, and that is the ridicule of one's self which one sees in one's own eyes. My reason makes mock of my faith and despises it.

And here I must have recourse to my Lord Don Quixote to learn how to face ridicule and overcome it, to best a ridicule he may perhaps—who knows?— not ever have known.

Yes, yes, of course my reason must smile at these pseudo-philosophical constructs of mine, these dilettante attempts at mysticism, which contain everything but patient study, objectivity, and method—scientific method. And nevertheless: *Eppur si muove!*

Eppur si muove! Yes! And I have recourse to dilettantism, to what a pedant would call *demi-mondaine* philosophy, as a refuge against the pedantry of specialists, against the philosophy of professional philosophers and the theology of the theologians. And who knows? . . . Progress usually comes from the barbarians, while there is nothing more stagnant than the philosophy of the philosophers and the theology of the theologians. And let them talk to us of Europe! The civilization of Tibet is parallel to our own, and men have lived and live there who disappear like ourselves. And over all civilizations hovers the shadow of Ecclesiastes, with the admonition of "how dieth the wise man?—as the fool" (2:16).

There is an admirable reply current among the people of my nation to the customary question "How are you?" and it consists in answering "One lives." And so it is—one lives, we live much as others do.

And what more can one ask? And what Spaniard would not know this verse?

> Every time that I consider
> that I am going to die
> I spread my cape upon the ground
> and sleep till life is by.

But no, not to sleep, rather to dream; to dream life, since life is a dream.

It is also proverbial to say that the point is to pass the time, that is, to kill time. And in fact we make time, find time—to kill time. But there is something else which has always concerned us as much or more than passing the time, which is a formula covering an aesthetic position, and that is to gain eternity, a formula covering the religious position. And in truth we jump from the aesthetic and the economic to the religious plane, passing over the logical and the ethical; we jump from art to religion.

A Spanish novelist, Ramón Pérez de Ayala, in his novel *La pata de la raposa*, tells us that the idea of death is a trap, while the spirit is the vixen, that is, the wary wisdom with which to step around the ambushes of fate, and he adds:

Caught in the trap, weak men and weak nations lie prone on the ground; and lying there they dream a cowardly dream, imagining that a bountiful and providential hand holds them down only to lead them to a new and more fortunate existence. Stout spirits and vigorous nations are shocked into clearheaded insight by the presence of danger. They gain a sudden insight into the enormous beauty of life, and put behind them forever their primitive wild carelessness; they slip the trap with muscles taut and ready for action, the wellsprings of their spirits more potent, effective, impelling.

*329**

But, wait, let us see: "weak men" . . . "weak nations" . . . "strong spirits" . . . "strong nations" . . . What does it all mean? I do not know. What I think I do know is that some individuals and nations have not yet seriously considered death and immortality, have not felt them; and that others have ceased to think about them, or rather ceased to feel them. And the fact that they have never passed through a religious age is not, I think, cause for boasting in either men or nations.

The "enormous beauty of life" is all very well in literature, and there are, indeed, people who resign themselves and accept life as they find it, and there are even those who would persuade us that the question of a trap is no problem. But Calderón told us:

> For ill luck it's no consolation—
> but an added bit of ill luck—
> to try to persuade its bearers
> that the ills they bear are not such.

And, furthermore, "nothing can speak to a heart but another heart," as Fray Diego de Estella wrote.

Not long ago, a statement of mine, replying to those who reproached us Spaniards for our scientific incapacity, appeared to scandalize a certain few. After having made the observation that electric light shines as brightly and locomotives run as well here as in the countries where they were invented, and that we make use of logarithms just as effectively as in the place where they were conceived, I exclaimed, notoriously, "Let others invent!" And I do not now retract that paradoxical expression. We Spanish ought to appropriate to ourselves in some good measure the sage counsels which Count Joseph de Maistre offered the Russians, a people cast in our likeness. In his admira-

ble letters to Count Rasoumowsky on public education in Russia, he wrote that a nation should not think
the worse of itself merely because it was not made for
science. The Romans had no proficiency in the mechanical arts, and they boasted of no mathematician;
but this fact did not prevent them playing their part
in the world. We should particularly take to heart
everything he said about that crowd of arrogant scio-
lists who act like idolators when confronted with foreign tastes, foreign fashions, and foreign languages,
and who are always ready to tear down whatever they
misunderstand, which is everything.

We have no scientific spirit, they say. What of it,
as long as we have some spirit? And who knows
whether our spirit is or is not compatible with the
scientific spirit?

Moreover, when I said "Let others invent!", I did
not mean to imply that we should content ourselves
with a passive role. Rather, let the others dedicate
themselves to science, and let us take advantage of
the results; meanwhile, let us cultivate our own spirit.
Defensive action is not enough, we must also attack.

But we must attack wisely and carefully. Reason
must be our weapon. Reason is the weapon even of
the fool and madman. Our sublime fool and madman,
our model, the exemplary Don Quixote, after destroying with two strokes of his sword the pasteboard visor
he had fitted to his steel helmet, "made it anew, placing certain iron bars within it, in such mode that he
stayed satisfied with its strength, without needing to
make any further trials, and he deputed it to be and
held it to be a most splendid piece of joinery." And
with the pasteboard visor on his head he made himself immortal. That is, he first made himself ridicu-

*331**

lous. For it was by making himself ridiculous that Don Quixote achieved immortality.

And there are so many ways of making ourselves ridiculous! . . . Cournot wrote: "It is best not to speak to either princes or peoples of the probabilities of death: princes will punish this temerity with disgrace; the public will revenge itself with ridicule." True, and therefore it is rightly said that one must live with the age. "Corrumpere et corrumpi saeculum vocatur," as Tacitus wrote.

One must know how to make oneself appear ridiculous, and not only in the eyes of others but also in one's own eyes. And more than ever today, when there is so much loose talk about our backwardness compared with other civilized peoples; today when a packet of shallow-pates who know nothing of our true history—which is yet to be written, after the webs of Protestant calumnies around it have first been swept away—tell us we have had neither science, nor art, nor philosophy, and no Renaissance either (though one would have thought we have had a little too much of the latter).

Carducci, who spoke of the "contorcimenti dell'affannosa grandiosità spagnola," "the contortions of zealous Spanish grandeur," also wrote, in *Mosche cocchiere*, that "even Spain, which never possessed hegemony of thought, can count on Cervantes." But was Cervantes a solitary phenomenon, perchance, isolated and rootless, without ancestral stock or foundation? It is understandable, after all, for an Italian rationalist, remembering it was Spain which reacted against the Italian Renaissance, to say that Spain "non ebbe egemonia mai di pensiero." But yet, was there nothing of importance, nothing akin to cultural hegemony, in the Counter-Reformation, of which Spain was the leader and which in point of fact began with the Spanish Sack of Rome, a providential chastisement of the city of pagan popes cast up by a pagan Renaissance? Leaving aside the question of whether or not the Counter-Reformation was good or bad, was there not something culturally hegemonic in Loyola and the Council of Trent? Previous to the Council, Italy was witness to an unnatural embrace and concubinage between Christianity and Paganism, or rather between immortalism and mortalism, a union entertained in the very souls of some of the Popes. Theological error served as philosophical truth, and everything was made right with the formula *salva fide*. But it was otherwise after the Council: then came the open and avowed struggle between reason and faith, between science and religion. And the fact that the change was wrought mainly by Spanish obduracy, is not this hegemonic?

Without the Counter-Reformation, the Reformation would not have taken the course it did; without the Counter-Reformation, the Reformation, lacking the buttress of pietism, might perhaps have waned in the gross rationalism of the *Aufklärung*, the Age of Enlightenment. Would the world have been the same without our Charles I, without our Philip II, our great Philip?

A negative labor ours, someone will say. And what is that? What is a negative labor? What is a positive labor? At what point in time—which is a line proceeding always in the same direction, from the past to the future—does the zero occur to mark the boundary between the positive and the negative? Spain, land of knights and knaves, they say—and both categories knavish—has been the country most calumniated in history precisely because it led the Counter-Reformation, and because its arrogance prevented it from appearing in the public forum, in Vanity Fair, to defend and justify itself.

Let us leave to one side Spain's eight centuries of warfare against the Moors, her defense of Europe against Mohammedanism, her labor of internal unification, her discovery of America and the Indies— for this was the work of Spain and Portugal, and not of Columbus and Vasco da Gama—let us leave all this and more aside, and it will be not a little leaving. Is it nothing in the cultural sphere to have created a score of nations, reserving nothing for oneself, and to have begotten, as the *Conquistadores* did, free men upon benighted Indian girls? And, apart from all these things, does not our mysticism count for something in the world of thought? Perhaps one day the people whose souls are ravished by Helen's kisses may have to return to our mysticism to search for their souls.

But—as everyone, of course, must know—Culture is composed of ideas and solely of ideas, and man is only an instrument of Culture. Man is made for the idea, and not the idea for man: the substance is made for the shadow. The end of man is to make science, to catalogue the Universe so that it may be handed back to God in good order (as I wrote in my novel *Amor y pedagogía*). Man is not, apparently, even an idea. And in the end, the human race will fall exhausted at the foot of a library of libraries, entire forests having been leveled to make the paper stored in the libraries in the form of printed books, fall at the foot of museums, machines, factories, laborator-

ies, which have been erected as a legacy for . . .
whom? For God will not receive them.

That terrible regenerationist literature, almost all
of it an imposture, which the loss of our last American
colonies provoked in Spain, led us into the pedantic
practice of writing about silent, persevering effort—
vociferating, silently vociferous—into the practice of
concerning ourselves with prudence, exactitude, moderation, spiritual fortitude, synteresis, equanimity, the
"social" virtues. And the chiefest vociferators were
those most lacking in these virtues. Almost all we
Spanish fell into the habit of this ridiculous genre,
some of us to a greater degree, some to a lesser. And
so it came about that the arch-Spaniard Joaquín
Costa, one of the least European spirits we have ever
boasted, invented the notion of our Europeanizing
ourselves and, while acting the Cid, he proclaimed at
the same time that we must lock up the sepulcher of
the Cid with the seven keys, and . . . conquer Africa!
And I myself, I uttered my cry of "Down with Don
Quixote!" This blasphemy, which meant the very opposite of what it seemed to mean (such was the state
we had gotten ourselves into at the time), led to my
writing *The Life of Don Quixote and Sancho* and to
my proposing the cult of Quixotism as the national
religion.

I wrote that book in order to think my way through
Don Quixote again, in the face of Cervantists and
scholars, and to resurrect a living work out of what
was and is a dead letter for most people. What do I
care what Cervantes did or did not mean to put into
that book or what he actually did put into it? The
living part of it for me is whatever I discover in it
—whether Cervantes put it there or not—and it is

whatever I myself put into or under or over it, and whatever we all of us put into it. And I sought to track down our philosophy in it.

For I increasingly harbor the conviction that our philosophy, Spanish philosophy, is to be found diffused and liquescent in our literature, in our collective life, in our action, above all in our mysticism, and not in any philosophical system whatsoever. And it is concrete. For that matter, is there not perhaps as much or more philosophy in Goethe, for example, than in Hegel? The "Elegy" of Jorge Manrique, the *Romancero*, *Don Quixote* itself, *La vida es sueño*, the *Subida al Monte Carmelo*, imply an intuition of the world and a concept of life, *Weltanschauung und Lebensansicht*. It was difficult for this Spanish philosophy to formulate itself in the second half of the nineteenth century, a period that was aphilosophical, positivist, technicist, devoted to pure history and the natural sciences, a period basically materialistic and pessimistic.

Our language itself, like any civilized language, implies a philosophy.

A language, in effect, is a potential philosophy. Platonism is the Greek language which speaks through Plato, developing in him its ancient metaphors. Scholasticism is the philosophy of the dead Latin of the Middle Ages struggling against the various vernacular languages. French discourses through Descartes; German through Kant and Hegel; English through Hume and John Stuart Mill. The logical point of departure for all philosophical speculation is not the I, nor is it representation (*Vorstellung*), that is, the world as it immediately appears to the senses, but rather is it a mediate or historical representation, humanly elaborated and given us principally in the

*336**

language through which we know the world; the point
of departure is not psychical but spiritual representation. Each one of us in thinking sets out from a point
of departure based—whether we know it or not and
whether we want to or not—on what others before
us or around us have thought. Thought is our inheritance. Kant thought in German, and into German he
translated Hume and Rousseau, who thought in English and French respectively. And Spinoza—did he
not think in his Judeo-Portuguese, inhibited by and
in contention with his Dutch?

Thought rests upon pre-judices, and prejudices are
embodied in the language. Bacon was right to ascribe
to language not a few errors of the *idola fori*. But is
it possible to philosophize in pure algebra or even in
Esperanto? One need only read Avenarius on the
critique of pure experience, *reine Erfahrung*, which
is a prehuman—that is to say, an inhuman—experience, to see whither that notion can lead. And even
Avenarius himself, who was obliged to invent a language, was forced to invent one based on Latin tradition, with roots which carry in their metaphorical
force a content of impure experience, of human social
experience.

All philosophy, then, is essentially philology. And
philology, with its great and fruitful law of analogical
formations, gives its head to chance, and to the irrational, to the absolutely immeasurable. History is not
mathematics, and neither is philosophy. And how
many philosophical ideas are due, strictly speaking, to
something akin to rhyme, to the necessity of correctly
placing a consonant! In Kant himself there is a great
deal of this aesthetic symmetry, of "rhyme."

Representation is, then, as is language, as is reason

itself—which is simply internal language—a social and racial product. "Race is . . ." Language!—the "blood of the soul," as Oliver Wendell Holmes, the Yankee, exclaimed and as I have often repeated.

It was in Athens, with Socrates, that our Western philosophy first matured, and became conscious of itself; and it arrived at this consciousness by means of dialogue, social conversation. And it is profoundly significant that the doctrine of innate ideas, of the objective and normative value of ideas, of what Scholasticism later knew as Realism, should have been formulated in dialogue. And these ideas, which constitute reality, are names, as Nominalism demonstrated; and the question is not whether they be no more than names, *flatus vocis*, but whether they be nothing less than names. Language is what gives us reality, and it does so not as a mere vehicle of reality, but as the true flesh of reality, of which all the rest, dumb-show or inarticulate representation, is merely the skeleton. And thus logic operates upon aesthetics, the concept upon the expression, upon the word, and not upon the brute perception.

And this is true even in the matter of love. Love does not discover that it is love until it speaks, until it says, "I love you!" It is with a profound intuition that Stendhal, in his novel *The Charterhouse of Parma,* makes Conte Mosca, furious with jealousy because of the love he believes unites the Duchessa Sanseverina with her nephew Fabrizio, say to himself: "I must calm myself; if I behave rudely, the Duchessa is quite capable, simply out of injured vanity, of following him to Belgirate; and there, or on the way there, a chance word may be spoken which will give a name to what they now feel for one another; and after that, in a moment, all the consequences."

And so it is: everything made was made by the word, and the Word was in the beginning.

Thought, reason, that is, living language, is an inheritance, and thus the solitary thinker invented by Aben Tofail, the Arab philosopher of Guadix, is as absurd as the ego of Descartes. The real and concrete truth, not the methodical and ideal, is *homo sum, ergo cogito*. To feel oneself a man is more immediate than to think. But, on the other hand, History, the cultural process, finds its perfection and full effectiveness only in the individual; the end of History and Humanity is man, each man, each individual. *Homo sum, ergo cogito; cogito ut sim Michael de Unamuno.* The individual is the end-purpose of the Universe.

That the individual is the end-purpose of the Universe is something we Spanish feel very strongly. The introspective individuality of the Spanish was sharply delineated by Martin A. S. Hume in his Preface to *The Spanish People*, and I commented on his book in my essay "Spanish Individuality."

And it is perhaps this same introspective individualism which has inhibited the growth on Spanish soil of strictly philosophical—or rather metaphysical—systems. And this fact is true in despite of Suárez, whose formal subtleties do not warrant the name of philosophy.

Our metaphysics, if it is anything, has been metanthropics, and our metaphysicians have been philologists, or rather, humanists, in the most comprehensive sense.

Menéndez y Pelayo, as Benedetto Croce truly said of him, was inclined toward metaphysical idealism, but he seemed to want to take something from other systems, even from empirical theories. For this reason, Croce considers that his work (he was referring to the *Historia de las ideas estéticas en España*) was weakened by a degree of uncertainty, given its author's theoretical point of view. Menéndez y Pelayo, a perfervid Spanish humanist, unwilling to disown the Renaissance, invented what he called Vivism, the philosophy of Luis Vives, and perhaps for no other reason than because he himself, like Vives, was an eclectic Spaniard of the Renaissance. The philosophy of Menéndez y Pelayo was, in truth, all incertitude: he had been educated in Barcelona in the uncertainties of the Scottish school as grafted on the Catalan spirit, in that uninspired philosophy of "common sense," which was anxious not to compromise itself and yet was all compromise, and which was well-exemplified by Balmes. And he always shunned any wholehearted inner struggle and formed his conscience upon compromises.

More happily inspired, in my opinion, was Angel Ganivet, a man all instinct and divination, when he proclaimed that Spanish philosophy was that of Seneca, the pagan Stoic of Córdoba, whom not a few Christians looked upon as one of themselves. This philosophy was lacking in originality of thought but splendid as regards tone and accent. Seneca's accent, in truth, was a Spanish, Latino-African accent, and not a Hellenic one, and there are echoes of Seneca in Tertullian—also so very Spanish—who believed in the corporeal and substantial nature of God and the soul, and who was a kind of Don Quixote of Christian thought in the second century.

But perhaps we must look for the hero of Spanish thought, not in any flesh-and-blood philosopher, but in a creation of fiction and yet man of action, more real than all the philosophers: Don Quixote. Doubtless there exists a philosophical Quixotism, but there is also a Quixotic philosophy. Is it not essentially that of the Conquistadores, of the Counter-Reformers, of Loyola, and, above all, in the order of abstract yet deeply felt thought, that of our mystics? What was the mysticism of St. John of the Cross but a knight-errantry in the divine sense?

And the philosophy of Don Quixote cannot, strictly speaking, be called idealism: he did not fight for ideas. It was of a spiritual order: he fought for the spirit.

Imagine Don Quixote given to religious speculation, as he himself once dreamed as a role for himself when he came across those images carved in bas-relief which some peasants were carrying for the high altar of their village church; imagine him meditating on eternal truths, and imagine him ascending Mount Carmel in the middle of the dark night of the soul, to watch from there, from its summit, the rising of the sun which never sets, and, like the eagle which accompanied St. John on the island of Patmos, gazing upon it face to face and scrutinizing its spots. For he leaves to the owl which in Olympus accompanies Athena— she, the goddess of the glaucous, or owl-like, eyes, who sees in the dark but is dazzled by the light of the moon—he leaves to Athena's owl the task of sharp-eyed searching among the shades for the prey to feed its young.

And speculative or meditative Quixotism, like Quixotism in practice, is a madness, a child of the madness of the Cross. And thus it is disdained by reason. Fundamentally, philosophy abhors Christianity, and well did the gentle Marcus Aurelius prove it.

The tragedy of Christ, the divine tragedy, is the tragedy of the Cross. Pilate, the sceptic, the man of culture, sought to make it into a comedy by making mock of it, and thought up the farce of the king with the reed scepter and crown of thorns, and he cried out "Behold the man!" But the people, more human than he and thirsting for tragedy, raised their own cry: "Crucify him!" The other tragedy, the human tragedy, the intra-human tragedy, is the tragedy of Don Quixote, whose face was daubed with soap that he might make sport for the servants of the Duke and Duchess, while the masters, who were as servile as their own servants, might cry out "Behold the madman!" And the comic tragedy, the irrational tragedy, is the passion following on mockery and ridicule.

The greatest height of heroism to which an individual, like a people, can attain is to know how to face ridicule; better still, to know how to make oneself ridiculous and not to fear the consequent ridicule.

I have previously mentioned the forceful sonnets of that tragic Portuguese suicide Antero de Quental. Sorrowing for his country at the time of the British ultimatum of 1890, he wrote:

> An English statesman of the last century, who was also indeed a perspicacious observer and a philosopher, Horace Walpole, said that for those who feel, life is a tragedy, and for those who think, a comedy. Very well, then: if we are destined to end tragically, we Portuguese, we who *feel*, we would far rather prefer this terrible, but noble destiny, to that which is reserved, and perhaps in a not too remote future, for England, the country which *thinks* and *calculates*, and whose destiny it is to end miserably and comically.

Let us leave to one side the assertion that England thinks and calculates, implying thereby that she does not feel, the injustice of which is explained by the provocative situation at the time, and also let us put aside the assertion that the Portuguese feel, implying thereby that they scarcely think or calculate, for our Atlantic-seaboard brothers have always presumed of a certain sentimental pedantry, and let us keep only the essence of this terrible idea, which is that some people, those who put thought above feeling, or as I would say, reason above faith, die comically, while those who put faith above reason die tragically. For the mockers die comically, and God laughs at them finally, and the tragic, noble fate is reserved for those who endured mockery.

And we, following in the footsteps of Don Quixote, must seek out mockery.

And shall we again be told that there has never been any Spanish philosophy in the technical sense of the word? And I say: what sense is that? And what does philosophy mean? Windelband, the historian of philosophy, in his essay on the meaning of philosophy, tells us that "the history of the word 'philosophy' is the history of the cultural significance of science." And he adds:

> When scientific thought attains an independent existence as a desire for knowledge for the sake of knowledge, it takes the name of philosophy; when subsequently integral knowledge divides into branches, philosophy becomes the general knowledge of the world, embracing all other knowledge. As soon as scientific thought stoops again to become a means to ethics or a medium for religious contemplation, philosophy is transformed into an art of living or into a formulation of religious beliefs. And then, when scientific life again regains its liberty, philosophy acquires once again its nature as an independent knowledge of the world, and whenever it begins to abandon the attempt to solve this problem, it is changed into a theory of knowledge itself.

Here we have a brief recapitulation of the history of philosophy from Thales to Kant, passing through the medieval scholasticism upon which it endeavored to establish religious beliefs. But has philosophy not perhaps some other role to play? May its role not also be to characterize the tragic sense of life itself, such as we have been studying it, to formulate the conflict between reason and faith, between science and religion, and deliberately to sustain this conflict?

Windelband goes on to say: "By philosophy in the systematic sense, not in the historical sense, I understand only the critical knowledge of values possessing a universal validity [*allgemeingiltigen Werten*]." But what values exist of more universal validity than that of the human will seeking before and above all else the personal, individual, and concrete immortality of the soul, that is, a human finality to the Universe, or than that of human reason denying the rationality and even the possibility of this desire? What values exist of a more universal validity than the rational or mathematical value and the volitional or teleological value of the Universe in conflict one with the other?

For Windelband, as for Kantians and neo-Kantians in general, there are only three normative categories, three universal norms: the true or the false, the beautiful or the ugly, and the morally good or evil. Philosophy is reduced to logic, aesthetics, and ethics, depending on whether the study is science, art, or morality. A further category remains excluded: that of the gratifying and the ungratifying, pleasing and the unpleasing, that is, the hedonic category is excluded. The hedonic cannot, according to them, pretend to universal validity, it cannot be normative. "Whoever places upon philosophy the burden of deciding the question of optimism or pessimism," wrote

Windelband, "whoever asks philosophy to render judgement on whether the world is more propitious for producing pain or pleasure, such a person, if he attempts to go beyond the position of a dilettante, labors on the phantom task of finding an absolute determination in a terrain where no reasonable man has ever sought one." It remains to be seen, however, whether this pronouncement is as clear as it seems to be, in the case of a man like myself, who am at the same time reasonable and yet nothing but a dilettante, which amounts to "the abomination of desolation."

With profound insight, Benedetto Croce, considering the philosophy of the spirit joined to aesthetics to be the science of expression and the philosophy of the spirit joined to logic as the science of pure concept, divided practical philosophy into two branches: economics and ethics. He recognizes, in effect, the existence of a practical order of spirit, purely economic, directed toward the singular and unconcerned with the universal. Iago and Napoleon are types of perfection, of economic genius, and this order of spirit remains outside morality. And every man passes through this order, because before all else he must wish to be himself, *qua* individual, and without this order, morality would be inexplicable, just as without aesthetics logic would lack meaning. And the discovery of the normative value of the economic order, which seeks the hedonic, was not unnaturally the work of an Italian, a disciple of Machiavelli, who speculated so fearlessly with *virtù*, practical efficiency, which is not exactly moral virtue.

But this economic order is essentially nothing but an inchoate religious order. The religious order is the transcendental, economic, or hedonic. Religion is a transcendental economy of hedonism. In religion, in religious faith, man seeks to save his own individuality, to make it eternal—something he cannot achieve through science, or through art, or through morality. Neither science, nor art, nor morality requires God; it is only religion which requires God. So that the Jesuits, with the insight of genius, speak of the grand commerce of our salvation. Commerce, yes, commerce, something in the economic, hedonistic order, albeit transcendental. We do not need God in order that He may teach us the truth of things, or their beauty, or that He may safeguard morality by penalties and punishments, but in order that He may save us, in order that He may not let us die utterly. And this singular longing, because it is a longing in each and every normal man—those who are abnormal by reason of their barbarism or their hyperculture do not count—is universal and normative.

Religion, then, is a transcendental economy, or a transcendental metaphysic, if you like. The Universe has for man, along with its logical, aesthetic, and ethical values, an economic value as well, which when thus made universal and normative, becomes the religious value. For us it is not solely a question of truth, beauty and goodness: it is also a question, above all else, of the salvation of the individual, of perpetuation, which those norms do not assure for us. So-called political economy shows us the most adequate, most economic mode of satisfying our needs, whether or not they be rational, beautiful or ugly, moral or immoral—a sound commercial transaction may amount to a swindle, something which in the long run destroys the soul—and the supreme human *need* is the need not to die, the need to enjoy forever the plenitude of one's own individual limitation. The Catholic eucharistic doctrine holds that the substance of the body of Jesus Christ is present whole and entire in the consecrated Host and whole and entire in each part of it, and this means that God is wholly and entirely in the whole Universe and also in each one of the individuals that compose it. And this principle is essentially not a logical, nor an aesthetic, nor an ethical one, but an economic principle of a transcendental or religious nature. And with this norm, philosophy is able to judge as to optimism and pessimism. *If the human soul is immortal, the world is economically or hedonistically good; if not, it is bad.* And the meaning which optimism and pessimism assign to the categories of good and evil is a meaning which is not ethical but economic and hedonistic. Whatever satisfies our vital longing is good, and whatever does not satisfy it is evil.

Philosophy, then, is also the science of the tragedy of life, a reflecting upon the tragic sense of life. And what I have attempted in these essays is an exercise in this philosophy, with its inevitable contradictions or inner antinomies. And the reader will not miss the fact that I have been operating upon myself; or that this work has been in the nature of self-surgery, without any anesthetic but the work itself. The pleasure of operating upon myself has sublimated the pain of being operated upon.

And as regards my other contentions, that what I have outlined above is Spanish philosophy, perhaps *the* Spanish philosophy, and that while if it was up to an Italian to discover the normative and universal value of the economic order, it is natural for a Spaniard to enunciate that this order is merely the beginning of the religious principle and that the essence of our religion, of our Spanish Catholicism, consists precisely in its being neither a science, nor an art, nor a morality, but a political economy of the eternal, that is, of the divine. The question of whether this is an essentially Spanish contribution I leave for another, historical, work. But for now, leaving aside the written and external tradition, the tradition expressed in historical documents, I merely express myself as a Spaniard, a Spaniard, moreover, who has scarcely ever been outside Spain, a product, therefore, of the Spanish tradition, of the living Spanish tradition, as transmitted in feelings and ideas that dream, rather than in texts that sleep.

The philosophy in the soul of my people seems to me the expression of an inner tragedy analogous to the tragedy in the soul of Don Quixote, the expression of a conflict between what the world appears scientifically to be and what we want the world to be in accord with the faith of our religion. And in this philosophy lies the secret of the judgement made of us to the effect that we are basically irreducible to *Kultur*: in other words that we will not submit to it. No, Don Quixote will not submit to the world, nor to its "truth," nor to science or logic, nor to art or aesthetics, nor to morality or ethics.

"The upshot of all this," I have been told more than once by more than one person, "is that you will only succeed in driving people to the most desperate Catholicism." Meanwhile I have also been accused of being a reactionary and even a Jesuit. So be it! And so?

Yes, I know, I know it is madness to try to drive the waters of a river back to their source, and that it is only the populace who rummages in the past for a cure to its ills. But I also know that whoever does battle for any ideal whatsoever, though the ideal seem to belong to the past, is a person who drives the world on into the future, and that the only reactionaries are those who find themselves at ease in the present. Any presumed restoration of the past is a pre-creation of the future, and if the past is a dream, something imperfectly known, so much the better. Inasmuch as we necessarily march into the future, whoever walks at all is walking into the future even if he walks backwards. And who is to say that this is not the better way to walk?

I feel within me a medieval soul, and I feel that my country's soul is also medieval, that this soul has perforce lived through the Renaissance, the Reformation, and the Revolution, learning from them, certainly, but never allowing the essence of the soul to be changed, always preserving intact the spiritual inheritance derived from the so-called Dark Ages. And Quixotism is simply the most desperate phase of the battle of the Middle Ages against its offspring the Renaissance.

And if some were to accuse me of being in the service of Catholic reaction, perhaps others, the official Catholics . . . well, but these, in Spain, scarcely notice anything and busy themselves only with their own dissensions and sectarian quarrels. And besides, poor folk, they have so little understanding!

But the truth is that my work—my mission, I was about to say—is to shatter the faith of men, left, right, and center, their faith in affirmation, their faith in negation, their faith in abstention, and I do so from faith in faith itself. My purpose is to war on all those who submit, whether to Catholicism, or to rationalism, or to agnosticism. My aim is to make all men live a life of restless longing.

Will such a purpose prove effective? Did Don Quixote, now, believe his purpose was of any immediately apparent effectiveness? It is very doubtful; in any event he did not repeat a second time—just in case—the experiment of slicing his pasteboard visor in two. And many passages in his history reveal that he did not consider it a matter of great moment to achieve immediate success in his purpose of restoring knight-errantry. And of what moment was it truly, so long as he lived as he would, and made himself immortal? And he must have guessed, and did in fact guess, that his labor possessed another and higher effectiveness, which was that it would have effective influence on all those who piously read of his exploits.

Don Quixote made himself ridiculous—but was he aware of the most tragic ridicule of all, the ridicule reflected in oneself, the ridiculousness of a man in his own eyes, in the eyes of his own soul? Imagine Don Quixote's battlefield to be in his own soul; imagine him fighting in his soul to save the Middle Ages from the Renaissance, fighting to save the treasury of his childhood; imagine him an inner Don Quixote—with his Sancho, an inner Sancho, too, and a heroic one as well, at his side—and then tell me if there is anything comic in this tragedy.

"And what has Don Quixote left us?" you may well ask. And I shall answer that he has left us himself. And a man, a living, eternal man, is worth all theories and philosophies. Other nations have bequeathed us, in the main, institutions and books, we have left souls. Teresa of Avila is worth any school or institute, any *Critique of Pure Reason* whatsoever.

Of course, Don Quixote reformed. Yes, only in order to die, the poor man. But the other Don Quixote,

350*

the real one, the one who remained on earth and lives among us, inspiring us with his spirit—that one never reformed, that one goes on inciting us to make ourselves ridiculous, that Don Quixote should never die. The Don Quixote who converted and reformed in order to die may have reformed because he was mad, and it was his madness, in any case, and not his reformation or his death, which made him immortal, earning him a pardon for the crime of having been born. *Felix culpa!* And his madness was not cured either: he merely exchanged one type of madness for another. His death was his final knightly adventure: with it he stormed heaven, which suffers violence.

Don Quixote, then, died and went down into Hell, which he entered, lance on rest, and there he freed all the condemned, as he had freed the galley slaves, and he closed the gates of Hell, and took down the inscription Dante saw there, "Abandon all hope!," and replaced it with one reading "Long Live Hope!" And then, escorted by the souls he had freed, and they laughing at him, he went to Heaven. And God laughed paternally at him, and this divine laughter filled his soul with eternal felicity.

And the other Don Quixote remained here, among us, fighting with desperation. For does he not fight from despair? Is it not only natural that among the words which English has taken from Spanish there should figure—among such words as *siesta, camarilla, guerrilla*—the word *desperado*? Is not this inward-turning Quixote of whom I spoke, a man conscious of his own tragic comical quality, is he not a *desperado*, a Spanish *des-esperado*? A *desperado*, indeed, like Pizarro and like Loyola. But "despair is the master of the impossible," as we learn from

Agustín de Salazar y Torres. And it is despair and despair alone which engenders heroic hope, absurd hope, mad hope. *Spero quia absurdum* is what we should say rather than *Credo quia absurdum*.

And Don Quixote, who lived alone, sought more solitude still; he sought the solitude of Peña Pobre, where, alone and without witnesses, he might give himself over to ever greater follies, for the relief of his soul. But he was not quite alone, for Sancho was at his side: Sancho the good, Sancho the believer, Sancho the simple. If, as some say, Don Quixote is dead in Spain and only Sancho lives on, then we are saved, for Sancho, his master dead, will become a knight-errant himself. Or at any rate he awaits some other mad lord to follow again.

And there is also the tragedy of Sancho. For there is no recorded evidence of the death of the Sancho who traveled with the Don Quixote who died, though there are those who believe he did die, a raving madman, calling for a lance and believing in the truth of everything his master had denounced as abominable lies at his deathbed conversion. But neither is it recorded anywhere that the graduate Samson Carrasco died, or that the curate did, or the barber, or the Duke and Duchess or the canons—and it is against them that the heroic Sancho must do battle.

Don Quixote traveled alone, alone with Sancho, alone with his solitude. And shall not we, his fond admirers, also travel alone as we forge a Quixotic Spain from out of our imagination?

And again we shall be asked: "What has Don Quixote bequeathed to *Kultur*?" And I shall answer: "Quixotism! Isn't that enough?" And it is a whole method, a whole epistemology, a whole aesthetic, a whole logic, a whole ethic, above all, a whole religion, that is to say, a total economy of the eternal and the divine, a total hope in the rationally absurd.

Why did Don Quixote do battle? He fought for Dulcinea, for glory, for life, for eternal survival. Not for Iseult, who is eternal flesh; not for Beatrice, who is theology; not for Margaret, who is the people; not for Helen, who is culture. He fought for Dulcinea, and won her, for he lives in her.

And his greatest attribute was that he was mocked and conquered: for being conquered was his way of conquering; he mastered the world by giving the world cause to laugh at him.

And now, today? Today he feels how comic, how vain were his feats on the temporal plane. He sees himself from outside himself—culture has taught him how to objectify himself, that is, how to alienate himself from himself, rather than how to steep himself in himself—and on seeing himself from outside, he has to laugh at himself, but with a certain bitterness. Perhaps the most tragic character would be a species of Margutte of the inner man, a Margutte who, like Pulci's, would die bursting of laughter, laughter at himself. "E riderà in eterno," and he will laugh through all eternity, as the Angel Gabriel said of Margutte. And do you not hear the laughter of God?

Dying, the mortal Don Quixote realized how comical he was, and he wept for his sins. But the immortal Don Quixote, understanding this same comical nature, superimposes himself upon the comedy and, without ever renouncing it, triumphs.

And Don Quixote will not surrender, because he is not a pessimist, and he fights on. He is not a pessimist because pessimism is the child of vanity and a question of fashion, pure snobbism, and Don Quixote is neither vain nor frivolous, nor modern in any way—and even less a modernist—and does not understand the meaning of the word "snob" unless it be explained to him in good Old-Christian Spanish. Don Quixote is no pessimist, for since he does not understand what is meant by *joie de vivre*, neither does he understand its opposite. And neither does he understand anything about futurist follies. In spite of Clavileño, he has not got as far as the airplane, which seems to carry a shipload of fools ever farther from heaven. Don Quixote has not arrived at the age of *taedium vitae*, which is commonly manifested among not a few modern spirits in the form of topophobia: these people spend their lives running at top speed from one place to another, not from any love of the place to which they are going, but from odium of the place they are leaving behind, thus fleeing all places, which is one of the forms of despair.

Don Quixote already hears the sound of his own laughter, and he hears the divine laughter too, and since he is not a pessimist, since he believes in life eternal, he is forced to fight without quarter against modern, scientific, inquisitorial orthodoxy, in the interests of restoring a new and impossible Middle Ages, dualistic, contradictory, impassioned. Like a new Savonarola—that Italian Quixote of the end of the fifteenth century—he does battle against this Modern Age which began with Machiavelli and will end in farce. He fights against the rationalism inherited from the eighteenth century. Peace of mind, conciliation between reason and faith, all of that—by the grace of a provident God—is no longer possible. The world will have to be as Don Quixote wants it to be,

and inns perforce will have to be castles, and he will
do battle with the world and he will, to all appearances, be bested, but in making himself ridiculous, he
will triumph. And he will triumph over himself by
laughing at himself, and making himself laughable.

"Reason speaks and feeling bites," Petrarch said.
But reason also bites, and it bites in the innermost
depths of the heart. And more light does not make for
more warmth. "Light, light, more light!" they say the
dying Goethe cried. "Warmth, warmth, still more
warmth!" we should cry, for we die of cold and not
of the dark. It is not the night that kills, but the hoar-
frost. And we must free the enchanted princess and
destroy Master Peter's puppet show.

And yet, may it not be just as pedantic to act the
part of Quixote, to imagine oneself ridiculed and
mocked? Kierkegaard said that the regenerate
(*Opvakte* in Danish) desire that the wicked world
should mock them, the better to assure themselves of
their own regeneracy as they see themselves mocked,
and thus to enjoy the advantages of being able to
chide the world's impiety.

If it is true that the natural man is only a myth
and we are all of us more or less artificial, then the
question is how to avoid the one pedantry or the other,
the one or the other affectation.

Romanticism! Yes, perhaps that is the word, in
part, for what we seek. And it serves us all the more
and all the better by reason of its very lack of precision. Against all this, against this romanticism, the
forces of rationalist and classicist pedantry, especially
in France, have lately been unleashed. Is romanticism,
then, another form of pedantry, a sentimental pedantry? Perhaps it is. In this world, a man of culture is

either a dilettante or a pedant: you have to take your choice. Yes, perhaps Chateaubriand's René, and Constant's Adolphe, and Sénancour's Obermann, and Byron's Lara were all of them pedants. The point is to seek consolation in desolation.

Bergson's philosophy, which is a matter of spiritualist restoration, essentially mystical, medieval, Quixotic, has been called a *demi-mondaine* philosophy. Take away the *demi*, and you have *mondaine*, mundane. Mundane, yes, a philosophy for the world and not for philosophers, just as chemistry ought not to be for chemists alone. The world wishes to be deceived—*mundus vult decipi*—either by the deception anterior to reason, which is poetry, or by the deception subsequent to reason, which is religion. And Machiavelli has said that whoever wishes to practice deception will always find someone willing to be deceived. And blessed are those who are easily duped! A Frenchman, Jules de Gaultier, said that it was the privilege of his countrymen not to be taken in, *n'être pas dupe*. A sorry privilege indeed!

Science does not give Don Quixote what he requires of it. "Then let him not make such demands," it will be said. "Let him resign himself, let him accept life and truth as they are!" But he will not accept them as they are, and he asks for some sign, urged on by Sancho, who is at his side. And it is not a question of Don Quixote's not understanding whatever is understood by those who speak to him of resignation and acceptance of a reasonable life and a rational truth. Not at all; the truth is that his needs are greater, his affective needs are greater. A piece of pedantry, someone says? Who is to say?

And in this critical century, Don Quixote, himself touched by the critical spirit, must struggle against himself, a victim of intellectualism and sentimental-ism, and the more he tries to be spontaneous, the more he appears affected. And he tries, unhappy man, to rationalize the irrational and irrationalize the rational. And he falls into the intimate despair of the critical century whose two greatest victims were Nietzsche and Tolstoy. And through despair he reaches the heroic fury of which Giordano Bruno spoke, that Bruno who was a Don Quixote of the mind escaped from a monastery, and he becomes an awakener of sleeping souls, *dormitantium animorum excubitor*, as the ex-Dominican said of himself. And Bruno also wrote: "Heroic love belongs to those superior natures called insane [*insane* in the Italian], not because they do not know [*non sanno*], but because they more-than-know [*soprasanno*]."

But Bruno believed in the triumph of his doctrines. Or, at least, the inscription placed at the foot of his statue in the Campo dei Fiori, not too far from the Vatican, states that the memorial is raised to him by the century he foresaw, *il secolo da lui divinato*. But our reborn Don Quixote, the self-searching Don Quixote conscious of his own comedy, cannot believe that his doctrines will triumph in this world, for his doctrines are not of this world. And it is better that they should not triumph. And if the world wished to make Don Quixote king, he would retreat to the woods in flight from the mob of king-makers and king-kill-ers, just as Christ withdrew to the mount when, after the miracle of the loaves and fishes, they sought to proclaim Him king. He left the title of king to be used as inscription above the Cross.

What, then, is Don Quixote's new mission in the world today? To cry aloud, to clamor in the wilder-ness. And the wilderness heeds, though men hear not, and one day it will grow into a resounding forest, and the solitary voice which falls like a seed upon the desert will bear fruit in the form of a gigantic cedar singing, with its infinity of tongues, an eternal hosanna to the Master of life and of death.

And as for you, graduate Carrasco of a pan-European regenerationism, you youths working with critical method, in the European fashion, you scientists, to you I say: create wealth, create nationality, create art, create science, create ethics, above all create—or rather transpose—*Kultur*, and thus kill off both life and death. Considering how long all that will last us . . . !

*   *   *

And on this note I temporarily break off—high time perhaps—these essays on the tragic sense of life in men and in nations, or at least in me—a man—and in the soul of my countrymen as it is mirrored in mine.

I trust, reader, that we shall meet again in the course of our tragedy, while the drama is being played out, in some interval between the acts. We shall recognize each other. Forgive me if I have disturbed you more than was necessary or inevitable, more than I intended when I took up my pen to distract you awhile from your distractions.

And may God give you no peace but glory!

Salamanca, in the year of grace 1912.

Afterword

Unamuno and the Contest
with Death

To re-read Unamuno—especially when one is reading to find where one stands at last with him—is itself to be in a contest. One emerges a little shaken and winded, for here is an author that insists upon coming at you head on. Yet the man himself is so simple, direct, beguiling—a true friend, but a troubling friend. He troubles us above all when we try to follow too straight a line in trying to pin him down. What I shall have to offer the reader here, I am afraid, will be my perplexities and questions—hesitations before the ultimate challenge he throws down to us.

Let us begin by remembering that Unamuno was for a long time professor of Greek at the University of Salamanca. This is a fact about his thought which we must not forget. True, there are other and deeper ways to characterize him as a man: a Basque who was Spanish to the core, "a Spanish consciousness, made in Spain"; or, as one genial interpreter put it, a man of "a Protestant mind and a Catholic heart"; or, as he liked to see himself, the knight of La Mancha on his own passionate quest through the modern wasteland ready to do battle with our latter-day ogres. All of these aspects dramatize the man and his mission; the quieter fact for his intellectual development was the experience of the Greek language and the Greeks—as decisive an exposure for him as, in a different way, for another significant modern thinker, Martin Heidegger.

Now, in Greek the word *agonia* means a contest, struggle. In English this root meaning has largely faded from the word. An agony is taken to mean merely physical or emotional pain. Yet if we reflect for a moment we shall find that this root meaning still lurks beneath the surface: when the blows of suffering fall, we must still be able to struggle and resist, or else we cease to be human altogether and collapse into a clinical lump. For Unamuno, life was unceasing conflict, out of the tension of which each human soul has to create its own fate and meaning. In this sense he would agree with the saying of the early Greek philosopher Heraclitus: "War [conflict] is the father of all things."

Consequently, when Unamuno speaks, as he does in many places, of "the agony of Christianity," we must understand that he can use this phrase only because for him Christianity is still something profoundly alive. What is in agony still lives, and lives powerfully. Christianity had this vitality for him largely because he had such a deep grasp of the *material* side of its symbols and images. Before Sir James Frazer and other anthropologists had made known the resemblances of Christian rites and symbols to those of primitive peoples, Unamuno perceived and savored this tie of Christianity with all that is earthbound and archaic in our nature. The symbols (through which this archaic nature speaks) live when taken as concrete and material, die when they become merely abstract signs.

In the history of Catholic theology, the definitions of dogma are called *symbola*, symbols. Unamuno was passionately interested in the history of dogma, and from the twists and turns in its evolution he finds proof for his belief that the vital current of life is not merely non-rational but actually anti-rational in nature. Perhaps he would have been more accurate to say anti-rationalistic. In any case, the point is central to his thought, and his argument deserves more objective appraisal than has been given to it. Unamuno advances it with the passion of a believer, but the lyricism of his writing should not mislead us, as it has often done many readers, about the sophistication of his thinking. The same argument can be stated coolly by the non-believer and in the objective terms of the behaviorial sciences. Despite all the research in these sciences we still have no coherent picture of human nature as a whole. It would seem, accordingly, to be sound procedure not to limit our samples of human behavior to man as a performing mechanism but to draw on all fields of human activity where our human nature may be revealing itself.

Now, over the millennia of its history, at each crucial stage where it was in difficulty and some easier and more rationalistic formula presented itself, the Church renewed itself by rejecting such formulae and choosing a doctrine more concrete and more paradoxical to reason. That is the evidence on which Unamuno bases his contention that the thrust of life must always carry us beyond reason. Consider three such occasions.

The conflict about Arianism in the fourth century turned on the question of the Incarnation. Jesus was true man and true God; but as man-God was he really one (consubstantial) with the Father? One would have thought Christianity already had enough stumbling blocks to put before the skeptical pagan intelligence without adding the doctrine, scandalous to reason, that God, the infinite, could become flesh as man, the finite. Arius arrived on the scene with a rationalistic simplification that would in effect have left Christianity a more or less straightforward theism, and therefore more acceptable to the philosophers. But Athanasius, his opponent, speaking for the people who were the body of the Church, triumphed; and the Incarnation became dogma. Here was a doctrine more concrete, physical, sensuous, even if altogether perplexing and enigmatic to the rational mind. At certain times the human need for the concreteness and the materiality of the symbol can be a craving as strong as physical hunger.

Later, in the ninth century, a controversy arose over the question of Transubstantiation. Was the wafer consecrated in the communion service actually transformed into the real body and blood of Jesus Christ? At the last supper, Jesus had simply said, "Whenever you do this [that is, break bread], do it in remembrance of me." The communion rite, accordingly, could be taken as a commemoration by the faithful of that last supper that Jesus shared with his disciples. Why not leave matters on this relatively simple and straightforward level? Why pile up more difficulties for the reason of the believer, particularly with a doctrine that links Christianity with those primitive rites of totemism in which the sacred animal is physically devoured? But here again, the craving for the sheer materiality of the symbol asserted itself against rationalism. A certain monk, Radbertus, advanced the doctrine that the wafer and wine used in communion are really transformed into the body and blood of Christ. Scotus Erigena, the greatest philosopher of the age, opposed this doctrine on rational grounds. But the craving for the concreteness of the symbol won out, and Erigena's fellow monks, according to historic legend, rose up and killed him.

Our third instance occurred in 1950, fourteen years after Unamuno's death, yet it was a faith he already held prophetically: the dogma of the Assumption of the Virgin. This *symbolon* tells us that the body of Mary has been taken up into heaven to reside with God the Father, Jesus, and the Holy Spirit. (That the body of woman should be so exalted, raised to the spiritual heights, and made to complete the male Trinity, led Jung to call the enactment of this dogma the most important event in Christendom since the Protestant Reformation. On the psychology of the matter Jung is undoubtedly right, but historically it remains to be seen whether the dogma did not arrive too late within Christianity.) To rationalists, of course, this dogma is worse than ridiculous.

But can we really take such incidents from the restricted sphere of ecclesiastical history as evidence of what our human nature and its needs are? The behavioral scientist, with his sampling techniques, will ask how fair a sample of human behavior this history represents. The answer is that it does in fact embrace a pretty large segment of *homo sapiens* of the West acting within that central area of his existence that is called religion. Of course, the fact that these instances are taken from the religious area of experience will make them immediately suspect to some minds. Does not such behavior merely belong to a superstitious past which mankind is now discarding? The assumption behind this attitude is that man in his modern secular and rationalistic form is to be taken as the measure of all things. But does not this assumption imply that our human nature and its needs have been altogether transformed within recent history? That is the question that Unamuno is constantly raising as he does battle with the positivism and rationalism of the nineteenth century.

Here the evidence from anthropology supplements

the history of religion. All history rests on the immensely longer past of pre-history, which it would be folly to neglect in any speculation about human nature. The anthropological findings have accumulated enormously since 1912, when Unamuno wrote *The Tragic Sense of Life*; and were he alive, there is no doubt but that he would be passionately immersed in this material. The overwhelming testimony from the ethnographers is that the primitive is the same human animal as us. Time and again, the fieldworker who at first encounter felt the ways of a tribe so foreign and strange will end with the statement, "They are so like us, after all." No doubt, between the cultures of these primitives and ours there is a great gulf, and their modes of being human may therefore be different from ours; but the human creature in both cases seems to be fundamentally the same. Now the savage mind, we are told, grasps its world as concrete, sacral, and totally meaningful (there are no loose ends or dangling facts that are not tied into a concrete matrix of meanings). Moreover, for the primitive there is a constant transaction, a process of give and take, between the dead and the living. (On another level, this same attitude is expressed in the Catholic doctrine of the Communion of All the Living and the Dead.) How far do these primitive attitudes express needs of our human nature that are still with us today? Has modern man succeeded in discarding these needs altogether? Or has modern culture merely suppressed them?

The time factor has some relevance here. Current paleontology tells us that man, *homo sapiens*, has been on this earth close to a million years. If we take the French Revolution as a conveniently arbitrary date when a public and deliberate program of secularization was unleashed on the Western world, then we may take the span of man's secular and rationalistic existence to be about two hundred years. Two hundred against a million! That is about one five-thousandth of man's existence on earth. If you imagine a clock running through the dial's cycle of twelve hours, then this span of man's programmed rationalization would amount to less than ten seconds.

How far do these last ticking seconds give us the measure of what our human nature is? Can we really believe that in these last ten seconds man has completely transformed himself and thrown off the weight of pre-history?

The weight of the sampling would seem to tilt the balance toward the immense stretch of anthropological and paleontological time. Moreover, the derangements and malaise in our contemporary life suggest that our rationalized technological civilization has come into conflict with our basic human nature. The discoveries of depth psychology in our century also warn us that the archaic and mythologizing animal—the creature that hungers for symbols—still lurks below the modern veneer.

*   *   *

It is this same hunger for the concrete and physical that explains Unamuno's longing for immortality. What he craves is not just the survival after death as pure consciousness or disembodied spirit, but survival in this flesh, these bones, this body. And so he hungers after a faith (which reason cannot supply) in the doctrine of the Resurrection of the Body.

The reader, according to his own faith, will or will

not follow Unamuno that far. The question of faith aside, we can, however, ask some philosophical questions about the meaning of death and the attitudes human beings take toward it. All philosophy, Socrates said, is a meditation upon death; yet the subject had received scant attention from his contemporary philosophers before Unamuno wrote *The Tragic Sense of Life*. Since that time, the movement of Existentialism arose and is still flourishing; and in its light (or darkness) Unamuno's own reputation as a man of vision has been considerably enhanced. Existentialism seems to mean many different things to different people; but at least one thing about it is clear: it has tried, and sometimes succeeded, in bringing questions of life and death back into philosophy. It is interesting to compare with Unamuno two thinkers within this movement, Heidegger and Camus, in whom the reflection upon death also plays a central role.

Time occupies the crucial position in Heidegger's philosophy. Man is the animal for whom Being spontaneously opens forward toward the future and backward toward the past. His Being is thus literally compounded of non-Being—the *Not*-yet of the future, the *No*-longer of the past. Only as he holds these two together in presence is he able to stand meaningfully within time; and only then can he go on to make chronometers and for practical purposes count off the hours, minutes, seconds. This clock time runs on; ticking away, it may even run away with our lives, even while we are trying to run away from it. In the end, time becomes real for each man only as the possibility of his own death looms before him. Then we know that man is truly finite, truly a Being-toward-death. From the moment he was born he has been delivered over to the possibility of death, and not just death in general, but his own, most individual, death.

How is the individual to bear such anxiety? Only, says Heidegger, if he lets this possibility of death— his own individual Being-toward-death—become disclosed to him in all its fullness can he acquire a certain resoluteness and freedom toward death that will liberate him from the servitude to petty cares, the daily fuss and fret, clock-time worries. As for immortality, that question lies altogether outside the scope of Heidegger's thought. Man has simply to learn to live with Non-being.

The pages in which Heidegger deals with time and mortality are written with a plodding power unrivaled in contemporary philosophy. Yet when we come later to the resolute and liberated *Dasein* (Man) I find the picture somehow unsatisfying. This creature is too solitary before his own death, too stiffly encased in the armor of his own resoluteness. To be sure, each of us must learn for himself that *he* (and not merely the others whose obituaries he reads in the papers) is mortal. But what about the death of another person? Is it always an external and neutral event happening out there in the world? Does not a man sometimes discover death, real death, in the agonizing thought that the woman he loves will someday die? Heidegger's view narrows the contest with death to a single player in unshatterable solitude. But there is another contest that involves the interplay of surrender and resoluteness; a contest in which we might want to trade a death for a death, our own for a beloved child or mate. In short, a contest of love and death.

Unamuno too might be taxed with this charge of egotism. He persistently speaks, especially in the earlier chapters, of his own personal and private longing for his own immortality, almost as if he were denying that the mortality of others might at some moments be a matter of greater anguish. The whole spirit and tone of the book speak against such egotism, however. The man is clearly so radiant with charity and compassion, so passionate to pour himself out to quicken the lives of others. (See, particularly, the chapter "Faith, Hope, and Charity.")

The early Camus (of the *Myth of Sisyphus*) had read some Heidegger and he sounds some of the same notes. Here is the same sense of our finite, time-bound, and mortal existence, and the same solitary existential ego confronting these facts in its own self-absorbed questioning. Time and death present themselves to Camus as threats to all human values. What are our highest cultural values—the works of a Shakespeare or a Goethe, for example—worth, if in ten thousand years they will not even be understood? Or if mankind no longer exists to read them? This vista of eventual Nothingness drove Unamuno into a frenzy; the young Camus, on the other hand, professes to confront it with an ironic and mock-Cartesian lucidity.

Camus could not remain in this aesthetic stance. The absurd man, confronting his own death with lucid courage, may strike an admirable posture; but he has nothing to say to the vast body of humanity that faces death day to day in the daily round of things. Camus had to pass from saying "I" in the face of death to saying "We." That is the progress from *The Stranger* to *The Plague*. Both novels deal with human mortality. But while the first presents the solitary man, stranger to his human brothers, who is pushed against the blank wall of death, the second shows us how some human beings can be drawn together under the threat of death. In the town that has been afflicted by a plague everybody stands under the sentence of death. The plague is thus but an image of the human condition, in which we all stand similarly condemned. Yet in that situation men learn for the first time that mortality makes them brothers, and that in the presence of death they can labor together to save life. The contest with death may be unequal, but it is worth waging.

Neither Heidegger nor Camus makes the leap toward immortality. They seem able to accept the fact of death, albeit with much anguish, without appealing to a life beyond. Unamuno could not rest with such stoicism, however much more rationally justifiable than his own attitude, simply because for him the acquiescence in death denies one part of our human nature: our absurd but unquenchable longing for everlasting life. Thrust this longing out the front door, he tells us, and it will return in some form through the back door. It could be argued that Camus virtually introduced a surrogate form of immortality in *The Plague* in the guise of the coherent community that persists beyond the death of its individual members. The individual can bear his own little light's flickering out in the great void if there will be others remaining for whom the light still shines.

Why is there death? Why did God introduce death into His creation? Theologians have asked these questions for centuries, and wearied themselves to death in answering. From the point of view of modern biology these questions do not appear quite so futile as once thought, and the biologists' answers, oddly enough, run parallel to the theologians'. Biologists have been able to fix in the long line of evolution the point at which death emerges for living beings. Below that point, among the simplest organisms, death does not occur: these very elementary creatures may be destroyed by a chemical or physical cause, but they do not die in the natural course of things as higher beings do. Now, at the point at which death enters the evolutionary scale, the differentiation of sex also occurs. Sex and death together! From the evolutionist's point of view, the biological use of these two phenomena is easily seen: sexual differentiation permits a wider capacity for variation in the offspring, while death's replacing one individual by another makes it possible for the offspring to surpass the parent. Here are two most efficacious devices on nature's part for enriching the evolutionary process.

But from the poet's or the philosopher's point of view, this evolutionary linking will suggest more intimate consequences in the life of man. Eros, which binds us most closely to one another, emerges in the scale of life coordinate with Death, which sunders us from all others. But are these two opposites to be separated so categorically from each other? In the life of man do they not play into one another inextricably? Does not the awareness of death bind humans closer in their love for each other? Since we are all brothers-in-death should we not love one another?

Tolstoi's story "The Death of Ivan Ilyich" has by this time become almost the classical reference on the subject of death, and yet its whole message is not usually grasped. (Heidegger, for example, bases his analysis of death on the first part, which deals with Ivan's breakdown, but he does not draw upon the reconciliation toward the end of the story.) Ivan Ilyich, an average bourgeois, has an accident and learns later that he is going to die. All his defenses are shattered; for the first time in his life he is thrown nakedly back upon himself. He, Ivan Ilyich, and not some other, is going to die. He is suddenly cut off from all the people he knew, and even from his own immediate family; he sees them all as alien and at an infinite distance. This is the imminence of death experienced as absolute solitude. Yet, toward the end of the story, he passes beyond that solitude to find love for another human being—in the person of the young peasant who comes to his bedside to keep him company. The near presence of death has enabled him to surrender to a larger life beyond his solitary ego. We die as individuals in order to join the possibly immortal life of mankind.

Unamuno, of course, wants more immortality than that. At this point perhaps the philosopher can only cheerfully part company with the man of faith. I do think, though, that Unamuno in the singleminded intensity of his passion does oversimplify the possible attitudes toward death. The natural craving (to live on and on) may take different forms and intensities in different people. At certain moments one does wish to live as oneself forever; at other moments, and without succumbing to nihilism or despair, one would be content to resign one's place. Besides, personal immortality offers some serious ambiguities of its own: it can be a terrifying rather than a comforting thought. So at least felt Kierkegaard, who in his *Sickness Unto Death* analyzes ultimate despair as the recoil from this possibility of having to be oneself, of not being able to escape oneself, through all eternity. Only an equally extreme faith, he argues, can enable the believing Christian to welcome such a future. Unamuno, a more robust man, seems never to have felt the same dismay.

The Tragic Sense of Life is to be read as a great

philosophical lyric. It expresses how one man—and an exemplary man—felt about death and immortality at a certain stage in his life. Those feelings, Unamuno repeatedly insists, cannot be justified logically; but neither can logic, and least of all logic, dismiss them. The reader will respond to Unamuno's passion with his own capacity for passion. But one thing that seems to me inarguable about this book is that it is also a *noble* lyric, the voice of a man, an *hombre*, speaking to his fellow men in the midst of our disheartened century. Nobody can come away from it without being quickened once again for that ceaseless contest with death—and particularly death of the spirit—that goes on day by day, and sometimes even hour by hour, in the lives of all of us.

WILLIAM BARRETT

Notes

Notes

The first Spanish edition of this work, *Del sentimiento trágico de la vida en los hombres y en los pueblos*, was published in Madrid in 1913 (320 pp. with a one-page index), by Renacimiento. (The first chapter had appeared in the magazine *La España Moderna*, beginning in December 1911, the second chapter in the January 1912 issue, in monthly installments, skipping the November issue, until the end.) It was followed by many other editions, by different publishers, the most important being in a two-volume edition of *Ensayos*, edited by B. G. de Candamo (Madrid, 1942), *Tomo* II, published by Aguilar. Then followed the first series of *Obras Completas* (*OC*[1] in our Notes) (Madrid, 1950), *Tomo* IV, published by Afrodisio Aguado; and then a second *Obras Completas* (*OC*[2] in our Notes), in sixteen volumes (Madrid, 1958), *Tomo* XVI, published by Vergara: all three editions have been used in our translation. In a third edition of *Obras Completas*, planned for ten volumes by Escelicer, Madrid, there appeared in their Vol. 7 (late 1969), the same text, only in clearer type. The book has been translated, in chronological order, into Italian, in two volumes (Milano, 1914, and Firenze, 1924), and into a one-volume edition (Firenze, 1937); into three French editions (Paris,

1917), translated "most of it in the trenches," by a medical doctor, and issued by the *Nouvelle Revue Française*, an edition in 1937 by Gallimard, and again in 1957; into English (London, 1921), into German (München, 1925, and Leipzig, 1933); into Czechoslovak (Praha, 1927); into Danish (Köben-havn, 1925); into Latvian (Riga, 1936); and into Japanese (Tokyo, 1971).

I. THE MAN OF FLESH AND BLOOD

3. *"Homo sum"*: Terence (c. 195–159 B.C.), *Heauton Timoroumenos*, 25, "I am a man; nothing human do I deem alien to me."

the real brother: It is this insistence on the total individual rather than the abstract man which aligns Unamuno with the existentialists, long before the term came into fashion.

featherless biped: Cf. Diogenes Laertius, *Lives and Opinions of Eminent Philosophers*, tr. R. D. Hicks (Loeb Classical Library, 1925), II, 43.

Aristotle: Politics, Book I, Ch. 2; the Greek, ζῷον πολιτικόν: "political animal."

a no-man: Cf. Unamuno's *Homo insipidus*, "who does not belong either here or there, is neither of the present nor the past, and is not of any time or place," in his *The Life of Don Quixote and Sancho*, Part II, Ch. 46 (Vol. 3, p. 234, in this edition).

5. *Kierkegaard*: Søren Kierkegaard (1813–55). It was in a book by Georg Brandes on Ibsen, whom Unamuno much admired (especially *Brand*), that Unamuno first came across the name of Kierke-gaard ("Ibsen y Kierkegaard," *OC*, IV; this edition, Vol. 5), and since he already knew German and some

Norwegian, it was not difficult for him to learn Danish. The discovery of Kierkegaard was one of the capital events in Unamuno's intellectual life, for in the Dane he found a soul-brother, one who had already expressed himself against implicit faith, religious "officialdom" and conformity, and those who set themselves up as purveyors of religious interpretations; Kierkegaard had already insisted on religion as subjective and passionate, and therefore recalcitrant to all definition, a *via crucis* rather than a reason for self-satisfaction. Unamuno's adoption of Kierkegaard as one of his favorite or "cardiac" writers makes of him the first Spaniard to study the Dane, and also one of the first, outside of Denmark, to understand his importance for modern thought. The Unamuno library boasts of the fourteen volumes of *Søren Kierkegaards Samlede Vaerker*, udgivne af B. A. Drachmann. J. L. Heiberg og H. O. Lange (Kjøvenhavn, 1901–06), many of which are profusely marked in Unamuno's hand, especially the volumes containing *Enten/Eller (Either/Or)*, *Stadier Paa Livets Vei (Stages on Life's Way)*, and the book he so often quotes in *The Tragic Sense of Life*, the *Afsluttende uvidenskabelig Efterskrift* or *Concluding Unscientific Postscript*.

The "leap" referred to here is one of Kierkegaard's central concepts, the leap from reason into faith.

6. *immortal leap: salto inmortal*. "There is a play here upon the term *salto mortal*, used to denote the dangerous aerial somersault of the acrobat, which cannot be rendered into English."—J. E. Crawford Flitch, in his translation (1921) of *The Tragic Sense of Life*.

Unamuno is playing with the famous "salto mortale" (Italian) of Kierkegaard: the leap from reason into faith, through will rather than logic. Quite in-dependently of Kierkegaard, William James had also understood the meaning of such a leap.

7. *William James*: The influence of William James (especially in *The Will to Believe*, *The Varieties of Religious Experience*, and *Pragmatism*) weaves its way through this and other works of Unamuno. In James, the Spaniard found substantiation of many of his own thoughts and feelings, e.g., that the temperament and affective needs of the thinking man contribute to molding his thought; the limitations of "objective certitude"; the creative power of faith; the notion of the "leap in the dark" from the empirical to the spiritual mode. Cf. Pelayo H. Fernández, *Miguel de Unamuno y William James, un paralelo pragmático* (Salamanca, 1961).

Consciousness or Conscience: Consciencia. "The same word is used in Spanish to denote both consciousness and conscience. If the latter is specifically intended the qualifying adjective '*moral*' or '*religiosa*' is commonly added."—J.E.C. Flitch.

8. *Hegel . . . framer of definitions*: This contempt for Hegel, in whose *Logic* Unamuno tells us he first began reading German during his university days in Madrid (1880–84), echoes Kierkegaard's own scorn for that systematic thinker. Already in *En torno al casticismo* (written as separate essays in 1895, five years before his discovery of the Danish writer), Unamuno refutes Hegel's idea that man defines himself in history.

Joseph Butler: (1692–1752), author of the *Analogy of Religion, Natural and Revealed* (1736). Unamuno has in his library the Everyman edition (London and New York, 1906). Of the several passages marked off by Unamuno, the one on p. 189 is of special interest: ". . . doubting necessarily implies some degree of evidence for that of which we doubt." Newman's judgment on Butler is given in the Introduction to the book in Unamuno's library.

11. *Fichte*: Johann Gottlieb Fichte (1762–1814), disciple of Kant, author (1800) of *Die Bestimmung des Menschen* (*The Vocation of Man*). Fichte attempted to rescue the "I" from eighteenth-century determinism, i.e., what we know of external things is what we know of our own mental processes.

12. *one of our ascetics*: Although J. E. Crawford Flitch attributes the notion to San Juan de los Angeles (1536–1609), and Giberto Beccari, the Italian translator of *The Tragic Sense*, attributes it to P. Alonso Rodríguez (1538–1616), it comes from *The Ascent of Mount Carmel* (*Subida del Monte Carmelo*, 1583), by St. John of the Cross (San Juan de la Cruz, 1542–91).

14. *Obermann*: A novel by Étienne Pivert de Sénancour (1770–1846), French Romantic; though in effect an *émigré* living in Switzerland at the time of his main work, he totally ignored the French Revolution and wrote as if it had not existed. *Obermann* (*Oberman*, in the first two-volume edition of 1804) was edited by Sainte-Beuve in 1833 and by George Sand in 1852; it was written in the Jura region, as a series of letters, and influenced later Romantic literature. This melancholy romantic novel was one of Unamuno's favorite books, endlessly quoted by him throughout his work. The words "And along with Obermann . . . everything," are, in the original French, from Letter XLV of Sénancour's *Obermann*: "Les lois générales sont fort belles, et je leur sacrifierais volontiers un an, deux, dix ans même de ma vie; mais tout mon être, c'est trop: ce n'est rien dans la nature,

c'est tout pour moi." As he often does, Unamuno here alters the original to suit his immediate purpose. For Unamuno and Sénancour, see Émile Martel, "Lecturas francesas de Unamuno: Sénancour," *Cuadernos de la cátedra de Miguel de Unamuno*, xiv-xv (Salamanca, 1964–65), 85-96.

16. *"shall lose it"*: Matt. 10:39.

17. *"help thou mine unbelief"*: Mark 9:24.

18. *"Para pensar cual tú, . . ."*:

> To think like you, all I need
> merely is to possess intelligence.

20. *unknowable*: The allusion here is to Herbert Spencer (1820–1903) and his school which relegated the religious to the area of the "unknowable." Unamuno fell under the spell of Spencer in the 1880s but eventually rejected his influence. Although he translated many of Spencer's essays, he considered his rejection of the Englishman one of the greatest victories of his life.

22. *men weighed down . . .* : It is noteworthy that the René of Chateaubriand and the Obermann of Sénancour, fictional characters, are considered as real as the long list of actual literary figures named here. These are Unamuno's "cardiac" writers, men whose hearts were as involved in their creation as their minds.

Spanish [proverb]: The Spanish proverb is "Piensa el ladrón que todos son de su condición" ("The thief thinks all men are thieves").

II. The Point of Departure

23. *the serpent—a model of prudence for Christ*: Cf. "And as Moses lifted up the serpent in the wilderness, even so must the Son of man be lifted up," John

3:14. And "John did not hesitate to compare Christ
with the Serpent because Christ had assumed the
whole economy of the exodus," Thierry Maertens,
Bible Themes (Brussels, 1962), I, 211; "Christ gave
it his full meaning by assimilating Himself to the
serpent," ibid., 176. In Mark 16:18, and Luke 10:
19, "it is one of the signs of the mission of the disciples
of Jesus that they have power over serpents," J. L.
McKenzie, *Dictionary of the Bible* (London-Dublin,
1965), p. 791. In the Old Testament, "the brazen
serpent was one of the objects of worship in the Temple—not a genuine idol, but a representation of God."
Cf. 4 Kings 18:4 and "the sign of the serpent, representing obedience to the Law"; cf. Wisdom 16:1-7,
Bible Themes, loc. cit. Cf., too, the double serpents
of Mercury's caduceus, where the tame serpent is a
counterpoise to the wild one. Jung, in his *Psychology
and Alchemy*, tr. R.F.C. Hull (Bollingen Series XX:
12, 2nd edn., Princeton, 1968), pp. 292-95, points
out that this double image suggests the concept of
homeopathy, cure by the cause, so that the serpent
is a source for curing the ill caused by the serpent.
It was thus a symbol of St. John the Evangelist and
appears next to a chalice. See Juan-Eduardo Cirlot,
A Dictionary of Symbols, tr. Jack Sage (London,
1962), p. 276. Cf. Simone Weil, speaking of Christianity in *Waiting on God* (London, 1952), p. 27:
"The bronze serpent must be lifted up again so that
whoever raises his eyes to it may be saved."

woman . . . life: It was Unamuno's conviction that
any system of education of women must take into account the fact that women gestate, give birth, and
nurse their children, and are structured toward these
three ends. Cf. "La educación: prólogo a la obra de
Bunge, del mismo título," *OC*, iii, 517.

31. *Mr. Balfour: The Foundations of Belief, being Notes Introductory to the Study of Theology*, by the Right Hon. Arthur James Balfour, London, 1895: "So it is with those persons who claim to show by their example that naturalism is practically consistent with the maintenance of ethical ideals with which naturalism has no natural affinity. Their spiritual life is parasitic: it is sheltered by convictions which belong, not to them, but to the society of which they form a part; it is nourished by processes in which they take no share. And when those convictions decay, and those processes come to an end, the alien life which they have maintained can scarce be expected to outlast them" (Ch. iv). A Conservative member of Parliament, Balfour became Foreign Secretary and prepared the Balfour Declaration, keystone to the legal creation of the state of Israel.

32. *it is not so much . . . Him*: There is an unmistakable echo here of the Kantian idea that the categorical imperative of morality leads to a belief in God.

33. *Max Stirner*: pseudonym of Johann Kaspar Schmidt (1806–56), author of *Der Einzige und sein Eigentum* (1845), translated as *The Ego and His Own* (1907). Stirner's work is a reaction against Hegel, an attack upon systematic philosophy. The only thing of which we have certain knowledge, Stirner held, is the individual who is unique and who must cultivate that uniqueness against all general beliefs and philosophies. Stirner was a forerunner of Nietzsche.

34. *"Act in such wise . . ."*: Kant, in *Grundlegung zur Metaphysik der Sitten* (1785). The translation by Thomas K. Abbott from *Fundamental Principles of the Metaphysic of Morals* (Indianapolis, New

York, 1949, p. 47) is: "There is therefore but one categorical imperative, namely, this: *Act only on that maxim whereby thou canst at the same time will that it should become a universal law.*"

Xenophon: Memorabilia and Oeconomicus, with an English translation by E. C. Marchant (Loeb Classical Library, 1959), *Memorabilia*, iii, xi.

Hodgson: Shadworth Holloway Hodgson (1832–1912), *Time and Space, a metaphysical essay* (London, 1865), p. 13.

36. *Spinoza*: 1632–77. Spinoza was not himself an exile; he was born in Amsterdam of a Jewish family that had come to Holland in the sixteenth century. The *Ethics* was published after his death. The translation by R.H.M. Elwes in *The Chief Works of Benedict de Spinoza: The Ethics* (New York, 1951), ii, 232, is: "A free man thinks of death least of all things; and his wisdom is a meditation not of death but of life."

"blessedness is not": op. cit., p. 270.

37. *Cicero's definition: De Officiis*, tr. Walter Miller (Loeb Classical Library, 1951), ii, 2, p. 172: "Sapientia autem est, ut a veteribus philosophis definitum est, rerum divinarum et humanarum causarumque, quibus eae res continentur, scientia; . . ." "Wisdom, moreover, as the word has been defined by the philosophers of old, is 'the knowledge of things human and divine and of the causes by which those things are controlled.' "

Clement of Alexandria: the edition in the Unamuno library is *Die Griechischen Christlichen Schriftsteller der ersten drei Jahrhunderte, Clemens Alexandrinus* (Leipzig, J. C. Hinrichs'sche Buchhandlung, 3 vols., 1905, 1906, 1909). The English translation is from *The Miscellanies*, ed. Rev. Alexander Roberts and

James Donaldson, *Ante-Nicene Christian Fathers*, Vol. XII, *Clement of Alexandria*, Vol. II (Edinburgh: T. and T. Clark, 1869), Book IV, Ch. XXII, pp. 202–03.

40. *poêle*: actually the *poêle* was a room heated by a stove. Cf. beginning of Part II of the *Discourse*.

cogito ergo sum, which St. Augustine . . . anticipated: In his copy of Adolf von Harnack's *Lehrbuch der Dogmengeschichte* (Freiburg i. B. und Leipzig; Akademische Verlagsbuchhandlung von J.C.B. Mohr [Paul Siebeck]), Vol. 3 (1890), p. 299, alongside of note 2 which reads "*Confess.* VII, 16 'Audivi (verba Ego sum qui sum) sicut auditur in corde, et non erat prorsus unde dubitarem; faciliusque dubitarem vivere me, quam non esse veritatem.' VI, 5" Unamuno penciled "Cf. cogito, ergo sum."

According to Étienne Gilson, *The Christian Philosophy of Saint Augustine*, tr. L.E.M. Lynch (New York: 1960), pp. 41-43, Augustine anticipates Descartes in several works, but especially in *De Libero Arbitrio*, in *De Trinitate*, and in *De Civitate Dei*. See the notes corresponding to the pages indicated.

III. THE HUNGER FOR IMMORTALITY

43. *legends on the theme*: In the *Phaedo*, Socrates is making his final observations before taking the hemlock, and has just given an account of the nature of the world and of the underworld, and of "they who are released . . . from confinement in . . . the earth, and passing upward to their pure abode, make their dwelling upon the earth's surface. And . . . such as have purified themselves sufficiently by philosophy live thereafter altogether without bodies, and reach habita-

tions even more beautiful, which it is not easy to por-
tray—nor is there time to do so now." And he concludes: "Of course, no reasonable man ought to insist
that the facts are exactly as I have described them."
But "We should use such accounts to inspire ourselves with confidence, and that is why I have already
drawn out my tale so long." *Phaedo*, tr. Hugh Tredennick, *The Collected Dialogues of Plato*, ed. Edith
Hamilton and Huntington Cairns, Bollingen Series
LXXI (Princeton, 1969), pp. 94-95.

44. *"He wants nothing of a god but eternity"*: "and
a heaven to throne in," *Coriolanus*, V. iv. (25). The
sense is that Marcius lacks only eternity to make him
a god, as Unamuno points out in the Spanish.

Pindar: Pythia, VIII, Epod 5, line 95.

45. *"If in this life . . . miserable"*: This is the
epigraph Unamuno chose for his culminating work,
the novelette *San Manuel Bueno, mártir*, *OC*, XVI,
in another volume of this edition.

The tragic Portuguese Jew . . . death: See herein,
note to p. 36.

46. *"in a matter . . . monster"*: No. 194 of Pascal's
Thoughts. Actually Pascal considers the "indifference" to be "monstrous."

47. *Amidst the delirium . . . immortality of the
soul*: "He [Robespierre] is President of the Convention; he has made the Convention *decree*, so they
name it, *décréter* the 'Existence of the Supreme Being,' and likewise *'ce principe consolateur* of the Immortality of the Soul.'" Cf. Thomas Carlyle, *The
French Revolution* (Leipzig, 1851), Vol. III, Book
XI, Ch. IV, p. 335, which Unamuno owned, read, and
finally translated entire. Throughout the book, Carlyle refers to Robespierre as the Incorruptible, some-

times as the Seagreen Incorruptible, which in his translation, *La revolución francesa*, published in Madrid, 1902, Unamuno renders as "*cetrino incorruptible*" (as: " 'A Republic?' said the Seagreen, . . . 'What is that?' . . . O seagreen Incorruptible, thou shalt see!" [Vol. 2, Bk. 4, Ch. 4], translated by Unamuno as: "¿República?—dijo el cetrino . . . — ¿qué es eso? ¡Ya lo has de ver, cetrino incorruptible!")

"*e quindi uscimmo a riveder le stelle*": last line of the *Inferno*: "And thence we issued forth to see again the stars," tr. Charles S. Singleton, *The Divine Comedy: Inferno*, Bollingen Series LXXX (Princeton, 1970), I, 369.

48. "*Every time*":

> Cada vez que considero
> Que me tengo de morir
> Tiendo la capa en el suelo
> Y no me harto de dormir.

"Strofa popolare andalusa," says the Italian translator G. Beccari, in a note at this point of his translation *Del sentimento tragico della vita negli uomini e nei popoli*, Prima parte (Milano, 1914), p. 46. Cf. *Our Lord Don Quixote*, Vol. 3 of this edition, p. xix.

49. "*Hell might afford my miseries a shelter*": From "Lines Written Under the Influence of Delirium," marked in Unamuno's own copy of *The Poetical Works of William Cowper* (London, 1889), p. 23.

Obermann: for the French, see herein, p. 282; on Sénancour, see the note to p. 14. We take the English from the version of J. Anthony Barnes (London and New York, 1915), II, 252, where the full quote begins: " 'Man is perishable,' is the response."

"*Abandon all Hope!*": "*Lasciate ogni speranza, voi ch'entrate!*" *Inferno*, Canto III, line 9.

50. *"Perì l'inganno estremo . . ."*: From "A se stesso" (*Canti*, Firenze, 1831):

> Or poserai per sempre,
> Stanco mio cor. Perì l'inganno estremo,
> Ch'eterno io mi credei.

Cf. *The Penguin Book of Italian Verse* (Harmondsworth, 1958), which gives a prose translation: "Now you will rest for ever, tired heart of mine. The last deception has perished which I believed eternal." Unamuno's version is totally different, and is surely what Leopardi had in mind.

The last line of this same poem is

> E l'infinita vanità del tutto.

"the close kinship . . . die": Cf. Leopardi's poem "Amor e morte."

> Fratelli a un tempo stesso, Amor e Morte
> Ingenerò la sorte.
>
> . . .
>
> Quando novellamente
> Nasce nel cor profondo
> Un amoroso affetto,
> Languido e stanco insiem con esso in petto
> Un desiderio de morir si sente. . . .

> Fate in one hour created Love and Death,
> Brothers to each other.
>
> . . .
>
> When freshly in the deepest heart
> A loving feeling springs,
> With it together in the breast is felt,
> Languid and weary a desire for death. . . .

The translation is from Leopardi's *Canti*, translated into English verse, with parallel text and an introduction, by John Humphreys Whitfield (Napoli, 1962), pp. 194 ff.

Unamuno's admiration for Leopardi's work never diminished throughout his lifetime; the author of the *Canti* was one of the Spaniard's "cardiac" writers, and when exiled to the island of Fuerteventura in 1924, Unamuno carried with him only three books: The New Testament in Greek, a copy of the *Divine Comedy*, and a volume of Leopardi's poetry. He had also translated Leopardi's "La ginestra" in 1899; cf. *OC*, xiii, 479-88.

"Beautiful risk!": Unamuno uses the Spanish "hermoso" (beautiful or handsome) to translate the Greek adjective, which is usually also rendered as "beautiful" in English. ("Risk" he changes to "chance"—"suerte" —for the substantive on the second invocation of the modifier.) "Glorious risk" might perhaps ring more roundly in English, however, and Hugh Tredennick, in his translation of the *Phaedo* (see herein, note to p. 43), translates the adjective as "noble," rendering the pertinent passage (which occurs after Socrates has described the good fortune after death of those who "have lived a life of surpassing holiness") as follows: "Of course no reasonable man ought to insist that the facts are exactly as I have described them. But that either this or something very like it is a true account of our souls and their future habitations— since we have clear evidence that the soul is immortal —this, I think, is both a reasonable contention and a belief worth risking, for the risk is a noble one."

51. *Pascal's famous argument of the wager*: Thought No. 233. The argument holds that since one is "embarked" in life there is no choice but to wager on whether God exists or not. It is wiser to wager affirmatively, since if He exists, then one wins all; if not, nothing has been lost.

"My I! They are stealing my I!" In his unpub-

lished doctoral thesis *Libros y lecturas franceses de Miguel de Unamuno* (Salamanca, 1964), Emile Martel says that Michelet is represented in Unamuno's work mainly by this quotation which neither Martel nor the present editors have been able to trace. Unamuno uses this quotation quite often in his work but the verb varies from "arrebatan" (used in the present quotation) to "arrancan" to "devuelvan," that is, from "they are stealing" (or "snatching away") to "they are tearing away." On p. 212 of his thesis, Martel says "After some early and partial contact with Michelet in 1887, Don Miguel seems to have become slowly more familiar with his work. It is probable that he read some of Michelet's books in 1900 and certainly read *L'Histoire de la France au Moyen Âge* in 1921." There is no book by Michelet in the Unamuno library in Salamanca.

53. *"stinking pride"*: is from Leopardi's "La ginestra," translated by Unamuno himself as "La retama" (*OC*, XIII, 482, line 106). The Italian context reads:

> Magnanimo animale
> Non credo io già, ma stolto,
> Quel che nato a perir, nutrito in pene,
> Dice, a goder son fatto,
> E di fetido orgoglio
> Empie le carte, . . .

Unamuno translated these lines as:

> Nunca creí magnánimo
> animal, sino necio
> el que a morir viniendo a nuestro mundo,
> y entre penas criado, aún exclama:
> "¡para el goce estoy hecho!"
> y de fétido orgullo
> páginas llena, . . .

And along with Obermann . . . : See herein, note to p. 14.

55. *the gods weave and accomplish the destruction of mortals*: In his *Diario íntimo* Unamuno notes:
"For a long time I kept in my room two portrait
sketches, one of Spencer, the other of Homer, drawn
by me; at the bottom of the latter I had copied out
the lines from the *Odyssey* which go 'The gods weave
and accomplish the destruction of mortals in order
that their posterity may have something to narrate'—
the quintessence of the shallow spirit of paganism, a
sterile aestheticism which kills all spiritual substance
and beauty." (Madrid, 1970), *Cuaderno* i, p. 16; and
also *Cuaderno* iii, p. 154, where the Homeric observation is followed by the notation: "Aestheticism is hor-
rible, a kind of death."

57. *There you have that "thief of energies"* . . .
courage: Here Unamuno has Nietzsche in mind, but
mistakenly if understandably attributes to the German writer part of a verse from the last stanza of
Arthur Rimbaud's "Les premières communions":
"Christ! ô Christ, éternel voleur des énergies!" There
are many passages in Nietzsche where Christ and
Christianity are condemned, and Unamuno confesses
that he knew Nietzsche only fragmentarily and
through references to and quotations from the German's work. He had read Henri Lichtenberger's *La
philosophie de Nietzsche* and Jules de Gaultier's *De
Kant à Nietzsche*, and if he considered Nietzsche a
great poet, he condemned him as an extremely weak
thinker. Cf. the essays "¿Para qué escribir?" and "Al-
go sobre Nietzsche" in *OC*, viii, and also the sonnet
"A Nietzsche" in *Rosario de sonetos líricos*, *OC*, xiii,
611.

In his exhaustive book, *Nietzsche en España* (Madrid, 1967), Professor Gonzalo Sobejano proves that
Nietzsche's influence on Unamuno is more in "man-

ner" than ideas, that Unamuno had probably read the *Zarathustra* by 1900 either in German, French, or in Spanish translation, and that numerous analogies between Unamuno and Nietzsche would disprove Unamuno's denial of any first-hand knowledge of the German writer.

"eternal recurrence": See Index to *Complete Works of Nietzsche*, ed. Oscar Levy (London, 1913).

58. *Boccaccio . . . virtue*: Cf. *Vita di Dante*, in Charles Allen Dinsmore, *Aids to the Study of Dante* (Boston and New York, 1903), p. 99.

Legenda trium sociorum: The Three Companions, a life of St. Francis of Assisi (middle of thirteenth century), written by Thomas of Celano, Italian friar of the thirteenth century, presumably the author of the *Dies Irae* hymn. An early follower of St. Francis, Celano was the author of two *Lives* of the saint (1229, 1247), the second of which is cited here (English translation by A. G. Ferrers, 1908).

59. *his life for his purse*: play on the robber's cry of "¡Manos arriba! La bolsa o la vida!" "Hands up! Your purse [money] or your life!"

60. *Émile*: Book iv, the section titled "The Creed of a Savoyard Priest," p. 231 of the translation by Barbara Foxley (London, 1963). It was this section outlining Rousseau's religious attitude that caused *Émile* to be banned and burned.

61. *a Stylite who erects himself into an image*: In his *The Penguin Dictionary of Saints* (1965), Donald Attwater points out how Simeon the Stylite's pillar became increasingly higher, so that over the years it grew to a height of sixty feet, and that while the purpose was ostensibly to remove Simeon from the press of the multitude, the opposite happened: as the column grew higher the crowds became greater. And cf.

Tennyson's poem "St. Simeon Stylites": "The silly
people take me for a saint," but also "Who may be
made a saint, if I fail here?" and "I will not cease to
grasp the hope I hold / Of saintdom" (lines 127, 48,
and 5-6).

The latest edition (Escelicer)of the *Obras Completas* reads "estilista": stylist.

Mr. X: Unamuno calls him "Fernández" which is a
very common Spanish name and may be translated
as "Mr. Smith," "Mr. X," or "John Doe."

62. *Abel . . . Cain*: The Cain-Abel theme is a
recurrent one in Unamuno, and was fictionalized by
him in the novel *Abel Sánchez* and the play *El Otro*.
Cf. Carlos Clavería, "Sobre el tema de Caín en la obra
de Unamuno," in *Temas de Unamuno* (Madrid,
1953).

"Death to me! Long live my fame!": "¡*Muera yo,
viva mi fama!*" Among the last words of Rodrigo
Arias, son of Arias Gonçalo, in the third act of the
Second Part ("Comedia Segunda") of the drama by
Guillén de Castro (1569–1631). Rodrigo Arias wins
the contest at arms against Don Diego Ordóñez de
Lara (though he dies, like his two brothers immediately before him) by driving Don Diego out of bounds
on the field of honor, so that, as Don Diego says,
"killing him I did not vanquish / and he in dying
vanquished me!" But later a formal sentence by the
judges has the effect of declaring them both victors.

Girolamo Olgiati: In his essay "Olgiati" of 1900
(in *OC*, viii, 666-69), Unamuno translates a long
passage from Jacob Burckhardt's *Die Kultur der Renaissance in Italien* (Leipzig, 1899), i, 61-62. Olgiati's exclamation comes at the end of that passage.
Our translation comes from *The Civilization of the*

Renaissance in Italy (London and New York, 1944), p. 38.

63. *"avidus malae famae"*: *The Annals of Tacitus* (Loeb Classical Library, 1962), ii, 28, pp. 424, 425: "Celebre inter acusatores Trionis ingenium erat avidumque famae malae." "Trio's genius, which was famous among the professional informers, hungered after notoriety."

Erostratism: or Herostratism. "Do you know who Herostratus was?" one character asks another toward the end of Unamuno's *Amor y Pedagogía.* "He was a man who burned down the temple of Ephesus to make his name imperishable. In the same way we burn down our felicity to bequeath our name, a vain sound, to posterity." Unamuno seems to have invented the word. Cf. "Dos cartas inéditas de Unamuno," by Dámaso Alonso, in *Spanish Thought and Letters in the Twentieth Century* (Nashville, 1966), pp. 4-5, where Alonso sums up the word's meaning as: "to do something, set fire to a temple, or create a great literary work, so as not to die, not to die altogether."

"Posterity . . . minorities": Cf. *Charles Gounod, Autobiographical Reminiscences with Family Letters and Notes on Music,* tr. The Hon. W. Hely Hutchinson (London, 1896), p. 197: "The only true and definite sentence, that of posterity, is but the accumulated judgment of successive minorities."

IV. The Essence of Catholicism

65. *Second Coming of Christ*: Cf. 1 Thess. 4:16-17: "For the Lord himself shall descend from heaven with a shout, with the voice of the archangel, and with the trump of God: and the dead in Christ shall

rise first: Then we which are alive and remain shall
be caught up together with them in the clouds to meet
the Lord in the air: and so shall we ever be with the
Lord."

66. *Harnack*: Adolf von Harnack (1851–1930),
eminent German Protestant theologian and church
historian, best known for his *Dogmengeschichte*
(English tr., 1894–99) which, along with other
books and essays by German liberal Protestant theologians, Unamuno read avidly in the last years of
the nineteenth century. The edition of Harnack's
work used by Unamuno is the *Lehrbuch der Dogmengeschichte von Dr. Adolf Harnack, dritte verbesserte
und vermehrte Auflage* (Freiburg i. B. und Leipzig,
Akademische Verlagsbuchhandlung von J.C.B. Mohr
[Paul Siebeck]). Of the three volumes making up
the total work, the first two are dated 1894, while
the third (containing the index to the three volumes)
is 1890, and therefore does not belong to the third
definitive edition.

These books are among the most annotated in the
Unamuno library. They are a monument of erudition,
and recount how early Christian faith hardened into
dogma as it encompassed Greek philosophy and
Roman law. Even the Reformation eventually became
involved with "ordinance, doctrine, and ceremony,"
and Harnack advocated a cleansing of all "non-essen-
tial" matter and a return to faith as "the beginning,
middle, and end of all religious fervor." The impact
of Harnack's research and concepts is patent throughout *The Tragic Sense of Life* and many other essays,
especially the important "La fe" ("Faith") of 1900.

It is of interest that Dietrich Bonhoeffer (1906–45)
was a member of Harnack's last seminar and spoke

at his teacher's memorial service on June 15, 1930, in Berlin.

Nemesius: (fl. c. A.D. 390), Christian philosopher, Bishop of Emesius, and author of the treatise *On Man's Nature*.

Lactantius: Lucius Caelius Firmianus Lactantius, 240?–320?, a native of Africa, has been called the Christian Cicero; he wrote treatises on the "handiwork" and the "wrath" of God, and a history tracing the effects of Divine Judgment on contemporary events.

67. *Hosea 11:1*: "When Israel was a child, then I loved him, and called my son out of Egypt."

68. *Rohde*: Erwin Rohde, *Psyche, Seelencult und Unsterblichkeit der Griechen* (Tübingen, 1907), Erster Band, p. 181. The translation is from *Psyche, The Cult of Souls and Belief in Immortality among the Greeks*, tr. W. B. Hillis (New York, 1966), I, 131. In a footnote concerning Rohde's book, Unamuno says "Up to the present this is the leading work dealing with the belief of the Greeks in the immortality of the soul."

Both the Titanic . . . jail: Rohde, op. cit., Zweiter Band, p. 121; tr. Hillis, II, 341-42: "The distinction between the Titanic and Dionysiac elements in man is an allegorical expression of the popular distinction between body and soul; it also corresponds to a profoundly felt estimate of the relative value of these two sides of man's being. According to Orphic doctrine man's duty is to free himself from the chains of the body in which the soul lies fast bound like the prisoner in his cell."

"an immortality . . . populace." Rohde, op. cit., Zweiter Band, p. 378; tr. Hillis, II, 538.

Pfleiderer; Otto Pfleiderer (1839–1908), German Protestant theologian. The quotation is from the third edition of *Religionsphilosophie auf geschichtliche Grundlage* (Berlin, 1896), p. 539.

69. *Weizsäcker*: Karl Heinrich von Weizsäcker (1822–99), German theologian and editor (1856–78) of *Jahrbücher für deutsche Theologie.* The quotation is from *Das apostolische Zeitalter der christlichen Kirche* (Freiburg i. B., 1892), p. 102. The translation made from the second and revised edition by James Millar, *The Apostolic Age of the Christian Church* (London and New York, 1897), I, 123, runs: "This we are entitled to call the earliest Christian theology. In Paul's case, it was a necessity; it supplied to some extent the want of personal acquaintance with Jesus. . . ."

70. *Justin Martyr*: born about A.D. 100 and beheaded about 165. Christian philosopher and apologist who opened the first Christian school in Rome. Cf. *Apologies*, ed. A.W.F. Blunt (Cambridge Patristic Texts, 1911), Apologia I, xlvi.

71. *Malebranche*: Nicolas de Malebranche (1638–1715). Malebranche emphasizes the notion referred to here in many other works of his: *Entretiens sur la métaphysique et la religion, Conversations chrétiennes, Recherches de la vérité.* For example, see *Traité de la Nature et de la Grâce*, édité par Ginette Dreyfus, *Œuvres de Malebranche*, Tome V (Paris, 1958), p. 43: ". . . there was no way of making men worthy of the glory they would possess one day comparable to that of allowing them all to be developed in sin, so that they might all receive mercy in Jesus Christ."

Council of Nicaea: The first Council of Nicaea. By order of Constantine, the council of all bishops of

the Roman world met in June of A.D. 325 and condemned the heresy of Arius.

Athanasius: St. Athanasius (c. A.D. 296–373). As
deacon he accompanied Bishop Alexander of Alexandria to the first council of Nicaea in 325; three years
later he became the bishop of the see of Alexandria
over which he presided for forty-six years with periods of exile for his opposition to Arianism, which
was supported by some of the emperors, especially
Constantius. Unamuno uses Harnack's work as the
basis for his discussion of Athanasius.

Socinian Protestantism: a forerunner of modern
Unitarianism, originating with the Italians Laelius
Socinus (1525–62) and his nephew Faustus Socinus (1539–1604). It spread from Poland to the
Netherlands to England, and in the eighteenth century to New England. The Socinians denied the doctrine of the Trinity and accepted Jesus solely as a
man, but chosen by God.

(*Orat. I. 39*): Cf. Harnack, op. cit., II, 203-04.

the Logos: Unamuno's note is "On this head, see,
among others, Harnack, II Teil, I Buch, VII cap., I."
That is, Vol. II, Book I, Ch. VII, I.

72. *Of this Christ . . . eschatology*: also *This
same Harnack . . . faith*; also "*The complete contradiction . . . contra-rational.*" Cf. Harnack, op. cit., II,
220 ff.

73. *Fray Pedro Malón de Chaide*: (1530–1589),
author of *Libro de la conversión de la Magdalena*, a
work on asceticism written in a popular and pictur-
esque style; the Prologue contains a graceful eulogy
of the Spanish language. The footnote by Unamuno
reproduced in *OC*, XVI, 193, erroneously ascribes the
quotation in question to Part IV, Ch. IX, rather than
to the correct Part IV, Ch. LVI. Cf. *La conversión de*

la Magdalena, ed. P. Félix García, Clásicos castellanos (Madrid, 1947), iii, 126-27.

74. ex opere operato: "By virtue of the thing done." In theology, a concept which substantiates the intrinsic merit of the sacraments irrespective of the virtue or merit of the priest.

Little wonder then: From St. Teresa's *Libro de las Relaciones Espirituales*, translated as *Spiritual Relations, Complete Works of St. Theresa*, tr. and ed. E. Allison Peers (London and New York, 1957), fifth impression, i, 351-52.

75. *Amiel, the Protestant*: Amiel writes, in *Fragments d'un Journal Intime* (Unamuno's library contains a marked copy of the Dixième Édition, Genève, 1908), Tome ii, pp. 122-23: "15 août 1871.—Relu une deuxième fois *La vie de Jésus*, de Renan, seizième édition populaire. Ce qui est caractéristique dans cette analyse du christianisme, c'est que le péché n'y joue pas de rôle. Or si quelque chose explique le succès de la Bonne Nouvelle parmi les hommes, c'est qu'elle apportait la délivrance du péché, en un seul mot le salut. Il conviendrait pourtant d'expliquer religieusement une religion, et de ne pas esquiver le centre de son sujet. . . . Il y a dans Renan un reste de ruse séminariste. . . ."

The entire passage, translated by Mrs. Humphry Ward, *Amiel's Journal* (New York, 1928), p. 252, runs in English: "Re-read, for the second time, Renan's 'Vie de Jésus,' in the sixteenth popular edition. The most characteristic feature of this analysis of Christianity is that sin plays no part at all in it. Now, if anything explains the success of the Gospel among men, it is that it brought them deliverance from sin —in a word, salvation. A man, however, is bound to explain a religion seriously, and not to shirk the very center of his subject. In Renan there are still some remains of a priestly *ruse*. . . ."

Renan's answers to Amiel are contained in his two articles on "Henri-Frédéric Amiel," written on September 30 and October 7, 1884, for the *Journal des Débats* and included in his *Œuvres Complètes*, ed. Henriette Psichari (Paris, 1948), Tome II, pp. 1140-61. Renan is harsh toward Amiel who, he says, in the face of the infinite number of tasks still to be accomplished in the world, fell back upon "devouring himself" and "doubting about life." In the second article, Renan argues: "It is not of sin, atonement and redemption that one must henceforth speak . . . it is of kindness, good cheer, indulgence, good humor and resignation. As hope in the other life disappears, we must accustom mortal beings to look upon life as tolerable, otherwise they will rebel. . . . Pessimism and nihilism are caused by the boredom of a life which, because of a defective social organization, is not worth living."

76. *Oliveira Martins*: Joaquim Pedro Oliveira Martins (1845-94), outstanding Portuguese historian, author of many works, among which the *História da Civilização Ibérica* was Unamuno's favorite, quoted by him many times. The translation is from *A History of Iberian Civilization* by Aubrey F. G. Bell (Oxford, 1930), p. 200.

Kaftan: Julius Kaftan (1848-1926), professor of religion at Berlin and representative of the Ritschlian "liberal" theology. His books *Dogmatik* (Tübingen, 1909) and *Die Wahrheit der christlichen Religion* (Basel, 1888) are both in Unamuno's library at Salamanca.

Ritschl: Albrecht Ritschl (1822-89), German Protestant theologian. In his most influential work,

Die christliche Lehre von der Rechtfertigung und Versöhnung (1870–74), he demonstrates his pivotal belief that Christianity is more a guide to life than a system of dogma; mysticism he held in low esteem. The quotation is from Dritter Band (Bonn, 1874), p. 436, while the translation is by H. R. Mackintosh and A. B. Macaulay, *The Christian Doctrine of Justification and Reconciliation* (New York, 1900), pp. 499-500. The translation is of the third volume only of Ritschl's work.

77. *Melanchthon's* Loci Communes: Cf. Wilhelm Herrmann's "Christlich-protestantische Dogmatik" in *Systematische Christliche Religion* von Ernst Troeltsch, Joseph Pohle, Joseph Mausbach, Cornelius Krieg, Wilh. Herrmann, Rein. Seeberg, Wilhelm Faber, Heinrich Julius Holtzmann; *Die Kultur Der Gegenwart* (ed. Paul Hinneberg), Teil I, Abteilung IV, 2, zweiter verbesserte Auflage (Berlin und Leipzig, 1909), p. 130.

Der Verkehr des Christen mit Gott: the edition in Unamuno's library is the third (dritte Auflage, Stuttgart, 1896). There exists a translation "from the second thoroughly revised edition with annotations by the author" done by J. Sandys Stanyon (London, 1895) called *The Communion of the Christian with God*.

"the effective knowledge": The reference is to Herrmann's essay "Christlich-protestantische Dogmatik," op. cit., p. 130.

78. *"The desire to save one's soul . . . salvation."*: ibid., pp. 130-31.

Ernst Troeltsch: (1865–1923), important Church historian who viewed Christianity within the context of history, not from without. Unamuno is referring to the following statement by Troeltsch: "Den grossartigsten Schmuck schliesslich empfing der Kultus durch das geistliche Konzert, das, von Schülerchören getragen, die lutherischen Kantoren zu einem Bestandteil der Kirche machte. Das Schönste, ja fast das Einzige, was die Kunst in diesem kirchlichen Zeitalter vollbracht hat, ist hier geschaffen worden. In Bach hat das Luthertum die tiefste Darstellung gefunden, die ihm überhaupt zuteil geworden ist." It is from the long essay "Protestantisches Christentum und Kirche in der Neuzeit," in *Die Kultur der Gegenwart* (ed. Paul Hinneberg), Teil I, Abteilung IV, 1: *Geschichte der Christlichen Religion*, zweite stark vermehrte und verbesserte Auflage (Berlin, 1909), p. 534.

The translation would be: "Religious worship received, finally, its most brilliant adornment in the sacred music which, executed by school choirs, made of Lutheran choirmasters an element of the Church. The finest, indeed the only, artistic accomplishment during this period of the Church was made in that area. It is in Bach that Lutheranism found the most profound representation it has ever achieved."

celestial music!: "The common use of the expression *música celestial* to denote 'nonsense, something not worth listening to,' lends it a satirical byplay which disappears in the English rendering" (J. E. Crawford Flitch, in his translation of *The Tragic Sense of Life*). Unamuno's tone-deafness was well known. Walter Starkie tells of how in Madrid "I also discovered that Unamuno was a-musical; to him sweet sound was but *música celestial*—the Spanish synonym for nonsense" (Introduction to *Our Lord Don Quixote*, this edition, Vol. 3, p. xviii).

Christ: For selections from *The Christ of Velázquez*, cf. *Poetry*, February, 1963.

Theologia Germanica: or *Theologia deutsch*, probably written in Frankfort about 1350 to explain the mystical experience to ordinary men. The author is supposed to have been a member of the association of the Friends of God that included Meister Eckhart, John Tauler, and the Blessed Henry Suso. The book was greatly admired by Luther, who published an incomplete edition of it in 1518. The translation used here is from *Theologia Germanica*, ed. Thomas S. Kepler (Cleveland and New York, 1952), p. 119.

79. *I am not moved, my Lord*:

> *No me mueve, mi Dios, para quererte,*
> *el cielo que me tienes prometido,*

sonnet formerly attributed to a variety of authors, from St. Ignatius Loyola to St. Teresa, but now proved to be the work of Miguel de Guevara (c. 1585–c. 1646), a Mexican friar.

80. *Pius IX*: reigned 1846–78.

Loisy: Abbé Alfred Firmin Loisy (1857–1940), Bible critic and author (1902) of *L'Évangile et l'Église* (a polemical refutation of Adolf von Harnack's *What is Christianity?*), a book which became the pivot of the Catholic Modernist movement, and which led to his eventual excommunication (1908). The quotation is from the second edition of *Autour d'un petit Livre* (Paris, 1903, pp. 211-13) in the same volume with *L'Évangile et L'Église*, third edition, 1904, 211-12.

81. *Vatican Council*: First Vatican Council (1869–70), defined "the traditional Catholic belief in the value of reason and of its rights in the field of religion . . ." and the infallibility of the pope; cf. Philip Hughes, *A Popular History of the Catholic Church* (New York, 1954), p. 243.

The recent struggle . . . Modernism: In 1907 Pius X issued his decree *Lamentabili sane exitu* and his encyclical *Pascendi*, condemning Modernists who argued against the "objective supernatural character [of Catholicism] . . . reducing it to a matter of individual religious psychology" (Hughes, op. cit., pp. 268-69).

Dogme et Critique: by Édouard Le Roy (1870–1954), French philosopher, successor to Bergson as professor of philosophy at the Collège de France. The book referred to was published in Paris, 1906, and Ch. v concerns itself with the problem of Christ's resurrection. Le Roy holds that the resurrection could not have been a real, material phenomenon in the ordinary sense: the resurrection—transcendental in meaning—cannot be linked to any physical or biological conditions, for it corresponds to another type of reality, psychological and spiritual in essence. Jesus' lasting effect is proof in itself of the resurrection for He is eternally resurrected in His Church and in the Eucharist.

Unamuno read the fourth edition (Paris, 1907).

82. *motiva credibilitatis . . . rationale obsequium*: Reason is the springboard from which one goes to faith which is beyond but not against reason. Therefore faith is reasonable, but not solely an act of reason.

fides praecedit rationem . . . per fidem ad intellectum . . . credo ut intelligam: Cf. Étienne Gibson, *The Christian Philosophy of Saint Augustine*, tr. L.E.M. Lynch (New York, 1960), for first quotation, p. 260, note 14; for second, p. 259, note 7; for third quotation, which is a transposition of Augustine's frequent *crede ut intelligas*, both those places and p. 261, note 17.

. . . *certum est, quia impossibile est*: Tertullian, *De Carne Christi*, 5.

Pascal's il faut s'abêtir: Thought 233. Unamuno used the edition *Blaise Pascal, Pensées*, d'après l'édition de M. Brunschvicg (London, Paris, n.d.).

Donoso Cortés: Juan Donoso Cortés (1809–53); during a short life he was a vigorous writer, speaker, and political figure; a conservative, his most important work, much cited by "libertarian anti-liberals" in the twentieth century, is his *Ensayo sobre el catolicismo, el liberalismo y el socialismo* (1851). He held up Catholicism as antithetical to "progressive" modernity. The quotation is from the 1851 Barcelona edition of this work, Book I, Ch. v, pp. 66–67: "Por el contrario, entre la razón humana y lo absurdo hay una afinidad secreta, un parentesco estrechísimo. El pecado los ha unido con el vínculo de un indisoluble matrimonio. Lo absurdo triunfa del hombre cabalmente, porque está desnudo de todo derecho anterior y superior a la razón humana."

Joseph de Maistre: 1754–1821, French diplomat and philosopher; in his *Du Pape* (*On the Pope*), 1819, he upheld the primacy of the Pontiff and examined schismatic groups; other works were *De l'Église Gallicane* (*On the Gallican Church*), 1820, and *Les Soirées de Saint-Pétersbourg* (*St. Petersburg Nights*), 1821.

Quod apud . . . traditum: quoted in Harnack's *Lehrbuch der Dogmengeschichte* (Freiburg i. B., 1888), I, 329. The translation of the entire quotation ("Nullus inter multos eventus unus est . . . quod apud multos unum invenitur, non est erratum sed traditum") by Neil Buchanan (*History of Dogma*, New York, 1958, II, 67–68) is "One event among

many is as good as none; but when one and the same
feature is found among many, it is not an aberration
but a tradition."

Lamennais: Hugues Félicité Robert de Lamennais (1772–1854), French ecclesiastic and philosopher; his early works were a defense of ultramonta-
nism, but he grew ever more unorthodox and died
refusing the sacraments; his *Essai sur l'indifférence
en matière de religion* (1817–23) is an attack on
the rationalistic thought following on the skepticism
of Voltaire and Rousseau; in this book Lamennais
held that all beliefs, especially religious, affect society and that therefore indifference is not acceptable;
he supported the cumulative opinion and belief of society against the individual's power of rationality; the
first part of this work was published in London
(1895) as *Essay on Indifference in Matters of Religion*, translated by Lord Stanley of Alderley. Lamennais's poetical *Paroles d'un croyant* (1834) was
condemned in an encyclical in the year of publication.
His final position favored "the Christianity of the human race" over that of the Vatican; no one man should
stand in his beliefs against the traditional ones held
by mankind. Unamuno cites him with frequency.

The entire quotation, of which Unamuno extracts
a part, is "La certitude, principe de vie de l'intelligence, résulte du concours des moyens et de la similitude des rapports; elle est, si cette expression m'est
permise, une production sociale. . . ." and comes from
Tome Deuxième of *Essai sur L'indifférence en matière de religion*, nouvelle édition (Paris, n.d.), p.
104. Note Unamuno's mistranslation of the first part
of the sentence. The English translation in the text,
nonetheless, follows Unamuno's wording.

"*I . . . true*": Joseph de Maistre, *Soirées de Saint-Pétersbourg*, X^e entretien, from *Œuvres Choisies* (Paris, 1909), II, 163.

83. *its supreme goodness or utility*: The concept reflects the influence of William James's pragmatism on Unamuno.

"*Since . . . none*": Lactantius, *Divin. Inst.*, lib. II, cap. IV; quoted by Lamennais, op. cit., quatrième partie, tome troisième, p. 161.

Henry Suso: the Blessed Henry Suso (1295?–1366), German mystical thinker and writer. The reference is to *Deutsche Schriften des seligen Heinrich Seuse*, Literarisches Institut von Dr. Max Suttler, München, 1876, Zweites Buch, neuntes Kapitel, p. 355, a book in Unamuno's library. Translation: *Little Book of Eternal Wisdom*, translated with an Introduction and Notes by James M. Clark (London, 1953), p. 79:

> THE SERVANT: Lord, everything is all that the heart could wish for, except one thing: Truly, Lord, when a soul is faint with longing for Thee, and for the sweet, loving converse of Thy presence, Lord, then Thou art silent, and speakest not a single word that one can hear. Alas, my Lord, is it not painful when Thou, gentle Lord, art the only chosen love of their heart, and yet dost behave like a stranger, and keep silence so completely?
> Reply of ETERNAL WISDOM: Do not all creatures proclaim that it is I? [Footnote explains "That I exist."]
> THE SERVANT: Ah, Lord, this is not enough for a longing heart.

Leo XIII: elected Pope in 1878, reigned until 1903. In his *Aeterni Patris* (1879) he restored St. Thomas Aquinas to his supreme place in Catholic philosophy and theology.

84. *faith of the charcoal burner*: "la fe del car-

bonero," proverbial expression to denote unblinking acceptance of religious dogma.

"Do not ask me . . . answer you": Part of the catechism of Gaspar Astete, S.J. (1537–1601), widely used in Spain; according to Unamuno it fostered passive acceptance of dogma and narrowness of thought.

"reservoir instead of river": Phillips Brooks (1835–93), American Episcopal bishop, orator, and writer. The quotation comes from "The Sufficient Grace of God," in *Sermons Preached in English Churches* (New York, 1883), p. 129.

"The victory of the Nicene Creed": Harnack, op. cit., II, 1 Kap., VII, 3, p. 274. Translated from the third German edition of Adolf Harnack, *History of Dogma* by Neil Buchanan (New York, 1958), vol. 4, p. 106.

85. *Pohle*: Joseph Pohle (1852–1922), professor of theology and philosophy. The quotation is from the essay "Christlich-katholische Dogmatik" from the collection *Systematische Christliche Religion*, in the series *Die Kultur der Gegenwart*, Teil I, Abteilung IV, 2.

Gnosticism: A many-faceted religious movement, tangential to primitive Christianity. A religion in its own right, its sources include the pagan *Corpus Hermeticum* and the oldest fonts of Jewish mysticism. In general it depreciates the cosmos and spurns atonement. "The sink of ancient spirituality . . . Gnosticism, that deathbed whereon all the myths of oriental and occidental antiquity crowded together for a last convulsion," Paul Elmer More, *The Greek Tradition, Christ the Word*, Vol. IV (Princeton, 1927), p. 70. In its Christian form, it developed into Manichaeism, a Gnostic world religion. Evil came to be represented as a break within the Godhead; eventually there was a division between the Creator and the highest God: the world, an evil, cannot be the work of a good God; the *pleroma* or realm of light is beyond this world; Valentinus and Basilides negated the humanity of Christ, and also rejected the Old Testament. (Cf. *A Vindication of the Counterfeit Basilides*, by Jorge Luis Borges, Englished by A. Kerrigan in *Transatlantic Review*, 27, London and New York, 1967–68. Borges judges the *Prophetic Books* of William Blake to be a rediscovery of the insights of Gnosticism.) Thomas Molnar, in his "Gnosticism: the Perennial Heresy," *Triumph*, July 1968, points out that for Gnostics, the Creator, or Demiurgos, was sometimes an anti-God, or the principle of materiality, and he goes so far as to label all materialist doctrines descendants of this heresy, categorizing Hegel and Marx as "neo-Gnostics," who recharacterized the Demiurgos as "reaction"; he also notes that God remains "powerless" in the struggle of the soul towards spirituality and that mankind alone can save itself: this is a partly Unamunian view ("Charity is the impulse . . . to liberate God."), but Unamuno's stand is not properly either meliorative or Gnostic.

Cf. Harnack, op. cit., on Gnosticism.

86. *as Herrmann says*: Wilhelm Herrmann, in his essay "Christlich-protestantische Dogmatik," op. cit., p. 161.

Channing pointed out: From "Objections to Unitarian Christianity Considered," 1819, in *The Complete Works of William Ellery Channing* (London, 1884), p. 303.

V. THE RATIONAL DISSOLUTION

88. *"immortality to light"*: The *Philosophical Works of David Hume Including All the Essays, etc.*,

in four volumes (Boston and Edinburgh, 1854), vol. 4, p. 547.

89. *Aristotle . . . substance: De Anima*, ii, 1, 2.

90. *devoted to pragmatism*: "Pragmatism, a New Name for Some Old Ways of Thinking," *Popular Lectures on Philosophy by William James* (London and New York, 1907), pp. 87-88.

94. *Cartesian dualism*: To Descartes, the mind was divorced from the external world of extended objects. Cf., for example, the *Principles of Philosophy*, Part i, Principle lxiii: "How we may have distinct conceptions of thought and extension, inasmuch as the one constitutes the nature of mind, and the other that of body," in *The Philosophical Works of Descartes*, rendered into English by Elizabeth S. Haldane and G.R.T. Gross (Cambridge, 1967), vol. i.

Curso de filosofía elemental: the quotation is from Tomo ii of the *Obras Completas* (Barcelona, 1925), section titled "Psicología," Capítulo ii ("Simplicidad del Alma").

Jaime Luciano Balmes (1810–48) was one of the first philosophers Unamuno read in his father's library as a very young man. In his *El protestantismo comparado con el catolicismo* (tr. as *European Civilization*, Baltimore, 1918), Balmes refuted Guizot's *History*, and held that Catholicism and progress were one; in politics, he advocated a union of Carlists and Liberals in Spain.

95. *feeling something: Treatise of Human Nature*, Book i, Part iv, Section vi, "Of Personal Identity," 1854 edn., i, 312: "For my part, when I enter most intimately into what I call *myself*, I always stumble on some particular perception or other, of heat or cold, light or shade, love or hatred, pain or

pleasure. I never can catch *myself* at any time without a perception, and never can observe anything but the perception."

96. *esse est percipi*: From George Berkeley (1685–1753), in *Treatise Concerning the Principles of Human Knowledge*, in *A New Theory of Vision and other Select Philosophical Writings* (London and New York, n.d.), p. 114: "For as to what is said of the absolute existence of unthinking things without any relation to their being perceived, that seems perfectly unintelligible. Their *esse* is *percipi*, nor is it possible they should have any existence, out of the minds or thinking things which perceive them."

97. *Bishop Joseph Butler*: See herein, note to p. 8.

paragraph 140: "In a large sense indeed, we may be said to have an idea, or rather a notion of *spirit*, that is, (1) we understand the meaning of the word, otherwise we could not affirm or deny anything of it. Moreover, (2) as we conceive the ideas that are in the minds of other spirits by means of our own, which we suppose to be *resemblances* of them: so we know other spirits by means of our own soul, which in that sense is the image or idea of them, it having a like respect to other spirits, that blueness of heat by me perceived has to those ideas perceived by another." From Berkeley, op. cit., p. 186, in Unamuno's library, marked and slightly indexed for his own use by Unamuno.

of the soul: "The natural immortality of the soul is a necessary consequence of the foregoing doctrine." Berkeley, op. cit., paragraph 141.

98. *Alexander of Aphrodisias*: or Alexandri Aphrodisei, Greek commentator on Aristotle, whom the humanists studied at the end of the fifteenth cen-

tury. His *De intellectu* was printed in the 1480s in Venice.

Pietro Pomponazzi: (1462–1524), Aristotelian philosopher, humanist, and teacher. His *De immortalitate animae* was published in Bologna in 1516. Pomponazzi argues that the immortality of the soul cannot be affirmed or denied by natural reason. The soul, however, operates and exists within the body, although in no special place; its essential operation is knowing and since it can grasp universals, it participates, in a way, in immortality.

two thick volumes: London and New York, 1903.

99. *Spencer*: Herbert Spencer (1820–1903). Cf. herein, note to p. 20. All of Part I of the *First Principles* is entitled "The Unknowable" which, in Spencer's words, means "that the reality underlying appearances is totally and for ever inconceivable by us; . . . ."

100. *Schleiermacher*: Friedrich D. E. Schleiermacher (1768–1834), German theologian and philosopher who held that since man is conscious and knows he cannot exist for himself, he consequently feels himself absolutely dependent; this feeling, he believed, is the source of all religion; all religion is positive because religious feeling is experienced through sense consciousness; the religion of reason, on the other hand, is a pure abstraction. His principal work is *Der christliche Glaube nach den Grundsätzen der evangelischen Kirche* (2 vols., 1821–22). In English: *The Christian Faith*, tr. H. R. Mackintosh and J. S. Stewart (Edinburgh, 1948; New York, 1963).

It seeks to arrest the flow.: an echo of Bergson's "durée."

In order to analyze . . . destroy it.: reminiscent of

Wordsworth's "we murder to dissect" from "The Tables Turned." In Unamuno's copy of Wordsworth, *The Poetical Works of Wordsworth* (a reprint of the 1827 edition, London and New York, n.d.), practically all the poems are marked ("The Tables Turned" has nine check-marks, corresponding, probably, to nine readings).

101. *appear and do not appear to be*: The last speech by the "venerable and awful" (as Socrates called him) Parmenides, in the *Parmenides*, is: "To this we may add the conclusion. It seems that, whether there is or is not a one, both that one and the others alike are and are not, and appear and do not appear to be, all manner of things in all manner of ways, with respect to themselves and to one another." To which Socrates says: "Most true," and the dialogue comes to an end. (From *Plato and Parmenides*, tr. F. M. Cornford, London, 1939, reprinted in *The Collected Dialogues of Plato*, ed. Edith Hamilton and Huntington Cairns [Princeton, 1969], pp. 920, 956.)

102. *Dean Stanley*: Arthur Penrhyn Stanley (1815–81), English theologian, professor of ecclesiastical history at Oxford, dean of Westminster. The quotation is from the first lecture in *Lectures on the History of the Eastern Church* (London, 1861), p. 27.

104. *Vinet*: Alexandre Rodolphe Vinet (1797–1847), Swiss theologian and critic, several of whose books were early translated into English: as, *Vital Christianity* (1846), *Outlines of Philosophy and Literature* (1865). The book here referred to by Unamuno was issued in English, translated by Thomas Smith, as *Studies On Pascal*, Edinburgh, 1859; his Englishing of the quoted passage reads

(p. 80): "Of the two wants with which human nature is continually distressed, that of happiness is not only the more universally felt, and the more constantly experienced, it is also the more imperious. And this want is not purely sensual; it is intellectual. It is not only for the *soul*, it is also for the *mind*, that happiness is a necessity. Happiness makes part of the truth."

105. *pacata posse mente omnia tueri: De Rerum Natura*, v. 1203. The entire passage runs: "O unhappy race of mankind, to ascribe such doings to the gods and to add thereto bitter wrath! What groans did they then create for themselves, what wounds for us, what tears for generations to come! It is no piety to show oneself often with covered head, turning towards a stone and approaching every altar, none to fall prostrate upon the ground and to spread open the palms before shrines of the gods, none to sprinkle altars with the blood of beasts in showers and to link vow to vow, but rather to be able to survey all things with mind at peace." From the Loeb Classical Library edition, p. 425.

1 Cor. 1:23: Unamuno gives, as Spanish for the Bible, "un escándalo para los judíos y una locura para los intelectuales."

odium generis humani: From *The Annals* (Loeb Classical Library, 1962), Tacitus IV, Book XV, 44, p. 282, where Christianity is called *exitiabilis superstitio* or "pernicious superstition." "Odio humani generis" appears on p. 285.

". . . *to come to conclusions*": Gustave Flaubert, *Correspondance*, troisième série, 1854–69 (Paris, 1919), p. 220.

The translation is from *Gustave Flaubert, Letters*, selected, with an Introduction, by Richard Rumbold, tr. J. M. Cohen (New York, 1951), p. 136. Between the word "ebony" and the sentence starting with "The gods . . ." there is a sentence which Unamuno omitted: "Pas de cris, pas de convulsions, rien que la fixité d'un visage pensif." "No cries, no struggles, only the fixity of the pensive gaze."

The letter to Madame Roger des Genettes was probably written in 1861.

106. *"This people who knoweth not the law are cursed"*: John 7:49.

Soloviev . . . hypocrisy: Vladimir Sergeevich Soloviev (1853–1900), Russian religious philosopher and poet; a friend of Dostoevski (he may have been the "original" of Aloysha in *The Brothers Karamazov*); a believer in the eventual deification of mankind, he influenced Nikolai Berdyaev and Aleksander Blok. The editors have been unable to trace present quotation.

Vogt: Karl Vogt (1817–95), German naturalist and materialist.

Haeckel: Ernst Heinrich Haeckel (1834–1919), German biologist and evolutionist; from "ontogeny recapitulates phylogeny," he developed a philosophy of materialistic monism.

Büchner: Friedrich K.C.L. Büchner (1824–99), German physician; his *Kraft und Stoff* (*Energy and Matter*), 1855, was a materialistic view of the cosmos.

Virchow: Rudolf Virchow (1821–1902), German anatomist, originator of the doctrine of germinal continuity.

108. *"Live for the day"*: Carpe diem, *quam minimum credula postero*, Odes, i, xi, 8, usually Englished as "Seize the day, and put as little trust as you can in the morrow."

Proposition XXI: The English given here is from *The Ethics* (*Ethica Ordine Geometrico Demonstrata*), tr. R.H.M. Elwes, *The Chief Works of Benedict de Spinoza* (New York, 1951), vol. II. All the Spinoza citations in English in this chapter are taken from this same source.

111. *"What good . . . feel it?"*: *The Imitation of Christ*, Part I, Ch. I. The Modern Library edition (carrying the generic title *The Consolation of Philosophy*) gives on p. 130 the following translation: "I desire rather to know compunction than its definition."

Diderot: "Lettre au sujet des observations du Chevalier de Chastellux sur le Traité du mélodrame," *Œuvres complètes de Diderot* (Paris, 1875), VIII, 509. The story is not precisely as Unamuno recounts it: the eunuch did not wish lessons in aesthetics, but simply advice on which girl to choose.

"the eternal recurrence": cf. Index to the *Complete Works* of Nietzsche, ed. Oscar Levy (London, 1913).

112. *a parte ante . . . a parte post*: An interesting parallelism of thought is to be found in a later-day poet:

> Time present and time past
> Are both perhaps present in time future,
> And time future contained in time past.
> If all time is eternally present
> All time is unredeemable.

T. S. Eliot, *Four Quartets*, "Burnt Norton," lines 1-5.

the laughing lion: *Thus Spake Zarathustra*, IV, LXXI, "The Greeting." Unamuno refers to the same "laughing lion" in his sonnet to Nietzsche, *Rosario de sonetos líricos* (*OC*, XIII, 611).

113. *Carducci*: Giosuè Carducci (1835–1907), Italian critic and poet, much admired by Unamuno, and recipient of the Nobel Prize for literature in 1906. (See Unamuno's essay "A propósito de Josué Carducci" in *OC*, iv, 890, in another volume of this edition.) "Idillio maremmano" can be found in *The Oxford Book of Italian Verse*, No. 344 (where it is spelled "Idillio Maremanno"); the poem is from *Rime nuove*, his fourth book (first edition 1887); the verse was written in September, 1872. A translation of this piece by G. L. Bickersteth, *Carducci* (London, 1913), p. 169, renders these lines as follows:

> Better by work to have forgot, than sought
> To solve, vast riddles that no man solved yet!

"Su Monte Mario," written in January of 1882, is from *Odi Barbare*, a collection of fifty-seven poems written between 1873 and 1889. Unamuno's Spanish translation of the poem, entitled "Sobre el monte Mario," is to be found in *Poesías* (1907), *OC*, xiii, 477-78.

114. *we* know *nothing*: the italics given here are found in the quoted lines from *Cain: A Mystery*, in *The Poetical Works of Lord Byron*, ed. E. H. Coleridge (London, 1905), pp. 628, 633, 639. Cf. herein, note to p. 146.

115. "*philosophy the illusion*": *Poems of Wordsworth*, chosen and edited by Matthew Arnold (London and New York, 1907), p. xix.

Brunetière . . . bankruptcy of science.: Ferdinand Brunetière (1849–1906), French critic. The expression comes from the article "Après une visite au Vatican" which appeared on January 1, 1895, in the *Revue des Deux Mondes* and was incorporated into the book *Questions actuelles* (Paris, 1907), pp. 3-

47. Partly in refutation of the scientific claims made by Renan in *L'Avenir de la Science*, published in 1890, Brunetière speaks of "banqueroutes" and "faillités" of science, its inability to enlighten us about man's destiny.

116. *the phenomenalism of Hume . . . Mill*: David Hume (1711–76) says in his *Treatise of Human Nature* (London, 1911), I, 5: "And, as the science of man is the only solid foundation for the other sciences, so the only solid foundation we can give to this science itself must be laid on experience and observation."

In his *System of Logic Ratiocinative and Inductive* (London, New York and Toronto, 1941, Book III, Ch. XXI, Sec. 4, p. 376) John Stuart Mill (1806–73) writes: "The uniformity in the succession of events, otherwise called the law of causation, must be received not as a law of the universe, but of that portion of it only which is within range of our means as sure observation, with a reasonable degree of extension to adjacent cases. To extend it further is to make a supposition without evidence, and to which, in the absence of any ground from experience for estimating its degree of possibility, it would be idle to attempt to assign any." The edition of the *System of Logic* in Unamuno's library is the 1872 edition published in London by Longmans, Green.

VI. In the Depths of the Abyss

118. *Parce . . . orbis*: "Spare the only hope of all the universe." The quotation from Tertullian is in Harnack, op. cit., I, 552.

Marcion: born about A.D. 85, raised a Christian, year of death unknown. To him, the mystery of

Christ was so tremendous that it aroused a sense of absolute estrangement: God is all love, man is helpless and wretched, and the Creator of the world cannot be identified with God. Thus Marcion rejected the Old Testament with its merciless creator. Christianity, he felt, was already falsifying the truth, and he attempted a critical sifting of the Gospels and the Epistles of Paul, and founded the Marcionite Church which spread widely.

119. *Doubt . . . function of method*: In his *Discours de la Méthode* (1637) Descartes rejected as false all opinions in any way open to doubt in order to arrive at something indubitable. And while he considered all things false, he arrived at the certainty that such doubt involved thought: I think, therefore I am.

hothouse doubt: Unamuno is again referring to the *poêle*, the room heated by a stove where Descartes elaborated his method. See Part II of the *Discours*.

120. *a provisional ethic*: Descartes's words are "une morale par provision."

121. *brother Kierkegaard*: from *Concluding Unscientific Postscript*: translated from the Danish by David F. Swenson, completed after his death and provided with Introduction and Notes by Walter Lowrie (Princeton, 1941), Book Two, Part Two, Ch. iii, pp. 267-68. The last sentence is in a footnote.

The Holberg mentioned in the passage is the Danish playwright Ludvig Holberg (1684–1754), while the play in question is referred to in French as *La Ruelle de l'accouchée* and in English as *The Lying-in Chamber*. There is no English translation of the play.

122. *Hegel . . . rationalist*: G.W.F. Hegel

(1770–1831) was as impersonal a thinker as Kierkegaard was subjective. Man, for Hegel, achieves concreteness only as a "moment" in the Absolute. Religion he considered a form of philosophy and Kierkegaard charged him with being essentially an atheist. In addition, the Dane inveighed against Hegel for absorbing the concrete individual into an abstract Absolute, for his concept of the individual only in terms of larger institutions such as State and Church; in short, for turning man away from the significance of his own existence.

123. *official State-philosopher*: for Hegel the State and its institutions embodied objective reason and rational freedom, and he glorified the Prussian state. He was called by that state to occupy the first chair of philosophy at Berlin (1818).

125. *"destructive barbarism"*: V. Troeltsch, *Systematische christliche Religion*, in *Die Kultur der Gegenwart* series. Unamuno himself supplies this information in a footnote to the text. The essay from which the quotation is taken is called "Wesen der Religion und der Religionswissenschaft," op. cit. (see herein, note to p. 78), p. 10.

Robert Browning: from "Bishop Blougram's Apology." Unamuno read and penciled (principally with the Spanish equivalents of the more difficult English words) practically every poem in the two large volumes of the *Poetical Works of Robert Browning* (London, 1905); the sections Unamuno used in his own work are generally indicated by a red line; the verses quoted here are to be found on page 531.

Vinet: See herein, note to p. 104. Vinet's laconic description of the "book" mentioned by Unamuno is a cutting minimization: "The author has only added an eloquent preface to the report which he made last year to the French Academy, on the autograph manuscript of the *Thoughts*" (Smith translation, p. 249). The title of the section—X—of Vinet's book dealing with Cousin is entitled (in Smith's English): "Literary Critique on M. Victor Cousin's Essay on the Thoughts of Pascal" (p. 248). Smith's wording of the passage we have quoted in Unamuno's text is: "Even the knowledge of the mind, *as such*, has need of the heart. Without the desire to see, we do not see. When the life and the thought are greatly materialized, we do not believe in spiritual things." *Studies in Pascal*, by Alexander Vinet, tr. Thomas Smith (Edinburgh, 1859), p. 274. Unamuno used *Études sur Blaise Pascal*, par A. Vinet, quatrième édition (Paris, 1904).

126. *Ritschl*: see herein, note to p. 76. The full title of the work quoted is *Die christliche Lehre von der Rechtfertigung und Versöhnung* (3 vols., 1870–74). We cite the passage from the English translation of this work, *The Christian Doctrine of Justification and Reconciliation*, Vol. III, translated by various hands (Ch. IV was rendered by H. R. Mackintosh), and edited by H. R. Mackintosh and A. B. Macaulay (Edinburgh, 1900), pp. 209-10. (This edition of Vol. III was published independently of the rest of the work.)

127. *The system of antithesis*: Kant held that when pure reason cannot handle categories beyond experiential phenomena, it comes up against contradictions that cannot be resolved. Hegel postulates that such contradictions or dialectical opposites (thesis and antithesis) are true in the more comprehensive synthesis.

The Analysis of Sensations: (*Die Analyse der*

Empfindigungen und Physischen zum Psychischen, 1886, I, Section 12, n.), translated from the first German edition by C. M. Williams, revised and supplemented from the fifth German edition by Sydney Waterlow (Chicago and London, 1914), p. 23, n.: "The scientist and scholar have also the battle of existence to fight, that the ways even of science still lead to the mouth, and that the pure impulse towards knowledge is still an ideal in our present social conditions."

Ernst Mach (1838–1916), Austrian physicist and philosopher, is perhaps best remembered in the field of ballistics, where he elaborated the properties of shock waves, so that the Mach reflection, Mach effect, and Mach stem are concepts used in studying the effects of atomic explosion.

128. *Kierkegaard*: in *Concluding Unscientific Postscript*, ed. Swenson and Lowrie, Part Two, Ch. III, p. 273. Unamuno's own footnote to this quotation reads: "I leave almost untranslated his original expression *Existents-Consequents*. It means existential or practical consequence, and not the consequence of pure reason or logic."

129: *Loyson*: Hyacinthe Loyson (1827–1912). Ordained a Dominican in 1851, entered the Carmelite Order in 1863, named to pulpit of Notre Dame in 1865. He opposed Vatican I, married a former Protestant woman in 1872, then left Carmel and finally the Church. Founded the Liberal Catholic Church in Geneva in 1873–74, then the Gallican Church in Paris in 1879.

For a full discussion of Loyson by Unamuno, see *The Agony of Christianity* in another volume of this edition.

Truth is whatever I feel to be truth: There are unmistakable echoes here of Kierkegaard's concept of truth as subjectivity.

130. *"What! . . . that he existed at all."* From Lamennais's *Essai sur l'indifférence en matière de religion*, Tome deuxième, Troisième Partie, Ch. 1, p. 83. All the Spanish editions give chapter 67, which is wrong. Cf. note on Lamennais herein, p. 82.

133. *Life of Don Quixote and Sancho*: see Vol. 3 of this edition.

134. *Francke*: August Hermann Francke (1663–1727), German pietist, Bible scholar, and educator, who founded the so-called "ragged school" of orphans and pauper students; his influence turned Halle into a center of pietism.

if . . . He actually existed: Albrecht Ritschl: *Geschichte des Pietismus*, II, Abt. 1 (Bonn, 1884), p. 251. Cf. herein, note to p. 76.

I should certainly exist too:

> *Sufro yo a tu costa,*
> *Dios no existente, pues si tú existieras*
> *existiría yo también de veras.*

Cf. "La oración del ateo," *Rosario de sonetos líricos* (1911), *OC*, XIII, 546; in another volume of this edition.

servum arbitrium: bondage of the will. In his book *The Bondage of the Will*, an answer to Erasmus's *The Freedom of the Will*, Luther argues that man is incapable by himself of willing himself into a proper relationship with God.

The difference between the "tragic sense" of Calvinism and the Catholic "temper" or *"talante"* is expertly handled by José Luis L. Aranguren in *Catolicismo y protestantismo como formas de existencia* (Madrid, 1952, 1957, 1963); see especially "Sobre el talante religioso de Miguel de Unamuno," pp. 193-211. Unamuno, says the author (pp. 198-99), "begins to err when, alongside of this 'Protestant desperation,' he affirms the existence of a 'Catholic desperation.' We know that there cannot be any 'Catholic desperation,' because the Catholic is the opposite of the 'despairing man.' What Unamuno calls [Catholic desperation] is either the temptation to despair, or the secularization of Protestant desperation, following the line of decreasing faith Luther-Pascal-Kierkegaard-Unamuno."

faith . . . charcoal burner: this is Unamuno's frequent way of referring to unblinking acceptance of dogma.

And what was that abyss, that terrible gouffre . . . il faut s'abêtir: All the prominent passages in Pascal have *abîme*; however, Baudelaire says "Pascal avait son gouffre. . . ." in his poem "Le Gouffre." For "il faut s'abêtir," see Pascal's Thought No. 233.

135. *Jansenism*: an ascetic religious movement based on the *Augustinus* (1640) of Bishop Jansenius (1585–1638), Dutch theologian and Bishop of Ypres. Its center was Port-Royal which under Angélique Arnaud became a retreat that received Pascal and other learned men. It was closed by Louis XIV in 1705 and destroyed in 1710.

Abbé de Saint-Cyran: Jean du Verger de Hauranne (1581–1643), friend to Jansenius, spiritual director at Port-Royal, born in Bayonne, and therefore of the French Basque country; consequently, according to Unamuno, "of the same race" as Loyola (1491–1556), founder of the Society of Jesus, born at the estate of Loyola in Guipúzcoa. Unamuno was, of course, also a Basque, born in Bilbao.

incredulous adulator: Voltaire. The line is from

his "Épître à l'auteur du livre des *Trois Imposteurs*."

136. *immortality is no less so*: Cf. Kierkegaard, *Concluding Unscientific Postscript*, ed. Swenson and Lowrie, pp. 152-58. For example (p. 154): ". . . the question of immortality is essentially not a learned question, rather it is a question of inwardness, which the subject by becoming subjective must put to himself. Objectively the question cannot be answered, because objectively it cannot be put, since immortality precisely is the potentiation and highest development of the developed subjectivity."

137. *"The time will come . . ."*: "Cantico del gallo silvestre" from *Operette Morali*. The translation is by J. H. Whitfield in *Leopardi: Poems and Prose*, ed. Angel Flores (Bloomington, 1966), pp. 225-26.

Spencer: Taking direction from Darwin and the embryologist K. E. von Baer, Spencer conceived of the evolution of all forms, organic and non-organic, from indeterminate homogeneity to more determinate heterogeneity, with an offsetting tendency toward integration into larger wholes or closer associations of men.

139. *Walt Whitman*: Whitman's *Leaves of Grass* was sent to Unamuno on April 30, 1906, by Prof. Everett Ward Olmsted of Cornell University. On August 6 of that same year, Unamuno published his story "El canto adámico" (included in the collection *El espejo de la muerte*, published in 1913 and included in *OC*, II; in another volume of this edition) in which the author translates some of Whitman's verses to a friend. This, as Manuel García Blanco points out, gives Unamuno first place among Spanish writers who concerned themselves with the American poet. For a full discussion of Unamuno and Whitman, consult the chapter "Walt Whitman" in García Blan-

co's *América y Unamuno* (Madrid, 1964), pp. 368-405.

143. *"life is a dream"*: The reference is to Calderón's drama *La vida es sueño*, which Unamuno uses as a point of reference throughout his works.

145. *progressives . . . European thought*: Unamuno, who had been an *europeizante* in his earlier period, a partisan of bringing Spain up to the level of France, England, and Germany, became, by the turn of the century, the enemy of such attitudes, and proposed that Spain "hispanize" Europe. One need only compare his "En torno al casticismo" (written in the form of five articles in 1895 and published in book form in 1902, *OC*, III, 157-303, another volume in this edition) with the article "Sobre la europeización" (*OC*, III; included in another volume of this edition) and especially his *Life of Don Quixote and Sancho* (Vol. 3 of this edition).

cardiacal truth: "Cardiacal" is an adjective Unamuno also frequently applies to certain of his favorite writers—who composed as much with their hearts as with their minds—such as Sénancour, Kierkegaard, Pascal.

VII. Love, Pain, Compassion, and Personality

146. *Byron*: The Cain and Abel theme is central to Unamuno's thought and work. Cf. the novel *Abel Sánchez* and the play *El Otro* (other volumes of this edition).

as Leopardi sang:

> Fratelli a un tempo stesso, Amor e Morte
> Ingenerò la sorte.

from *Amor e morte*. See herein, note to p. 50.

148. *The love of money . . . evil*: 1 Tim. 6:10.

And some people . . . flesh: Cf. *La tía Tula* (*OC*, IX; another volume in this edition).

149. *this child . . . falls sick and dies*: It is of significance to point out here that a few months after his birth in October 1896 Unamuno's third child, Raimundo Jenaro, suffered an attack of meningitis and developed hydrocephalia. Grief over his child's misfortune aggravated Unamuno's feelings of guilt at having lost his faith and brought on the famous "crisis of 1897" of which he writes in many letters and which is best reflected in his *Diario íntimo*, started about the time of the child's illness.

The crisis erupted one night in March of 1897; when Unamuno's wife, Concha, saw the grief and suffering of her husband, she cried out "¡Hijo mío!" ("My son!" or "My child!"), a scene which appears in several novels and plays by Don Miguel, and accounts for the statement (page 150) "And in woman all love is maternal."

151. *Isabel . . . Lorenzo*: From Keats's "Isabella or The Pot of Basil," in *The Poetical Works of John Keats* (London, 1899), p. 183 (a book much marked by Unamuno, in his library).

152. *That distant star . . . existing*: Cf. the poem "Aldebarán" (*Rimas de dentro*, 1923, *OC*, XIII, 882-86).

155. *Dante*: The lines quoted are from the *Inferno* of Dante's *Divine Comedy*, Canto V, verses 121-23, here in the translation of Charles S. Singleton (Princeton, 1970):

"There is no greater sorrow than to recall, in wretchedness, the happy time; . . ."

Herodotus: The English here is from *The His-*

tories of Herodotus, tr. George Rawlinson, ed. E. H. Blakeney (London and New York, 1964), p. 281.

156. *Giambattista Vico*: (1668–1744), Italian cultural historian, who postulated a cyclical development of history and retraced the evolution of the earliest myths. His "new science" is a milestone in the philosophy of history, the theoretical history of science and the history of ideas. The quotations from his work are from *Della metafisica poetica*, Book ii, of *Scienza nuova*; the English given here is from the translation by Thomas G. Bergin and Max Harold Fisch, in their *The New Science of Giambattista Vico*, translated from the third edition, 1744 (Ithaca, 1958), pp. 104, 105, 106.

157. *Tacitus*: the quotation here is from *Annals*, v, 10.

It was useless . . . positivism: Auguste Comte (1798–1857), father of Positivism, divided the history of man into three stages: theological, metaphysical, and positivistic.

158. *Memorabilia*: in *Memorabilia and Oeconomicus* (Loeb Classical Library, 1923), pp. 5-7 (*Memorabilia*, i, i, 6-9, as mentioned by Unamuno); the Anaxagoras reference is in iv, vii, 6, pp. 349-55.

Aristotle . . . necessity: Physics, ii, viii. Aristotle does not mention Zeus, but see note on Aristophanes, below.

159. *Bergson*: Henri Bergson (1859–1941), French philosopher and winner of the Nobel Prize for Literature in 1927. The foreign philosopher most widely read by such members of the generation of 1898 as Azorín, Machado, Unamuno. The reference here is to Bergson's *Évolution créatrice* (1907) which, along with other works, represents a reaction against the positivism, determinism, and evolutionism

of the late nineteenth century, in favor of intuitionism.

Richard Avenarius: Richard H. L. Avenarius (1843–1896), German philosopher and professor of philosophy at Zurich, originator of a positivist system known as "empiriocriticism (attacked by Lenin in his tract *Materialism and Empirio Criticism*, 1909). The quotation comes from *Kritik der reinen Erfahrung* (Leipzig, 1888), p. xix.

160. *The Clouds*: lines 367-89. Cf. the translation by William Arrowsmith (Ann Arbor, 1962), pp. 34-35; "*Strepsiades*: Then *who* makes it rain? . . . *Sokrates*: Why, the Clouds, of course. . . . *Strep.*: But who makes them move before they collide? Isn't that Zeus? *Sokr.*: Not Zeus, idiot. The convection-principle! *Strep.*: Convection? That's a new one. Just think. So Zeus is out and convection-principle's in. Tch. Tch. But wait: you haven't told me who makes it thunder. . . ."

161. *Berkeley*: Cf. herein note to p. 96.

Hartmann: Karl Robert Eduard Von Hartmann (1842–1906), German philosopher, author of *Die Philosophie des Unbewussten* (1869), English translation, *The Philosophy of the Unconscious* (1884). In his view, will and existence are sin, and a collective reason must eventually lead to a collective effort to will non-existence; civilization involves the annulment of the will to live and the freeing of the unconscious from its suffering.

162. *Lamarck*: Jean Baptiste de Monet, Chevalier de Lamarck (1744–1829), French naturalist who believed in the inheritance of acquired characteristics and formulated a theory of evolution from imperfect to perfect beings, stemming from the perfecting power of nature and responding to the changes in environment. Darwin recognized that Lamarck had drawn at-

tention to the probability that organic change was the result of law and not miracle.

platter Empirismus: *Schopenhauer-Briefe*, ed. Ludwig Schemann (Leipzig, 1893), p. 325.

163. *the inner, essential force*: Unamuno is here echoing Bergson's *élan vital*.

166. *material things . . . hunger*: Unamuno wrote a prologue (in *OC*, VII, 384-93) to the book of the Catalan biologist Ramón Turró, *Orígenes del conocimiento (el hambre)*, first published in French (1914; this French edition was sent to Unamuno by the author with a dedication, and is profusely marked by Unamuno), and later in German, and finally in Spanish (Madrid, 1921) in which he says "When I read this book in its French edition (since it was published in German and French before it was in Spanish, the language in which it was written), I was struck by how certain of its outstanding psychological ideas coincided with ideas which I have long held and expounded in some of my books. The principal idea is the one which is expressed in a synthetic phrase— therefore lending itself to misinterpretation—to the effect that the external world of the senses is revealed to us by hunger; as knowledge, it is the handiwork of hunger. Of hunger, which is individual, and of love, which is the hunger of the species. . . ."

167. *"And what is truth?"*:. Cf. *"¿Qué es verdad?"* in *OC*, III; in another volume of this edition.

169. *Emanuel Swedenborg*: (1688–1772), the Swedish scientist and theologian, postulated a system of "correspondence" in which everything on the material plane corresponds to its aspect among the spiritual realities; the reality, thus, is spiritual, and the material aspect but a reflection or correspondence. Swedenborg, then, is the inverse of the classical

"spiritualist." The English given here is taken from *Heaven and its Wonders and Hell: from Things Heard and Seen*, the Everyman edition of 1911, p. 22, in Unamuno's library at Salamanca, used and marked by Unamuno. No translator is given on the title page, but the Introduction states: "The translation of the present volume has been revised by Mr. F. Bayley, M.A., on the basis of the F cap. 8vo. edition issued by the Swedenborg Society. . . ." An earlier edition, also consulted, is the version of Samuel Noble, 2nd edn. (London, 1851), p. 20, where the wording is roughly similar.

"God . . . eternal": Concluding Unscientific Postscript, p. 296.

Mazzini: Giuseppe Mazzini (1805–72), political writer born in Genoa, champion of Italian unity and independence, spent most of his life in exile. The quotation from the essay "Ai giovani d'Italia" ("Dio è grande, perchè pensa operando") is from *Scritti Scelti*, a cura di J. White Mario, nuova presentazione di Cesare Federico Goffis (Firenze, 1964), p. 258. Unamuno has in his library the original edition (Firenze, 1901) with the same pagination.

170. *Scripture . . . made*: Cf. John 1:1-4.

For to believe in God is . . . to create Him, even though He creates us beforehand.: "Porque creer en Dios es . . . crearle, aunque El nos cree antes." This rhetorical device, paronomasia, is a play on the verbs *creer*, to believe, and *crear*, to create; apart from the sound play, or sound-similarity play, there is also the double-edged ambiguity of the last verb, *cree*, which could be either the present indicative of *creer* or the present subjunctive of *crear* (which is the sense in which we have taken it).

VIII. FROM GOD TO GOD

172. *timor fecit deos*: Statius, Vol. I (Loeb Classical Library, 1928), *Thebaid*, III, line 661: "primus in orbe deos fecit timor!" translated as "Fear first created gods in the world!" pp. 500, 501. (Cf. " 'Twas only fear first in the world made gods," Ben Jonson, *Fall of Sejanus*, Act II.)

Schleiermacher's theory: Cf. herein, note to p. 100, also *The Christian Faith*, English translation from the 2nd German edition, ed. H. R. Mackintosh and J. S. Stewart (Edinburgh, 1948), p. 12: "The common element in all howsoever diverse expressions of piety, by which these are conjointly distinguished from all other feelings, or, in other words, the self-identical essence of piety, is this: the consciousness of being absolutely dependent, or, which is the same thing, of being in relation with God."

175. *Robertson Smith: The Prophets of Israel* (London, 1895), Lecture I, p. 36.

176. *Vinet*: From Smith translation (Edinburgh, 1859), p. 184: "To know that a thing is, without knowing what it is, is very often to know nothing. Separated from its mode, existence is but a word." Unamuno owned the fourth edition of the original French (Paris, 1904). Cf. herein, note to p. 104.

Scotus Erigena: (c. 810-877), Irish philosopher and theologian, a luminary of the Carolingian Middle Ages (tautologically named: Scotus from Scotia, Erigena from Erin, the Irish being then called Scots); he translated the Pseudo-Dionysius; his own thought postulated theophanies, manifestations of the Godhead: man himself is a theophany, and, like God, shares His unknowability. The quotation is "Dum ergo incomprehensibilis intelligitur, per excellentiam nihilum non immerito vocitatur." From *De Divisione Naturae*, in *Joannis Scoti, Opera*, ed. H. J. Floss, *Patrologiae Cursus Completus*, J.-P. Migne, 1853, Vol. 122, p. 681A.

Dionysius the Areopagite: The actual person described by this name, a supposed disciple of St. Paul at Athens, acquired a posthumous reputation as author of ten short letters and four treatises, probably forgeries; a central theme is the ascent of the soul by the negative way, in which the senses are obliterated, as are thoughts and reasonings, until the soul achieves "the darkness of unknowing," wherein it is enlightened by "the ray of divine darkness." The quotation Unamuno refers to is "Divina caligo est inaccessibile lumen, in quo habitare Deus dicitur. . . ." From *Sancti Dionysii Areopagitae, Epistolae Diversae, Joannis Scoti, Opera*, ed. H. J. Floss, Migne, op.cit., p. 1178C.

do not care to recall: a paraphrastic echo of the opening sentence of Cervantes' *Don Quixote*.

177. *Laplace*: Pierre Simon de Laplace (1749–1827), French astronomer and mathematician who attempted to explain away all the anomalies of Newtonian physics, especially the notion of divine intervention. The "phrase" is his celebrated reply to Napoleon's query about the absence of God from his theory.

178. *the watch and the watchmaker*: The argument that as the watch presupposes an intelligent being who produced it, the existence of the universe requires the existence of a Maker, is from William Paley (1743–1805), English theologian and philosopher whose most important work is *Natural Theol-*

ogy, or Evidences of the Existence and Attributes of the Deity collected from the Appearances of Nature (1802).

181. *Lamennais*: Cf. herein, note to p. 82. The citation is from *Essai sur l'indifférence*, quatrième partie, chapitre VIII, tome troisième, p. 177, in the four volume edition (n.d.) in the Unamuno library at Salamanca: ". . . la raison humaine est comme la Religion, une, universelle, perpétuelle, sainte." Lactantius is mentioned on p. 196, p. 235; Heraclitus on p. 162; Aristotle on p. 163; Pliny on p. 164 (from *Paneg. Trajani*, LXII); Cicero (*De natura deorum*, Book III, Ch. II, 5 and 6) on p. 241.

182. *an ancestral dogma*: *Metaphysics*, Lib. VII, Cap. VII.

Herrmann: Cf. herein, note to p. 77. The quotation is from the essay "Christlich-protestantische Dogmatik" in *Systematische Christliche Religion*, in the series *Die Kultur der Gegenwart*, I, iv, 2 (Berlin und Leipzig, 1909), p. 166.

Augustinian sentence: The quotation here, which is indeed redolent of Augustine, is from Pascal's *Le Mystère de Jésus*, Thought 553: "Console-toi, tu ne me chercherais pas, si tu ne m'avais trouvé." It is also the first line of Sonnet IV, from *Andanzas y visiones españolas*, in *OC*, XIII, 808.

183. *Ritschl writes*: Cf. herein, notes to pp. 76 and 126. The quotation is from *Rechtfertigung und Versöhnung*, III, Ch. IV. The translation is from *The Christian Doctrine of Justification and Reconciliation*, English translation ed. H. R. Mackintosh and A. B. Macaulay (New York, 1900), p. 322.

184. *the Nothing-God of Scotus Erigena*: See herein, note to p. 176 on Scotus Erigena.

the hypothesis of ether: Cf. "The Vertical of Le Dantec" in another volume of this edition.

186. *image and likeness*: Crawford Flitch, in a footnote to his translation, pertinently quotes Voltaire's statement "Si Dieu a fait l'homme à son image, l'homme le lui a bien rendu"; he might have added the well known "Si Dieu n'existait pas, il faudrait l'inventer," which bears on the same point of the relation between the inventor and the invented, the Maker and the Made, and on the question of which is which.

Lactantius: See herein, note to p. 66; the citation here is from *Divinarum Institutionum*, II, 8. Cf. *The Divine Institutes*, *The Ante-Nicene Fathers*, Vol. VII (Grand Rapids, 1951), Book I, Ch. VII, p. 17: "But because that which exists must of necessity have had a beginning, it follows that since there was nothing before Him, He was produced from Himself before all things. . . . God of His own power made of Himself."

and we may say . . . being created by man: The idea is beautifully put by Rainer Maria Rilke in one of the poems from his *Das Stundenbuch* (*The Book of Hours*):

> Was wirst du tun, Gott, wenn ich sterbe?
> Ich bin dein Krug (wenn ich zerscherbe?)
> Ich bin dein Trank (wenn ich verderbe?)
> Bin dein Gewand und dein Gewerbe,
> mit mir verlierst du deinen Sinn.

187. *The logical theory . . . concept*: See herein, note to p. 94, for Descartes's distinction.

Hegel . . . identical: Georg Wilhelm Friedrich Hegel's *Wissenschaft der Logik*, *Werke*, Dritter Band (Berlin, 1841), *Erstes Buch*, *Die Lehre vom Seyn*, p. 72: "Seyn, reines Seyn,—ohne weitere Bestimmung. In seiner unbestimmten Unmittelbarkeit ist es nur sich selbst gleich, und auch nicht ungleich gegen Anderes. . . ." The edition is in Unamuno's library.

188. *the absolutely indefinable*: an echo of the Kierkegaardian concept of God as the "absolutely different." Cf. *Philosophical Fragments*, tr. David Swenson, revised by Howard V. Hong, second edition (Princeton, 1962), p. 55.

191. *Demosthenes . . . goddesses: On the Crown.*

192. *"that which is divine"*: "Porque *el* dios no es más que *lo* divino." Flitch translates the sentence: "For the masculine concrete god [*el* dios] is nothing but the neuter abstract divine quality [*lo* divino]." This version has an obvious merit of its own, although less literal than the version chosen in the present translation.

Socinian: See herein, note to p. 71.

195. *"If of two men . . . to God": Concluding Unscientific Postscript*, pp. 179-80: "If one who lives in the midst of Christendom goes up to the house of God, the house of the true God, with the true conception of God in his knowledge, and prays, but prays in a false spirit; and one who lives in an idolatrous community prays with the entire passion of the infinite, although his eyes rest upon the image of an idol: where is there most truth? The one who prays in truth to God though he worships an idol; the other prays falsely to the true God, and hence worships in fact an idol."

198. *Frederick William Robertson*: (1816–53). Anglican preacher noted for his independent views and his non-scientific theology. The citation is from his *Sermons*. Unamuno possessed and marked the Tauchnitz (Leipzig) edition, in 4 volumes, Volume I, Sermon III (June 10, 1849), "Jacob's Wrestling," pp. 46-47.

199. *Browning*: the verses quoted here are in "Christmas Eve and Easter Day."

Saul: from the *Dramatic Lyrics*, Vol. I of *The Poetical Works*, XVIII, p. 280.

202. *"The wicked man . . . God."*: "The fool hath said in his heart, There is no God." Psalms 14:1, also 53:1.

IX. FAITH, HOPE, AND CHARITY

204. *Tacitus*: the epigraph from Tacitus reads, in the English of William Peterson, *The Dialogues of Publius Cornelius Tacitus* (Loeb Classical Library, 1914): "[It is] more religious and more reverent to believe in the works of Deity than to comprehend them." And cf., in Tacitus, *Germania*, ed. J.G.C. Anderson (Oxford, 1938), p. 167, where, in a note, the opening phrase is given as ". . . more in accordance with piety and reverence."

". . . create what we do not see!": The play on words of the Spanish locution is lost in translation, the original reading: "Creer lo que no vimos, ¡no!, sino crear lo que no vemos." The essay written "a dozen years ago," is "La fe," 1900 (*OC*, XVI, 99; another volume of this edition). (In the quotation from the essay given in *OC²*, XVI, 313, *crear* is mistakenly printed as *creer*, thus making *creer* appear twice in the sentence and changing the meaning. *OC¹*, IV, 609, 1950, gives the correct wording.)

205. *"faith in faith itself"*: From the same essay referred to in the previous note, "La fe" in which he used some passages of an earlier essay "¡Pistis y no gnosis!" dated January 1897 (*OC*, IV, 1019-25).

206. *Seeberg*: Reinold Seeberg; the citation is from *Christliche-protestantische Ethik* in *Systemati-*

sche Christliche Religion, published in the series *Die Kultur der Gegenwart*, p. 202. See herein, notes to pp. 77, 78, 85 for information on this series.

208. *Phillips Brooks*: (1835–93), American Episcopal clergyman and preacher (Unamuno calls him a Unitarian, perhaps mindful of the fact that he was a Broad Churchman, more concerned with humanity as a whole than with the Church as God's instrument), Bishop of Massachusetts, and author of several collections of sermons. Unamuno owned the London edition of *The Mystery of Iniquity and Other Sermons* (1900). The passage cited is from Sermon XVI (not XII, as all editions of Unamuno in Spanish have it), pp. 278-79.

210. *makes us live it.*: Cf. St. Thomas Aquinas, *Summa*, secunda secundae, quaestio IV, art. 2. [Note by Unamuno.]

Cournot: Antoine Augustin Cournot (1801–77), French mathematician and economist. From *Traité de l'enchaînement des idées fondamentales dans les sciences et dans l'histoire* (written in 1861, the edition in the Unamuno library is Paris, 1911), p. 373.

211. *So that St. Augustine could say*: The English given here is from *Confessions*, Book I, 1, in the translation of R. S. Pine-Coffin, in the Penguin edition, 1968. Unamuno omitted the phrase "because we have had preachers to tell us about you."

212. *Vanni Fucci . . . insulting God with obscene gestures: Inferno*, XXV, 1-3:

> At the end of his words, the thief raised up his hands with both the figs, crying, "Take them, God, for I aim them at you!"

Vanni Fucci was a violent partisan of the Neri Guelfs of Pistoia. According to one account, Fucci, with two accomplices (both of whom were similarly named

Vanni), broke into and plundered the treasury of San Jacopo in the church of San Zeno at Pistoia in 1293. (See Singleton, *Inferno*, translation and commentary.) The "figs" are an obscene and insulting gesture made by thrusting the thumb between the first and second fingers.

213. *"Go ye therefore and teach all nations!"*: In a letter to his friend Pedro Jiménez Ilundain, dated May 25, 1898, Unamuno recalls: "Many years ago, when I was still a child, at a period when I was most imbued with the religious spirit, I came home from taking communion, and I got the idea of opening the gospel at random and placing my finger on some passage. And it was this one: 'Go ye therefore and teach all nations [Matt.: 28:19].' This made a very deep impression on me; I took it to be a command to become a priest.

"But since I was already about fifteen or sixteen at the time, and was already betrothed to the girl who is now my wife, I decided to try again for clarification. When I again took communion, I went home, opened the Gospel once more, and came upon verse 27 of Chapter ix of Saint John: 'He answered them, I have told you already and ye did not hear: wherefore would ye hear it again?' I cannot tell you the effect this had on me." From Hernán Benítez, *El drama religioso de Unamuno* (Buenos Aires, 1949), pp. 267-68. Unamuno recalls these incidents in other writings of his.

216. *In a previous essay*: Cf. "What is Truth?", *OC*, iii, 992 (in English in this edition); first published in *La España Moderna*, March 1906, Vol. 207.

portico . . . temple: Cf. the essay "El pórtico del templo," of July 1906, in *OC*, iv; in English in this edition.

217. *"Poesy is the illusion . . ."*: from *Concluding Unscientific Postscript*, ed. Swenson and Lowrie, pp. 408-09.

"desperate way out": Kierkegaard, op. cit., p. 96.

all eternity . . . point: With regard to Kierkegaard's treatment of the *Instant* or *Moment*, cf. *The Concept of Dread* (Princeton, 1957), pp. 74 ff., and *Philosophical Fragments* (Princeton, 1962), pp. 72 ff.

224. *Will . . . suffering*: Whether consciously or otherwise, Unamuno is using here for his own purposes Schopenhauer's concept that irrational will underlies all aspects of life, especially the need for self-perpetuation, and at the same time that it is the source of frustration and suffering.

226. *"Be nought, and thou shalt be more than aught that is"*: This quotation comes from *Diálogos de la conquista del espiritual y secreto Reino de Dios* (Madrid, 1912), and is from the Third Dialogue (8), p. 69. Cf. herein, Ch. I and see note to p. 310.

"Do I exist at all?": cf. Unamuno's own experience, e.g., in the inception of the famous religious crisis of March 1897 as related in the *Diario íntimo*, in its second entry: he had started this diary on Wednesday of Holy Week, and on the next day, Holy Thursday, he wrote: "My terror has been annihilation, nullification, the nothingness beyond the tomb." Quoted by Emilio Salcedo in his *Vida de Don Miguel* (Salamanca, 1964), p. 86; in the same book, pp. 84-85, Salcedo relates the details of Unamuno's cardiac crisis of a few days before. And cf. the interpretation placed on the event by Charles Moeller, in "Quelques aspects de l'itinéraire spirituel d'Unamuno," in *Unamuno a los cien años* (Salamanca, 1967), p. 81, where he calls the experience, a "séisme intérieur,"

and says the religious crisis as Unamuno felt himself seized "in the claws of the angel of nothingness" was "provoquée par un spasme cardiaque," thus affirming the well-known James-Lange theory of affect, in which a high state of emotion generally follows from awareness of a physiological alteration. In his *Retrato de Unamuno* (Madrid, 1957), Luis S. Granjel writes (p. 156) that the crisis set Unamuno definitely upon his course of finding out who he really was.

227. *as Spinoza taught us*: See herein, notes to pp. 36, 108.

228. *"The Soul of the Universe . . ."*: The translation of Plotinus here is from *The Enneads*, tr. Stephen McKenna, New York and London, 1962.

230. *"sweet-tasting dolor"*: for Unamuno's "dolor sabroso" which is his paraphrase of St. Teresa's "esta pena tan sabrosa" from the *Life*, Ch. XXIX, "this pain so sweet."

235. *an irrational system*: OC^2 has "sistema racional" but OC^1 and the Candamo (Aguilar) edition of *Tragic Sense of Life* (Vol. II, p. 922), both have "irracional," which makes more sense.

X. Religion, Mythology of the Beyond, and Apocatastasis

236. *Phaedo*: See *The Collected Dialogues of Plato*, ed. E. Hamilton and H. Cairns, p. 44.

Cicero: De natura deorum, lib. I, cap. XLI. The English translation is that of H. Rackham (Loeb Classical Library, 1933).

Miguel de Molinos: (1628–96), Spanish priest who developed his extreme Quietist outlook and practice in Rome and died there in an Inquisition prison; his impulse to suppress the will to the point where

God took over and worked His own way led him to accept any sexual temptation or aberration as the work of the Devil upon a passive, and therefore sinless, believer, who was thereby intensified in his quiet repose in God; at his trial he admitted to his antinomianism, as revealed in his correspondence, and, as was natural in a Quietist, in the end proffered no defense.

Through its influence on Madame Guyon, Quietism came into France and deeply affected Fénelon (1651–1715). The heresy was denounced by Bossuet, and Fénelon was condemned by the Pope in 1699. See herein, note to p. 245.

237. *Tacitus: Hist.* lib. v, cap. iv. "The Jews regard as profane all that we hold sacred; on the other hand, they permit all that we abhor"; in the English of Clifford H. Moore: Tacitus, *The Histories* (Loeb Classical Library, 1931), Bk. v, Ch. iv, p. 179. The next phrase is from Bk. v, Ch. xiii, where the English is given (p. 197) as: "a people which, though prone to superstition, is opposed to all propitiatory rites." (*OC²*, but not *OC¹* and Candamo, give "conversa" for "concessa".) Unamuno gives the source for the two final Latin quotations in his paragraph as *Ab. excessu Aug.* (i.e., *The Annals*, which Tacitus first called *Ab. excessu divi Augusti*, though he also spoke of them as *Annales*), Bk. xv, 44, where the Latin passage is given (in Tacite, *Annales*, Traduit par Henri Goelzer, Paris, 1957, p. 491) as "multitudo ingens haud proinde in crimine incendii quam odio humani generis conuicti sunt"; the English for which (in Tacitus, *The Annals and The Histories*, tr. A. J. Church and W. J. Brodribb, Chalfont St. Giles, 1966, p. 257) is given as: "an immense multitude was convicted, not so much of the crime of firing the city, as of hatred against mankind." The previous

Latin phrase, Unamuno's "existialis superstitio" (in all Spanish editions) is given by all authorities (cf. edition by H. Furneaux, Oxford, 1907, p. 375) as "exitiabilis superstitio."

Schleiermacher: Cf. herein, note to p. 172.

Herrmann's statement: from the essay "Christlich-protestantische Dogmatik" in *Systematische Christliche Religion*, in the series *Die Kultur der Gegenwart*, I, IV, 2, p. 140. See herein, note to p. 77.

Cournot: see herein, note to p. 210; the citation is from *Traité de l'enchaînement des idées fondamentales dans les sciences et dans l'histoire*, §396. In the Paris (Hachette) edition of 1911, p. 450, the orginal reads: "Les manifestations religieuses sont la suite nécessaire du penchant de l'homme à croire à l'existence d'un monde invisible, surnaturel et merveilleux: penchant que l'on a pu regarder, tantôt comme la réminiscence d'un état antérieur, tantôt comme le pressentiment d'une destinée future."

238. *"Whoever . . . religion"*: from Goethe's *Zahme Xenien aus dem Nachlass*:

> Wer Wissenschaft und Kunst besitzt,
> Hat auch Religion;
> Wer jene beiden nicht besitzt,
> Der habe Religion.

239. *Guía espiritual*: Unamuno furnishes the full title of the work and the source for the quote in a footnote: *Guía espiritual que desembaraza al alma y la conduce por el interior camino para alcanzar la perfecta contemplación y el rico tesoro de la paz interior*. The source is given as "Libro III, cap. XVIII, párrafo 175." Flitch gives the paragraph as 185, whereas the paragraph in question is neither the one nor the other, but 176 in Molinos. The translation given here is

made from the Madrid, 1935, edition of the book (Imprenta de Galo Sáez, Espasa-Calpe in the series *Biblioteca de filósofos españoles*), together with some borrowing from Flitch. In his library Unamuno has the following edition of the book: *Guida spirituale del dottore Michele di Molinos* (Napoli, 1908). The *Guía* was originally written in Italian.

Flaubert: The quotation is from *Par les Champs et par les Grèves, Pyrénées, Corse* (Paris, 1910), p. 153.

240. *Francesco de Sanctis*: (1817–83), leading Italian literary critic of his century; together with Benedetto Croce, his editor, and the much earlier Giambattista Vico, he was one of a line of unorthodox Neapolitan philosophers of history; his *Storia della letteratura italiana* was first issued in 1870. English translation by Joan Redfern, 1931; the English given here is from *The History of Italian Literature* (New York, n.d.), I, 28-29.

St. Bonaventura: (1221–74); a doctor of the Church. His theology was basically mystical, and he did not scorn playing the divine fool, which would naturally imply certain affinities with Unamuno. His life of St. Francis was rendered into English in 1904, and his *The Mirror of the Blessed Life of Jesus Christ* in 1926. See also *The Philosophy of St. Bonaventura*, by Étienne Gilson (1938).

241. *Cicero*: "(*Tuscul. Quaest.* XVI., 36)" in Unamuno's text. In the Loeb edition (1927) of the *Tusculan Disputations* (*Tusculanarum Disputationum*), Bk. I, XVI, 36, in the English of J. E. King, the passage reads: "resting upon the agreement of all races of mankind we think that souls have an abiding life. . . ." The second citation, in the next sentence, is from Bk. I, XI, 25. But the Loeb edition cited here

(p. 30) reads in Latin: "Adensio illa omnis elabitur," rather than the Latin of the three principal editions of Unamuno in Spanish; the English for the passage (p. 31) reads: ". . . somehow I am sorry to find that I agree while reading, yet when I have laid the book aside and begin to reflect in my own mind upon the immortality of souls, all my previous sense of agreement slips away."

242. *Swedenborg*: Unamuno possessed and marked the Everyman edition of *Heaven and Hell* (London and New York, 1911), in the translation first issued by the Swedenborg Society and revised by F. Bayley, where, on pp. 80-81, we read: "The same is true of a belief in the life of man after death. He who speaks about it without any learned cogitations respecting the soul or the doctrine of its reunion with the body, believes that after death he is to live as a man and among angels if he has lived well; and that then he will see magnificent things and experience great joy: but as soon as he reverts to the doctrine of re-union with the body, or to the common hypothesis about the soul, and doubt arises whether the soul is of such a nature, and thus the question is raised, *whether it is so*, his former idea is dissipated."

Cournot: Traité, §297, p. 343, in the edition cited above.

Julius Kaftan: Dogmatik, von D. Julius Kaftan (Tübingen, 1909). The quotation is: "Das verlangt der sittliche Charakter des christlichen Glaubens und Hoffens." *OC*² has "688" pages, which is incorrect.

245. *Fénelon*: François de Salignac de la Mothe Fénelon (1651–1715), Archbishop of Cambrai, a synthesist of Christian mysticism; a mystic himself (eventually), he assigned priority for achieving the mystic experience to renunciation of self until a pas-

sive state, which was love, was attained (Quietism).
His *Télémaque* (1699) embodied his innate abomination of despotism; an account of the adventures of
Telemachus in search of his father Ulysses, the book
constitutes a political novel interspersed with passages
of prose poetry. In an incisive entry in the *Encyclo-
paedia Britannica* (1967 edition) by François Varil-
lon, the commentator writes that Fénelon remains for
us the man who wrote, "Everything about us is vain,
except the death of self, which is brought about by
Grace." Unamuno's textual quotation is from *Télémaque*, and constitutes the beginning of the first sentence of the book; the English here given is from *The
Adventures of Telemachus, The Son of Ulysses*, tr.
from the French by John Hawkesworth (Dublin,
1791), fourth edition, p. 1. Cf. herein, the note to
p. 236 on Molinos.

246. *Swedenborg observed*: In the Everyman edition of *Heaven and Hell* in Unamuno's library at Salamanca (paragraphs 158 and 160) §158: "I have
been informed from heaven why there are such
changes of state. The angels said that there are many
reasons. The first is that the delight of a heavenly
life due to the Lord's gifts of love and wisdom, would
gradually lose its value if they were always in its full
enjoyment: this indeed is actually the case with those
who are in the enjoyment of unvarying delights and
pleasures. Another reason is, that angels have a selfhood as well as men; this consists in loving themselves,
and all who are in heaven are withheld from their
selfhood and enjoy love and wisdom so far as they
are withheld from it by the Lord. Now in proportion
as they are not so withheld they are drawn to the
love of self, and since every one loves his selfhood
and is attracted by it, therefore they experience these

successive alternations of state. A third reason is that in this way they are perfected, for they thus become accustomed to be maintained in love to the Lord and to be withheld from the love of self; and the perception and sense of what is good is rendered more exquisite by such alternations of delight and sadness. . . ." §160: "When the angels are in the last of these states, that is, when the influence of their selfhood is felt, they begin to grow sad. I have conversed with them when they were in this state and have noticed their sadness; but they said that they hoped soon to return to their former state, and thus, as it were again to heaven; for it is heaven to them to be withheld from their selfhood."

Bossuet: Jacques Bénigne Bossuet (1627–1704), French Catholic theologian and polemicist; chiefly known for his funeral orations and sermons; he engaged in polemical activity against Quietism as represented principally by Fénelon (see herein, notes to pp. 236 and 245); like Unamuno, he was acutely conscious of the paradox between the grandiose and the ephemeral in the human condition; his rhetoric and style have been much admired by the French, including such writers as Paul Valéry. A. J. Krailsheimer (in the *Encyclopedia of Philosophy*, New York and London, 1967, p. 354) concludes that "Bossuet earns his place in history above all else as a public figure, 'the eagle of Meaux.' In the *grand siècle* Bossuet was the church just as Louis was the state."

The present citation is attributed by Unamuno to *Du culte qui est dû à Dieu*, without further indication. It is not, however, in the sermon "Sur le culte dû à Dieu" nor in the section called "De Dieu et du culte qui lui est dû" from *Pensées chrétiennes et morales sur différents sujets.*

247. *Judges*: The English of Judges 13:22 (in the King James version) reads: "And Manoah said unto his wife, We shall surely die, because we have seen God."

St. Teresa: Chapter 20 of *The Life*. Cf. the English of David Lewis, in his translation of *The Life of St. Teresa of Avila* (London, 1962), Ch. 20, where the context can be found in English, and further, in Ch. 38; the entire work is well indexed. And cf. *The Life*, in *The Complete Works of Saint Teresa of Jesus*, tr. and ed. E. Allison Peers (London, 1946), where even the "Principal Figures of Speech Used by the Saint," as well as her "Scriptural Quotations," are indexed. For Unamuno's quotation farther down, from the *Moradas sétimas*, see Peers, Vol. II, *Seventh Mansion*, Ch. II, p. 335, for his English of the saint's subtle figures of speech concerning the wax tapers, the rain and the river, and the two windows, where the translator is less literal, but the meaning perhaps made clearer.

248. *Jakob Böhme*: (1575–1642), German mystic who strove to reconcile the divided world of Good and Evil, of Yes and No, and show how it would be made one, just as the three-fold God had sprung from one source; a shoemaker by trade, and with little schooling, he produced twenty-nine titles, which attracted later thinkers from Nietzsche and Heidegger to Berdyaev and Tillich, and influenced such contemporary irregulars as Henry Miller.

Moradas sétimas: see herein, note on St. Teresa, above.

249. *the silence of thought*: Unamuno's paraphrase

is synoptical. Paragraph 129 of Ch. xvII of Book
One of the *Guía espiritual* (Madrid, 1935), reads:
"Tres maneras hay de silencio. El primero es de palabras, el segundo de deseos y el tercero de pensamientos. En el primero, de palabras, se alcanza la virtud;
en el segundo, de deseos, se consigue la quietud; en
el tercero, de pensamientos, en interior recogimiento.
No hablando, no deseando, no pensando se llega al
verdadero y perfecto silencio místico, en el cual habla
Dios con el ánima, se comunica y la enseña en su
más íntimo fondo la más perfecta y alta sabiduría."
The second sentence of Unamuno's paraphrastic re-
statement of Molinos is taken from Paragraph 187
of Ch. xx of Book Three (*OC*[1] and *OC*[2] wrongly
print the citation as from "cap. xx, párr. 186," which
paragraph is, in fact, in the preceding chapter): "El
camino para llegar a aquel alto estado del ánimo
reformado, por donde inmediatamente se llega al
sumo bien, a nuestro primer origen y suma paz, es
la nada. . . ."

Journal intime: Unamuno used the *Fragments
d'un Journal Intime*, précédés d'une étude par Ed-
mond Scherer, dixième édition (Genève, 1908), 2
vols. *Nada* is used both times in Vol. II, pp. 4 and 194
respectively: "Tu avais besoin de te donner à quelque
grand amour, à quelque noble but; tu aurais voulu
vivre et mourir pour l'idéal, c'est-à-dire pour une sainte
cause. Une fois cette impossibilité démontrée, tu n'as
repris coeur sérieusement à rien et tu n'as plus fait
que badiner avec une destinée dont tu n'étais plus
dupe, *Nada*!" And: "Est-ce que toutes mes paperasses
réunies, ma correspondance, ces milliers de pages in-
times, mes cours, mes articles, mes rimes, mes notes
diverses sont autre chose que des feuilles sèches? A
qui et à quoi aurai-je été utile; est-ce que mon nom

durera un jour de plus que moi et signifiera-t-il quelque chose pour quelqu'un?—Vie nulle. Beaucoup d'allées et de venues et de griffonnages pour rien. Le résumé: *Nada!*"

249-50. *acquiring differentiated knowledge*: At this point Unamuno says: "Hence Lessing's famous saying, already cited." The quotation Unamuno is referring to is indeed from Lessing, although never previously cited, and comes from Kierkegaard's *Concluding Unscientific Postscript*, p. 97. The quotation in German reads: "Wenn Gott in seiner Rechten alle Wahrheit, und in seiner Linken den einzigen immer regen Trieb nach Wahrheit, obschon mit dem Zusatze mich immer und ewig zu irren, verschlossen hielte, und spräche zu mir: wähle! Ich fiele ihm mit Demuth in seine Linke und sagte: Vater, gieb! die reine Wahrheit ist ja doch für dich allein!"

251. *Plotinus: Enneads*, II, 9. See McKenna translation, p. 139.

Bossuet: Traité de la Concupiscence, Œuvres Complètes de Bossuet, ed. F. Lachat (Paris, 1862), Vol. VII, Ch. XI, p. 438: "L'homme donc étant devenu pécheur en se cherchant soi-même, il est devenu malheureux en se trouvant. . . ."

Carlyle: Past and Present (Chicago and New York, n.d.), p. 276. This is the edition in Unamuno's library.

252. *Seneca*: Cf. *Moral Essays* II, "To Marcia On Consolation," XXVI, 6, in the English of John W. Basore (Loeb Classical Library, 1932), where the related passage (p. 97) reads: "Then also the souls of the blest . . . when it shall seem best to God to work once more this ruin—we, too, amid the falling universe—shall be changed again into our former elements."

Unamuno, like so many others, considers Seneca a Spaniard because he was born in Cordoba around 4 B.C.

Job: 19:25-7: "For I know that my redeemer liveth, and that he shall stand at the latter day upon the earth: And though after my skin worms destroy this body, yet in my flesh shall I see God: Whom I shall see for myself, and mine eyes shall behold, and not another; though my reins be consumed within me."

253. *Ulysses*: Homer's *Odyssey*, Book x, 488-92; in the English of E. V. Rieu (Harmondsworth, 1967) the passage reads: ". . . 'to consult the soul of Teiresias, the blind Theban prophet, whose understanding even death has not impaired. For dead though he is, Persephone has left to him, and him alone, a mind to reason with. The rest are mere shadows flitting to and fro.' "

Aristotle: Ethics, X, B, 7.

St. Thomas Aquinas: Summa Theologica, I-IIae, IV, 1, New York and London, 1966.

254. *Dante*: Cf. the poetic and finished English of the standard verse translation by Dorothy L. Sayers and Barbara Reynolds of *Paradise* (Harmondsworth, 1967), Canto XXXIII, 58-63 (pp. 344-45):

> As from a dream one may awake to find
> Its passion yet imprinted on the heart,
> Although all else is cancelled from the mind.
> So of my vision now but little part
> Remains, yet in my inmost soul I know
> The sweet instilling which it did impart.

and for the next sentence of the Italian

> So the sun melts the imprint on the snow, ...

255. *Ethics*: Propositions XXXV and XXXVI and finally Proposition XLII of Part Five of *The Ethics*;

the English given here is that of R.H.M. Elwes, translated from the Latin; in *The Chief Works of Benedict de Spinoza*, Vol. ii (New York, 1951), pp. 264-65, and 270.

the heart also has its reasons: "*Le cœur a ses raisons que la raison ne connaît point.*" "The heart has its reasons of which reason knows ought." Blaise Pascal, *Pensées*, Thought No. 277.

256. *Bernard Brunhes: La Dégradation de l'Énergie* (Paris, 1912), ive Partie, Ch. xviii, 2, pp. 261-62.

Gratry: Auguste Joseph Alphonse Gratry (1805–72), French priest and professor at the Sorbonne; opponent of idealist pantheism and rationalism.

257. *Cauchy*: Augustin Louis, Baron Cauchy (1789–1857), French mathematician, who made important contributions in numerous fields, ranging from astronomy to optics; his collected works, *Œuvres complètes d'Augustin Cauchy*, have been published in twenty-seven volumes.

258. *Brunhes calls*: op. cit., Ch. xxvi, par. 2, p. 381: "les théologiens du monisme."

258-59. "*The world built to last . . . without Him*": Brunhes, op. cit., Ch. xxvi, par. 2, p. 380.

259. *the comments of Ritschl . . . cited before*: see herein, note to p. 126. And also cf. pp. 76-77, above, and notes.

as Papini called him: In *Il Crepuscolo dei filosofi*, Società Editrice Lombarda (Milano, 1906), p. 186 (in his chapter on Spencer), Papini calls Spencer "L'ingegnere licenziato diveniva filosofo." And a little later on (p. 188), Papini adds: "la filosofia spenceriana si presenta a noi, innegabilmente, come l'opera paziente e faticosa di un *meccanico disoccupato*." It may be recalled that Spencer was a railway engineer from 1837 until 1841.

Ardigò: Roberto Ardigò (1828–1920), principal Italian positivist; he received an "anti-revelation" while staring at the red color of a rose, and left the priesthood convinced that knowledge originated in sensation; Ardigò's differences with Spencer hinged on his substituting an indistinct-distinct relationship in the formation of all reality for Spencer's homogeneous-heterogeneous relation, and in assuming an infinity for the indistinct, or, as Unamuno puts it, assuming that the heterogeneous is eternal.

In a letter to his friend Pedro de Múgica, dated November 23, 1891, shortly after beginning his career as professor of Greek at Salamanca, Unamuno announced he was reading the *Opere Filosofiche* of Roberto Ardigò whom he considers comparable to the best philosophers of his day, worthy of standing alongside of Spencer, Taine, and Wundt. Cf. *Cartas inéditas de Miguel de Unamuno*, ed. Sergio Fernández Larrain (Santiago de Chile, 1965), p. 155.

261. *Leopardi . . . "La Ginestra"*: Leopardi's original (lines 124 and 125 of "La Ginestra") reads:

che de' mortali
È madre in parto ed in voler matrigna.

which Unamuno translates (lines 127 and 128 of *La Retama*, *OC*, XIII, 482) as:

de los mortales
madre en el parto, en el querer madrastra.

Cf. *The Penguin Book of Italian Verse*, edited by George Kay (Harmondsworth, 1958), where the full Italian title is translated as

The Broom
or
The Flower of the Desert,

and the lines in question are translated by Kay (p. 296), in prose at the foot of the Italian original, as ". . . the mother of humankind in bearing them, and their stepmother in feelings."

Antero de Quental: (1842–91), one of the most important Portuguese poets of the nineteenth century. Like Unamuno, he was brought up in an orthodox Catholic household, came in contact with modern European ideological currents—political, philosophical, religious, literary—during his years at Coimbra, and was tormented for the rest of his life by enthusiasms and disillusionments, along with deplorable health which led him to suicide. His most important collections of poetry are the *Odes Modernas* (1865) and especially his *Sonetos* (1861, 1881, 1886), philosophical, abstract, un-musical but moving in their intense sincerity.

Unamuno's enthusiasm for Antero de Quental was such that he grouped him with his other "cardiac" writers: Sénancour, Leopardi, and Kierkegaard (cf. "La literatura portuguesa contemporánea" in *Por tierras de Portugal y de España, OC,* I, 362). For a comprehensive discussion of Unamuno-Antero de Quental, see Ch. IX, "El sentimiento trágico de Antero de Quental," in Julio García Morejón, *Unamuno y Portugal* (Madrid, 1964).

The "two superb sonnets" translated by Unamuno (*OC,* XIV, 929-30) are:

"Redención"

(Dos sonetos de Antero de Quental, "traducidos a la letra y no en verso".)

Voces del mar, de los árboles, del viento
cuando a veces en sueño doloroso
me cuna vuestro canto poderoso
juzgo igual al mío vuestro tormento.

Verbo crepuscular e íntimo aliento
de las cosas mudas, salmo misterioso,
¿no serás tú, quejumbre vaporosa,
el suspiro del mundo y su lamento?

Un espíritu habita la inmensidad;
un ansia cruel de libertad
agita y mueve las formas fugitivas;

y yo comprendo vuestra lengua extraña,
voces del mar, de la selva, de la montaña,
almas hermanas de la mía, almas cautivas.

* * *

¡No lloréis, vientos, árboles y mares,
coro antiguo de voces rumorosas,
de voces primitivas, dolorosas,
como un llanto de larvas tumulares!

. . . .

Rompiendo un día surgiréis radiosas
de ese sueño y esas ansias afrentosas
que expresan vuestras quejas singulares.

Almas en el limbo aún de la existencia,
despertaréis un día en la conciencia,
y cerniéndoos, ya puro pensamiento,

veréis las formas, hijas de la ilusión,
caer deshechas como un sueño vano
y acabará por fin vuestro tormento!

262. *Antonio Machado*: (1875–1939), chief poet of the Generation of 1898. The lines are from his long somber ballad "La tierra de Alvargonzález" (p. 167 of *Antonio Machado, Obras, Poesía y Prosa*, ed. Aurora de Albornoz y Guillermo de Torre, Buenos Aires, 1964):

¡Oh tierras de Alvargonzález
en el corazón de España,
tierras pobres, tierras tristes,
tan tristes, que tienen alma!

Though closely reasoned, Machado's verses are a species of "*objets trouvés*," a finding, perhaps, as above, of the quintessence of Castile, more by fortuitous paradoxical juxtaposition than by development of poetic logic, which latter was the manner of Unamuno in his verse. Machado's simple selectivity, while eschewing the abstractions of categories, abstracted the psychic character of objects and places in more concrete terms than others of his time. Often he coincides with Unamuno and other members of the Generation of 1898 in finding, say, death, to be the genius of Castile ("Castilla de la muerte"). And, like Unamuno, he sensed the dream-meaning of life: from memory the only worthwhile re-creation was that of its dreams ("De toda la memoria sólo vale / el don preclaro de evocar los sueños"). He also shared with Unamuno a sense of ironical paradox, as in the lines quoted in the text here by Unamuno, where sorrow creates soul, the soul of the hard landscape; finally, like Unamuno, he could be called a "visceral" poet.

One of the greatest poetical tributes paid to Unamuno is Machado's poem "A don Miguel de Unamuno" (op. cit., p. 228). Cf. also "Las cartas de Antonio Machado" plus appendices in Manuel García Blanco, *En torno a Unamuno* (Madrid, 1965), pp. 215-91. For a complete discussion of the relations between the two writers, see Aurora de Albornoz, *La presencia de Miguel de Unamuno en Antonio Machado* (Madrid, 1968).

Espronceda: José de Espronceda (1808–42), Spanish poet in the Byronic manner and one of the most curious lyric talents. The original of the lines given are:

> Aquí, para vivir en santa calma,
> o sobra la materia o sobra el alma.

It is from *El diablo mundo*, Canto I; cf. the edition by Jaime Gil de Biedma (Madrid, 1966), p. 159.

264. *Plotinus: Ennead* II, 9:7.

266. *In the end . . . apocatastasis*: Cf. Harnack, op. cit., I, 631.

267. *anything but law*: The original Spanish reads: "eso que llaman derecho penal, y que es todo menos derecho." The word *derecho* means not only "law" but "right" and "straight," so that Unamuno is using a double-barreled word.

Lamennais: Œuvres de F. de Lamennais, Essai sur l'indifférence en matière de religion, nouvelle édition, tome troisième, quatrième partie, ch. VII, p. 111: "Dieu est juste et nous sommes punis, voilà tout ce qu'il est indispensable que nous sachions; le reste n'est pour nous que de *pure curiosité*" (Lamennais's italics). Cf. herein, notes to pp. 82, 130, 181.

269. *St. Augustine: Confessions*, Book VII. For full discussion on this head see Étienne Gilson, *The Christian Philosophy of Saint Augustine*, tr. L.E.M. Lynch (New York, 1960), p. 144 and corresponding notes.

Franklin: The Autobiography of Benjamin Franklin (London, 1903), p. 2: "This good fortune, when I reflect on it (which is frequently the case), has induced me sometimes to say, that, if it were left to my choice, I should have no objection to go over the same life from its beginning to the end; requesting only the advantage authors have of correcting in a second edition the faults of the first. So would I also wish to change some incidents of it for others more favourable. Notwithstanding, if this condition was denied, I should still accept the offer of recommencing the same life."

Leopardi: To Leopardi this world was a valley of tears, without a God, full of suffering and tedium, and it was better not to have been born, while death was a favor ("Grazia il morir," line 84 of "Sopra un basso rilievo antico sepolcrale"). Cf. herein, notes to pp. 50, 53.

271. *Browning*: This citation is from "Easter Day," Vol. I, VII, p. 498, of the collected edition in Unamuno's library (see herein, note to p. 125).

Inferno: The appropriate lines, covering the entombment of the Epicureans, are in Canto X, lines 10-15:

> "All shall be closed when from Jehoshaphat they return here with the bodies which they have left above. In this part Epicurus with all his followers, who make the soul die with the body, have their burial-place."

The Divine Comedy: Singleton translation, I, 99. Unamuno interpreted the passage liberally, combining the two stanzas in his own way, though the Canto does begin in the area where the Epicureans are buried. "Sepolcreto degli Epicurei" (in the commentary and according to the Canto headings by Siro Chimenz, Turin, 1962).

Aeneid: Book VI, 426-29. In his prose translation, W. F. Jackson Knight (Harmondsworth, 1968), p. 160, gives the passage as follows: "Immediately cries were heard. These were the loud wailing of infant souls weeping at the very entranceway; never had they had their share of life's sweetness, for the dark day had stolen them from their mothers' breasts and plunged them to a death before their time."

272. *Charles Bonnefon: Dialogue sur la vie et sur la mort*, 3ᵉ édition (Paris, 1911), passim. Although Bonnefon has disappeared without apparent trace in the histories of thought and encyclopedias, there is a very moving letter from him in the Unamuno files, dated *10 janvier 1915*(?) from Nîmes,

in which he signs himself "ancien correspondant du Figaro à Berlin, auteur du Dialogue sur la Vie et la Mort; soldat."

274-75. *two pietists of Protestant origin*: Johann Jakob Moser (1701–85) and Friedrich Christoph Oetinger (1702–82). Both quotations that follow are from Albrecht Ritschl, *Geschichte des Pietismus in der lutherischen Kirche des 17. und 18. Jahrhunderts*, 3 vols. (Bonn, 1880, 1884, 1886).

275. *Spener*: OC^1 and OC^2 both have "Spencer"; the Candamo edition (Madrid, 1958) has "Spener." Unamuno obviously meant Spener, as Flitch has it, as also do the Italian translator G. Beccari, and the French translator Marcel Faure-Beaulieu. Philipp Jakob Spener (1635–1705) was a leading German pietist; his *Pia desideria* (1675) was published in an English edition in 1964. In order to revitalize the Church, he organized *collegia pietatis*, or associations of piety, through which, very much in the spirit of the evangelical movements which also swept England and America in the eighteenth century, he hoped to revive the spirit of Christ in the lives of men, to leaven formal theology by true faith. Pietism exercised an influence on the Moravian Church and on such men as Kant and Schleiermacher. Ritschl discusses Spener in the work cited above.

276. *Browning*: The couplet quoted is from Section xv, of "The Flight of the Duchess," p. 420 of the edition in Unamuno's library (see herein, note to p. 125).

277. *He is among them*: Matt. 18:20: "For where two or three are gathered together in my name, there am I in the midst of them."

278. *speranza*: Dante's *Inferno*, Canto iii, line 9: *Lasciate ogni speranza voi ch'entrate*: usually trans-

lated as: "All hope abandon, ye who enter here." In her version of the *Inferno* (Harmondsworth, 1949), Dorothy L. Sayers translates the tercet (terzain), in the style of Dante's *terza rima*, as follows:

NOTHING ERE I WAS MADE WAS MADE TO BE
SAVE THINGS ETERNE, AND I ETERNE ABIDE;
LAY DOWN ALL HOPE, YOU THAT GO IN BY ME.

279. *doubt: "incertidumbre": OC*² reads "*muchedumbre*," a howling typographical error.

felicity: Unamuno is, of course, inverting Dante's well-known tercet: "There is no greater grief than to recall past happiness in an unhappy time" (*Nessun maggior dolore / Che ricordarsi del tempo felice / Nella miseria; Inferno*, v, 121).

280. *desperate way out*: Although *OC* says *Afsluttende uvidenskabelig Efterskrift* (*Concluding Unscientific Postscript*), II, I, Ch. I, it is actually in II, I, Ch. II, 3 (p. 97 in the Princeton edition cited previously).

No wonder . . . madness of the Cross: 1 Cor. 1:23. Cf. herein, note to p. 105.

Holmes . . . "asylums": Actually Holmes is quoting himself at this point, not "one of the characters in his . . . conversations." See *The Autocrat of the Breakfast Table*, in the edition by Eleanor M. Tilton (New York, 1961), p. 47. Unamuno used the Everyman Edition (London, 1906, 1908), p. 41.

281. *Obermann*: Cf. the epigraph to Chapter Eleven and its translation from the French on p. 286 of the text. The full translation, from *Obermann*, by Étienne Pivert de Sénancour, tr. J. Anthony Barnes (2 vols., London and New York, 1910, 1915), Vol. II, Letter XC, p. 252 reads: " 'Man is perishable,' is the response. That may be; but let us perish resisting, and if annihilation must be our portion, let us not make it a just one."

unique problem: Unamuno uses *único*, which may be translated as *unique* or *sole*, in either case it means, as Unamuno repeated again and again, that the problem of personal immortality is the only *real* problem that confronts us.

XI. THE PRACTICAL PROBLEM

282. *Obermann*: see the translation from the French herein, p. 286; see also the note to p. 281 on *Obermann*.

Jeremiah: 15:10: "Woe is me, my mother, that thou hast borne me a man of strife and a man of contention to the whole earth!" Unamuno has "Job" in all editions; French and Italian editions preserve "Job."

283. *Fouillée . . . idea forces*: Alfred Fouillée (1838–1912), French philosopher and sociologist who wished to reconcile traditional metaphysical thought with natural science through his concept of the *idée-force*, i.e., that thought or mind is always behind action. His central work is *Psychologie des idées-forces* (Paris, 1893), 2 vols. Unamuno has in his library Fouillée's *Critique des Systèmes de Morale Contemporains* (Paris, 1883), of which *livre premier*, ch. II is called "L'évolution des idées et des sentiments moraux selon la philosophie idéaliste des *idées-forces*. Complément psychologique du naturalisme."

285. *Pascal*: Thought No. 233.

Johann Jakob Moser: Cf. herein, note to p. 274.

286. *Obermann*: The English given here is that of J. Anthony Barnes in his version of the book. See herein, note to p. 281 on *Obermann* for full source. For Sénancour, see herein, note to p. 14 on

Obermann. It is interesting that Albert Camus used the same quotation as epigraph to the fourth letter of his *Lettres à un ami allemand*.

"*Whatever . . . destroyed*": *Faust I*, lines 1339-40.

287. *The Nation*: (London), Vol. xi, No. 14, July 6, 1912, p. 504.

288. *H. G. Wells*: (1866–1946), the English novelist (*The Time Machine*, 1895; *The War of the Worlds*, 1898) and popular historian (*The Outline of History*, 1920, rev. 1931), had a period of belief in the supernatural (*God: the Invisible King*, 1917). Unamuno used and marked the Tauchnitz edition of *Anticipations* (Leipzig, 1902), p. 285.

290. *Windelband*: Wilhelm Windelband (1848–1915), German historian of philosophy and philosopher. The reference is to *Präludien: Aufsätze und Reden zur Einführung in die Philosophie*, published in 1884 in 2 volumes. Unamuno's copy of the work is Tübingen, 1911, and the chapter referred to is "Über Friedrich Hölderlin und sein Geschick," i, 239-59.

Life is a Dream: *La vida es sueño*, Acto III, escena 4.ᵃ:

> Que estoy soñando y que quiero
> obrar bien, pues no se pierde
> el hacer bien aun en sueños.

and Acto III, escena 10ᵃ

> acudamos a lo eterno
> que es la fama vividora,
> donde ni duermen las dichas
> ni las grandezas reposan.

Some Spanish texts omit the division into scenes, as in Candamo (*OC²* gives an erroneous act in the first instance) and in Pedro Calderón de la Barca, *Tragedias* (I), edición de Francisco Ruiz Ramón (Madrid, 1967), pp. 128 and 148.

293. *Epistle to the Ephesians*: The fourth chapter in its entirety is addressed more or less to those in the "vocation wherewith you are called."

"*I am a Roman citizen!*": Acts 16:37-38; Acts 22:25-29; Acts 25:11. Anyone who possessed citizenship rights in the Roman Empire could, if he uttered the words "I am a Roman citizen," demand to appeal to the emperor.

296. *my own official bureaucratic capacity*: Unamuno was rector of the University of Salamanca for the first time from 1900 to 1914.

297. "*dies on them*": " 'se les muera,' y no sólo 'se muera' ": the Spanish phrase is by natural usage more vivid: it conveys the intimate colloquial sense of personal loss.

ethical sense . . . religious one: An echo of Kierkegaard's three stages on life's way: aesthetic, ethical, and, the loftiest, religious.

298. *anonymous societies*: Unamuno speaks merely of the ". . . *sociedades y empresas industriales anónimas*," which are the Spanish equivalent of the American "Inc." (incorporated societies) and the British "Ltd." (limited companies): we take the liberty of adding the equivalents in the two languages.

299. "*in the sweat of thy face*": Gen. 3:19.

301. *Fourier*: François Marie Charles Fourier (1772–1837), French philosopher who proposed life in socialist units called Phalansteries where there would be division of labor and sharing of profits.

305. *Be ye . . . is perfect*: Matt. 5:48.

306. ". . . *help Thou my impotence!*": An echo and paraphrase of "Lord, I believe; help thou mine unbelief" (Mark 9:24).

Fray Thomé de Jesus: Portuguese friar and mystical writer who accompanied his king, D. Sebastião, to Africa and was captured; while in prison, where he died in 1582, he wrote his *Trabalhos de Jesus*, or *The Sufferings of Jesus*, published posthumously, the first part in 1602, the second in 1609. The quotations are from the First Part (Lisboa, 1865), pp. 3 and 82.

307. *morality of slaves*: Nietzsche's *Sklavenmoral*. Cf. *Genealogy of Morals*, also *Will to Power*.

308. *Milton*: The English text used here, from "On His Blindness," is taken from the *Oxford Book of English Verse* (Oxford, 1957), p. 352.

309. *an egotistical poet of an avaricious people*: the poet was Alfred de Musset (1810–57) and the people, the French. The line is from *La coupe et les lèvres, Premières Poésies*: "Mon verre est petit, mais je bois dans mon verre."

"Be ye . . . is perfect": Cf. above, note to p. 305.

John 17:21: "That they all may be one; as thou, Father, art in me, and I in thee, that they also may be one in us."

Romans 12:5: "So we, being many, are one body in Christ, and every one members one of another."

310. *Fray Juan de los Angeles*: See herein, note to p. 226. The citation given here is from his *Diálogos de la conquista del espiritual y secreto Reino de Dios, Obras místicas de Fr. Juan de los Angeles* (Nueva Biblioteca de Autores Españoles, 1912), p. 69: "No seas, y podrás más que todo lo que es."

311. *Concluding Unscientific Postscript*: We translate here directly from Unamuno's Spanish, instead of quoting from the Swenson-Lowrie translation hitherto cited, where the English is a violation of the textual sense. Cf. op. cit., Book Two, Part Two, Ch. IV, Sect. II. A, 3, p. 479.

Windelband: op. cit., "Das Heilige," II, 297.

312. *Goethe: Gespräche mit Eckermann*, 4. Februar 1829. The translation is from *Conversations of Goethe with Eckermann*, tr. John Oxenford, ed. J. K. Moorhead (London, 1946), p. 287.

the Thebaid: the desert region around Thebes to which the earliest Christian hermits retired. Unamuno is referring to the monastic ethic.

313. *Domingo de Guzmán*: St. Dominic (1170?—1221).

the Piarists: founded by St. Joseph of Calasanz (c. 1557–1648), a Spaniard from Aragón, who established his first primary school in Rome; forerunners of the Christian Brothers, or de La Salle Order, the Piarists were therefore among the first priests to teach in schools.

314. *. . . exclaimed St. Teresa*: Although Unamuno attributes this quotation to the *Life* (*Vida*) of St. Teresa, it is actually from the *Camino de perfección*. The translation is from the *Book Called Way of Perfection, Complete Works of Saint Teresa of Jesus*, translated and edited by E. Allison Peers from the critical edition of P. Silverio de Santa Teresa, C.D. (London and New York, 1957), II, 79.

Fray Luis de León: (1527–91), Augustinian friar, religious poet and humanist, professor at the University of Salamanca. His prose work *De los nombres de Cristo* (*On the Names of Christ*), published in 1583, expounds meanings of the names given to Christ in the New Testament. Unamuno passed by his statue every day and was one of his great admirers. The reference in the text is to the above work, in the edition in Unamuno's library (*Biblioteca Salvatella*, Barcelona, 1885), Libro I, p. 61.

315. *Annie Besant*: (1847–1933); British social reformer, sometime Fabian socialist, theosophist, and Indian independence leader. The quotation is from

Annie Besant. An Autobiography (London, 1908), p. 335.

316. *Plato . . . knowledge: Meno*, 87.

318. *Descartes . . . described*: The reference here is to the clash between Unamuno and José Ortega y Gasset in 1909. When Azorín wrote his article "Colección de farsantes" for the newspaper *ABC* of September 12, 1909, to defend his country against foreign detractors, Unamuno wrote him a private letter of congratulations which found its way into the same newspaper. Unamuno referred to the "simpletons" (*papanatas*) fascinated by Europeans. "It is time," he said, "to declare that we are their equals and perhaps even better in quite a number of things." And he added: "If it were impossible for one nation to produce both a Descartes and Saint John of the Cross, I would opt for the latter." In answer, Ortega wrote his article "Unamuno y Europa, Fábula" in which he refers to St. John of the Cross as a "handsome little monk with an incandescent heart who wove lacework of ecstatic rhetoric in his cell," and calls Unamuno a "wild man" (*energúmeno*) who cannot see that without Descartes "we would remain in darkness and see nothing, certainly not the dark robe [*pardo sayal*] of Juan de Yepes [St. John of the Cross]." The article is in the *Obras completas* of José Ortega y Gasset (Madrid, 1957), Vol. I.

319. *Krausism*: The ideas of the German philosopher Karl Christian Friedrich Krause (1781–1832), as propagated by Julián Sanz del Río (1814–69), had enormous influence in Spain. Sanz del Río studied in Heidelberg with disciples of Krause, and when he assumed his chair of philosophy at the Central University of Madrid, he attracted many enthusiasts to his Krausist system. Briefly, he held that it was the duty of Humanity, through rational

effort, to carry out on earth God's harmonious design and to resolve all differences. The Krausists' view of God had nothing to do with dogma or revelation, or indeed even Christianity, but imbued many men with a sense of mission: e.g., Francisco Giner de los Ríos founded the independent secular Institución Libre de Enseñanza, a landmark in Spanish "idealist" educational reform. The definitive history of Krausism is to be found in Vol. I of *La Institución Libre de Enseñanza* by Vicente Cacho Viu (Madrid, 1962). (And cf. review in English of this book in "The University Bookman," Winter, 1964.) Menéndez Pelayo judged that "In Spain we have been Krausist by chance, thanks to the intellectual gloom and slovenliness of Sanz del Río." And: the Krausists "more than a school, were a lodge, a mutual benefit society . . . something tenebrous and repugnant to all independent souls. . . . Whenever they were in command they divided up the professorships like seized booty; they all spoke alike and dressed alike. . . . They were all sullen, lowering, somber; they all reacted according to formula, even in the pettiness of practical daily life. . . ." *Heterodoxos* (Buenos Aires, 1951) Vol. VII, p. 363. "Underlying nebulous Krausist philosophizing was a paradisiacal millenarianism, a vague and abstracted sentimentalism," wrote Azorín in the *ABC* (May 15, 1908). And the poet Ramón de Campoamor defined the doctrinal content of the school as: "in philosophy, an all-nothing, pantheism gone to seed; in morality, calculated indifference; in politics, communism: in the arts, indeterminism; and in literature, sheer chaos." In sum: "Artists, poets, and writers may come from all known philosophical systems except Krausism." *Obras completas* (Madrid, 1901) III, pp. 17 and 154.

Notes

XII. Don Quixote in the Contemporary European Tragicomedy

322. *Böhme . . . Aurora: Aurora oder die Morgen-röthe* von Jacob Böhme (Amsterdam, 1620), Ch. xi, paragraph 75, p. 113, and paragraph 83, p. 114. See herein, note on Böhme, p. 248.

323. *which Carlyle called a Fortress of Ignorance:* "fortaleza de la ignorancia, . . ." Unamuno was probably recalling (and paraphrasing) from *Sartor Resartus*, where Carlyle puts the matter rather differently, speaking of Salamanca as a type of "Castle of Indolence": "And yet, in such winter-seasons of Denial, it is for the nobler-minded perhaps a comparative misery to have been born, and to be awake, and work; and for the duller a felicity, if like hibernating animals, safe-lodged in some Salamanca University, or Sybaris City, or other superstitious or voluptuous Castle of Indolence, they can slumber through, in stupid dreams, and only awaken when the loud-roaring hailstorms have all done their work, and to our prayers and martyrdoms the new Spring has been vouchsafed." From "Pedagogy," *Sartor Resartus, Heroes and Hero-Worship, and Past and Present* (London, 1888), p. 82, a book in Unamuno's library.

Frenchman of letters . . . university: Unamuno is referring to the critic Remy de Gourmont (1858–1915), whom he mentions by name in his speech "Lo que ha de ser un rector en España" ("Conferencia leída en el Ateneo de Madrid el 25 de noviembre de 1914," *OC*, vii, 870). Unamuno was especially outraged by the preface Remy de Gourmont wrote for a book of poetry by the Argentinian Leopoldo Díaz (*Las Sombras de Hellas, Les Ombres d'Hellas*, avec la traduction en vers français par F. Raisin, préface de

Remy de Gourmont, Genève, Paris, 1902) which
Unamuno reviewed for the Madrid paper *La Lectura*
("Los sonetos de un diplomático argentino" in *OC*,
VIII, 236-41). In his preface, Gourmont says that the
Spanish language is flourishing not in Spain, but in
South American literature, which owes nothing to
Spain but its language, since its ideas are European
and its intellectual capital is Paris. Leopoldo Díaz,
adds the French critic, sings in the purest "langue
néo-espagnole" which is "plus souple que le rude
castillan classique, . . . aussi plus claire; . . ." Unamuno has red marks alongside of "Sa capitale intel-
lectuelle est Paris" and "Cette langue, plus souple que
le rude castillan classique, . . ."

Archer M. Huntington: "Mister Archer M. Hunt-
ington, poeta—"; Huntington (1870-1955) was not
widely known as a poet, although he did translate the
verse of *El Cantar de Mío Cid*. He was an art col-
lector, philanthropist, and ardent Hispanist, founder
of the *Hispanic Society of America* (1904). The
Italian translator (Beccari) puts the matter which we
have placed in parentheses into a footnote in the
Italian edition. The sentence quoted here is from a
letter to "My dear Unamuno" written on the sta-
tionery of the Hotel du Palais, Biarritz, undated (but
probably 1911), in the Unamuno archives in Salamanca.

324. *in 1604: The Tragical History of Doctor*
Faustus was entered on the Stationer's Books in
1600–01, probably written before 1590; Unamuno's
copy of the play (in the Everyman's Library) was
"From the Quarto of 1604," the earliest known edition.

325. *Marlowe's* Faust: In *The Plays of Chris-*

topher Marlowe with an Introduction (dated 1909) by Edward Thomas (London and New York, n.d.); the verse quotation given here is on p. 154.

326. *Simon Magus*: this Simon appears for the first time in Acts 8:9-24 as the Samarian sorcerer converted to Christianity by the evangelist Philip, and who then offered Peter and John money for the powers of those to whom the Holy Ghost was given. Then Peter upbraided him and urged him to repent. In ecclesiastical tradition, Simon (who gave his name to "simony") developed into a magician and heretic, and Justin Martyr speaks of him as a native of Gitta in Samaria who was considered God by his fellow countrymen and was accompanied by a woman named Helen, formerly a prostitute, and whom he called "the first intelligence" proceeding from him. This tradition was taken up by Irenaeus, Tertullian, and others, Helen becoming assimilated to Helen of Troy.

schibolet: in his essay "Faith," in another volume of this edition, Unamuno plays upon variants of the word, speaking of *"chiboletes," "schibolet," "sibolet,"* and the sectarian and geographical significance of the differences between the pronunciation of the word. Cf. Judges 12:5-6:

> . . . If he said Nay, then they said to him, Say now Shibboleth, and he said Sibboleth, for he could not frame to pronounce it right. Then they took him and slew him. . . .

The Italian translator, Beccari, adds: *"Tres Ensayos,* Madrid, 1900 pagg. 58 e ss. L'A. si riferisce a un episodio poco noto della Bibbia, della lotta di Jefte contro gli Efraimiti *(Giudici,* XII, 6) e divenuto poi materia di proverbio."

327. *When Galileo . . .* : From the letter "A Leo-

poldo d'Austria in Innsbruck," in *Galileo Galilei, Frammenti e Lettere*, con introduzione e note di Giovanni Gentile (Firenze, n.d.), seconda edizione, pp. 262-63. The letter was written "23 maggio 1618."

"Eppur si muove!": "Yet it does move!" This phrase, attributed to Galileo, was supposed to have been said after he was forced to recant his doctrine that the earth moves around the sun.

329. *Every time* . . . :

> Cada vez que considero
> Que me tengo de morir
> Tiendo la capa en el suelo
> Y no me harto de dormir.

Cf. herein, note to p. 48, and Vol. 3 of this edition, pp. xix and 218.

Pérez de Ayala: Ramón, Spanish novelist (1880–1962), identified with Unamuno on many issues in Spanish culture; a master stylist, he reflected the preoccupations of the Generation of 1898 (the contradiction between dream and reality, among others, and he was dubious about the value of pure thought). *La pata de la raposa* is a semi-autobiographical novel. The quotation here is taken from the Spanish text of the Buenos Aires (Austral) edition of 1966, p. 174. Unamuno wrote a review of the book for *La Nación* of Buenos Aires, August 13, 1912. We give the complete passage from the novel; Unamuno excerpted it.

330. *Calderón*: The quotation is from the dramatist's *Gustos y disgustos no son más que imaginación*, *Act.* I, *esc.* IV:

> *No es consuelo de desdichas,*
> *es otra desdicha aparte,*
> *querer a quien las padece*
> *persuadir que no son tales.*

Fray Diego de Estella: (1524–78), celebrated

orator and confessor to Cardinal Granvelle. The quotation is from his *Tratado de la Vanidad del Mundo* (1574), Ch. xxi.

330-31. *In his admirable letters*: Joseph de Maistre wrote *Cinq lettres sur l'Education Publique en Russie à M. Le Comte Rasoumowsky, Ministre de l'Instruction Publique*, to be found in *Considérations sur la France, Mélanges* (Paris, 1909), iv, 182-92. Here Unamuno refers to "Lettre 1," where de Maistre expatiates on the lack of science in Russia and the apparent incapacity of that country to absorb science at that point in history. Cf. herein, note to p. 82.

331. *pasteboard visor*: in *Don Quixote*, Part i, Ch. i.

332. *Cournot wrote*: in his *Traité de l'enchaînement des idées fondamentales dans les sciences et dans l'histoire*, etc. (Paris, 1911) par. 510.

Tacitus: in *Germania*, 19. The translation by Sir William Peterson in the Loeb Classical Library, 1920, p. 291, is: "No one laughs at vice there; no one calls seduction, suffered or wrought, the spirit of the age."

". . . *grandiosità spagnola*": from Carducci's *Del rinnovamento letterario in Italia*. Unamuno used and marked *Prose di Giosuè Carducci, MDCCCLIX–MCMIII* (Bologna, 1905), where *Mosche cocchiere* appears on p. 1353 through p. 1372. Unamuno has, in a handwritten index of his own at the back of the book, noted "Cervantes . . . 1364"; on that page the Italian is to be found: ". . . anche la Spagna, che non ebbe egemonia mai di pensiero, ha il suo Cervantes." Cf. herein, note to p. 113.

333. *Charles I*: the Emperor Charles V of the Holy Roman Empire.

334. *Amor y pedagogía*: Unamuno's satire of so-

ciological pedagogy and "scientism" in general, published 1902; in *OC*, II.

335. *regenerationist literature*: in the wake of Spain's defeat by the United States in 1898 and the loss of its last important colonies, came many articles and books analyzing the causes of Spanish decline and proposing concrete remedies for national regeneration.

Joaquín Costa: (1846–1911), scholar, writer, and reformer ("regenerationist") who denounced the corruption and stagnation that kept Spain from catching up with the rest of Europe through political, industrial, agricultural, and educational reform. For him, the figure of the Cid, hero of the great Spanish epic dating from c. 1140, could teach Spain many lessons, if correctly interpreted, and Costa interpreted the Cid's actions and words as pointing to constitutional monarchy, separation of Church and State, social justice, in short, meliorist change in keeping with basic traditions and the genius of the Spanish nation. Only when the Cid was used as a symbol for intransigent statist absolutism did Costa ask, on several occasions, that a "double lock" be put on his tomb. However, as Unamuno himself put it, "that man always thought about keeping North Africa for Spain, and perhaps even more, about conquering it totally." ("Discurso en el homenaje a Joaquín Costa, en el Ateneo de Madrid, el 8 de febrero de 1932," *OC*, VII, 1031.) Cf. also "Sobre la tumba de Costa," *OC*, III, 1127-45.

acting the Cid: "poniéndose a *cidear*"; the French translation (by Marcel Faure-Beaulieu) gives "se mit à 'faire le Cid' "; while the Italian translator (Beccari), after giving "si mise a cidear," adds a clarifying note: "Da Cid, verbo creato dall'A.: significa 'fare el Cid,' cioè il bravo." Flitch, in his English translation, avoids the complication of Unamuno's play on words by apparently avoiding Unamuno's phrase; in any case, it is omitted.

"Down with Don Quixote!": On June 25, 1898, Unamuno published in the *Vida Nueva* his article "¡Muera Don Quijote!" (*OC*, v, 712) in which he advocated the elimination of the madness of quixotic undertakings in favor of solid, continuous work; Spain was enslaved to its spectacular history and should shake off that hypnosis, forget its overseas ambitions and concentrate on its workaday tasks.

Life of Don Quixote and Sancho: in Vol. 3 of this edition.

336. *"Elegy" of Jorge Manrique*: the "Coplas por la muerte de su padre don Rodrigo" (1476), the great elegy written for his father by Jorge Manrique (1440–79), splendidly translated into English by Longfellow.

Romancero: medieval Spanish ballads, among the most beautiful in the world.

La vida es sueño: Life is a Dream, the best-known drama of Pedro Calderón de la Barca (1600–81).

Subida del Monte Carmelo: the great work (1578–83) of St. John of the Cross (1542-91), consisting of eight stanzas accompanied by prose commentaries.

337. *pre-judices*: "pre-juicios."

Bacon was right . . . : In his *Novum Organum* (Book i), "Aphorisms Concerning the Interpretation of Nature and the Kingdom of Man," Francis Bacon says "There are four classes of idols which beset men's minds" and proceeds to call them Idols of the Tribe, Idols of the Cave, Idols of the Market-place, and Idols of the Theater (xxxix). The Idols of the Market-place (or *"idola fori"*) are those formed "by the intercourse and association of men with each other," and the author says that "the ill and unfit choice of words wonderfully obstructs the understanding. Nor do the definitions or explanations wherewith in some things learned men are wont to guard and defend themselves, by any means set the matter right. But words plainly force and overrule the understanding, and throw all into confusion, and lead men away into numberless empty controversies and idle fancies" (XLIII).

Avenarius: see herein, note to p. 159.

337-38. *as is reason itself*: *OC*² gives "como la raza misma"; but the early edition in the Unamuno library (Madrid, 1938) gives "como la razón misma" (as do *OC*¹ and the Candamo edition).

338. *Oliver Wendell Holmes*: The exact words of the "Yankee," given here, are from *The Professor at the Breakfast-Table* (Everyman's Library, London and New York, 1906), p. 38; his copy much marked by Unamuno and with numberless pencilled marginal translations into Spanish of the more esoteric "Yankee" words.

Stendhal: The English given here is in the translation from the French by C. K. Scott-Moncrieff of *The Charterhouse of Parma* (New York, 1962), pp. 142-43. The passage is marked in Unamuno's own copy of *La Chartreuse de Parme* (Paris, n.d.), p. 130-31.

339. *Aben Tofail*: also spelled Ibn Tufail and Ibn Tofayl (cf. index and note to p. 370 in Vol. 3, this edition). He was a twelfth-century writer, born in Guadix (Granada province); the solitary thinker is the hero of a romance written on the theme of a child brought up in isolation from the world. Unamuno was taken with this theme, which finds a slightly different, but equally theoretical—and absurd—development, in his *Amor y pedagogía*, where the child is brought up in accordance with "scientific" formulae, independent of reality.

Unamuno had in his library the book *El filósofo autodidacto de Abentofail*, novela psicológica traducida directamente del árabe por D. Francisco Pons Boigues, con un prólogo de Menéndez y Pelayo (Zaragoza, 1900).

Martin A. S. Hume: The Spanish People, their Origin, Growth and Influence (London, 1901). Unamuno says that Hume refers to the "individualidad introspectiva" of the Spaniard in his Preface. This is a mistake, since in his essay "El individualismo español," *OC*, III, 617, he says that the phrase "the introspective individuality of the Spaniards" occurs in Ch. x, p. 375, which is the right place.

Suárez: Francisco Suárez (1548–1617), Jesuit, commonly considered the most important systematic philosopher produced by Spain before the twentieth century, although he wrote all of his many works in Latin. Of special significance and influence is his *Disputationes metaphysicae* (1597).

metanthropics: "metantrópica" in *OC*[1] and Candamo, but *OC*[2] has, erroneously, "misantrópica."

Menéndez y Pelayo: Marcelino Menéndez y Pelayo (1856–1912), considered the father of modern Spanish historical research and criticism. He studied at the University of Barcelona with Manuel Milá y Fontanals (1818–84) who more than anyone else was responsible for Menéndez y Pelayo's formation in scientific research. An indefatigable worker, he became Professor of Spanish Literature at the University of Madrid in 1878; in 1881 he was elected to the Royal Spanish Academy; and in 1898 he left his teaching post to become Director of the National Library. An impassioned genius of great culture, at home with the major European languages, he was deeply religious and a traditionalist, and although he modified his views somewhat in his later years, he felt that Spanish greatness coincided with its orthodoxy. The author of many highly significant works, his *Historia de las ideas estéticas en España* (*History of Aesthetic Ideas in Spain*) was published in 1883–91.

as Benedetto Croce truly said of him: in Croce's *Filosofia dello spirito, I, Estetica come scienza dell' espressione e linguistica generale*, terza edizione riveduta (Bari, 1909), pp. 558-59. For a detailed analysis of the literary relations between Unamuno and Croce (1866–1952) see Manuel García Blanco, "Benedetto Croce (Historia de una amistad)," in *En torno a Unamuno* (Madrid, 1965), pp. 425-67. The correspondence between both writers started in 1911 when Unamuno sent the Italian his prologue to the Spanish translation of the *Estetica* ("Prólogo a la versión castellana de la *Estética* de B. Croce," *OC*, VII, 242-64) which he had read in Italian. The correspondence continued very sporadically until 1921. In one of his letters dated 16-X-12, Unamuno states that it was through Croce that he came to De Sanctis and Windelband.

340. *Luis Vives*: Juan Luis Vives (1492–1540), Spanish humanist and philosopher, friend of Sir Thomas More and Erasmus. Born in Valencia, he died in Bruges, having spent a good deal of his life outside of Spain, in England, France, and the Low Countries. The author of many works in Latin on diverse subjects, he fought the errors of Aristotelianism and advocated observation of nature. José Fer-

rater Mora (*Diccionario de filosofía*, Buenos Aires, 1965, 5th edition, II, 916) says: "As Menéndez y Pelayo has pointed out, the philosophy of Vives is a critical philosophy, but also an eclectic philosophy: anti-Aristotelianism in dialectic, Aristotelianism in metaphysics, Stoicism and Platonism in ethics, naturalism in physics, experimentalism and rationalism in the science of the soul, all presided over by the sincerest Christian belief. . . ."

Scottish school: the Scottish philosophy of common sense, originated by Thomas Reid (1710–95), whose *An Inquiry into the Human Mind on the Principles of Common Sense* (1764) defended common sense against philosophical paradoxes and skepticism. Others associated with this school were Dugald Stewart (1753–1828), whose books were read widely in France and America, and Sir William Hamilton (1788–1856), who proclaimed the sovereignty of common sense as the test of truth.

Balmes: see herein, note to p. 94.

Angel Ganivet: (1865–98), Spanish essayist and novelist, known mainly for his seminal *Idearium español* in which he develops the idea that Spanish philosophy "was that of Seneca," along with other theories in an attempt to analyze the Spanish temper and Spanish history. He and Unamuno met in Madrid in the spring of 1891 while both were waiting to take the oral examinations for teaching posts. After about two months of close friendship, they never saw each other again. Some five years later, Unamuno read Ganivet's articles in *El defensor de Granada*, and they corresponded from 1896 to 1898, when Ganivet took his own life. They exchanged public letters published in the same newspaper, dealing with the purpose and future of Spain, which Unamuno republished in 1912 under the title of *El por-venir de España* (*OC*, IV, 953–1015). Cf. "Ganivet, Philosopher" in Vol. 3 of this edition, pp. 368-73.

Tertullian: See herein, note (Credo quia absur-dum) to p. 352, below.

341. *the high altar of their village church*: In Ch. 58 of the Second Part of Cervantes' *Don Quixote* and the same chapter in Unamuno's *The Life of Don Quixote and Sancho* (Vol. 3, p. 247, of this edition).

Mount Carmel: see herein, previous note to p. 336, for *Subida del Monte Carmelo*. The poem commented on in that work is commonly known as the *Dark Night of the Soul*.

Athena's owl: It is interesting that one of the symbols José Ortega y Gasset uses in advocating clarity and precision is that of the owl. See herein, note to p. 318 (Descartes . . . described) on the relations between Unamuno and Ortega.

Unamuno himself was caricatured as an owl.

342. *ultimatum of 1890*: The ultimatum referred to was issued by England in 1890 threatening a sev-erance in relations with Portugal should certain dis-puted African territories not be evacuated by Portu-gal. Portugal was forced to accede.

he wrote: Unamuno supplied a bibliographical footnote to the text: "In an article which was to have been published on the occasion of the ultimatum, and of which the original is in the possession of the Conde do Ameal. This fragment appeared in the Portuguese review *A Aguia* (No. 3), March, 1912." It was pub-lished in Porto, vol. 1-2ª serie, p. 68. For Quental, see herein, note to p. 261.

343. *"the history of the word 'philosophy'. . ."*: From *Präludien* by Wilhelm Windelband (Tübingen, 1911), I, 20.

344. *"By philosophy in the systematic sense . . .":*
See *Präludien*, p. 29.

"Whoever places upon philosophy the burden . . .":
Windelband, p. 39.

345. *"the abomination of desolation":* Matt. 24:
15.

Benedetto Croce: Unamuno is here referring to the
three parts of Croce's *Filosofia dello spirito:* 1. *Estetica come scienza dell'espressione e linguistica generale*
2. *Logica come scienza del concetto puro* 3. *Filosofia
della pratica economica ed etica.* All three (Bari,
1909) are in Unamuno's library along with the later
fourth part, *Teoria e storia della storiografia* (Bari,
1917). Cf. earlier note on Croce, herein, p. 339.

virtù, *practical efficiency:* Unamuno's definition of
the Italian word is somewhat original.

350. *slicing his pasteboard visor in two:* In Part I,
Ch. 1, Don Quixote constructed a pasteboard visor,
because he was lacking a real one, and then, to test
its strength, "unsheathed his sword and delivered two
blows, and with the first one, and at one point, undid
the work of a week." He then reconstructed it with
iron cross-strips, but desisted from putting it to the
test again: ". . . unwilling to experiment with it further, he commissioned it and held it to be a most
excellent fitted visor."

351. *the crime of having been born:* the reference
is to Calderón's play *La vida es sueño:* ". . . for a
man's greatest crime is to have been born" ("pues
el delito mayor del hombre es haber nacido"), Jornada primera, Escena II.

Felix culpa!: Latin: "Happy sin," in reference to
the Fall of Man, which made possible his redemption.

which suffers violence: a reference to Matt. 11:12:
"And from the days of John the Baptist until now

Notes

the kingdom of heaven suffereth violence, and the violent take it by force." Cf. Vol. 3 of this edition, pp. 29 and 247, with their corresponding notes. Cervantes also echoed the Biblical sentence.

as he had freed the galley slaves: in *Don Quixote*, Part I, Ch. 22.

352. *Agustín de Salazar y Torres*: (1642–75), Spanish poet; in his *Elegir al enemigo*, acto 1, he writes "es la desesperación dueña de los imposibles."

Credo quia absurdum: a phrase by Tertullian (c. 155–c. 222), earliest of the ancient Church writers in the West. Some texts give "Credo quia impossibile," "I believe because it is impossible," which in itself is an adaptation of "Certum est quia impossibile est," "It is certain because it is impossible" (*De Carne Christi*, V). Unamuno paraphrases yet again, changing the main verb: "I hope because it is absurd."

the solitude of Peña Pobre: In Part I, Ch. 25, Don Quixote goes through his own form of penance in the Sierra Morena, in imitation of his hero Amadís de Gaula, who had withdrawn to the Peña Pobre for the same purpose.

the curate . . . the barber . . . the canons: the well-known figures in *Don Quixote*, who, for Unamuno, represent all that Don Quixote is not: common sense, sanity, moderation. The Duke and Duchess may be said to represent the undynamic lack of tension (to use Ortegan terms) of the powers-that-be in Spain.

Kultur: Unamuno often used this spelling to underline his contempt for German science, scholarship, and militarism.

353. *for he lives in her*: "pues que vive." The French translator (Faure-Beaulieu) gives: "puis-

482

qu'elle vit," that is, Dulcinea lives. But Unamuno has just said that Dulcinea is the life-principle, so it is more likely he means that Don Quixote lives because he fought for her, and won life. We give a combination of the two possible meanings, a rendering which in any case does not violate the Unamunian idea.

Margutte: a half-giant who dies, in his turn, of laughing overmuch when Morgante dies from the bite of a mere crab; the giant Morgante is the squire of Orlando (Roland), a knight in the service of Charlemagne; all these characters appear in a burlesque heroic poem, *Morgante Maggiore*, by Luigi Pulci (1432–87), a mordant Florentine poet.

354. *modernist*: Unamuno is here referring to the *modernista* movement in Hispano-American and Spanish literature, which received its main impetus from the Nicaraguan poet Rubén Darío (1867–1916), and was strongly influenced by the French Parnassians and Symbolists. Although their style was often over-refined and artificial, the modernists effected a revolution in literary style and theme. Unamuno never failed to show his disapproval of the school and of Rubén Darío, for he believed them too far removed from the central spiritual questions, too interested in form rather than matter, too aesthetic and "Frenchified."

Old-Christian Spanish: "cristiano viejo español." This is a play on the mania for "pureza de sangre," for blood free from Jewish or Moorish strain, thus pure Old-Christian stock (ironically, therefore, of stock closest in point of time to the Hebrew original of the newer religion), as opposed to that of the New Christians, mainly converted former Jews. There is no Old-Christian Spanish, of course, since the language of the oldest Christians is impregnated with pagan-Latin, Muslim-Arabic, and other roots. The translation "good old-fashioned Spanish," is probably a sensible working rendering, except that Unamuno liked to hear the echoes of irony in his writing.

Clavileño: The wooden horse upon which Don Quixote imagined that he and Sancho were carried through the air in order to aid some "ladies in distress." (*Don Quixote*, Part II, Chs. 40 and 41.)

355. *and inns perforce will have to be castles*: On several occasions Don Quixote held that certain inns were castles.

Master Peter's puppet show: in *Don Quixote*, Part II, Ch. 26, the puppets depict the freeing of the legendary Melisendra, captive of the Moors, until Don Quixote breaks up the show by unsheathing his sword and setting about among the puppet-Moors, finally destroying the stage and the actors.

Kierkegaard: the reference is to *Concluding Unscientific Postscript*, Book II, Part II, Ch. IV, Section II, B. The translation by Swenson and Lowrie in the edition we have been using (Princeton, 1941, p. 503) is: "The 'awakened' religionists are often enough busied about the ungodly world which derides them—though from another point of view this is after all just what they themselves would wish, for the sake of being well assured that they are the 'awakened' . . . seeing that they are derided, and then again for the sake of having the advantage of being able to complain of the world's ungodliness."

the forces . . . pedantry: the allusion here is to the movement headed by Charles Maurras (1868-1952) who fought individualism, liberalism, and romanticism, and espoused the causes of monarchy, Roman

Catholicism, and classical reason as forces of discipline. Along with Léon Daudet (1868–1942), Maurras founded *L'Action française*, which Unamuno particularly detested.

356. Byron's Lara: In Unamuno's copy of the 1905 (London) edition of the one-volume *Poetical Works of Lord Byron*, "Dedicated by Gracious Permission to his Majesty the King of the Hellenes," "Lara: A Tale" is marked marginally, as is the rest of the volume. A footnote to the poem in this edition clarifies the Spanish reference: "The reader is appraised that the name of Lara being Spanish . . . the word 'Serf,' which could not be correctly applied to the lower classes in Spain, who were never vassals of the soil, has nevertheless been employed to designate the followers of our fictitious chieftain. [Byron, writing to Murray, July 14, 1814, says, 'The name only is Spanish; the country is not Spain, but the Moon.'—*Letters*, 1899, iii, 110]."

Machiavelli . . . deceived: *The Prince*, Ch. xviii.

Jules de Gaultier: (1858–1942). Unamuno read Gaultier's *De Kant à Nietzsche* in the *Mercure de France* of 1899-1900. The "n'être pas dupe" undoubtedly is a paraphrase of a section concerning the superiority of France as regards their religious and spiritual maturity, which Unamuno marked in the margin. The general trend of the passage is found in the following: "C'est un grand bonheur pour un peuple posséder une religion qui a passé le temps de sa fermentation. Par la bienfaisance de ce privilège, la race française est actuellement la mieux préparée à voir éclore les modalités les plus intellectuelles de la Vie. . . ." *Mercure de France*, octobre, 1899, *No.* 118, *Tome* xxxii, 142-47. *De Kant à Nietzsche* was published in book form in 1900.

357. *Giordano Bruno*: (1548–1600), born in Nola; in 1565, at the age of seventeen, he entered the Dominican friary of San Domenico in Naples, where he troubled the authorities. He fled, shed his habit, and started his long years of wandering and creativity. Burned in Rome as a heretic.

And Bruno also wrote: In the third dialogue of his *De Gli Eroici Furori*, Bruno describes heroic love as having divinity as its object: a certain divine beauty, which is reflected in the soul, whence it extends to the body. ("Tutti gli amori (se sono eroici, e non son puri animali, che chiamano naturali e cattivi alla generazione, come instrumenti de la natura in certo modo) hanno per oggetto la divinità, tendeno alla divina bellezza, la quale prima si comunica all'anime e risplende in quelle; e da quelle poi, o per dir meglio, per quelle poi si comunica alli corpi. . . ."); p. 336 of Unamuno's copy of *Dialoghi Morali, con note di Giovanni Gentile* in the series Classici della filosofia moderna a cura di Benedetto Croce e Giovanni Gentile, vol. ii (Bari, 1908). In the fourth dialogue there is a discussion of the intellect and how it achieves divine beauty. In the same fourth dialogue there is a discussion of *anima* and it is then we have the talk of *insano* and *soprasape*. When the *anima* becomes too intense, there results an *insano* condition, because, according to the subsequent conversation, the *anima* knows too much (*soprasape*), p. 354. Obviously, Unamuno has compressed and paraphrased the third and fourth dialogues to combine both the qualities and nature of heroic love and *anima*. Since Bruno himself extends heroic love to *anima*, Unamuno apparently does not feel compelled to take one step at a time, but leaps grandly from one stage to the other.

il secolo da lui divinato: the inscription on the

plinth of the large dark statue to Bruno in the Campo
dei Fiori reads: A BRUNO IL SECOLO DA LUI DIVI-
NATO QUI OVE IL ROGO ARSE MDCCCLXXXIX (To
Bruno, the century he foresaw, here where his pyre
burned, 1889).

Index

Index

A page number followed by *n* refers to the notes at the end of the text. If the item which is indexed appears only in a note, the page number is given as, for example, 23*n*. If the item appears in the text and in a note, the form is 23 & *n*.

Index

historical development, 124*f*; immortality in, 70*f*, 83, 288; Judaic influence, 65*ff*, 69; Kierkegaard on, 217 & *n*; morality of slaves, 307; Oriental, 79; philosophy abhors, 341; primitive, 311*f*; primitive elements in, 362, 364; sense of honor and, 32; suffering God in, 223; symbols of, 362; Tacitus on, 105 & *n*, 237 & *n*. *See also* Catholicism; Protestantism

Church, A. J., 237*n*

Cicero, 105, 181*f* & *n*; *De natura deorum*, 181*n*, 236 & *n*; *De officiis*, 37 & *n*; on immortality, 241*f* & *n*; philosophy, definition of, 37 & *n*; on piety, 236; *Tusculan Disputations*, 241 & *n*

Cid, the, 335 & *n*

Circe, 253

Cirlot, Juan-Eduardo: *A Dictionary of Symbols*, 23*n*

Clark, James M., 83*n*

Claudius, Emperor, vii

Clavería, Carlos: *Temas de Unamuno*, 62*n*

Clavileño, 354 & *n*

Clement of Alexandria, 37, 39; *Stromata*, 37*f* & *n*

cloisters, life in, 63, 293, 313*f*, 327

cogito ergo sum, 40*ff*

Columbia University, xxiv, 90

Columbus, Christopher, 334

comedy: people abominate, 320; tragedy and, 341*ff*

common sense, 28, 340 & *n*

communion of saints, 263, 275*f*, 366

Communist Party: French, xix; Spanish, xviii*f*

Cómo se hace una novela (M. de U.), x, xvi

compassion: beauty and, 222; charity and, 229*f*; knowledge and, 155; love and, 149-153, 165, 225, 229; morality and, 162; for suffering, 155*f*, 229*f*

Comte, Auguste, 157 & *n*

concept, extension and comprehension of, 187 & *n*

conduct: motives for, 283*ff*; as proof of doctrine, 284*f*

Confession (sacrament), 75

conflict, life as, 362

Conquistadores, 334, 341

conscience, 129, 138

consciousness, 90, 95*ff*, 213*ff*, 233; of all living beings, 156; of cells in body, 163*f*; collective, of human race, 193; compassion and, 153, 155*f*; of consciousness itself, 159; dependent on body, 88*f*; as disease, 22; eternal, 252*f*; of God, 264*f*; good and evil affecting, 269; of guilt, 315*f*; individual, and immortality, 277*f*; infinite, 265*f*; of self, 154*f*, 161; social, 166; suffering and, 231*f*, 307; Supreme, 164, 169*ff*; Universal, 241, 309*f*; varied, births and deaths of, 164; will and, 162; world made for, 16*f*

Consciousness (Conscience) of the Universe, God as, 7 & *n*, 136, 154, 161, 164, 166, 168, 193, 200*f*, 208, 214

383